Maoist People's War
in Post-Vietnam Asia

Studies in Insurgency and Terrorism No. 1
Series Editor: Thomas A. Marks

Maoist People's War in Post-Vietnam Asia

Thomas A. Marks

White Lotus Press

White Lotus Co., Ltd
G.P.O. Box 1141
Bangkok 10501
Thailand

Tel.   (66) 0-38239-883-4
Fax   (66) 0-38239-885
E-mail   ande@loxinfo.co.th
Website   http://thailine.com/lotus

Printed in Thailand

Designed and typeset by COMSET Limited Partnership

ISBN   978-974-480-106-7   pbk.

For Mike and Joe,
who knew me best—
and have passed the torch
to
Michael Joseph

Contents

List of Figures

Preface

My earlier volume *Maoist Insurgency since Vietnam* (1996) is the foundation on which this volume has been constructed. It remains, nevertheless, a life's work in progress. There are some groups that change so quickly, such as the Maoists of Nepal, that no study can hope to keep up. Thus the work here was completed by the end of 2005, but April 2006 brought dramatic new developments in Nepal that have further complicated the situation. I will touch upon these but leave in-depth assessment for later publications.

It is the case of Nepal that emphasizes the need to return to the Maoist approach even as there remain some groups, such as the Indian Maoists, that I am still researching and hence have relegated to passing mention. Likewise, there are groups, such as *Fuerzas Armadas Revolucionarias de Colombia* or FARC (Revolutionary Armed Forces of Colombia), that use people's war forms and need to be explored, but not here.

In an age of terrorism, why talk about insurgency, much less a form of insurgency now ostensibly become but history, "people's war"? This is a reasonable question. The initial element contained within the query can be met with an answer just as reasonable because driven by unassailable logic: insurgency has never become history, something of the past, and is with us today. Hence it must be studied.

As to the second element: "people's war" is the most sophisticated form of insurgency devised. It should come as no surprise that it also is with us today. Nepal knows this. Built on mass mobilization, people's war started in Mao's mind with a recognition that initially he had nothing except a desire to construct a better world. He faced the complex task of forming a counter-state with which to challenge the state.[1] To do this, ideologically informed leadership would have to mobilize grievance-driven manpower.

Beginning as but a few intellectuals, moving beyond terror to guerrilla war, then to mobile war (also termed maneuver or main force warfare), and finally to war of position (often termed "conventional war" in Western terminology),[2] Mao and like-minded individuals transitioned from the primitive to the modern, from the "war of the flea" to the clash of huge armies. All was built on mobilizing individuals into an organizational matrix that directed their action, that convinced them it was their interests that were being furthered.

In revisiting this topic, it is not my intention to fold all manifestations of mass-based insurgency into a single category labeled "people's war." This would have the character of Liddell Hart's approach in his famous *Strategy*, whereby all martial success came to illustrate the "indirect approach," all failure something else.[3] Rather, I will use an approach (Chapter 1) that is bounded in time. The original title of the book on which this work is based sets the stage by using the words "since Vietnam." I have provided necessary particulars of the Chinese and Vietnamese cases (Chapter 2), but either of these could support separate treatments. This book is built on several case studies, specifically the insurgencies that took place or are ongoing in Thailand (Chapter 3), the Philippines (Chapter 4), Sri Lanka (Chapter 5), and Nepal (Chapter 7). I have, however, found it necessary to discuss the Peruvian case in a shorter, intervening, chapter (Chapter 6), to set the stage for the case of Nepal. The cases have been chosen both for applicability to my discussion and to illustrate the framework outlined in Chapter 1. Nepal has been added to my earlier cases, but even those have been completely rewritten to incorporate continuing research. Only the parameters of the Thai case remain largely as they previously were.

These points have certain consequences that must be spelled out. My cases are not universal. I have made no effort to include all people's wars but have focused on what emerged as the major cases of self-proclaimed Maoist people's wars in Asia following the conclusion of the Vietnam War. As indicated, even as I write one could argue that the various Indian Maoist organizations have entered this category. Unfortunately, by the time a third treatment becomes necessary, it will certainly have to include them.

How then can the likes of Sri Lanka appear in a study of Maoist people's war? In answering, the first point above becomes salient. Sri Lanka is virtually a study in itself, containing both an avowedly Maoist insurgency—that of the JVP, now a legal political party despite having twice surfaced in armed form to convulse the island—as well as the on-going Tamil insurgency, itself once far more complicated and avowedly Marxist-Leninist, with a strong people's war influence. That the two threads existed in the same space and were often intertwined dictates that they both be explored.

This study is both historical and thematic. There is a logical progression to the presentation. It essentially follows a temporal sequence (allowing for thematic linkage of the cases): Thailand (defeated; turning-point in insurgency: 1982); the Philippines (residual insurgency; high point: 1987); Sri Lanka (JVP II crushed by 1990; Tamil phase on-going with the mobile warfare phase launched in 1991); Peru (insurgent remnants; turning-point: 1992); and Nepal (on-going; inspired by Peru, with 1996 the declaration of people's war and April 2006 the turning point).

The study is written from the perspective of strategy and operational art. People's war is a strategic approach to war-fighting that is conducted in a manner dissimilar to conventional (regular) war. Yet it is implemented through the same process of operational art, lines of operation comprised of campaigns. These are multi-faceted rather than solely martial and conducted overwhelmingly amidst human rather than military terrain. Tactics, then, are mentioned only as necessary to the narrative.

Mao Tse-tung himself would surely agree with this last point. His works cited in the following chapters are focused on strategy and operational art to the virtual exclusion of tactics. (The contrast with the pedestrian work of Che Guevara could not be more glaring.[4]) He understood fully that all of the technical finesse in the world could not redeem incorrect approach and implementation. It is a lesson, we shall see, that both insurgents and their opponents have been slow to learn.

Notes

[1] Referred to more commonly by the term "clandestine infrastructure," the concept of the counter-state apparently entered into the literature of internal war in the 1960s. See, for example, Luis Mercier Vega, *Guerrillas in Latin America: The Technique of the Counter-State* (New York: Praeger, 1969). More recently, the concept has been used by Arthur Mitchell, *Revolutionary Government in Ireland: Dail Eireann, 1919–22* (Dublin: Gill and Macmillan, 1995), as well as by Gordon McCormick, Naval Postgraduate School (Monterey, California) in unpublished work.

[2] For a comprehensive treatment of terminology, particularly as used by the Russians/Soviets, hence as undoubtedly passed on via the Soviet advisory effort to the Chinese during the crucial interim between the great wars, see Richard W. Harrison, *The Russian Way of War: Operational Art, 1904–1940* (Lawrence: University Press of Kansas, 2001). Also useful

for background is V. K. Triandafillov, *The Nature of the Operations of Modern Armies*, ed. Jacob W. Kipp (London: Frank Cass, 1994).

[3] For the original as republished and still widely available, see B. H. Liddell Hart, *Strategy: The Indirect Approach* (New York: Meridian Books, 1991); for cogent commentary, Brian Holden Reid, *Studies in British Military Thought: Debates With Fuller and Liddell Hart* (Lincoln: University of Nebraska Press, 1998).

[4] Quick reference may be made to David Rooney, *Guerrilla: Insurgents, Patriots and Terrorists from Sun Tzu to Bin Laden* (London: Brassey's, 2004), pp. 199–220 (chapter entitled "Che Guevara and Guerrilla War"). See also Paul J. Dosal, *Commandante Che: Guerrilla Soldier, Commander, and Strategist: 1956–1967* (University Park: Pennsylvania State University Press, 2003). For Che's benchmark work, Che Guevara, *Guerrilla Warfare*, ed. Brian Loveman and Thomas M. Davies, 3rd edn. (Wilmington, Delaware: Scholarly Resources, 1997).

Abbreviations

AI: Amnesty International
AIADMK: *Anna Dravida Munnetra Kazhagham* ("*Anna* DMK")
AIS: Administrative Inspectorate System
AFP: Armed Forces of the Philippines
AMRS: Association of Major Religious Superiors
AO: Area of Operations
APC: All-Party Congress
APF: Armed Police Force
APRA: *Alianza Popular Revolucionaria Americana* (American Popular Revolutionary Alliance)
ARD: Accelerated Rural Development
ARVN: Army of the Republic of Vietnam
ASIC: All Source Intelligence Center

BCG: *Base contra guerilla*
BPP: Border Patrol Police

CAFGU: Citizen Armed Forces Geographical Units
CC: Central Committee
CCO: Chief Coordinating Officers
CCOMPOSA: Coordination Committee of Maoist Parties and Organisations of South Asia
CCP: Chinese Communist Party

Abbreviations

CDO: Chief District Officer
CIA: Central Intelligence Agency
CO: Coordinating Officers
COIN: Counter-insurgency
COLAR: Colombian Army
COMINTERN: Communist International
CPM: Civil-Police-Military
CPN(M): Communist Party of Nepal (Maoist)
CPP: Communist Party of the Philippines
CPT: Communist Party of Thailand
CPS: Communist Party of Siam
CSOC: Communist Suppression Operations Command
CYS: Communist Youth of Siam
CZ: *Comite Zonal*

DC: District Committee
DEA: Drug Enforcement Agency
DGU: District Guerilla Unit
DMK: *Dravida Munnetra Kazhaghan*

ECCSTP: European Coordinating Committee for Solidarity with the Thai People
EGP: *Ejercito Guerilla Popular* (Popular Liberation Army of People's Liberation Army)
ENLF: Eelam National Liberation Front
EPRLF: Eelam People's Revolutionary Liberation Front
EROS: Eelam Revolutionary Organisation of Students
ETA: *Euzkadita ta Askatasuna* (Basque Homeland and Freedom)

FARC: *Fuerzas Armadas Revolucionarias de Colombia* (Revolutionary Armed Forces of Colombia)
FBIS: (US) Foreign Broadcast Information Service
FF: Fighting Front
FGU: Front Guerilla Unit
FMLN: *Frente Faribundo Marti de Liberacion Nacional* (Faribundo Marti Liberation Front)
FPU: Front Partisan Unit
FWAC: Front White Area Committee

GA: Government Agent
GDP: Gross Domestic Product
GMA: Gloria Macapagal Arroyo

HPF: High Powered Firearm
HUMINT: Human Intelligence

IAFP: International Association of Filipino Patriots
IGP: Inspector General of Police
INSEC: Informal Sector Research and Study Centre
IPC: Island Party Committee
IPFK: Indian Peacekeeping Force
ISDP: Integrated Security and Development Programme
ISOC: Internal Security Operations Command
ITBF: Indo-Tibetan Border Force
IW: Information Warfare

J-2: Office of the Assistant Chief of Staff for Intelligence
JOC: Joint Operations Center
JVP: *Janatha Vimukthi Peramuna*
(People's Liberation Front)
KDP: Union of Democratic Filipinos
KMT: Kuomintang

LCM: Local Communist Movement
LGU: Local Guerilla Unit
LIC: Low Intensity Conflict
LPRP: Lao People's Revolutionary Party
LTTE: Liberation Tigers of *Tamil Eelam*

MACV: (US) Military Assistance Command, Vietnam
MCC: Maoist Communist Centre
MDD: Movement for a Democratic Philippines
MGU: Main Guerilla Unit
MILF: Moro Islamic Liberation Front
MNLF: Moro National Liberation Front
MOS: Military Occupational Specialty

Abbreviations

MP: Member of Parliament
MRTA: *Movimiento Revolucionario Tupac Amaru* (Tupac Amaru Revolutionary Movement)

NDF: National Democratic Front
NFF: Northern Fighting Front
NFPC: Northern Front Party Committee
NLFT: National Liberation Front of *Tamil Ealam*
NPA: New People's Army (CPP)
NSC: National Security Council
NUC: National Unification Commission
NVA: North Vietnamese Army

OC: Organizing Committees
OG: Organizing Groups
OM: Organized Masses
OIC: Organisation of the Islamic Conference
OMM: Open Mass Movement

PACT: Philippine American Cooperation Treaty (of 1991)
PANAMIN: Presidential Assistant on National Minorities
PB: Party Branch
PC: Philippine Constabulary
PIRA: Provisional Irish Republican Army
PIRPC: Panay Island Regional Party Committee
PFLP: Popular Front for the Liberation of Palestine
PKM: *Partido Komunista ng Philipinas* (Communist Party of the Philippines)
PLO: Palestine Liberation Organisation
PM: Prime Minister
PMA: Philippine Military Academy
PNP: Philippine National Police
POT: Political Organizing Team
PRC: People's Republic of China
PSB: Public Security Bureau
PWG: People's War Group

RAs: Reaffirmists

RAW: Research Analysis Wing
RIM: Revolutionary Internationalist Movement
RJs: Rejectionists
RMA: Revolution in Military Affairs
ROE: Rules of Engagement
RPA: Revolutionary Proletarian Army
RTA: Royal Thai Army
RTG: Royal Thai Government
RUC: Regional Unified Command
RUFG: Regional United Front Group

SAS: Special Air Services
SLFP: Sri Lanka Freedom Party
SRA: Strategic Research and Analysis Division
SRI: Stanford Research Institute
STF: Special Task Force
SZ: *Sub Zonales*

TCP: Thai Communist Party
TELA: *Tamil Eelam* Liberation Army
TELF: *Tamil Eelam* Liberation Front
TELO: *Tamil Eelam* Liberation Organisation
TERA: *Tamil Ealam* Republican Army
TFDP: Task Force Detainees of the Philippines
TIC: Thai Information Center

TNA: Tamil National Army
TOE: Tables of Organization and Equipment
TPLA: Thai People's Liberation Army
TULF: Tamil United Liberation Front

UML: United Marxist-Leninists
UNP: United National Party
UP: University of the Philippines
UPFA: United People's Freedom Alliance
URPC: United Revolutionary People's Council
USARPAC: United States Army, Pacific

Abbreviations

VC: Vietnamese Communists
VCP: Vietnam Communist Party
VDC: Village Development Committee
VFA: Visiting Forces Agreement
VIC: Virtual Information Center
VISSA: Visayas Secretariat for Social Action
VOPT: Voice of the People of Thailand

Chapter 1

Introduction

To draw upon Biblical inspiration, "to rise up," as with "the poor," has always been with us. That is, as long as there has been humankind, there have been those who have felt obliged to strike out against their rulers, to revolt. The Bible is a useful reference, for it is replete with instances of such rebellion. Similarly, it contains numerous examples of revolt directed against occupying powers, so-called wars of resistance or wars of liberation.

The fusion of these two notions, striking out against those within and against those who have occupied from without, makes the Maoist approach so powerful.[1] It states simply that the two categories of oppressor are one and the same, that those who behave in such fashion as to spark revolt are likewise "occupiers" in their own land and thus rightfully to be resisted. The existing order—the old-regime (a*ncien regime*)—must be overthrown.

In order to implement such sentiment requires more than verbiage. By its very definition, revolt is something initiated by those in a position of societal disadvantage, by those on the bottom. Not having the resources available to those in power, they have been forced to rely upon the weapons of the weak—asymmetric weapons—those maximizing their strengths and striking at the enemy's weaknesses: terror and guerrilla war.

Terror is not to be confused with "terrorism" as the term is currently used. The former is a tool, a weapon designed to foster fear in pursuance of a larger organizational end, such as popular control or mobilization into a counter-state. The latter takes the tool and makes it the end itself. Any organizational consequence is incidental. Terror, put another way, is a tactic; terrorism is tactic, operational art, and strategy. In terrorism there is little beyond the terror. Effective rebels have recognized that such is quite ineffective, whatever damage it may inflict.

To avoid semantic gymnastics, scholars increasingly use terror and terrorism interchangeably, even as they are careful to draw a distinction between terrorism as a method of action and terrorism as a logic of action.[2] Terrorism is distinguished by the latter; insurgency incorporates the former. The key element of terrorism is the divorce of armed politics from a purported mass base, those in whose name terrorists claim to be fighting. Little or no meaningful effort goes into constructing a counter-state, which is the central activity of insurgency. In contrast, insurgencies, while also armed expressions of organic, internal political disaffiliation,[3] use terrorist action principally as one weapon among many to facilitate constructing the counter-state.

The second major tactic mentioned above, guerrilla war, necessarily involves an element of terror but is distinct in that it is the mode of warfare most often adopted by those who can not wage war in the manner of their oppressors. It is, as the very Spanish language term, *guerrilla*, states, a "little war." It is "unconventional," because it does not choose to be "conventional." It apes military forms and ends without adopting them. In particular, it does not seek to hold position on the battlefield and thus make of itself a vulnerable target. Guerrillas attack the enemy's military power and then fade away.

Such a mode of operation presupposes areas for rest and regroupment, areas that are in touch with a population that, even if not wholly sympathetic, is not overtly hostile, particularly to the extent of informing the authorities. This necessitates a modicum of positive interaction. At times, throughout history, certain legendary bandits—England's Robin Hood and Scotland's Rob Roy come immediately to mind—achieved the desired blend of popular support, guerrilla action, and terror-in-moderation necessary to thwart their adversaries and emerge victorious.

They emerged victorious, however, only within societal parameters. Robin Hood, in the legend, is redeemed by the return of the good king who sees to it that justice is carried out; Rob Roy sees justice done only through the intercession of a benighted member of the elite, the evil representatives of which he has risen up against. All that has changed is personalities, not the structure whereby the principals relate to each other. Absent a "good man," the dynamic is likely to occur again.

Insurgency as Strategic Choice

This reality is explicitly recognized by insurgents, those for whom politics is wedded to revolt. Insurgency is often used as but a synonym for revolt, but in modern parlance it has rather more specifically come to mean revolt aware of the structural issues at stake, of the need to change not merely personalities but institutions and their interaction. This has required building a counter-state in which the new order can be made real.

This is the essence of politics: the process whereby society decides and implements "who gets what," with "what" further delineated as rights, resources, privileges, and obligations. Politics, then, sets society's rules of the game. To revolt with such an end in mind is very different from the traditional lashing out that has driven most rebels prior to the modern era.

And it was with the modern era that insurgency appeared, its first instance being the American Revolution, also termed (in Britain) the War of American Independence. In its discussions, documents, and in the very "orders of the day" read out to the troops, the notion was set forth that what was at hand was not a mere rising up but the fashioning of a new order. What was at hand was violence in support, strategically, of a political goal; operationally, of a political infrastructure, a counter-state; tactically, of local political domination.

It is worth noting, too, that the name of the conflict raises yet another key issue, that of revolution. "Revolution" as a term has seen a variety of meanings attached to it. Yet in the modern era it has meant something very specific: the fundamental overturning of what is, "the world turned upside down," as the British band is reputed to have played at the climactic surrender to the Patriots at Yorktown.[4] In the conceptual framework of Max Weber, the father of sociology, this meant—since all existence could be conceptualized within three systems of stratification, economic, status, and politics—the overturning of those systems.[5]

The debate as to whether "revolution" is a proper label for the American War of Independence stems from precisely this point: What actually changed, and how quickly did it do so? The common currency in historical thought contends that nothing much changed at all, although research over the past several decades has thoroughly laid this notion to rest. Hence, the issue is a temporal one. In political science, a "revolution" is held to be akin to an earthquake, a massive upheaval bounded in time and place, the place a particular nation-state, the time undetermined but "short."

A convincing body of research now holds that what went on during the eight years of the American Revolution was so profound that the product was indeed, certainly within a decade of the formal peace being signed, a society so unlike that which began the conflict that "revolution" is appropriate.[6] Be this as it may, the crucial element, as concerns us here, is that not only was an insurgency carried out, as opposed to a mere revolt, but also what we may call a revolutionary war, war waged specifically to create a revolution.

This separates the American Revolution from the other profound upheaval more normally associated with the term, the French Revolution. As there was in the latter no insurgency *per se*, there could be no revolutionary war.[7] Instead, there was an upheaval that swept away the *ancien régime*, the old-order,[8] followed by counter-revolution and the Napoleonic era.

That era, specifically Napoleon's "Spanish Ulcer" of 1808–12 (or 1808–09 to 1813–14, depending upon precise periodization), returned attention to the concept of *guerrilla* and gave that style of resistance its particular name.[9] Ironically, the two phenomena, insurgency and revolution, proceeded on virtually separate tracks for a considerable period of time. Marx, in his invention of "Marxism," expounded an explicit theory of revolution based on economic disparity,[10] while Lenin subsequently "invented" the means whereby Marx's vague notions could be realized.[11]

Though his thoughts on the "secret party" were little different from the organizational lessons that had been an essential part of the American revolutionary movement, he added particulars, such as democratic centralism, that divorced his approach from democratic process and made it a more viable tool for subversion. It is noteworthy, though, whatever his embrace of violence as inherent to his approach, Lenin felt compelled to speak out against the unstructured and incoherent use of terror, as embodied, most particularly, in the campaigns of the anarchists. Absent explicit organizational construction, he observed, terror was a deviation from the correct path for seizing state power.

It is just as appropriate to note that Lenin had little to say of guerrilla warfare save as an adjunct to conventional power. The key was to form military units that could drive their opponents from the field. Society could then be molded to accord with revolutionary prerequisites. The battle began among the proletariat, in urban centers, and then, by subversion and mobilization of the workers, advanced against the centers of enemy power.

This was the approach adopted by those who sought to follow Lenin's dictates, from Germany to China, where a new synthesis appeared, one that in and of itself was to have a revolutionary impact on insurgency as a form of warfare.

Although not yet addressed explicitly, a reality lurks behind what has been said above: the thoughts and actions of individuals drive events. To engage in politics is to choose courses of action. Societal structure will influence these, facilitate and constrain, shape the field of battle, yet, when all is said and done, reality only exists as it is made so by human agency.

"Revolution in the Revolution"

If there were any single work that should have influenced research on insurgency, it was an often overlooked piece by James C. Scott, "Revolution in the Revolution: Peasants and Commissars."[12] Scott addresses what for analysts is a classic query: Have societal causes produced activism, or has activism taken advantage of societal causes? Opponents of the *status quo* normally opt for the former, proponents for the latter. In a sense, the query itself is irrelevant, and the distinction in causation need not be made: the two processes are complementary, not mutually exclusive. As Scott perceptively notes, all insurgent movements necessarily contain two elements: leadership ranks comprised of members drawn generally from a society's elite, followers taken from the masses. The same "causes" motivate them but in very different ways. The leadership normally perceives injustice and attempts to deal with it by ideological solution. The followers, in contrast, who historically have been drawn overwhelmingly from the peasantry, attempt to deal with justice by correcting those immediate wrongs (that is, grievances) that are identified.

Insurgent movements, therefore, involve a continuous process whereby the two elements, the leadership and the followers, establish links and interact with each other. Societal causes are a necessary but not sufficient factor for the insurgency. First, the causes must lead to alienation of both potential leadership and potential insurgent manpower. Secondly, the two must establish a relationship. Only when this has been accomplished does a potential insurgency exist.

But a constant tension is present. If the ideological approach of the leadership is able to hold sway, insurgency will result. The movement will go on to pursue political goals, normally the effort to remake the system, either defensively (e.g., separatism) or offensively (e.g., revolutionary war, the purposive effort "to make a revolution"). If, however, the resolution of immediate grievances wins out, as normally desired by the manpower, then rebellion results.

The point is crucial. If an insurgency is judged as essentially a coalition of various local rebellions, then examination must focus on the sources of unrest, whether driven by "moral economy" or "rational" inspiration. If, however, infrastructure (the counter-state) tightly controls and regulates the insurgency, recruiting manpower from a wide variety of strata, then the research focus needs to shift to the mechanisms of organization. This has not often occurred, not, in any event, in the politicized academic world of Vietnam and after.[13]

It can readily be seen that these two perspectives are hardly value-neutral. In the first case, rebellion can be said to come from "within," in the second, from "without." The first case inherently presupposes a certain legitimacy in the uprising; the second lends itself to an explanation of "manipulation by outsiders." These are, respectively, the basic positions of the political spectrum's left and right wings. The first came to dominate research on popular upheaval of any sort. Predictably, however, a fusion of the two approaches, with special attention paid to the evolution of a movement over time, yields the most satisfactory results.[14]

In such examination, scale is important, as is the changing relationship over time between three elements: terror, recruitment, and infrastructure (counter-state). The vaster a country, particularly its rural sector, the more marginal areas are there in which revolutionary political activity can operate with minimal fear of government intervention. The effect of this physical space is often magnified by the "political space" created through government miscues and omissions. As time passes and the counter-state becomes more established, invariably using terror to stifle opposition, the original grievances assume less importance. Instead, the organizational mechanisms become paramount. At one extreme, potential recruits see the movement as a viable alternative for social participation; at the other, they simply recognize that it effectively has become the state and thus must be obeyed. It socializes and controls.

No insurgent movement, in particular those of the Cold War era, ever was wholly an ideological creature. Then, as now, it was the parameters of the relationship between the leaders and the followers that were critical to understanding the nature of any insurgency and in dealing with it.[15] The essence of insurgency lies in mobilization. Scott's observation is so telling precisely because it states what should be obvious but seems to have been forgotten: those in organizations, whether insurgent or any other, are there for many different reasons and stay for a variety of reasons. Throughout the Cold War, leaders thrown up by societal issues looked to Marxist ideology for both explanations of their situations and for operational guidance. They looked, too, for followers.

These, however, rarely if ever experienced alienation in the same way as the leaders and were not much interested in Marxist conceptualizations. They wanted tangible progress toward redress. As classic "grievance guerrillas," they were willing to give into movement demands for participating in Marxist forms to the extent that the movement seemed to answer to their needs. Those needs could include ethnicity or national identity. They could also include any number of other factors. The key was neither the Marxist ideology nor the specific grievances of the manpower but, rather, the "negotiated relationship" between the leaders and the followers.[16]

Ideological Blueprint for Seizing State Power

What Mao did was to recognize that the solution to the challenge of seizing state power lay in forming a counter-state, an alternative infrastructure grounded in the same "nation in arms" as had come to characterize conventional warfare but a nation created from scratch. To that end, he developed an approach that, as will be discussed below, was not laid out in the neat formulation[17] comprised of the five essential components given here:

(1) *Mass line*: organizing an alternative society through the construction of clandestine infrastructure, that is, a counter-state. Local socio-economic grievances and aspirations are to be addressed by cadre, who then connect solutions to the party's political mechanism. As with all political action, appeal to perceived needs (not only grievances but also hopes and aspirations) seeks to win allegiance for the purpose of target mobilization. The approach seeks a mass base.

(2) *United front*: making common cause with those, individuals and groups, who share concerns but not necessarily party goals. That an armed political movement is able to address perceived needs does not necessarily carry with it enough momentum to overcome natural fear of participation in what, after all, is an illegal, underground, dangerous endeavor. "Fellow traveler" status (even if itself concealed by the organization concerned) offers an alternative route and may, in fact, provide some benefits to the insurgency in the form of advancing legal, open organizations that swell the mass base.

(3) *Violence*: The new alternative society, existing as it does illegally and clandestinely, necessarily relies upon armed action to maintain its security within and without. The "liberation" struggle progresses through three strategic phases, which are quite logical. Initially, the revolutionary movement will be on the defensive, then achieve stalemate, finally go on the offensive. During each phase, a particular form of warfare will drive the dynamic, although not necessarily quantitatively. During the strategic defensive, terror and guerrilla actions will lead. During the strategic stalemate, mobile warfare (maneuver warfare) will dominate. This will see insurgent "main force" units, equivalents of government formations, take the field but not seek to hold territory. The final phase, the strategic offensive, will see such seizure of ground, the so-called "war of position."

(4) **Political warfare**: using nonviolent methods, such as participation under-mining the morale of enemy forces or offering to engage in negotiations, as an adjunct to violence. These methods could be implemented at all three levels of war: strategic, operational, or tactical. Unlike the united front, Mao conceived of political warfare means as those specifically intended to force-multiply. The united front was a line of operation unto itself.

(5) **International action**: Although not as prominent an element during Mao's struggle as it was to become later in the hands of pupils, international pressure upon the state, or in favor of the insurgents, was recognized as an important element in the equation.

That the Americans, or any other subsequent historical actors we might be able to identify (for example, Sandino and his followers in Nicaragua, or Zapata and his mass base in Mexico), had in fact applied just these elements is correct. What Mao did that was revolutionary was to combine the parts into a systematic whole, complete with doctrine, in a manner that put any state at risk. Indeed, the combination, built as it was upon an ideological mobilization of inferiority, proved so baffling that for a time it appeared well-nigh unstoppable.[18] Then, just as had happened with another startling martial innovation from the same era, German *Blitzkrieg*, people's war was analyzed and beaten on its own terms. Not surprisingly, this occurred at the hands of states with far more will than might to resist.

One way to proceed in the present study would be to take the five elements above and assess a number of case studies within the framework. This would be mind-numbing, and only in the Nepal case itself, where the insurgents were almost transparently determined to copy what had gone before, will the template be brought explicitly to bear.

There is also a central issue that can be obscured by relying on a neat outline (such as that above). Mao's strategy itself did not spring full-grown from his mind. To the contrary, what has been set forth above did not appear in any Maoist text as a systematic display of approach. Just as Che Guevara could produce his celebrated, and spectacularly unsuccessful, *foco* theory only by ignoring reality,[19] so much that has come to be associated with people's war emerged as Mao and his followers projected onto their past the purported logic and intent that was in reality as much the exception as the rule during actual events. It was this sanitized, homogenized rendering of the past that subsequent revolutionaries sought to adopt.

In the event, only by fits and starts did people's war as doctrine emerge as a formidable method. As such, it really has several parts, and the relationship between them is not always appreciated. Specifically, during the Jiangxi Soviet period, 1930–34, techniques of tactics and operational art, as well as for dealing with the masses, were developed. Yet these proved insufficient to prevent the Jiangxi Soviet from being crushed by Chiang Kai-shek's five encirclement campaigns.[20] Subsequently, during the Yenan period, that following the Long March but prior to full-scale war with Japan, further "mass line" techniques were developed (that is, developing a counter-state that could support maintenance and projection of revolutionary force). Only with the Japanese occupation, however, could a synthesis between guerrilla warfare and mass organization emerge that we would recognize today as "Maoist insurgency" or people's war.

Despite the controversy over the role peasant nationalism played in the mobilization process, Chalmers Johnson is obviously correct in judging that without the Japanese occupation there would not have been Maoist insurgency.[21] One need not even enter into the debate as to whether it was nationalism or social action that activated the peasantry. Both were important and played varying roles depending upon the specific region in question; the real key was the destruction of the Kuomintang (KMT) resource and manpower base by the Japanese, a reality that meant the state, incomplete and inefficient although it was, even after the Northern Expedition, was no longer able to muster the power that had previously proved quite sufficient to crush the communists, most tellingly in the Fifth Encirclement Campaign. It is not an overstatement to posit that without the Japanese invasion, there might well have been no Mao. The collapse of the KMT in the 1945–49 civil war was an anti-climax. The Nationalist cause was mortally wounded before the battle was joined.[22]

Finally, from the struggle against the Japanese came Mao's actual people's war framework. Here, we see all of the diverse pieces fit together to form a picture. What was crucial was that in Mao's final product his earlier techniques were subsumed by the larger strategic approach that rested upon a very particular world view, that of the insurgent battling within the imperialist context. Lacking that, the pieces did not necessarily hang together. This, too, was to pose problems for those who would seek to use the model.

Let us look at this more carefully. By perfecting the notion of the clandestine party of revolutionaries, Lenin removed the Marxian revolution from its position as a course of action open only to advanced capitalist societies and placed it within the realm of possibility for any state, provided a revolutionary situation existed and a revolutionary party could guide the population toward consciousness. Mao took this lesson and applied it to China, producing a movement far more grounded in the masses than anything Lenin envisaged. Mao thus demonstrated the need for revolutionaries to bend Marxism to their particular situation, rather than attempting to fit the situation to Marxism.[23] Would-be revolutionaries frequently overlooked this lesson.

Mao's greatest contribution was to recognize that in a country where the working class was unavailable or unable to participate in the revolutionary movement, other classes in a relationship with the dominant class similar in quality/nature to that between the proletariat and the bourgeoisie might have class consciousness and, therefore, revolutionary potential. In China, the class Mao specifically had in mind was the peasantry, the overwhelming majority of the Chinese population. The revolution, to be sure, would still have to be guided by the representatives of the working class (the party), but the relationship between the party and the masses was to be far more symbiotic than proposed by Lenin. Even as the party raised the consciousness of the peasants, it was to learn from the people and thus to modify its approaches. Only by pursuing such a process of interaction could a correct strategy be developed.

This "going to the masses" is often mistaken as democratic action. It is anything but. Rather it is a technique to maximize mobilization of manpower for a counter-state by using a carrot rather than a stick. The masses needed to be brought into decision-making, but their deliberations would be guided in the direction chosen by the party. Early efforts to build revolutionary power on a proletarian base in China had foundered on the most logical of explanations: There was insufficient human material in the urban centers of proletarian concentration to build a potent movement. The peasantry was where the bodies were.

Mao's recognition of the need to mold Marxism to fit China's unique circumstances had a profound effect in another area, that of the analysis of the revolutionary situation. While agreeing with Lenin that there were major and minor contradictions in a society, Mao recognized that there might arise special circumstances so extreme in character that there was the chance that the very society that gave rise to the contradictions, and therefore the opportunity for revolutionary action, might be eliminated. The special circumstances would thus have to take priority over the contradictions; that is, the special circumstance in itself became the major contradiction, and all other contradictions became minor.[24]

At the time Mao wrote this analysis, China was caught up in two great contradictions, that of feudalism *versus* the masses of the people, and that of China *versus* imperialism, as represented by Japan. The contradiction between China and Japan had been principal, because the Japanese invasion threatened to wipe out Chinese society. The nature of class relations was changed, since all classes faced the issue of survival. The need to resist the common threat made possible bonds that could not have existed previously. The struggle against imperialism had to take priority; and since this was a struggle of the Chinese people as a whole, the entire population could be viewed as a revolutionary class.

Mobilizing this class required a united front against the imperialists. Mao welcomed into his united front all except "enemy classes." To ensure harmony within the front, certain concessions not involving "issues of principle" were made. Most significantly, the goal of a "workers' and peasants' republic" was broadened to include all allied elements in a "people's republic."[25] The united front, therefore, had become for Mao an integral step in a process of societal transition, rather than a mere maneuver, to use Trotsky's term, to be used to advantage under certain circumstances (i.e., a mere element of political warfare). It was not a "temporary makeshift." Through it, the revolution could be propelled to a new stage.

The key was the mobilizing the counter-state so as ultimately to be able to project superior combat power against the state. Even while participating in a united front, the Communist Party was directed to proselytize, to win over to its way of thinking "the middle forces." It was within this context that Mao was able to create the mass organization that ultimately allowed him to defeat the Kuomintang. The mass line was the foundation on which all else was built. As Mao wrote:

> All correct leadership is necessarily from the masses, to the masses. This means: take the ideas of the masses (scattered and unsystematic ideas) and concentrate them (through study turn them into concentrated and systematic ideas), then go to the masses and propagate and explain these ideas until the masses embrace them as their own, hold fast to them and translate them into action, and test the correctness of these ideas in such action. Then once again go to the masses so that the ideas are preserved in an endless spiral, with the ideas becoming more correct, more vital and richer each time. Such is the Marxist-Leninist theory of knowledge, or methodology.[26]

Such a philosophy would be familiar to any political party in a democracy. What made it more than that, a weapon of war, was the goal of mass mobilization for armed action. Always, the end was to strengthen the insurgent organization; and at no time were the people to be allowed to veer off along self-selected paths. Tactical compromises, to be sure, were allowed, even encouraged, but only if they produced results that would strengthen the counter-state's overall ascent.

Closely related to the mass line was Mao's emphasis on self-reliance. Not only were the masses the ultimate source of revolutionary rectitude, but upon them the revolutionaries in China also depended for their sustenance. There were no foreign sanctuaries as had sheltered Lenin and his compatriots. Neither did the Chinese bourgeoisie state seem to be in straits as desperate as those into which Russia entered after years of martial defeat in the First World War.

We now know this part of Mao's reasoning to be inaccurate in one sense: The Japanese intrusion, in fact, had shattered the KMT state. Nonetheless, in the immediate matter of military confrontation, the "die-hard forces" (i.e., the anti-communist forces) remained powerful *vis-à-vis* the communists. To counter them it was necessary for Mao to engage the third operational aspect of his approach, the "protracted war."

The strength of the national bourgeoisie, and later also the strength of the Japanese imperialists, was initially overwhelming compared to that of the communists. This meant that the party was faced with two tasks: first, construction of a viable military apparatus; and, secondly, to use this apparatus to engage in a protracted war of the "three stages" discussed above. Hand-in-hand with the violence inherent to military action was to go what the Chinese termed "political warfare," the use of non-violent techniques as elements of combat power.

Although the united front could in a sense be so considered, what Mao (and later the revived forces of Chiang Kai-shek on Taiwan) had in mind was a more direct use of non-violent operational art and tactics (for example, a campaign to ensure troop motivation, in the first instance; preventing the deployment of enemy units to the battlefield through a transportations strike, in the second). The united front was both strategy and strategic environment.

What emerges clearly from this fact is the relevance of the international context. People's war was an approach developed by a Marxist-Leninist party committed to waging revolutionary war. As such, imperialism, as a higher form of capitalism, was inevitably the strategic environment within which struggle would take place. The only issue was which capitalist power was the dominant foe at any juncture in history. This foe and its allies could be dealt with by the same techniques associated with the united front, ranging from strategic isolation, so as to neutralize efforts to aid counter-insurgents, to tactical action, using action by friendly foreign forces to block the provision of arms and equipment to a state undergoing insurgency.

This aspect of Mao's contribution was to have enormous impact on liberation movements throughout the "developing world." As he struggled to continue the revolution and to create a new society in post-1949 China, Mao viewed the primary threat to the Chinese Revolution no longer as the Japanese but the Americans. His answer to the threat lay in people's war. Speaking as a surrogate for Mao, Lin Piao, in his "Long Live the Victory of People's War,"[27] published in 1965 to commemorate the twentieth anniversary of Japan's defeat in the Second World War, clearly set forth the need for self-reliance and the organic as opposed to expedient role the united front was to occupy in the process.

More to our point, a cardinal theme that ran throughout the work was that, just as the invasion of China by the Japanese imperialists had caused a transformation of the principal and secondary contradictions, so the situation in an Asia ripe for revolution had been transformed by America's assumption of the Japanese imperial role. During the national-democratic revolutionary phase, "imperialism and its lackeys" were thus the principal enemy. American imperialist aggression presented the Asian communist parties with the opportunity "to rally all anti-imperialist patriotic forces, including the national bourgeoisie and all patriotic persons" in an anti-imperialist united front. Those from the exploiting classes who joined the struggle against the imperialists thereby played a progressive historical role and transcended their own reactionary essence.

In short, analyzed Lin Piao and Mao, the strategic setting was ripe for seizing the initiative, and through the united front against the imperialists, Asia's communists would be able to mobilize their countrymen in such a way as to advance the revolution itself, just as Mao had in China. The intervention of American imperialism was not a setback but a boon, for it created the historical conditions for realizing the national united front. Just as importantly, this intervention was not a chance occurrence, but rather a stage in the historical decline of capitalism, a permanent reality that was to be overcome and used to further the revolution.

Hence, Maoist techniques for waging revolutionary war, while conceivably viable when taken in isolation, were intended to function within a very special context. In particular, the mobilization of the oppressed depended upon two necessities: first, carving out liberated areas (i.e., soviets) of such size that the alternative society could function to incorporate the masses; and, secondly, convincing these same masses that the feedback mechanisms of the Leninist structure were a sufficient form of democracy. Lacking either of these, the only realistic alternative to effect mobilization was terror. This, in fact, became increasingly prominent in movements that sought to use Maoist insurgency. They were to be caught in strategic misjudgment, because Mao's assessment of the situation, grounded as it was in the economic determinism of Marxism, failed to discern the larger structural dynamic at work: the growth of popular demand for democratic governance.

Small wonder that those adopting the Maoist model, rather than recognizing this strategic reality, often fell into emphasizing techniques. Most such students copied from afar, absorbing a filtered view of the Maoist strategy. Still not completely understood, however, and thus discussed but little in this work, is the extent to which the Chinese sought to pass on directly their understanding of what they were about in making revolutionary war (as opposed to imparting technical training, particularly in cadre procedures and military tactics). In salient cases examined here, Thailand, the Philippines, Sri Lanka, and Peru, it is now established that cadre either actually trained in China or were in contact with Chinese personnel posted abroad. We have long known of the instruction given to Thai communists in China, but only more recently has information surfaced on training trips made to China by Philippine and Peruvian insurgents. The picture is incomplete as concerns the Sinhalese component of the Sri Lankan uprising, although contact did occur with overseas Chinese representatives. What remains yet to be researched is the precise balance struck in this training between technique and approach, which is to say, the relative weight given to the tactical, operational, and strategic components of the Maoist approach.

At the end of the day, what should be clear is how very far the Maoist approach is from what we persist in calling guerrilla warfare. To the contrary, it was a multidimensional approach for assaulting the state, with the "weapons" at its disposal as varied as terror and massed battalions, as violence and persuasion, as cooperation and assault. Not only did Mao return time and again to the theme that guerrilla warfare could not be decisive, but he also developed a sophisticated template for mobilizing ever more powerful forces across an entire spectrum of techniques fielded at the three levels of war.

So complete was what Mao advanced compared to what had gone before that it stands as a Revolution in Military Affairs (RMA). This is not the place to discuss this issue in depth. Suffice to say that an unfortunate tendency has emerged that equates RMA, as distinguished from the more elemental Military Revolutions (MR), with technologically driven upheavals in the application of military power. Witness the application of the term RMA to describe as US forces combine technological prowess with intelligence integration and decentralized lethality guided by competent leadership to produce a military machine unlike anything the world has seen before.[28] But it will not have gone unnoticed that two of the three elements just mentioned (that is, integration and leadership) are intertwined with human action, which is precisely the point. Mao's innovation, people's war, was so fundamental in what it did to the science and practice of internal war that it must be recognized as a true RMA.[29]

Notes

[1] This point would in an earlier decade have been stated as matter of fact and left at that. It is perhaps better to highlight it now, because a growing body of work has emerged from US commentary on the Iraq insurgency that advances the notion that counter-insurgents functioning as occupiers are locked into a position that fundamentally changes the essence of insurgency and counter-insurgency. Maoist insurgents would find this notion quaint. For the original statement of the issue under discussion, see Steven Metz and Raymond Millen, *Insurgency and Counterinsurgency in the 21st Century: Reconceptualizing Threat and Response* (Carlisle, Pennsylvania: Army War College, 2004). The same argument may also be found, under the same title, in Metz and Millen in *Special Warfare*, 17.3 (February 2005), 6–21.

[2] The precise terminology here is that of Michel Wieviorka, "Terrorism in the Context of Academic Research" in Martha Crenshaw, ed., *Terrorism in Context* (University Park: Pennsylvania State University Press, 1995), 597–606. See also Wieviorka's benchmark *The Making of Terrorism*, trans. David Gordon White (Chicago: University of Chicago Press, 1993).

[3] This insightful definition was coined by Larry Cable in his "Reinventing the Round Wheel: Insurgency, Counter-Insurgency, and Peacekeeping post-Cold War," *Small Wars and Insurgencies*, 4.2 (Autumn 1993), 228–62.

[4] For a discussion of this conflict within an analytical framework useful for understanding the approach advanced here, see Ira Gruber, "The War for American Independence: The People at War," Chapter 2 (29–68) in Robert A. Doughty et al., *American Military History and the Evolution of Warfare in the Western World* (Lexington, Massachusetts: D. C. Heath, 1996). Indispensable as well are John S. Pancake, *1777: The Year of the Hangman* (Tuscaloosa: University of Alabama Press, 1977), and *This Destructive War: The British Campaign in the Carolinas, 1780–1782* (Tuscaloosa: University of Alabama Press, 2003).

[5] Most accessible for explicating this formulation, which I find extraordinarily useful, is a basic text, Mark N. Hagopian, *Regimes, Movements, and Ideologies—A Comparative Introduction to Political Science* (New York: Longman, 1984), especially Chapter 6, "Society and Polity" (223–58), and Chapter 7, "Social Movements and Revolution" (259–300). See also Hagopian's *The Phenomenon of Revolution* (New York: Dodd, Mead, 1974).

[6] A recent treatment of this topic is Gordon S. Wood, *The American Revolution: A History* (New York: Modern Library, 2003).

[7] Particularly useful in examining the origins of the American insurgency is Pauline Maier, *From Resistance to Revolution: Colonial Radicals and the Development of American Opposition to Britain, 1765–1776* (New York: Norton, 1991).

15

⁸ On clandestine processes, see Olivier Bernier, *Words of Fire, Deeds of Blood: The Mob, the Monarch, and the French Revolution* (New York: Anchor Books-Doubleday, 1989).

⁹ On the Spanish *guerrilla* itself, three short works are particularly good: Richard Humble, *Napoleon's Peninsular Marshals* (New York: Taplinger, 1973); David G. Chandler, *On the Napoleonic Wars: Collected Essays* (London: Greenhill Books, 1994), Chapter 10 "Wellington and the Guerrillas," 166–80; and Gunther Rothenberg, *The Napoleonic Wars* (London: Cassell, 1999), Chapter 5 "The Peninsular War: Wellington and the Guerrillas 1809–13," 132–55. In the latter, the final section, "Guerrilla War: An Assessment" (152–55) is as fine a summary of the particulars and issues as one is likely to find. To the latter should be added Charles J. Esdaile, *Fighting Napoleon: Guerrillas, Bandits and Adventurers in Spain, 1808–1814* (New Haven: Yale University Press, 2004). Also useful are John Lawrence Tome, "Napoleon's Uncongenial Sea: Guerrilla Warfare in Navarre during the Peninsular War, 1808–14," *European History Quarterly*, 26.3 (1996), 355–82, and Don W. Alexander, *Rod of Iron: French Counterinsurgency Policy in Aragon during the Peninsular War* (Wilmington, Delaware: Scholarly Resources, 1985). See related material in Milton Finley, *The Most Monstrous of Wars: The Napoleonic Guerrilla War in Southern Italy, 1806–1811* (Columbia: University of South Carolina Press, 1994).

¹⁰ See Karl Marx, *On Revolution*, ed. and trans. Saul K. Padover (New York: McGraw-Hill, 1971), and Robert C. Tucker, *The Marx-Engels Reader*, 2nd edn. (New York: Norton, 1978).

¹¹ For the life of Lenin, see Robert Service, *Lenin: A Biography* (Cambridge: Belknap Press of Harvard University Press, 2000). On context, see Sheila Fitzpatrick, *The Russian Revolution*, revised edn. (New York: Oxford University Press, 1994). Possibly the best insight into Lenin's thought comes from Alexander Solzhenitsyn's novel, *Lenin in Zurich* (New York: Farrar, Straus, and Giroux, 1975).

¹² James C. Scott, "Revolution in the Revolution: Peasants and Commissars," *Theory and Society*, 7.1–2 (January–March 1979), 97–134. Scott's signal contribution to our understanding of peasant behavior, particularly the forms peasant resistance to the state has taken, is understood; and most in this field have at one time or another used his *The Moral Economy of the Peasant: Rebellion and Subsistence in Southeast Asia* (New Haven: Yale University Press, 1976), wherein he described a peasantry that became involved in upheaval because its traditional norms of justice were violated.

¹³ It was only late in the game that the precise relationship between peasant rebellion and insurgency was dealt with explicitly. Rather, it remained a simmering debate in the literature. While Scott approached the subject theoretically, his important insights, which are discussed here, did not initially inspire a body of empirical work. Ben Kerkvliet, for instance, an important figure interested in many of the same research areas as Scott, raised the issue, only

quickly to abandon it, in his "Patterns of Philippine Resistance and Rebellion," *Pilipinas*, 6 (Spring 1986), 35–52 (see especially note 4). Nevertheless, in the post-Vietnam era, virtually all works in the field, consciously or otherwise, adopted a position. See Kerkvliet's *The Huk Rebellion: A Study of Peasant Revolt in the Philippines* (Berkeley: University of California Press, 1977).

[14] This has been recognized in recent years in any number of intelligent studies. See David Stoll, *Between Two Armies in the Ixil Towns of Guatemala* (New York: Columbia University Press, 1993); Eric Selbin, *Modern Latin American Revolutions*, 2nd edn. (Boulder, Colorado: Westview Press, 1999); and Timothy P. Wickham-Crowley, *Guerrillas and Revolutions in Latin America: A Comparative Study of Insurgents and Regimes since 1956* (Princeton, New Jersey: Princeton University Press, 1993). Also useful for illustrating the point are: John Womack, *Rebellion in Chiapas: An Historical Reader* (New York: The New Press, 1999); Neil Harvey, *The Chiapas Rebellion: The Struggle for Land and Democracy* (Durham, North Carolina: Duke University Press, 1998); Daniel Nugent, ed., *Rural Revolt in Mexico: US Intervention and the Domain of Subaltern Politics* (Durham, North Carolina: Duke University Press, 1998); Wunyabari O. Maloba, *Mau Mau and Kenya: An Analysis of a Peasant Revolt* (Bloomington: Indiana University Press, 1993); Lynn Horton, *Peasants in Arms: War and Peace in the Mountains of Nicaragua, 1979–1994* (Athens: Ohio University Center for International Studies, 1998); and Yvon Grenier, *The Emergence of Insurgency in El Salvador: Ideology and Political Will* (Pittsburgh: University of Pittsburgh Press, 1999). Highlighting the point being made, Grenier has even titled her third chapter (67–96), "Revolution Within the Revolution."

[15] See Tom Marks, *Making Revolution: The Insurgency of the Communist Party of Thailand in Structural Perspective* (Bangkok: White Lotus Press, 1994) and Thomas A. Marks, *Maoist Insurgency since Vietnam* (London: Frank Cass, 1996), wherein I build on my doctoral work dealing with the Thai insurgency to look also at the insurgencies of the Philippines, Sri Lanka, and Peru.

[16] Although not the explicit focus of his work, Gregory T. Knouff highlights the point for Revolutionary War insurgents in his *The Soldiers' Revolution: Pennsylvanians in Arms and the Forging of Early American Identity* (University Park: Pennsylvania State Press, 2004).

[17] In this, one is reminded of Napoleon's approach as related by David D. Chandler: "The chief difficulty which every would-be commentator meets in his researches is the fact that Napoleon never really *formulated* a precise system of war—at least not on paper," *The Campaigns of Napoleon: The Mind and Method of History's Greatest Soldier* (New York: Scribner, 1966), 134.

[18] Anthony Joes uses this naïve awe articulated by some, notably Douglas Pike in a

noteworthy gaffe (claiming that people's war has never been defeated), for an appropriate chapter title, "The Myth of Maoist People's War" in his *Resisting Rebellion: The History and Politics of Counterinsurgency* (Lexington: University Press of Kentucky, 2004), 191–208. The chapter, although making its point, does not actually discuss the people's war approach, especially what made it, if not unstoppable, nevertheless so powerful.

[19] On this approach, see Matt D. Childs, "An Historical Critique of the Emergence and Evolution of Ernesto Che Guevara's *Foco* Theory," *Journal of Latin American Studies*, 27, Pt. 3 (October 1995), 593–614; for the death, Henry Butterfield, *The Fall of Che Guevara: A Story of Soldiers, Spies, and Diplomats* (New York: Oxford University Press, 1998); for the relationship between the urban and rural components: Roman L. Bonachea and Marta San Martin, *The Cuban Insurrection, 1952–1959* (New Brunswick, New Jersey: Transaction, 1974), and Julia E. Sweig, *Inside the Cuban Revolution: Fidel Castro and the Urban Underground* (Cambridge, Massachusetts: Harvard University Press, 2002).

[20] I have dealt with this topic in my *Counterrevolution in China: Wang Sheng and the Kuomingtang* (London: Frank Cass, 1998). See especially Chapters 2 and 3.

[21] The debate was begun by the publication of Chalmers Johnson, *Peasant Nationalism and Communist Power in China* (Berkeley: University of California Press, 1962). For a critique of his approach, see Donald G. Gillin, "Review Article: 'Peasant Nationalism' in the History of Chinese Communism," *Journal of Asian Studies*, 23.2 (February 1964), 269–87. Johnson himself considers the controversy and discusses his point further in "Peasant Nationalism Revisited: The Biography of a Book," *China Quarterly*, 72 (December 1977), 766–85. For presentation of the Yenan approach, see another Johnson critic, Mark Selden, *The Yenan Way in Revolutionary China* (Cambridge, Massachusetts: Harvard University Press, 1971). Also useful is his earlier "The Guerrilla Movement in Northwest China: The Origins of the Shensi-Kansu-Ninghsia Border Region," Parts I and II, *China Quarterly*, 28 (October–December 1966), I: 63–81; 29 (January–March 1967), II: 61–81. Carl E. Dorris suggests modification of the "Yenan thesis" in his interesting "Peasant Mobilization in North China and the Origins of Yenan Communism," *China Quarterly*, 68 (December 1976), 697–719. A recent exploration of the entire controversy is Suzanne Pepper's "The Political Odyssey of an Intellectual Construct: Peasant Nationalism and the Study of China's Revolutionary History—A Review Essay," *Journal of Asian Studies*, 63.1 (February 2004), 105–25

[22] An excellent work on the damage inflicted upon the KMT by the Japanese invasion is Hsi-sheng Ch'i, *Nationalist China at War* (Ann Arbor: The University of Michigan Press, 1982). For the civil war period, see Suzanne Pepper, *Civil War in China* (Berkeley: University of California Press, 1978). Fine consideration of the KMT regime, its strengths and weaknesses, is found in two works by Lloyd E. Eastman: *The Abortive Revolution: China under Nationalist Rule, 1927–1937* (Cambridge, Massachusetts: Harvard University Press, 1974)

and *Seeds of Destruction: Nationalist China in War and Revolution, 1937–1949* (Stanford: Stanford University Press, 1984).

²³ This discussion is based principally upon *The Selected Works of Mao Tse-tung* (hereafter *SWM*), 5 vols. (Peking: Foreign Languages Press, various dates); Stuart Schram, *Mao Tse-tung* (Harmondsworth: Penguin Books, 1966); and Schram, *The Political Thought of Mao Tse-tung*, revised edn. (New York: Praeger, 1976).

²⁴ Mao: "Two contradictory things can be united and can transform themselves into each other, but in the absence of these conditions, they cannot constitute a contradiction, cannot coexist in the same entity and cannot transform themselves into each other." See "On Contradiction" (August 1937), *SWM*, I: 311–47.

²⁵ See Lyman P. Van Slyke, *Enemies and Friends—The United Front in Chinese Communist History* (Stanford, California: Stanford University Press, 1967).

²⁶ "Some Questions concerning Methods of Leadership" (1 June 1942), *SWM*, III: 117–22.

²⁷ For a complete text see Lin Piao, "Long Live the Victory of People's War," *Peking Review*, No. 32 (4 August 1967), 14–35. On the author himself, see Martin Ebon, *Lin Piao: The Life and Writings of China's New Ruler* (New York: Stein and Day, 1970).

²⁸ As John Shy and Thomas W. Collier have astutely noted in Chapter 27 of the revised edition of *Makers of Modern Strategy*, "Revolutionary War": "In 1941, when the Princeton seminar in military affairs began the work that led to the original *Makers of Modern Strategy*, the subject of this essay did not exist . . . Evidence of the rising interest in revolution, and of the close connection between outbreaks of revolution and military theory, is scattered through the essays of the first *Makers of Modern Strategy*. But nowhere in that volume, not in the essays on Marx, Trotsky, or the strategists of French colonial warfare, do we find a systematic treatment of ideas for the use of armed force in effecting radical political and social change. The gap was not the fault of Professor Earle and his colleagues; rather, it reflects the fact that in 1941 no such body of theory existed; or, more correctly, that no such theory was seen to exist or, if it existed, to deserve space in a book surveying military thought from Machiavelli to Hitler." See Peter Paret, ed., *Makers of Modern Strategy—From Machiavelli to the Nuclear Age* (Princeton, New Jersey: Princeton University Press, 1986), 815–62. Similarly, as careful a scholar as Azar Gat, in his *A History of Military Thought* (New York: Oxford University Press, 2001), does not even discuss thought pertaining to internal war. (To be fair, his title is misleading, because the work discusses *Western* military thought, but the subhead reads, "From the Enlightenment to the Cold War.") The single best work on the evolution of guerrilla war from tactic to operational art and ultimately strategy is Walter Laqueur's *Guerrilla Warfare: A Historical and Critical Study*, 3rd printing (new Introduction) (New Brunswick, New Jersey: Transaction, 2002).

[29] On the subject or RMA and MR, see MacGregor Knox and Williamson Murray, eds. *The Dynamics of Military Revolution, 1300–2050* (New York: Cambridge University Press, 2001), especially the jointly authored first chapter, "Thinking about Revolutions in Warfare," 1–14.

Chapter 2

Origins of a Model: Insurgency in China and Vietnam

Chapter 1 highlighted the fact that people's war did not spring full-blown from the mind of Mao Tse-tung but, rather, was an approach that emerged only gradually during the course of what we now know as the Chinese Revolution, a process that began even before the 1911 collapse of the Qing (Ch'ing, Manchu) dynasty that brought an end to imperial rule.[1] There followed the chaotic years of the warlords, a time of bloodshed and suffering, tempered, at least partly, only in 1927 with the consolidation of the Republic. It was a republic, however, that did not even dominate its core area of provinces centered on the great treaty ports such as Canton and Shanghai. It was these that had been seized in the so-called Northern Expedition, headed by the emerging star of the Kuomintang (KMT), Chiang Kai-shek, the leading party figure following the death, in 1925, of the "Father of the Republic," Sun Yat-sen. From the moment of Sun's passing, Chiang had increasingly dominated the KMT and the future of China.

Growth of Insurgent Challenge to the Old-Regime

This future was anything but clear in 1927, because the revolutionary endeavor, the drive to replace the old-regime with something new, had early on splintered into two contending forces, both Soviet advised, the Kuomintang and the Chinese Communist Party (CCP). The CCP was not yet, in those early years, led by Mao Tse-tung, and so was not "Maoist." What it sought was a Marxist-Leninist solution to China's problems, the most salient of which were a loss of national independence and internal socio-economic-political structures so flawed that they made life, to use the apt Hobbesian phrase, "nasty, brutish, and short."

In the chaotic post-imperial world, it was the local elite, or gentry, who increasingly determined the rhythms of existence. Although ultimately beholden to regional warlord power, the gentry were thrust to the fore by China's very vastness and the size of her population. Of necessity, warlord power was concentrated in urban centers. The gentry were masters of their localities and the directors of the forces of local order. Predictably, too, they were the CCP's targets. Neither could the gentry gain protection from the KMT, at least initially. Far from being their ally, the KMT also saw them as a counter-revolutionary force, a link with the past standing in the way of the new structures needed to restore China to her previous glory and rightful place in the family of nations. It was logical that the CPP and the KMT initially worked together against the warlords and, by implication, their local representatives (i.e., structurally if not actually), the gentry.

This marriage of convenience ended, however, even as the Northern Expedition drew to a close. In 1927 and 1928, estranged by the CCP's efforts to emphasize class struggle and mobilize into its ranks forces Chiang saw as a threat, the KMT leader turned on his erstwhile allies and purged them. In disarray, the CCP fled from the cities, where, following its Marxist-Leninist doctrine, it had focused its efforts, to the only place where it could find safety, the countryside. There, Mao, who had early on attempted to reorient the party toward the teeming rural millions who dwarfed in numbers any purported, doctrinal "proletariat," was ultimately to emerge as CCP helmsman. And there, the KMT, needing to mobilize force to do battle with the communists, turned to the gentry in an alliance that was to last throughout an increasingly more widespread and bitter civil war.

Chiang Kai-shek, in other words, sought to build upon the structures that were embedded in Chinese society; Mao Tse-tung worked to mobilize new forces for the creation of new structures. To reiterate, it was not in the rural hinterlands that the CCP first attempted to make its movement a going concern. Instead, it was in southern China's urban centers, particularly Canton and Shanghai, where a proletariat could be found that needed only the leadership of a Leninist revolutionary party to throw off its chains. Only with their hammering in the cities did it become necessary for the would-be revolutionaries to go to the masses who comprised the peasantry. Mao and a host of lesser known, local would-be revolutionaries were already there. Most of these individuals, to include Mao himself, had sprung from the gentry. More often than not they were teachers and students, who used the existing institutions and structures of Chinese society to build their movements.

Once they gained a certain following, they went to work among those they judged to be the exploited, particularly the landless poor.[2]

Initial recruits, however, as we now know from a wide body of material, were not drawn from the masses *per se* but from fringe elements of the populace, especially secret societies, bandits, and linguistic minorities located in locales of minimal official presence, such as border areas.[3] Only when the revolutionary movement became a going concern was it able to exploit the mechanisms and contradictions in the old-regime, as it did in Jiangxi, where the communists were to have their most important pre-Second World War "liberated areas," or soviets (see Figure 2.1). The structural shortcomings of the old-regime in China, in other words, were not sufficient in and of themselves to cause the communist insurgency.[4]

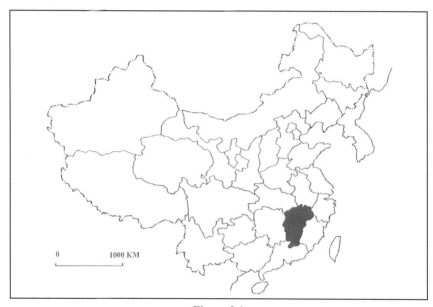

Figure 2.1

The contrary has been a dominant theme in American scholarship on China, but it sidesteps the important roles of human agency (voluntarism) and strategic implementation. When all is said and done, communist revolutionary warfare in China was a technique for purposive action. It was a means to an end: political power to be seized for the purpose of overthrowing the existing order. It was not, as many of its misguided adherents claimed, an alternative form of democratic governance.[5] To the contrary, as will become clear in the course of this work, democratic empowerment has been the most viable counter to the Maoist approach.

CCP insurgency, hence, was about politics. It was the conscious effort to supplant one political structure with another, to mobilize a counter-state with which to overthrow the existing one. Taken to its logical end, it became that what Mao claimed to be waging, revolutionary warfare, the conscious effort by insurgents "to make a revolution" by seizing state power using politico-military means radically to reshape it. Those who resisted the effort, such as the KMT, by definition were engaged in counter-revolutionary warfare. They were counter-insurgents.[6] In all these endeavors, it was human beings who comprised revolution and counter-revolution. Structural circumstances meant nothing save they were made real through human action. External manifestations of insurgency or counter-insurgency, such as terror or guerrilla war, were but tools to accomplish the political end.

Constructing the Counter-State

Mao's use of these tools, his approach,[7] was not accepted initially even by his own party. Only with the loss of its urban elements was the CCP forced to retreat to the hinterland, where Mao and others had been active from at least 1925. There, safe from the preponderance of KMT power, the "Maoists" had already carved out fledging base areas (i.e., territory "liberated" from state control) and used these to mobilize manpower. Given strategic priority, this effort blossomed. A counter-state was created to challenge the state.[8]

The battle that was joined was one for control of Jiangxi, a province of 81 counties or *hsien* (see Figure 2.2). There were 28 provinces, excluding Tibet and Outer Mongolia, and approximately 1,964 *hsien* nationwide.[9] Jiangxi itself at this time had a reported 13,794,159 inhabitants in 173,089 square kilometers,[10] an area, it is impressive to note, larger than Nepal (140,797 sq. km) but only slightly smaller than the state of Kansas (177,848 sq. km).

A *hsien* was its own miniature world, comprised of villages. Longnan, for instance, which achieved some fame later as the birthplace of KMT stalwart Wang Sheng,[11] was 80,000 people living in five districts embracing twenty-two small towns or villages. Most of the homes were sun-baked mud brick structures, tiled roofs and wooden frames. Subsistence activities were the norm. Rice-growing provided the livelihood for most, augmented by vegetables and fruit. As cash crops, the

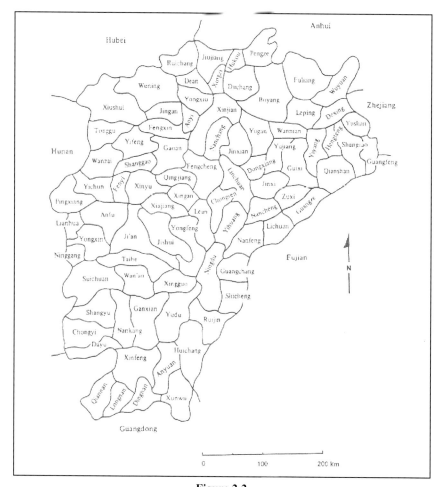

Figure 2.2

inhabitants processed cotton, tobacco, sugarcane, peanuts, and beans.[12] Although Longnan in the early days of the struggle was not in the main area of confrontation, the counties around it were. To the west was the CCP's Hunan-Quangxi base area, to the east the key Central Soviet base area. This main "Jiangxi Soviet," as it was called, with its capital in Ruijin, controlled most of sixteen counties and three million people at the beginning of 1934.[13]

Mao began with the obvious: an insurgent movement seeking to make revolution in a poor, backwards country dominated in numbers by the peasantry needed to center its mobilization effort in the rural areas. Harsh living conditions made the peasants ready for recruitment by a political movement that sought to address their grievances and aspirations. In other words, the "subjective forces" (i.e., voluntarism) needed to exploit the "objective forces" (i.e., structural conditions). This could be done only through meticulous planning and execution and would necessarily be a protracted affair since the state would not sit idly by as it was challenged.

Further, observed Mao—in a contention that sparked a fierce ideological battle only gradually resolved in his favor—mobilization needed to proceed systematically in area after area, with each "base area" serving as a platform for further expansion. The opposing position held that the insurgency should seek to exploit grievances nationwide in order to prepare the populace for an ultimate rebellion. In contrast, in Mao's formulation, within base areas, new societal structural arrangements would mobilize the people, who would provide the manpower for armed contingents, as well as their sustenance.

Armed manpower, being at considerable disadvantage in the face of government power, would initially engage principally in guerrilla action, complemented by terror carried out against societal enemies in areas of operation. Since they were dynamic bodies, always seeking to become as potent as possible, guerrilla units would grow in strength and operational reach. Ultimately, they would become "regular forces" (i.e., main forces), in effect copies of government regular units.

As Mao simultaneously advanced a strategic framework for using these armed forces, their nature and role has occasioned no little confusion. The strategic framework,[14] when stripped of jargon, stated simply that the revolutionary forces would first be on the strategic defensive, then fight the enemy to stalemate, and finally go over to the strategic offensive. Within each strategic phase, however, tactical and operational art were driven by the imperative of the offensive. Only in the final phase would all three levels of war merge in offensive action.

The forces involved, however, were not mutually exclusive. US sources in particular have tended to conflate their own phases of guerrilla war, as taught in American Special Forces, with Mao's tripartite structure.[15] They could not be more different. US Special Forces doctrine, drawn from the experience of Second World War Europe—teams entering a hostile zone to aid in the formation of resistance groups—divides the life-cycle of a "guerrilla" movement under three headings: organizational, guerrilla, and conventional. Mao's typology is guerrilla, mobile, and war of position, with each form of warfare the driving force (i.e., "driver") during each phase.[16] That is, guerrilla warfare is used to carve out base areas and to provide the shield behind which political work can proceed. This is done, when considering the effort as a whole, where the state is weakest, in unincorporated space. In China, this meant the rural areas. As base areas grow and further areas are contested, incorporated space (in China, the cities) is surrounded.

When the enemy responds with his military to assist restoring his local position, he finds himself compelled to disperse his forces to deal with guerrillas—but then defeated in detail by regular units that have been formed by gradual strengthening of local units.[17] Until the final strategic phase, however, combat remains a fluid affair, conducted according to a force-on-force imperative: destroying enemy plans and forces is the goal.[18] In contrast, in the final phase, positions are taken and held.

Mobile warfare, then, was the key to bringing Phase II to fruition. The phase did not commence because stalemate had been achieved; it grew out of the conditions of local domination (i.e., establishing base areas) that were the hallmark of Phase I. In Phase II, regular units engaging in mobile warfare were capable of destroying government regular units, hence bringing about the neutralization of the government's position. The logical result would be the going over to the regular war offensive in Phase III.

Mao recognized that this scheme of action, simple in concept, was fraught with difficulties in execution. It was common sense that "to transform guerrilla units waging guerrilla warfare into regular forces waging mobile warfare" manpower could be gained by direct recruiting or by "amalgamating small units." Both would go on, but the latter would be the more likely. Yet this would serve to accentuate the tension between those demanding emphasis on local action, with its symbiotic link between guerrillas and political transformation, and those who saw the regular forces as key.[19]

Time and again in his works, Mao hammered home that he was not positing an either/or position:

> They do not realize that the development of guerrilla warfare into mobile warfare means not the abandonment of guerrilla warfare, but the gradual formation, in the midst of widespread guerrilla warfare, of a main force capable of conducting mobile warfare, a force around which there must still be numerous guerrilla units carrying on extensive guerrilla operations. These guerrilla units are powerful auxiliaries to the main force and serve as inexhaustible reserves for its continuous growth.[20]

27

In this, Mao was advancing a disposition of forces that had been recognized throughout history by Western armies, the need for regular operations to be complemented by irregular operations, for operations to exist as supported by special operations. What was distinct was that all of the CCP's forces would grow from the dynamic expansion of the counter-state. They were not ends unto themselves but means to an end: implementing the new socio-economic-political order. As such, they were too valuable to waste. Consequently, Mao fiercely advocated using time and space to neutralize enemy thrusts. The trick was to fall back into China's fastness, scattering before the enemy and drawing him in, then massing overwhelming strength at points of weakness. Done time and again, this would serve to destroy any enemy campaign.

Nevertheless, the issue in the clash of forces remained that of contending battle-field strengths. Guerrilla action could cause the erosion of the enemy's strength but could not in and of itself be decisive. For that, regular warfare (i.e., main force warfare) was necessary. Mao was adamant that what was necessary was powerful forces manned by motivated, revolutionary manpower.[21] They were to be used according to the maxim: "With regard to the whole, mobile warfare is primary and guerrilla warfare supplementary; with regard to the parts, guerrilla warfare is primary and mobile warfare supplementary."[22] Or, put another way: "Guerrilla warfare is basic, but lose no chance for mobile warfare under favourable conditions."[23]

This approach was to remain constant in Mao's military writings, as was his emphasis on the symbiotic relationship between the new society and the projection of insurgent power. Constructing the counter-state gave substance to the mobilization effort.[24] The objective conditions of the old-order had paved the way for subjective exploitation.[25] Non-violent methods, deployed systematically in political warfare, could serve as force-multipliers in violent action. (A strike, for instance, used as a weapons system, could prevent enemy troops from reaching a battlefield just as effectively as direct military action.)[26]

State Response to Insurgent Challenge

Since the proffered CCP solution was one that saw the overthrow of existing institutions, it was the gentry with whom the Party rapidly came into confrontation. As the conflict grew in scope and violence, the gentry's need for enhanced resources, particularly trained manpower, resulted in appeals to higher rungs of government for assistance. These responded, with the result that the contest that emerged was characterized by alternative modes of mobilization.

What is of most significance in this process is that, because it was a political battle between rival infrastructures, state *versus* counter-state, with each side marshalling armed power to protect its organizing efforts, the outcome in any particular area was never a forgone conclusion. Grievances thrown up by structural injustice, to include widespread gentry abuse of the populace,[27] could be used by the insurgent leadership to mobilize manpower, but the process could work for the counter-insurgents in support of the *status quo*, as well, particularly if the gentry could be made to ameliorate their excesses. Where the two sides differed fundamentally was in the use they were willing to make of existing societal structures.[28]

Initially, the KMT attempted to deal with the advance of the CCP counter-state by imposing a Western-style police structure, established in September 1928, upon Jiangxi in the form of a Public Security Bureau (PSB) in each county. Nominally under its control was a paramilitary body, the county Police Force, recruited to deal with law and order problems such as the communists.

Since the impetus for this capability came from above, however, it proved quite ineffective, causing Nanjing to turn to the traditional source of local order, the gentry-recruited militia. These numerous bodies were gathered under one system, the *baowei tuan*,[29] ordered to be in place by the end of August 1930. Answering to the county magistrate, this organization "conscripted all able-bodied men between the ages of twenty and forty into tactical militia units organizationally corresponding to the neighborhood, village, district, and county self-governing institutions set up by the government."[30]

Although more rooted in society, the *baowei tuan* also did not work out well. This and the government's defeat in the First Encirclement and Suppression Campaign (19 December 1930 to 3 January 1931),[31] led Nanjing to revive yet another traditional approach, the *baojia* system, based upon organizing the entire populace in decimal hierarchies of mutual guarantee and collective responsibility. The PSB's were given the task of implementing the system; the *baowei tuan* was used to organize a truly universal militia. By 1934 the government had an available manpower pool of more than two million.

Meantime, three more unsuccessful encirclement campaigns had taken place, the fourth ending in April 1933. While unsuccessful, the causes of these defeats had little to do with either insurgent popular mobilization or skillful guerrilla tactics, as is so frequently lauded. To the contrary, the main source of KMT disaster stemmed from the mixing of units, task organizing assault forces from diverse warlord and KMT divisions that failed to support each other and consequently suffered defeat in detail when faced with superior CCP operational and tactical defensive moves.

Entire "government" divisions were lost in operations that had little to do with "guerrilla tactics" so much as sound military fundamentals.[32]

The point is important, because it was not mass mobilization stemming from structural inequity that was allowing the CCP to win on the field of battle; it was military skill resulting in good tactics and sound operational designs. Neither was there anything uniquely "guerrilla" about these, unless drawing the enemy ever deeper so that he could be ambushed and cut up piecemeal was to be considered "guerrilla." Where mobilization came into play was in the production of manpower for the communist armies. Even in this facet, control of the "Jiangxi Soviet" and other base areas was not a matter of communist counter-state gradually subverting and finally capturing an area. Instead, areas in contention were normally captured by CCP columns issuing from secure areas, *then* organized as part of the counter-state. What this meant was that the communists, as an alternate, fledging state, which could not yet match the Republic in resources, were vulnerable to a competently prosecuted counter-revolutionary campaign. This was not long in coming.

The Second Encirclement and Suppression Campaign (1 April to 30 May 1931) had been essentially a rerun of the First Campaign, but beginning with the Third Campaign (1 July to 20 September 1931), external factors played as important a role as communist defensive action in the actual defeat of the government forces; in the case at hand, the Canton Secessionist Movement (May 1931) and the Mukden Incident (18 September 1931). The former threatened Nanjing's already tenuous hold on power; the latter resulted in the alienation of Manchuria to Japan. Likewise, the Fourth Campaign (1 January to 29 May 1933) was halted because of renewed Japanese aggression.[33]

Already, following the Third Campaign, Chiang Kai-shek had used the occasion of the Five Province Bandit Suppression Conference at Lushan, Jiangxi to announce a "Three Parts Military and Seven Parts Politics Policy" that focused upon popular mobilization through the strengthening of administrative structure and efficiency.[34] Under the guidance of a Chiang Kai-shek intimate, Hsiung Shih-hui (Xiong Shihui), who was Jiangxi governor from 15 December 1931 to 1941, counties were grouped under thirteen intermediate bodies in an Administrative Inspectorate System (AIS). The inspectorates, in turn, reported to Nanchang, where Chiang Kai-shek had his military headquarters for most of the 1927–35 period.

Wholesale personnel changes followed, as did training for government personnel at all levels. Socio-economic initiatives, such as fostering cooperative societies and promoting the "New Life Movement,"[35] played a secondary role but were a logical outgrowth of Chiang Kai-shek's emphasis upon the primacy of values and behavior in producing viable structures for a new, revolutionary order. The results were mixed, but when the Fourth Campaign was accompanied by a communist offensive outside the "Jiangxi Soviet" area, as well as the inauguration of an aggressive CCP policy for land redistribution, the pieces of a viable government approach fell into place. Aroused at last by the communist menace to their position, the gentry—and their ability to mobilize local resources—moved decisively to the government side. The *sanbao* ("three *bao*'s") strategy, adopted in April 1933, sought to expand the *baojia*, revitalize the *baowei tuan*, and construct *baolei* (blockhouses) to blockade the soviet base area.[36]

In conception, the KMT's approach to popular mobilization was the opposite of that adopted by the CCP in that it sought to use existing structures, improved in honesty and administrative efficiency, to tap the manpower pool. In contrast, the communists built new structures by bringing into political play popular forces marginalized by the existing system. Both approaches were alike, however, in that they were strategic initiatives adopted by the contending elites, revolutionary and counter-revolutionary. Both, we may further note, involved co-opting local movements: the gentry-led social structure and militia, by Nanjing; regional insurgent groups rooted in parochial disaffection, by the CCP hierarchy.

In the Fifth Encirclement Campaign (16 October 1933 to 14 October 1934), the KMT demonstrated its ability to derive greater power in this contest of mobilization capabilities. It used the militia to build and man a blockade of the "Jiangxi Soviet" area, enforcing population and resources control as regular military units moved the network of blockhouses and barriers inexorably forward. The results for the CCP "liberated area," always a questionable economic entity even at the best of times, were catastrophic. In autumn of 1934, the communists abandoned their would-be state and launched upon the epic "Long March" that led them, a year later, to the wilds of Yenan.[37]

Stay-behind units remained, however. Consequently, a continuing task for the KMT was the complete pacification of Jiangxi. To effect this counter-insurgency goal required ensuring that the government infrastructure was impervious to assault from within and without. Initially, Military Pacification Regions were established, but these proved unwieldy, and their functions were transferred to the AIS, reorganized from thirteen to eight inspectorates. Within them, the *baojia* was extended and used both for control and reconstruction. From its rolls, all able-bodied men, 18–45 years old, were enrolled in militia units called everything from the Peace Preservation Corps to Righteous Warriors Communist Suppression Squads. As William Wei observes, "While in the militia, they received a modest education and a heavy dose of political indoctrination. On the eve of the War of Resistance against Japan, there were over one hundred eighteen thousand men in these paramilitary units."[38]

Apparently, the KMT had put together a winning combination. As it moved to finish the job by seizing Yenan, an external variable interjected itself into the equation: the Japanese invasion. Chiang Kai-shek found himself held hostage by a group of regional officers demanding that the impending Sixth Campaign against the communists be called off in favor of a war of national resistance. The campaign was cancelled, even as the Japanese made the entire business virtually a moot point by using the Marco Polo Bridge Incident in July 1937 as an excuse to launch all-out military penetration into the Chinese interior and to seize important coastal areas, such as Shanghai. Intense fighting mauled key KMT units, dealing Chiang Kai-shek a blow in the power stakes from which he never recovered.

Change in the strategic environment brought to the fore a new element in CCP approach, the united front. True, the CCP and KMT had made common cause before against the warlords, but the powerful presence of alien forces threatening the very existence of Chinese society dictated a strategic unity of hitherto hostile elements. This meant temporarily setting aside the most radical elements of the CCP platform in the interests of the common good, but not to the extent that revolutionary impulse was becalmed. Indeed, the situation proved filled with opportunity for the CCP. "Within a year," Jonathan D. Spence has written, "the Japanese overran east China, depriving the Guomindang of all the major Chinese industrial centers and the most fertile farmland, and virtually severing China's ties to the outside world. Chiang's new wartime base, Chongqing [Chungking], became a symbolic center for national resistance to the Japanese, but it was a poor place from which to launch any kind of counterattack."[39]

In other words, although Chiang remained China's "ruler," he was anything but that, maintaining his position through inertia and the disarray of his domestic opponents. The vastness of China's human and physical geography prevented the Japanese from delivering a knockout punch.[40] Yet the Japanese absorption of the KMT's coastal heartland had exposed the fatal flaw in the structural make-up of the Republic of China. The very manner in which the Northern Expedition had consolidated KMT power, co-opting warlords rather than ousting them and mobilizing new social forces, as advocated by the CCP and the KMT's own left wing, resulted in a paucity of individuals committed to revolution. The only means to get around this roadblock was to educate the young.

This certainly was the communist solution. The difference was that the CCP chose to create new institutions altogether to carry out the national revolution by tapping the forces of the welling social revolution. The KMT sought only a national revolution, to staff its modifications of the old structure with new blood schooled in traditional values and virtuous in thought and behavior.[41]

This lay behind Chiang Kai-shek's support for his newly formed Youth Corps and even such shadowy and much-misunderstood bodies as the *Lixingshe* or Blue Shirts.[42] Constantly disappointed that the "old blood" with which he was surrounded, particularly in the revolutionary party, the KMT, was unable to remake itself in the mold necessary for internal restoration and national liberation—the failure of the so-called "New Life Movement" must be seen in this context— he sought to invest in the future by molding young minds to a calling in every sense analogous to that of the Christian priesthood.

If the very structure Chiang Kai-shek sought to modify may be deemed tragically flawed, as it has been by so many, his efforts were doomed to failure. Yet this would hardly seem to be a foregone conclusion. Most at issue was not the structures but rather the temporal element: Could the Republic survive a contest of resource mobilization with other contenders even as it struggled to acculturate and train new personnel, who, if nothing else, would move into the structure as the old officeholders died off or were put out to pasture?

While the KMT still had access to resources in the pre-War of Resistance years, it did successfully withstand challenges to its position and extend its domain. Once, however, as noted above, it was cut off from these resources by the Japanese, it was vulnerable. In the event, it was CCP mobilization that provided the knockout blow, because the communist method of organizing proved the more appropriate to the radically altered environment of Japanese occupation.

Insurgent People's War Victory

Mobilization of the masses was the CCP aim, but mobilization only so that it could carry out a Marxist revolution. As it had demonstrated time and again, in both its activities in the field, as well as in its negotiations with the government, the CCP would do whatever was necessary tactically to assure itself of strategic success. This success, Mao knew, could only be based on military power deployed to protect the Leninist party structure intended to guide the masses through successful completion of the revolution.

The war had been a boon, because Yenan had been a safe haven from both the Japanese and the KMT. After the 1940 Hundred Regiments Campaign, the CCP was not to launch a major operation again, content instead to build up its guerrilla forces behind Japanese lines (in the process eliminating Kuomintang units and any other rivals), its mobile forces and party structure in Yenan. Potentially divisive redistributive policies were downplayed in favor of "united front" appeals. The New Fourth Army incident in early 1941 ended whatever potential existed for actual cooperation; thereafter it was a contest of mobilization for the ultimate reckoning.[43]

Certainly the KMT had the tougher time, for not only did it have to maintain some semblance of a functioning state in order to continue receiving important foreign aid, but its forces were also consistently mauled by the Japanese even as the regime was cut off from its power base in occupied China. This left Chiang Kai-shek in an ever more precarious situation.

The war's sudden conclusion caught him virtually flat-footed. In the rush to accept the surrender of the more than a million Japanese troops who remained on Chinese soil, emphasis was given to reclaiming the traditional centers of KMT support along the coast. Poor conduct on the part of the liberating forces, though, cost the government much of the good-will it might have reaped had its representatives behaved with a modicum of civility and grace. Standing in stark contrast to such behavior was the deportment of the CCP's soldiers as they, too, moved to take advantage of the vacuum created by the Japanese collapse.

Their prime goal, however, was Manchuria, occupied by the Soviets in August in the closing days of the war.[44] Soviet forces were not particularly helpful to the CCP due to Stalin's suspicions of Mao's independent bent, as well as his pragmatic judgment that the CCP had little chance of emerging victorious. Still, they allowed large amounts of surrendered weapons to be seized and stuck to their business of looting, giving the Chinese communists full reign to mobilize the countryside. This they did behind a Soviet shield that refused access to KMT forces and did not depart until April 1946.

By that time, the CCP had built up a truly formidable position, complete with a considerable force comprised of picked troops who had entered the region immediately at war's end via forced march, as well as guerrillas now "regularized" into more conventional units. As events were to transpire, so solid were the communist preparations that the government, despite airlifting (on American planes) to Manchuria some half million of its best troops (few of whom were from the region), was never able to dislodge the CCP from the area north of the Sungari River, with its main urban center of Harbin. To the contrary, as perceived by at least some American advisors, the move greatly overextended the KMT's lines of supply and communication.[45]

That this was even more so the case than even the Americans anticipated became clear when the full extent of CCP guerrilla force organization in former Japanese-held areas was appreciated. These very areas, concentrated in north China, sat astride the lines of communication necessary to support the troops in Manchuria. Additionally, the troops themselves added to their isolation by behaving badly to the population and hugging the urban areas. The results, once battle was joined in earnest in mid-1947, were predictable. By late 1948, Chiang Kai-shek had lost the cream of the only forces remaining to him that could really be considered "govern-ment." Thereafter, Nanjing was forced to rely upon less loyal, less well-trained units that collapsed like decks of cards in some of the most massive conventional battles ever seen in the history of warfare.

Crucial to the CCP's success, of course, was the mobilization that allowed it to field forces capable of besting the Nationalists. This process, however, has occasioned no little analytical confusion. True, solution to "the land problem" was the element on which the communists were able to build their power base. Yet their "solution" was not that called for in their dogma; neither did it occur in competition with other alternative mobilization efforts. Rather, shielded by the Soviet military presence, the CCP had the field to itself and could adopt a divide-and-conquer approach that pitted some elements of the community against others to the extent necessary to achieve inroads.

Skillful use of cadre and an absolute preponderance of force, with a substantial percentage comprised of outsiders, particularly Koreans, gave the communist campaign a self-sustaining quality once underway. The point is that whatever worked in Manchuria because of the peculiarities of that former Japanese puppet state did not necessarily have anything to do with "the land problem," or any other structural dilemma, in China. What resulted, however, was that the CCP was able to build a potent martial instrument in a very particular post-colonial vacuum, and with it destroy the lynchpin of what remained of the KMT military institution.[46] Those KMT units yet to join the battle, while impressive in sheer numbers, were unimpressive in every other respect and scarcely put up credible resistance.[47]

That even many good units performed poorly could hardly be surprising. The disastrous financial trends mentioned earlier reached such a state[48] that anyone on a fixed income, such as officers and men, was in an impossible situation.[49] Morale was further broken by fragmentation on the home front. Large numbers of students and intellectuals deserted the regime. A virulent peace movement pressured the government, fanned by communist infiltrators. Factionalism within the government was serious.

Small wonder, therefore, that of the 4.9 million men reportedly lost by the Nationalists between mid-1946 and the end of 1948, three-quarters had either defected or been captured. Entire armies simply broke. As Harrison has observed, "Equally devastating, some 105 of 869 Nationalist generals defected to the Communists."[50] It was later revealed that even the Nationalist Deputy Chief of the General Staff, Wu Shih, was a longtime communist agent.

In contrast to Chiang Kai-shek, Mao was able to avoid strategic and operational distraction, to see that a solution that worked needed to be pressed home regardless of the events, external and internal, demanding otherwise. In retrospect, this gave the Maoist insurgency its inevitability, when, in reality, it was anything but. Chiang Kai-shek, on the other hand, continually expressed his frustration to achieve perfection by endeavoring to come up with new organizations and approaches, even while leaving the old in place. Mao saw the disastrous implications of such clutter and thus kept his lines of command and implementation clean and focused. In the end, the results were a CCP responsiveness, the very quality Chiang Kai-shek sought from the KMT.

To look at the problem from another angle, Chiang Kai-shek was a bad Leninist. As he pointed out any number of times, he had urged adopting the "political officer" system after his three-month visit to Russia in late 1923 and early 1924.[51] Sun Yat-sen was already working with Moscow to strengthen the Kuomintang. It was at the behest of Russia's chief representative, Michael Borodin, for example, that the First Congress was called on 20 January 1924.[52] Chiang Kai-shek convinced Sun Yat-sen that the Russian system of "commissars," instituted to insure the loyalty of military commanders in a Red Army that still contained many "Whites," had applicability to a KMT revolutionary army grappling with similar problems of internal cohesion and fealty.

Consequently, a Party Representative had been made co-equal with the Whampoa Academy Commandant (Liao Chung-k'ai and Chiang Kai-shek, respectively), a Political Department had been established (whose most famous head Chou En-lai was appointed in April 1925), and a system of party representatives had been established in the military. For some decades this system of party oversight in the units culminated in a Political Department under the KMT Military Committee; later the system was shifted to the Ministry of Defense under the 1944 American-inspired reorganization scheme (the same impetus behind the plan to reconstitute 39 divisions, to which the Youth Army contributed nine). The American distaste of

Soviet forms was indulged by redesigning the Political Department as the Information Bureau with a more narrow scope of responsibility.

The innumerable permutations through which the system went were of little consequence save one: unlike its Maoist equivalent, the KMT structure of political officers remained haphazard, incomplete, and quite ineffective. As was the case with the Youth Army, Chiang Kai-shek never saw the project through to fruition by steadily building unit upon loyal unit. Instead, he attempted to push the political officers into the already existing system without backing them up with coercive power, as was the case in the communist system. To the contrary, he repeatedly emphasized the primacy of his military commanders even while denouncing their lack of revolutionary spirit.

As early as the fourth Whampoa class, which began in 1926, functional specialization within the corps of cadets included the choice of becoming a political officer. Likewise, a special class of 120, trained at the same time as the fourth class by the Whampoa Political Department, consisted entirely of military officers, especially returned graduates from Whampoa's own second and third classes. The KMT political instruction courses that followed were also military-dominated. Although civilians were included, it was not until the setting up of the Youth Corps that a system of political instruction as comprehensive as that available in the military was attempted for party members at large.

That Chiang Kai-shek should adopt this approach stemmed from his constant disappointment with civil society as opposed to its military counterpart. His emphasis on values and correct conduct leading to institutional probity took, in his judgment, its most concrete form in the revolutionary military. "Now the party is about to complete the second phase of the revolution and establish a new China," he told the assembled students and staff at the 5 May 1944 official opening of the Central Cadre Academy. "What is necessary for completion of this second phase is military discipline."[53]

What he constantly sought was a society that would match the military in its commitment and sense of mission. When this proved impossible, as noted above, he tended to lose heart and interest. Dissimilarly, Mao knew that he had the key and was thus willing to endure any degree of internal turmoil and momentary ineffectiveness to achieve his ends. It was precisely these lapses, during which the system was being purged and righted, that Chiang Kai-shek never felt he could afford in the world of dog-eat-dog warlord politics. Given the fate of CCP efforts at popular mobilization when they were actually subject to the brunt of KMT military power (Canton, Shanghai, Jiangxi), Chiang may well have been correct.

What could not be brought together was the Kuomintang itself, which continued to be afflicted with debilitating factionalism. The KMT had copied the form of a Leninist party, but it never implemented the most important element, the principle of democratic centralism, whereby decisions reached through democratic debate (at least in theory) were enforced through party discipline so that the body presented a unified face, both theoretically and actually. Consequently, while Mao Tse-tung was building a focused, disciplined body to implement his strategic approach, Chiang Kai-shek presided over an amorphous, fractious mass and concentrated on fostering individual discipline. Needless to say, the former made the more potent weapon. James Harrison has perceptively summed up the situation:

> Given the diversity and limitations of all the Nationalist groups and the problems they faced, it is perhaps understandable that no effective Nationalist government could be realized in China after the war. Many individuals in the Kuomintang and the independent groups were extremely able, but they were not backed by effective organization.[54]

One of the consequences of this was that those individuals who proved themselves especially able were increasingly in demand as tasks arose. They held multiple positions and shuttled from spot to spot, serving as the government's fire brigade. Although this could be quite good for their careers if they were consistently successful, it deprived an already weak system of whatever stability it might have been able to gain from competent individuals remaining in position long enough to make a significant impact.

Indeed, there was no time for any reforms to take root, for events proceeded at breakneck pace. Negotiations with the communists, pushed strenuously by the Americans under the guidance of "Special Representative to China" George C. Marshall, had gone on throughout 1945 and 1946, with heavy fighting breaking out from mid-1946.[55] Conflict occurred amidst the soaring inflation detailed earlier[56] and a concerted CCP effort to infiltrate all groups it thought could be useful to its own campaign. In particular, these were student, youth, and intellectual bodies, together with labor unions.

Of necessity, these groups were concentrated in urban areas, those most affected by inflation and already swollen in population because of the continued presence of refugees. Taking advantage of the declining purchasing power that reduced students and faculty to virtual beggary, the CCP was able to use them to spearhead a variety of "peace" campaigns, to include a "GI's Leave China" movement.[57] The alleged rape of a university girl in Peking by an American serviceman proved an issue sufficient to support widespread youth protest in December 1946 and January 1947, into which was folded denunciation of US support of the government and Nanjing's alleged insistence upon waging civil war. These protests increased still further when, on 4 July 1947, general mobilization was decreed to fight the communists.

Organizationally, the KMT was on the ropes. More seriously, by early 1948 the Chinese economy was in such serious shape that any hope the government had in restoring order, whether by the party or any other means, had disappeared. As prices continued to soar throughout 1947, a wave of communist-instigated strikes rolled over major urban centers. The government promised wages indexed to the cost of living but, in reality, could do little save keep its printing presses running. Hyperinflation reached such an extent that ordinary transactions could not be carried out. In early 1948 a point was reached at which notes could physically not be created fast enough to keep up with price increases. Many shops simply closed. For all practical purposes, China had become a barter economy.[58] Hence, there was no saving the old-regime. On 8 November 1948, the communists launched the battle for Hsu-chou, the key to the Yangtze and the approaches to Shanghai and Canton themselves. As the Nationalist armies crumbled, so, too, did the country's finances, fatally undermining morale and purchasing power. As Eastman summarizes:

In just two weeks [following the unfreezing of prices] the wholesale index rose over sixteen times. . . Early in 1949 the gold yuan began to depreciate uncontrollably. . . By April, the price index stood at over 3,000,000 and the National Government—now having fled to Canton—desperately attempted yet another currency conversion, replacing the gold yuan with a new silver yuan. In just eight months, therefore, the gold yuan had lost virtually all value, just as the fa-pi before it.[59]

It was a simple matter of time before the end came. Massive battles in the north during autumn and early winter 1948–49 had already decided the military issue.[60] Fruitless negotiations made clear that the CCP would settle for nothing short of unconditional surrender and the punishment of leading "war criminals," to include Chiang Kai-shek, his wife, and leading members of the Soong and Kung families.[61] On 21 January 1949, Chiang resigned the presidency and retired to his native town, Chikow in Fenghua County of Zhejiang (Chekiang) Province, south of Shanghai. He was succeeded by his vice-president, Li Tsung-jen, who sought to revive peace talks. The next day, the Nationalist forces in Peking surrendered.[62]

From the above discussion, it should be immediately clear that any insurgent group seeking a template for seizing state power would find the going rough. The elements outlined in Chapter 1 as constituting people's war, although in evidence, were fielded in coherent fashion only when history was filtered selectively to support the case study. Indeed, the very bitterness shown by many former comrades toward Mao Tse-tung stemmed precisely from the fact that he had been wrong as often as right in his insurgent efforts but had proved adept, in the fashion of a true politician, at deflecting blame and projecting his own flaws onto others. Ironically, where Mao emerged as a great commander was in the very area where Hannibal and Napoleon faltered: he was much better at the big picture, and thus the successful culmination of the strategic "Long March" with his seizure of state power, than in the areas of operational art or tactics. In his rapid assessments of the changing strategic environment, he was invariably correct. Hence mistakes at lower levels did not prove fatal. Only once, in Jiangxi, did his inability to provide an answer to the Fifth Encirclement campaign very nearly lead to physical elimination of the revolutionary effort. But the collective nature of CCP leadership allowed him to escape blame by pinning on his opponents for party leadership the alleged military mistakes that had resulted in defeat. In fact, Mao produced no better answer for the operational conundrum the Fifth Encirclement Campaign presented than anyone else. The reality was that the "encirclement" was carried out carefully, inexorably, and physically, much in the manner one associates with Roman sieges. Mass mobilization within the counter-state provided no answer to the state's superior mobilization.

The depth of the animosity on this topic is manifest in possibly the most important memoir of the period, that by COMINTERN[63] representative Otto Braun.[64] At heart, Braun's complaint is that Mao did not aid in efforts by the CCP leadership to arrive at a viable counter to the inexorable advance of the Chiang Kai-shek's blockhouse lines. To the contrary, not only did he refuse to participate in strategy sessions but also cast blame for defeats upon others, even as his own usual method of drawing in the enemy so that he could be defeated piecemeal was manifestly inappropriate to the slow strangulation approach of the KMT. By refusing to take part, one way or another, in the campaign to save Jiangxi, Mao was subsequently able to claim that he was "right" by the simple expedient of disclaiming participation in a strategy that had not worked. That a "wrong" approach had not been successful, went the logical end of the argument, stemmed from ideological deviation that made necessary a change of leadership.[65]

Neither, it is important to highlight, would Mao's subsequent "Yenan Way" have become an exemplar for revolutionary organization and mystique had Japanese intervention not drawn off state combat power. In the KMT *versus* CCP contest, sheer brute strength was an issue, and the KMT had demonstrated its ability to amass such. Not even political warfare had proved able to slow the inexorable advance of "blockhouse warfare." What did matter was domestic pressure that produced the united front, combined with international pressure that supported it and sought constantly to pressure the state into an unrealistic "compromise" for which there simply was no basis. That the CCP, whatever the united front agreements, carefully and systematically instructed its cadre to maintain their ideological focus, as well as institutional integrity, was well known to the KMT. Once the battles of the civil war were joined, in the new strategic environment created by the Second World War, there was little margin for the KMT to survive operational or even tactical errors. The result was cataclysmic defeat, defeat that, we should bear in mind, did indeed come at the hands of a powerful new doctrine of internal war (unsystematic though it might have been). What should also be highlighted, though, is the extraordinary role played by intervening variables. It was in labeling these as scientifically predictable (that is, through Marxist-Leninism) that Mao sought to deny contingency and trumpet human agency employed within structural matrix.

Vietnam and People's War

Still, what came to be called simply "Maoist insurgency" or "people's war" emerged as a central force in future insurgencies stemmed not only from what happened in China, but also just as importantly due to how events unfolded in what we may call "the southern sector," namely, Indochina, or, more specifically, Vietnam. There, Mao's lack of precision was rectified and made more relevant to circumstances that did not necessarily correspond to China's, especially its vastness.

The presence of Ho Chi Minh in China, as a representative of the COMINTERN during the formative years of Maoist insurgency, meant Vietnamese people's war advanced simultaneously with the Chinese original. Ho Chi Minh regularly sent reports to his comrades in Indochina. They, in turn, worked to implement what they derived from them and in the process made doctrine more systematic.[66] Above all, they emphasized that operationally and tactically, what was at hand was the "war of interlocking." That is, all forms of warfare occurred simultaneously, whether violent or nonviolent, political or military, rural or urban. Furthermore, they were to build to a "general uprising," though even this was integrated more seamlessly than the term implied, with strategic, operational, and tactical aspects.

Vietnamese insurgency progressed little, however, until the Second World War shattered French colonial power in the same manner the war and the Japanese had eviscerated the KMT. Indeed, the *Viet Nam Doc Lap Dong Minh Hoi* (League for an Independent Vietnam) or Viet Minh, remained largely a guerrilla threat until the Chinese communists consolidated their hold on the mainland in 1950, especially the border area with Vietnam.

Moving rapidly and pursuant to Chinese advice, the Viet Minh seized French positions on the border, set up training camps inside China, and by January 1951 fielded a five-division main force of 81 battalions. One of the divisions was a so-called "heavy division." Included in the battalion count were twelve heavy weapons battalions and eight engineer battalions. Wrote Bernard B. Fall: "According to one French officer, Captain Jacques Despuech, author of *Le Traffic des piastres*, the table of equipment for a French battalion in Indochina provided for 624 rifles, 133 submachine-guns, 41 BARs, 4 81mm mortars and 8 60mm mortars, while the corresponding battalion of the 304th Viet-Minh Division counted 500 rifles, 200 submachine-guns, 20 BARs, 8 81mm mortars, 3 recoilless cannon and 3 bazookas."[67] Since this insurgent combat power was but the apex of the guerrilla structure, the French were outgunned in all respects, from main force warfare to special operations. Fighting a multi-dimensional war (terror, guerrilla war, war of movement, war of position), the Viet Minh knocked the French off the playing field.[68]

America had already become deeply enmeshed in the struggle even prior to the French withdrawal,[69] and its commitment to the independence of a non-communist South Vietnam saw the period 1955–64 dominated by the efforts of advisors, both civilian and military, to prevent the replication in the South of what had occurred in the North, where most action had been centered during what came to be called (in the West) the First Indochina War.[70] For the first five years, 1955–60, Saigon under President Diem did a reasonable job at consolidating its position. North Vietnam was preoccupied with "building socialism in one country" (i.e., in Hanoi's jurisdiction). Diem's consolidation with US help, however, aroused the nationalist sentiments that had inspired the Viet Minh forces there (much smaller than in the North but "there" nevertheless) during previous struggle.[71]

North Vietnam had to struggle to keep the Southern insurgents from precipitating a military clash prematurely, because priority of effort, the communists in Hanoi felt, had to go to building up that state with its regular North Vietnamese Army (NVA) using Soviet doctrine. Pressure from below ultimately led to a formal decision to reactivate Viet Minh networks and bases in the South, as well as to send cadre (and some weapons). The impetus for the insurgency, however, came from aroused Southerners, those in the Viet Cong or "Vietnamese Communists."[72]

The approach used successfully in the North was copied,[73] with North Vietnam, Cambodia, and Laos serving the sanctuary role previously provided by China. Additionally, numerous base areas were already in existence in South Vietnam. Terror was used prominently (2,000 officials assassinated in 1963 alone),[74] augmented by guerrilla warfare that fairly rapidly morphed into mobile warfare. Operational intent was classic "seize the rural areas to isolate the urban areas," although the Viet Cong also set up urban cells. By 1964, the decision had been made to transition to the war of position and endeavor to deliver a knockout punch before US main forces could enter the conflict.[75] Thus assassinations of officials dropped to "only" 500 in 1964, because main force war had assumed the leading role. To augment the power of VC battalions, which were regularly knocking off ARVN (Army of the Republic of Vietnam) battalions, NVA battalions were infiltrated.[76]

By the time of US intervention with its main forces, March 1965, there were more some 96 VC battalions and more than 40 NVA battalions in South Vietnam. The US had some 18,000 advisors. US main forces ultimately grew to some 82 army infantry battalions and 24 Marine battalions, plus numerous artillery, armor, others battalions.[77] Most US forces, though, were for support. General Westmoreland, as the overall theater commander, did not have the manpower needed to take on both main forces and guerrillas, so he elected to use US main forces to attack communist main forces, while ARVN was to deal with the guerrillas (who were in the populated areas).[78]

ARVN had been created in the US image and proved maladroit in its counter-guerrilla performance. US main forces, on the other hand, had seized the strategic initiative within a year of commitment. At this point, rather than shifting gears to strengthen and then solidify ARVN's counter-guerrilla posture, and thus domination of the population, Westmoreland kept focus upon the main forces. This was because there were still plenty of them, and because killing them ("body count") had become the war's measure of success.

For its part, the Vietnamese communist leadership developed tactics for minimizing main force exposure to US firepower while locked in combat ("hugging") and implemented an operational campaign of luring US main forces into largely unpopulated areas for force-on-force encounters. This (largely) NVA effort (increasingly enlarged and sustained by NVA battalions coming down and supplied from North Vietnam, via Cambodia and Laos through the so-called Ho Chi Ming Trail) was planned as attrition warfare and designed to produce US casualties and thus a backlash in the US itself. VC main force battalions, while they did clash regularly with US battalions, ensured guerrilla domination of the population.

"Tet of '68" was an effort to move to war of position but was specifically planned around different levels of outcome (i.e., minimum, medium, and maximum goals). It was to incorporate the "popular uprising," but this, too, was not intended as the English rendering of the term implies. The "popular uprising" was the use of "organized masses" (OM) as a force multiplier, but these organized masses had strength levels like any military unit. What happened is well known—"coming out in the open" led to the decimation of the all-important VC main force units without which the exposed guerrilla infrastructure, the counter-state, could not resist US/ARVN pressure, especially since many guerrilla units had amalgamated to augment VC battalion power—and thus had been decimated themselves.[79]

A US change-of-command, to General Abrams, and a reorganized structure to more adequately balance the various components, civil and military, of the US effort led to several years of steady progress in South Vietnam's (i.e., Republic of Vietnam, or RVN) gaining control of the population. Simultaneously, the communists were patiently rebuilding their position, as they had done after their premature switch to war of position during the First Indochina War, when formations were decimated attacking the Red River Delta in 1951.[80] The US gradually withdrew from Southeast Asia, "Vietnamizing" the war. There followed two more communist "war of position" offensives: Spring 1972 and Spring 1975. Enough US firepower (mainly air) remained in the first case to back up ARVN in repelling an NVA multi-divisional attack, but not in the second case, when Saigon in April went to the communist forces, approximately ten years after the initial US main force commitment.

Although the precise role played by the antagonistic stance of the US media and anti-war groups in forcing US departure remains ambiguous, it is certainly the case that both put tremendous pressure, post-Tet '68, on the US leadership to disengage. Internal upheaval caused by the civil rights and "flower power" movements reinforced this, as did weak but psychologically significant domestic terrorism within the US. The North Vietnamese approach, using a combination of population control measures and exploitation of nationalism, faced few such pressures.[81] With a steady supply of war material from the USSR and PRC, Hanoi could implement an effective, theater-wide strategic approach,[82] even as the US both artificially divided the battlefield into independent countries, and even commands, and made mistakes. These existed at every level, from lack of unity of command to allowing a single operational element (defeating the main forces) to become strategic imperative.[83]

As might be expected, the communists incorporated the lessons of victory into doctrine further refined. Just as the Chinese documents associated with Maoist people's war had been translated into a host of languages, so, too, were those of the Vietnamese variant. From Thailand to Colombia, the Philippines to Nepal, Sri Lanka to Peru, the tactics, operational art, and strategy of highly refined people's war were available in local tongues, as frequently was training in either China or Vietnam.

Notes

[1] Edmund S. K. Fung's *The Military Dimension of the Chinese Revolution* (Vancouver: University of British Columbia Press, 1980) is useful for the military antecedents to this chapter.

[2] See esp. Stephen C. Averill, "Party, Society, and Local Elite in the Jiangxi Communist Movement," *Journal of Asian Studies*, 46.2 (May 1987), 279–303, as well as his "Local Elites and Communist Revolution in the Jiangxi Hill Country," Chapter 11 in Joseph W. Esherick and Mary Backus Rankin, eds., *Chinese Local Elites and Patterns of Dominance* (Berkeley: University of California Press, 1990), 282–304.

[3] A fine treatment of a minority case is Xiaoyuan Liu, *Frontier Passages: Ethnopolitics and the Rise of Chinese Communism, 1921–1945* (Stanford, California: Sta..ford University Press, 2004).

[4] Roy Hofheinz, Jr also reached this conclusion in his "The Ecology of Chinese Communist Success: Rural Influence Patterns, 1923–45" in A. Doak Barnett, ed., *Chinese Communist Politics in Action* (Seattle: University of Washington Press, 1969), 3–77. He finds the most significant factor in explaining whether an area became involved in the insurgency to be the presence of CCP cadre themselves. William Wei agrees with this in his "Insurgency by the Numbers I: A Reconsideration of the Ecology of Communist Success in Jiangxi Province, China," *Small Wars and Insurgencies* (London), 5.2 (Autumn 1994), 201–17, but emphasizes, too, the importance of structural factors. He points out that the role of these factors becomes evident when statistical measures are used to analyze available data, as he has done, rather than relying solely upon map comparison, as in Hofheinz. I have addressed the viability of ecological explanation in my "Insurgency by the Numbers II: The Search for a Quantitative Relationship between Agrarian Revolution and Land Tenure in South and Southeast Asia," *Small Wars and Insurgencies* (London), 5.2 (Autumn 1994), 218–91.

[5] See, for example, Mark Selden, "People's War and the Transformation of Peasant Society: China and Vietnam" in Mark Selden and Edward Freedman, eds., *America's Asia*, offprint (nfd). In one telling passage, he observes: "The thesis of this essay is as follows:

Out of the ashes of military strife which enveloped China and Vietnam in protracted wars of liberation emerged a radically new vision of man and society and a concrete approach to development. Built on foundations of participation and community action which challenge elite domination, this approach offers hope of more *humane* forms of development and of effectively overcoming the formidable barriers to the transformation of peasant societies" (emphasis in original).

[6] For an overview of the entire period under discussion, see Tibor Mende's *The Chinese Revolution* (London: Thames & Hudson, 1961), an older, still useful, work.

[7] Mao's methodology is contained in a number of works authored at the time and in subsequent years. For sake of clarity, since that is the product we are after rather than the historiography, these will be considered as a whole. All are contained in *Selected Works of Mao Tse-tung* (Beijing: Foreign Languages Press, 1967): "Report on an Investigation of the Peasant Movement in Hunan," [March 1927], 1: 23–59; "A Single Spark Can Start a Prairie Fire," [5 January 1930], 1: 117–28; "Problems of Strategy in China's Revolutionary War," [December 1936], 1: 179–254; "Problems of Strategy in Guerrilla War against Japan," [May 1938], 2: 79–112; "On Protracted War," [May 1938], 2: 113–94. These texts can also usually be found at various internet sites.

[8] Numerous works are available on this early period. Among the most useful, in discussing soviet formation, are Linda Grove, "Creating a Northern Soviet," *Modern China*, 1.3 (July 1975), 243–70, and Shinkichi Eto, "Hai-lu-feng—The First Chinese Soviet Government," Parts I and II, *China Quarterly*, 8 (October–December 1961), I: 161–83; 9 (January–March 1962), II: 149–81. For the Jiangxi period in general, see Philip C. C. Huang, Lynda Schaefer Bell, and Kathy Lemons Walker, *Chinese Communists and Rural Society, 1927–1934*, Chinese Research Monograph No. 13 (Berkeley, California: Center for Chinese Studies, 1978). Particularly good for Jiangxi specifics are the two works by Stephen C. Averill already cited above; likewise, James M. Polachek, "The Moral Economy of the Kiangsi Soviet (1928–1934)," *Journal of Asian Studies*, 42.4 (August 1983), 805–29. One may also profitably consult Mao Tse-tung's own *Report From Xunwu*, released in a new edition, Roger Thompson, ed. and trans. (Stanford, California: Stanford University Press, 1990). His introduction is useful. In dealing with the KMT counter-insurgency, no research approaches that of William Wei, *Counterrevolution in China: The Nationalists in Jiangxi During the Soviet Period* (Ann Arbor: University of Michigan Press, 1985).

[9] See Hung-mao Tien, *Government and Politics in Kuomintang China 1927–1937* (Stanford, California: Stanford University Press, 1972), especially Chapter 5: "Provincial and County Government: An Overview," 89–95. Commenting generally on the administrative setup of the Republic, Tien notes: "China's provinces differ greatly in size and population. In the 1930s the areas of the 28 provinces varied from about 39,000 square miles to over

633,000 square miles; and their populations ranged from about 400,000 to over 50,700,000. There were also significant differences in the number of counties each province had. The total number of counties in the 28 provinces in 1935 was *estimated* [emphasis added] to be 1,964. Szechwan had the most, 148 counties, and Ningsia the least, 11. At the county level, too, variations in size and population were considerable. Counties ranged from 28 square miles to over 225,300 square miles and from 234 to 1,568,492 residents. The size and population of some counties actually exceeded those of some provinces. Thus, when speaking of a province or a country [*sic*], we must be constantly aware of the great range of individual differences" (89–90).

[10] Figures are those given for 1940 in Hollington K. Tong, ed., *China Handbook, 1937–1943: A Comprehensive Survey of Major Developments in China in Six Years of War* (New York: Macmillan, 1943), 1–2. The actual compilation of the book was carried out under the auspices of the Chinese Ministry of Information.

[11] See my *Counter-Revolution in China: Wang Sheng and the Kuomintang.*

[12] Interview with Chung Li-Jieh, former resident of Longnan (dob: 28 September 1912), 22 July 1993 in Taipei.

[13] Philip C. C. Huang, "The Jiangxi Period: An Introduction" in Huang, Lynda Schaefer Bell, Kathy Lemons Walker, *Chinese Communists and Rural Society, 1927–1934*, Chinese Research Monograph No. 13 (Berkeley, California: Center for Chinese Studies, 1978), 1–4.

[14] See Mao, "Problems of Strategy in China's Revolutionary War."

[15] See, for example, US Army Special Forces, *Special Forces Qualification Course Branch Training: Advance / Summary Sheets, Phase IV* (Fort Bragg, North Carolina: various imprints), "Fundamentals of Unconventional Warfare" (August 1997), especially SS-7, SS-8. There, the three phases are given as: I, latent or incipient; II, guerrilla warfare; III, mobile warfare or war of movement. Lest such a flawed approach be seen as a product of but narrow military thinking, it is useful to consult a work by the highly regarded Martin Van Creveld, *The Art of War: War and Military Thought* (London: Cassell, 2000). His treatment of "guerrilla warfare" (204–12) is the weakest discussion in an otherwise solid text. Indeed, while he may be judged limited in his treatment of both T. E. Lawrence and Mao, his discussion of the latter is particularly ill-informed and misrepresents even the phases of the approach.

[16] Mao does not use this "driving force" (or "driver") terminology, of course, and at times he can be quite confusing, as when he claims that "guerrilla war" dominates the mobile war phase (which may also be translated as maneuver war phase). What he intends, however, as he makes clear in his various texts, is that guerrilla *tactics* will dominate; i.e., that "hit and run" will be the essence of the campaign, not the holding of territory.

[17] "Since the war is protracted and ruthless, it is possible for the guerrilla units to undergo the necessary steeling and gradually to transform themselves into regular forces, so that their mode of operations is gradually regularized and guerrilla warfare develops into mobile warfare," Mao, "Problems of Strategy in Guerrilla War against Japan," 107.

[18] Mao uses different phraseology that obscures this simple reality: "Mobile warfare is the form in which regular armies wage quick-decision offensive campaigns and battles on exterior lines along extensive fronts and over big areas of operation." Mao, "On Protracted War," 171. Ironically, given his near-universal association with "guerrilla warfare," the same point is made, although often overlooked, by Che Guevara in *Guerrilla Warfare*.

[19] "In amalgamating small units, we must, on the one hand, guard against localism, whereby attention is concentrated exclusively on local interests and centralization is impeded, and, on the other, guard against the purely military approach, whereby local interests are brushed aside," Mao, "On Protracted War," 107–08.

[20] *Ibid*, 108.

[21] "To raise the quality of the guerrilla units it is imperative to raise their political and organizational level and improve their equipment, military technique, tactics and discipline, so that they gradually pattern themselves on the regular forces and shed their guerrilla ways. Politically, it is imperative to get both the commanders and the fighters to realize the necessity of raising the guerrilla units to the level of the regular forces, to encourage them to strive toward this end, and to guarantee its attainment by means of political work. Organizationally, it is imperative gradually to fulfill all the requirements of a regular formation in the following respects—military and political," *Ibid*.

[22] *Ibid.*, 115.

[23] *Ibid.*, 116.

[24] ". . . that is, the policy of establishing base areas; of systematically setting up political power; of deepening the agrarian revolution; of expanding the people's armed forces by a comprehensive process of building up first the township Red Guards, then the district Red Guards, then the county Red Guards, then the local Red Army troops, all the way to the regular Red Army troops, of spreading political power by advancing in a series of waves, etc., etc. Only thus is it possible to build the confidence of the revolutionary masses throughout the country," Mao, "A Single Spark Can Start a Prairie Fire," 118.

[25] See Mao, "Report on an Investigation of the Peasant Movement in Hunan," for a detailed discussion of this point.

[26] See Marks, *Counter-Revolution in China*.

[27] See Phil Billingsley, "Bandits, Bosses, and Bare Sticks: Beneath the Surface of Local Control in Early Republican China," *Modern China*, 7.3 (July 1981), 235–88.

[28] William Wei, *Counterrevolution in China* describes this process thus: "The actions of the Guomindang indicate that, while it recognized the need for a mass movement, it was averse to Communist approaches that sought to generate popular support by restructuring society and making it more equitable. Rejecting radical agrarian measures that might have preempted the CCP's popular base, the Guomindang chose to extend and intensify its local administrative authority and to rely on its military-civil bureaucracy and upon the manipulation of traditional types of authority, specifically the elite sector of society, to gain compliance of the people. The Nanjing government was convinced that 'the strength of the rural communities rested upon the old gentry and that at all costs the power of the gentry should be restored.' Nationalist leaders appreciated the fact that since the collapse of the Qing dynasty, power had steadily devolved into the hands of the local elite. They would seek to take advantage of the elite's normative and coercive influence in rural society to mobilize the masses to carry out its blockade-blockhouse strategy. The principal agencies used to accomplish this end were elite-controlled security forces" (3–4). (The internal quotation used by Wei is from James C. Thomson, Jr., *While China Faced West: American Reformers in Nationalist China, 1928–1937* [Cambridge: Harvard University Press, 1969], 31.)

[29] *Baowei tuan*: literally, "safeguarding corps"; generally translated as "official militia."

[30] Wei is the basic source for all of the organizational details contained in this discussion of the evolving KMT security apparatus. See also Hung-mao Tien.

[31] For military particulars and maps see William W. Whitson with Huang Chen-hsia, *The Chinese High Command: A History of Communist Military Politics, 1927–71* (New York: Praeger, 1973), especially 268–91.

[32] See Wei, "Warlordism and Factionalism in the Guomindang's Encirclement Campaigns in Jiangxi," ," in *Illinois Papers in Asian Studies 1983, Pt. II: Kuomintang Development Efforts During the Nanking Decade* (Urbana: Center for Asian Studies, University of Illinois, 1983), 87–120.

[33] See Wei, "Five Encirclement and Suppression Campaigns (1930–1934)" in Edwin Pak-wah Leung, ed., *Historical Dictionary of Revolutionary China, 1839–1976* (New York: Greenwood Press, 1992), 121–23.

[34] See Wei, "The Guomindang's Three Parts Military and Seven Parts Politics Policy," *Asian Profile* (Hong Kong), 10.2 (April 1982), 111–27.

[35] See Eastman, *The Abortive Revolution*, 66–70.

[36] For details, again refer to Wei.

[37] Considerable confusion exists in the literature concerning the inspiration for this successful KMT approach. As correctly ascertained by Wei, "The Role of the German Advisers in the Suppression of the Central Soviet: Myth and Reality" in Bernd Martin, ed., *The German Advisory Group in China: Military, Economic, and Political Issues in*

Sino-German Relations, 1927–1938 [or *Die deutsche Beraterschaft in China 1927–1938*] (Dusseldorf: Droste, 1981), the operational particulars were not drawn from foreign advice but rather from historical precedent, particularly the suppression of the Nien Rebellion in the mid-nineteenth century. See Mary C. Wright, *The Last Stand of Chinese Conservatism: The T'ung-chih Restoration, 1862–1874* (Stanford, California: Stanford University Press, 1957); Teng Ssu-yu, *The Nien Army and Their Guerrilla Warfare, 1851–1868* (The Hague: Mouton, 1961); Chiang Siang-tseh, *The Nien Rebellion* (Seattle: University of Washington Press, 1954); and Elizabeth J. Perry, *Chinese Perspectives on the Nien Rebellion* (Armonk, New York: M.E. Sharpe, 1981).

[38] Wei, *Counterrevolution in China*, 137. The actual text reads "One the eve," clearly a misprint.

[39] Jonathan D. Spence, *The Search for Modern China* (New York: Norton, 1990), 437.

[40] For a far more hostile appraisal of Chiang Kai-shek's wartime role, see Sterling Seagrave, *The Soong Dynasty* (New York: Harper & Row, 1985).

[41] For greater discussion of this matter, see the benchmark work by Mary C. Wright, "From Revolution to Restoration: The Transformation of Kuomintang Ideology," *Far Eastern Quarterly*, 14.4 (August 1955), 515–32.

[42] Basic works include: W. F. Elkins, "'Fascism in China: The Blue Shirts Society, 1932–1937,'" *Science and Society*, 33.4 (1969), 426–33; Lloyd E. Eastman, "Fascism in Kuomintang China: The Blue Shirts," *China Quarterly*, 49 (January–March 1972), 1–31; Eastman, *The Abortive Revolution*, specifically Chapter 2 (31–84), "The Blue Shirts and Fascism"; Maria Hsia Chang, *The Chinese Blue Shirt Society: Fascism and Developmental Nationalism*, Chinese Research Monograph No. 30 (Berkeley, California: Center for Chinese Studies, Institute of East Asian Studies, 1985); and Eastman, "The Rise and Fall of the 'Blue Shirts': A Review Article," *Republican China*, 13.1 (November 1987), 25–48.

[43] Although written from the communist perspective, a useful work on this period, valuable for both its text and copious photos, is Zhang Chengjun and Liu Jianye, *An Illustrated History of China's War of Resistance Against Japan* (Peking: Foreign Languages Press, 1995). Tables provide a wealth of data, to include order of battle information and personalities.

[44] See Steven Levine, *Anvil of Victory: The Communist Revolution in Manchuria, 1945–1948* (New York: Columbia University Press, 1987).

[45] A detailed discussion of this campaign may be found in Harold M. Tanner, "Guerrilla, Mobile, and Base Warfare in Communist Military Operations in Manchuria, 1945–1947," *Journal of Military History*, 67.4 (October 2003), 1177–222. This article must be approached with some care. Its use of sources to arrive at military particulars is superb, but its effort to graft onto the discussion another, dealing with doctrinal development of the insurgents, is inadequate. Terminology is not used correctly, and specifics of Maoist "doctrine" are misstated.

[46] James Pinkney Harrison has put this well in his *The Long March to Power: A History of the Chinese Communist Party, 1921–72* (New York: Praeger, 1972), 394: "Reliance on activists among the people for recruits, supplies, intelligence, and general support had been a basic feature of Communist strategy since the mid-1920's, but the propaganda, organizational, and military techniques for 'people's war' that had been worked out over two decades really bore fruit in the 'third revolutionary civil war.' Naturally, they did so unevenly and primarily in certain areas where the Communists were able to consolidate their support. In most of the country, traditional practical concerns continued to prevail, but in crucial areas in the late 1940's, especially in North China and Manchuria, the Communists were able to use the 'mass line' as a decisive weapon."

[47] Numerous sources are available for the military particulars of the civil war, among them: Whitson; Liu; E. R. Hooton, *The Greatest Tumult: The Chinese Civil War, 1936–49* (New York: Brassey's UK, 1991), and Trevor N. Dupuy, *The Chinese Civil War* (New York: Franklin Watts, 1969).

[48] The discussion on inflation in Jonathan D. Spence, 498–504, is quite useful, especially the tables. They demonstrate that between September 1945 and February 1947, the Shanghai wholesale price index went from 100 to 3,090; pegged again at 100 in May 1947, it reached 11,100 by July 1948; returned to 100 in August 1948, it was 40,825 by February 1949. For the long-term consequences, see Chang Kia-ngau, "War and Inflation" in Pinchon P.Y. Loh, ed., *The Kuomintang Debacle of 1949: Conquest or Collapse* (Boston: D. C. Heath, 1965), 23–26. Therein he provides startling figures, "based on statistics compiled by Directorate-General of Budgets, Accounts and Statistics" (see especially Table 27, p. 24). The Shanghai index, for example, with January–June 1937 pegged at 100, had reached 4,635,700 by September 1947 ("the last month for which the wholesale price indexes of major cities were published by the government"). In a city such as Tsingtao, it was at 6,304,000. Principal causes of this spiral were uncontrolled government spending financed in the main by the printing of bank notes. For the war years specifically, see Arthur N. Young, *China's Wartime Finance and Inflation, 1937–1945* (Cambridge, Massachusetts: Harvard University Press, 1965).

[49] This aspect of inflation has been considered directly for the years of the Second World War by Arthur N. Young, *China's Wartime Finance and Inflation, 1937–1945*, 318–20. His observations for 1937–45 are appropriate in a discussion of the civil war period, as well, when the trends he identifies became still worse. He notes, in part (pp. 318–19; emphasis added): "The heaviest burden of inflationary finance fell upon those receiving salaries or payments that were more or less fixed; and first and foremost of these was the army. . . The effect on the army's morale and value as a fighting force was grave. . . About 20 officers *monthly* were deserting from one division [observed by two European Red Cross doctors 1941–42] for economic reasons."

51

[50] Harrison, 424.

[51] See, for example, Chiang Kai-shek's 16 April 1926 speech at Whampoa as related in Heinlein, *op.cit.*, 172–74.

[52] Dan N. Jacobs, *Borodin: Stalin's Man in China* (Cambridge: Harvard University Press, 1981).

[53] See Chiang Kai-shek, "*Chung-yang kan-hsiao ch'eng-li tian-li chi yen-chiu-pu ti-yich'i k'ai-hsueh tian-li hsun-tz'u*" ("Address at the Ceremony Establishing the Central Cadre Academy and First Research Class") in *Chung-yang kan-pu hsueh-hsiao yen-chiu-pu ti-yi ch'i pi-yeh shih-chou-nien chi-nien t'e-k'an* (*Special Issue Commemorating the Fortieth Anniversary of the Graduation of the First Research Division of the Central Cadre Academy*), 11–14.

[54] Harrison, 369–70.

[55] For details see Harrison, Chapter 18 ("The Third Revolutionary Civil War Begins"), 366–93.

[56] *Ibid.*, 391: "Some seventy per cent of the Nationalist budget was still going to military expenses, and, by the end of 1946, the government had lost one-half of its gold reserves. During the same year, prices rose 700 per cent."

[57] In the immediate aftermath of the Second World War, the US had some 113,000 troops in China, 53,000 of whom were Marines. Most were concentrated in the north pursuing missions connected with the surrender and repatriation of Japanese armed forces, which in China alone numbered more than a million men. Aside from residual contingents, however, all American forces had been withdrawn by early 1947. See *Ibid.*, 391; Spence, 488–91.

[58] Eastman, *Seeds of Destruction*, 173 states: "The economy of Nationalist China during 1947 and much of 1948 was in a terrible state: the fabric of rural society was faltering; the transportation system was in a state of continual disrepair (largely owing to Communist sabotage); and inflation was daily eroding the value of the fa-pi, the national currency."

[59] Eastman, *Seeds of Destruction*, 194–95.

[60] See Harrison, 423–24.

[61] Spence, 510: "Mao's eight points were stark: (1) punish all war criminals; (2) abolish the invalid 1947 constitution; (3) abolish the Guomindang's legal system; (4) reorganize the Nationalist armies; (5) confiscate all bureaucratic capital; (6) reform the land-tenure system; (7) abolish all treasonous treaties; (8) convene a full Political Consultative Conference to form a democratic coalition government."

[62] Li Tsung-jen's efforts to negotiate with the CCP had come to nothing. He gave in to a number of communist demands, among them that the Bandit-Suppression National-Reconstruction Corps be disbanded, but there was no middle ground to be had. *Ibid.*, 426 states: "On April 21, Liu Po-ch'eng's Second and Ch'en Yi's Third Field Armies crossed the Yangtze

on a 300-mile wide front and took Nanking on May 27, Foochow on August 17, and Amoy on October 17. On May16–17, Lin Piao's Fourth Field Army captured the Wuhan cities and moved south, taking Changsha on August 5, Canton on October 14, Kweilin on November 22, Nanning on December 4, and, finally, in April 1950, Hainan Island, which since the 1920's had been partly controlled for the Communists by Feng Pai-chu."

[63] Communist International (COMINTERN)—the body used by Moscow to direct the affairs and campaigns of international communist parties. See Kermit E. McKenzie, *Comintern and World Revolution, 1928–1943: The Shaping of Doctrine* (New York: Columbia University Press, 1964); and Edward H. Carr, *Twilight of the Comintern, 1930–1935* (New York: Knopf, 1983).

[64] Otto Braun, *A Comintern Agent in China, 1932–1939* (St Lucia: Queensland University Press, 1982).

[65] As a committed revolutionary, Braun finds such Machiavellianism ideologically repugnant if not morally grotesque.

[66] See Greg Lockhart, *Nation in Arms: The Origins of the People's Army of Vietnam* (Boston: Allen and Unwin, 1989).

[67] Bernard B. Fall, *Street Without Joy* (New York: Praeger, 1961), 94 (pagination as per 1967 reprint).

[68] Excellent for its fresh focus upon operational art is Martin Windrow, *The Last Valley: Dien Bien Phu and the French Defeat in Vietnam* (Cambridge, Massachusetts: Da Capo, 2004). Discussion of Vietnamese doctrine as compared to classic Maoism can at times be misleading but does not contradict my own presentation herein. See also *Ibid*, as well as Bernard B. Fall, *Viet-Nam Witness, 1953–66* (New York: Praeger, 1966); especially useful is the discussion in Chapter 3, "The Failure of the Navarre Plan," 30–40. To gain an appreciation not only of the particulars of this period but also where it fits within the longer span of conflict under discussion, see William J. Duiker, *The Communist Road to Power in Vietnam*, 2nd edn. (Boulder, Colorado: Westview Press, 1996). Important background discussion is in David G. Marr, *Vietnam 1945* (Berkeley: University of California Press, 1995).

[69] See Ronald H. Spector, *The United States Army in Vietnam—Advice and Support: The Early Years, 1941–1960* (Washington, DC: Center of Military History, US Army, 1985).

[70] An understanding of the US role during the latter portion of this period, prior to the commitment of American main force units, can be gained by inspecting of the individual contributions to Harvey Neese and John O'Donnell, eds. *Prelude to Tragedy: Vietnam, 1960–1965* (Annapolis, Maryland: Naval Institute Press, 2001).

[71] For an examination of the long-term changes, see Hy V. Luong, *Revolution in the Village: Tradition and Transformation in North Vietnam, 1925–1988* (Honolulu: University of Hawaii Press, 1992).

[72] Excellent discussion may be found in Carlyle A. Thayer, *War by Other Means: National Liberation and Revolution in Viet-Nam 1954–60* (Boston: Allen and Unwin, 1989).

[73] The best single work on the Vietnamese approach prior to the launching of the war of attrition against US forces in the Second Indochina War is Truong Chinh, *Primer for Revolt: The Communist Takeover in Viet-Nam*, ed. Bernard B. Fall (New York: Praeger, 1963). See also Strategic Research & Analysis Division (SRA), Office of the Assistant Chief of Staff for Intelligence (J-2), US Military Assistance Command Vietnam (MACV), *Truong Chinh on Revolutionary Warfare*, SRAP-669 mimeo (Saigon: 31 December 1969); and Rod Paschall, "Low-Intensity Doctrine: Who Needs It?", *Parameters*, 15.3 (Autumn 1985), 33–45. No consideration is complete without reference to the benchmark works by Douglas Pike, *Viet Cong: The Organization and Techniques of the National Liberation Front of South Vietnam* (Cambridge, Massachusetts: MIT Press, 1966); and *PAVN: People's Army of Vietnam* (Novato, California: Presidio Press, 1986). Very useful discussion may be found in appropriate sections of Wray Johnson, *Vietnam and American Doctrine for Small Wars* (Bangkok: White Lotus Press, 2000).

[74] Pike, *Viet Cong*, 102, lists the assassination figures per year as follows: 1957–60, 1,700; 1961, 1,300; 1962, 1,700; 1963, 2,000; 1964, 500—By 1964 the party controlled two-thirds of the country's 2,500 villages. The nature of these killings is revealed by two representative analyses: J-2/MAC-V, *Studies of the National Liberation Front of South Vietnam* : VC Cadre—"Our purpose was not only to eliminate those who could be harmful to the movement but also with a view toward making the people afraid and to prevent them from co-operating with the government." Malcolm W. Browne, *The New Face of War* (New York: Bobbs-Merrill, 1965): "The hamlet chief in this instance had been tied to a stake in the middle of the market place in full view of the assembled villagers. The man was slowly disemboweled, his children decapitated, and his pregnant wife then tied to the same stake and similarly disemboweled" (103).

[75] For overview see especially Merle L. Pribbenow, "North Vietnam's Master Plan," *Vietnam* (August 1999), 30–36.

[76] For particulars, see J. W. McCoy, *Secrets of the Viet Cong* (New York: Hippocrene Books, 1992).

[77] An excellent discussion of the entire period, with discussion framed in such manner as to facilitate understanding of our discussion here, is George Herring, "The Vietnam War, 1961–1975: Revolutionary and Conventional Warfare in an Era of Limited War," Chapter 21 (633–66) in Doughty et al. For tactical particulars, see Robert A. Doughty, *The Evolution of US Army Tactical Doctrine, 1946–76* (Washington, DC: Center for Military History, 2001).

[78] The matter of Westmoreland's strategic approach remains controversial to this day. A trenchant critique is typical: Lewis Sorley, *A Better War: The Unexamined Victories and*

Final Tragedy of America's Last Years in Vietnam (New York: Harcourt, 1999). More measured but nonetheless critical are: Peter Brush, "The War's 'Constructive Component'," *Vietnam* (February 1997), 36–41; and Brush, "Uncommon Ground: Interservice Rivalry in I Corps," *Vietnam* (October 1999), 23–28. Useful is John M. Carland, "Documents of Note—Winning the Vietnam War: Westmoreland's Approach in Two Documents," *Journal of Military History*, 68.2 (April 2004), 553–74. For an earlier discussion on the same topic by Garland see the final chapter, "Summing Up" (Chapter 16), in his *United States Army in Vietnam—Combat Operations: Stemming the Tide, May 1965 to October 1966* (Washington, DC: Center of Military History, US Army, 2000), 355–68; as well as Bruce Palmer, Jr., *The 25-Year War: America's Military Role in Vietnam* (Lexington: University Press of Kentucky, 1984). For the best single treatment of Vietnamese "war of position," see Dale Andrade, *America's Last Vietnam Battle: Halting Hanoi's 1972 Easter Offensive* (Lawrence: University Press of Kansas, 2001). Andrade is presently in the process of completing an article, tentatively titled "Westmoreland Was Right: A Reexamination of America's Vietnam War Strategy, 1965–66," which will include consideration of the three strategic phases of revolutionary war.

[79] The best single discussion of this topic is Ngo Vinh Long, "The Tet Offensive and its Aftermath" in Marc Jason Gilbert and William Head, eds., *The Tet Offensive* (Westport, Connecticut: Praeger, 1996), 89–123.

[80] See Peter Brush, "Reassessing the VC Role after Tet," *Vietnam* (February 2002), 34–43.

[81] Particularly useful is William J. Duiker, *Sacred War: Nationalism and Revolution in a Divided Vietnam* (Boston: McGraw-Hill, 1995).

[82] See The Military History Institute of Vietnam, *Victory in Vietnam: The Official History of the People's Army of Vietnam, 1954–1975*, trans. Merle L. Pribbenow (Lawrence: University Press of Kansas, 2002).

[83] The best single overview of this subject is Marc Jason Gilbert, ed., *Why the North Won the Vietnam War* (New York: Palgrave, 2002).

Chapter 3

Form over Substance:
The Communist Party of Thailand

In one of the final scenes of the 1983 film *Under Fire*, Nick Nolte, as journalist Russell Price, joins in the celebration as the Sandinistas march triumphantly into Managua. To his disgust, he finds beside him a mercenary acquaintance who, throughout the film, has kept popping into his life, alternately amusing and shocking him. Price wants nothing to do with the man and makes his exit. As he does, the mercenary calls out after him, "See you in Thailand." This sentiment was shared by more than a few over the years. Early on in the Vietnam War, books began to appear with titles such as *Thailand: Another Vietnam?* and *Thailand: The War That Is, The War That Will Be* ("A first-hand report of another Vietnam in the making," read the subtitle). It was only a matter of time, such analyses predicted, before the next domino found itself wobbling. The script writers for *Under Fire* obviously agreed with them.

Still, the film barely had time to hit the theaters before Bangkok had won its war with the insurgents of the Communist Party of Thailand (CPT) and begun its move to becoming a viable democracy and market economy. It had, indeed, been "the next Vietnam," but the state emerged victorious. The failure of the Thai insurgents highlights the difficulty of replicating a successful approach. Although it had studied people's war in detail, to the point of copying its approaches and campaign elements precisely, the CPT proved unable to reproduce the results.[1]

Growth of Insurgent Challenge to the Old-Regime

One of the few states to avoid the loss of its independence in the nineteenth- and early twentieth- century imperial scramble that divided up the globe, Thailand (see

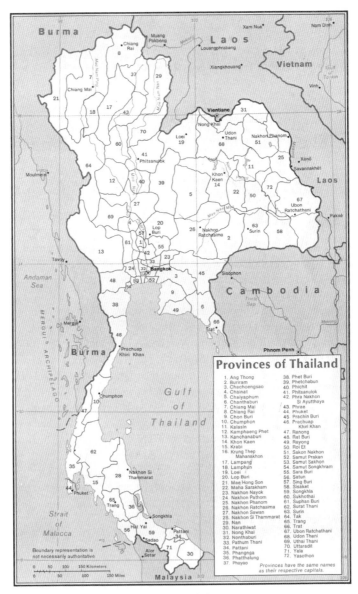

Figure 3.1

Figure 3.1) nonetheless emerged from the episode a greatly changed society. Not only was its economy integrated into the world market, but its political system, following the 1932 overthrow of the absolute monarchy, also institutionalized rule by the bureaucratic elite, dominated by the military, a form of governance that has been called a bureaucratic polity. (That is, political interplay took place within the bureaucracy itself.)

In its geographic boundaries, this polity had shrunk considerably, as both the French and British had lopped off outlying areas. This latter circumstance, however, was a plus, because it made the kingdom more ethnically and culturally homogenous. Its basic socio-cultural orientation remained traditionally Buddhist and Thai, both formally and in fact. That is, in the kingdom there was a common thread of belief in Buddhist conceptions of life and correct conduct, as well as agreement on the legitimacy of the established order, the old-regime.

At the apex of that order was the king, who, despite having lost his position as an absolute monarch in 1932, regained, in the decades that followed, prominence in both social life and politics through his role as one who could stand above the fray and serve the interests of Thailand alone. Similarly, the notion that the Thai government ruled with the blessing of the king, even at his pleasure, increasingly became a political fact that no coup group could ignore, the coup having become, in the post-1932 world of Bangkok, the accepted method for changing the government. To be perceived as having failed to obtain royal assent was to insure failure.

In addition to his resurgent political position, the king was formally the chief patron and protector of Buddhism, represented by a vibrant Buddhist order (*Sangha*). The *Sangha* impacted on all levels of Thai society, and scarcely a major village in the kingdom did not have in its boundaries a *wat* (temple) with, as required, a group of monks in residence. The monks were an important element in the continual renewal of culture, because they comprised a transient group, moving in and out of the population. It was considered every young man's duty to spend at least a three-month period in the saffron robe.[2] Members of the *Sangha* were present at all major government functions, and the king himself engaged in activities dictated by the religion as giving strength and unity to the kingdom (for example, the ritual plowing ceremony before the spring planting).

The result was to intertwine religion and polity integrally. This was not merely a formal relationship. Numerous anthropological studies[3] found community of belief and practice that linked all classes and groups. The value structure was shared by both elites and the populace at large. Among the more central elements were a shared perception that position was a function of merit accumulated in past lives; that it was the duty of those more well-off to share with and care for those not as well endowed (a major tenet of ubiquitous patron-client relationships); and that all members of the polity were at the most basic level members of a unique community linked by that which was "Thai."

Beliefs such as these served qualitatively to shape the impact of "modernization" even while, structurally, conditions grew during the twentieth century that were fraught with conflict. Increasingly, as the bureaucratic polity stifled the constitutive system,[4] forces of the left offered radical solutions to issues of policy, of which there were many, ranging from increasing poverty and landlessness to lack of avenues for political participation. Ultimately, after the Second World War, the Communist Party of Thailand (CPT) emerged as the primary opposition to the Royal Thai Government's socio-economic-political policies. As such it challenged the legitimacy of the Buddhist-sanctioned order.

The Thai government had long been viewed communism as a threat. The Russian Revolution had served as an early example of the menace of the philosophy, involving as it did regicide, attacks on religion, and assaults on the existing order. What damned Marxism still more was its association with the Chinese immigrant problem: the earliest communist proselytism was carried out amongst the Chinese community by agents sent from China. Similarly, other communist activities involved resident foreign communities. Vietnamese communist cadre, for instance, worked amongst the Vietnamese refugee groups in the Thai northeast, and Ho Chi Minh was in the kingdom for more than a year after leaving China. For a time, in fact, when French pressure became intense during the 1931–33 period, the Vietnam Communist Party temporarily shifted its headquarters to the Thai northeast.[5]

Still, it was a schism within the ethnic Thai community that led to the 1933 promulgation of an anti-communist statute. The overthrow of the absolute monarchy in 1932 had occurred in response to, and amidst, economic and social crisis brought on by worldwide depression, yet the coup plotters had no coherent plan for dealing with this crisis. When Pridi Panomyong, a brilliant member of the inner coup group, produced an economic strategy that, it was claimed, advanced "socialist" principles, he was attacked. The plan served as the catalyst for factionalism, and ultimately Pridi found it discreet to leave the country for a time. So broad was the resulting "1933 Act Concerning Communism" that all radical thought was effectively outlawed. So it was, in the years leading up to the Second World War, that communism was suppressed.

Only during the worldwide struggle was Thai communism able to gather momentum. Then, fascinated by the Fascist phenomenon, the military-led regime appropriated many of the notions and trappings of the ideology, including adopting the name "Thailand" to replace Siam and formally siding with the Japanese after they invaded the kingdom in December 1941. The declaration was at best a half-hearted exercise, however, and government officials maintained regular contact with the resistance movement led by Pridi. The communists, too, organized as the Communist Party of Siam (CPS) and the Communist Youth of Siam, participated in resistance, although the entire business remained rather low key. In December 1942, ethnic Chinese communists, joined by some Thai of the CPS, met in what was later called the First Party Congress. Among the various outcomes of this gathering was the formation of the party Politburo (at the time called the "Executive Committee").

Such was the party's focus on the Chinese community that it was forced to operate as two sections, one for Chinese, the other for non-Chinese Thai. The "Thai Section" later became the Thai Communist Party (TCP). At the 1952 Second Party Congress the name was formally changed to the Communist Party of Thailand (CPT). It was there that the Maoist influence became clear. Given Mao's victory in China and the model his approach presented, this was hardly surprising. Furthermore, the CPT hierarchy, especially the Politburo and the Central Committee, was almost exclusively Sino-Thai in ethnic composition. In the wake of the Second Congress, talk about "liberation forces" became standard CPT fare. During the late 1950s Thai were for the first time taken out of the country for training in China, North Vietnam, and Laos.

By the time of the Third Party Congress in 1961, the Maoists within CPT ranks were firmly in control, supporters of the Soviet Union banished. A formal resolution was passed declaring that armed struggle was the proper strategy for revolution in Thailand. Plans were laid to implement the resolution. These included establishing a Northeast Region Jungle Headquarters in 1962, together with front organizations to support the guerrilla forces, such as the Farmer's Liberation Association. The clandestine CPT radio, "Voice of the People of Thailand" (VOPT), also began broadcasting in 1962. Virtually until the end of the insurgency, it would serve as a principal means for disseminating party directives and theory. In 1963, VOPT commenced issuing CPT statements designed to foster the impression that a budding united front, a key component of the Maoist approach, was forming. The first clash between government and CPT forces occurred in the Northeast on 7 August 1965, thereafter annually celebrated by the CPT as the date its people's war commenced.

The insurgency grew in step with the American war in Vietnam. Indeed, Bangkok was so concerned with the strategic threat that it committed major forces to ground combat in both Laos and South Vietnam, with smaller numbers seeing covert action in Cambodia. In Thailand, conflict was centered in three major areas: the Northeast, North, and South. Each area possessed local features that fostered unrest. Throughout the insurgency's history, however the Northeast was to remain the primary area of conflict, because CPT campaigns in the North and South attracted mainly ethnic minorities that did not pose the same threat to the government as did action among the Thai-Isaan of the Northeast.

Significantly, while the government viewed the insurgency as an integral part of China's strategy for "liberating" Southeast Asia—and North Vietnam as an instrument to that end—the thrust behind the CPT, whatever the region, in reality originated from within the kingdom itself, in those "internal contradictions" that existed. Most of the rank and file individuals involved were not communists, therefore, but individuals who for various reasons were alienated from the existing system. Government repression was the CPT's best recruiting tool.

Of importance in considering these three main areas of conflict was the fact that little evidence could be found of coordination or even liaison between them below the strategic level. Geography undoubtedly played a role in this, yet the CPT's inability to surmount obstacles to unified effort led to an ever-expanding reliance for support on external sources and a constant danger of degeneration from indigenously supported insurgency to externally supported partisan warfare.[6]

Initially, external links were salutary. The CPT's long-standing ties with the stronger communist parties in the region gave it access not only to the usual training and propaganda assistance but also to the formal mechanisms of support developed to fuel Indochina's "liberation." Of these, the most important was the western portion of the Ho Chi Minh Trail system under the auspices of the 35th PL/95th NVA (Pathet Lao/North Vietnamese Army) Combined Command. Apparently already in existence by 1961–62, this logistics network had possibly been constructed as early as the end of the Second World War. Its expansion went on simultaneously with the improvement of the Ho Chi Minh Trail's main routes dedicated to the support of operations in South Vietnam.

Nevertheless, their common purpose notwithstanding, neither the Chinese nor the Vietnamese or Lao were willing to allow the other to encroach into self-proclaimed spheres of influence. The 35th PL/95th NVA Combined Command, for instance, served the Northeastern insurgency, while the conflict in the North was supplied by the Chinese using Second World War era infiltration routes and a newly constructed road network in northern Laos.[7] Regular troops of both sides were so positioned as to stake out their preserves. The South was so far away that it was all but forced to become self-reliant and thus remained something of a backwater throughout most of the insurgency. In the main theaters of operation, the North and the Northeast, the Sino-Vietnamese rivalry limited the amount of support reaching the CPT and hampered its coordination efforts within Thailand itself.

Thus the growth and intensity of the insurgency were in many respects dependent on the machinations of these outside supporters, because "in-country" the communists consistently failed to achieve inroads among the lowland population of the kingdom's central core and capable of making the movement self-sufficient. By 1970 internal sources, in fact, were incapable of meeting minimum logistical needs, and, from that date, external sources of weaponry predominated in the CPT supply system. Obviously, the revolutionary conjuncture posited by communist doctrine as necessary for the overthrow of the government had yet to arrive.

Constructing the Counter-State

This lack of absolute success did not mean the CPT insurgency was not a relative threat. To emphasize a point: The CPT had long sought to engage in revolutionary action and finally did so in the post-Second World War years. Maoist people's war was adopted as its strategy. In this conception the state's greater military power was to be negated by mobilizing the people against it. This was to be done through creating a counter-state, using the mass line and the united front, in particular. Eventually, the counter-state would become strong enough to contend militarily for power.

Power, then, was the insurgents' strategic goal. Tactically, this was sought through local guerrilla operations that challenged government control of specific areas. Operationally, the link between the two was a political infrastructure rooted in base areas. Indeed, the principal purpose of insurgent armed force was to protect and facilitate expansion of this counter-state. Conversely, for the Thai government seeking to retain state power, to combat revolutionary warfare was to combat the insurgent counter-state.

As with all organizations, the CPT had to have a beginning. Its foreign origins have already been noted: it was an ethnic Chinese and Vietnamese creation. Party members were not originally targeted against Thai society but sent to raise funds amongst their ethnic compatriots for the liberation movement in the motherland. Consequently, the CPT was from its inception very much attuned to the strategic designs of other regional communist parties. It remained so oriented throughout the struggle. Its Secretary General at the time hostilities broke out (1965), in fact, Thong Chaemsiri, was a Thai-Vietnamese who had come to the kingdom as a refugee from North Vietnam in 1930s. When he arrested in 1968 (he was later released in 1974 and rejoined the Politburo), his place was taken by Charoen Wanngarm, a Chinese who immigrated to Thailand in the years just before the Second World War.[8]

Four other members of the seven-man ruling Politburo—Deputy Secretary General Wirat Angkathavorn, Song Nopakhun, Udom Srisuwan, and Damri Ruengautham—were also Sino-Thai.[9] All came from what we may be called elite backgrounds. Charoen, for example, first joined the CPT in 1945 and then worked for two years on the editorial board of *Mahachon*, a Bangkok socialist newspaper.[10] Similarly, Udom first gained notoriety as a writer for the economic newspaper *Sethisarn*, "whose articles served to inspire activists and intellectuals of the period."[11] Though some of these top-ranking CPT figures joined the party in the post-Second World War years (Udom, for instance, was arrested and held without trial during a 1958 roundup of communist suspects; he did not flee into the jungle until his release seven years later), it was the war and the anti-Japanese resistance that provided the political space for the CPT to emerge from the shadows.

Too much should not be made of the party's wartime resistance activity. Thaddeus Flood, for example, claims a massive organization supported by wide-spread popular mobilization,[12] a contention few scholars would support. Still, the foundations for later expansion were laid. Developments in Trang and Phatthalung Provinces in the South were typical.[13] Following the First Party Congress in 1942, the CPT (though it had not yet adopted the title) mobilized Sino-Thai for work against the Japanese. When fighting ended, many of these individuals remained with the party's forces, which then set about expanding. In Trang, for example, particular organizational efforts were carried out in Muang, Kantang, and Palian Districts. These included the abortive formation of a labor union (later ordered by the party to disband) and of a farmers' association, as well as having a party member openly stand as a parliamentary candidate in the 1957 general elections. (He was not elected.) Significantly, in this two-province effort, a number of personalities were active who in later years would become important CPT figures, notably Wirat Angkathavorn, future Deputy Secretary General.

Following the 1961 decision of the Third Party Congress to opt for people's war, additional cadre were sent to the rural areas with instructions to develop further the covert infrastructure; others left for training in North Vietnam. As proselytizing bore fruit, the CPT established three camps: North (07 Area), further divided into two sites, Rai Mai Camp and Khao Kaeo Camp; Central (09 Area); and South (08 Area). Their actual locations changed frequently, to avoid detection, but manpower grew steadily from the initial batch of sixteen persons housed at the Central Camp after fleeing into the jungle to avoid government actions. Ultimately, strength apparently reached nearly 500. So it went throughout peripheral areas of the kingdom, in unincorporated space: the North, Northeast, and South. Although not especially large, neither was the kingdom small. Its 514,000 sq. km (198,500 sq. mi) and 28 million population (1962) put it in the same league with a unified Vietnam, which ultimately absorbed a very considerable war. (Thailand was smaller in population but larger in area.)

As a tool for CPT expansion, terror was an essential ingredient, but it was selective, generally aimed at recalcitrant villagers or symbols of government authority (e.g., village headmen and school teachers). Appeal to grievances was the essence of the CPT approach. Consequently, as might be expected, CPT activity was concentrated in areas of rural poverty and political estrangement, above all in the Northeast (*Isaan*). That the Northeast was susceptible to revolutionary action was owing to economic, cultural, and political characteristics that distinguished it from Thailand's other regions.[14] It was the kingdom's largest and most populous yet poorest area, a fact owing principally to the physical environment. The land's carrying capacity was so minimal as to make even subsistence agriculture haphazard.[15] As a result, although most Northeasterners were owner-operators,[16] poverty was the norm. Per capita income was substantially less than the rest of the country.[17] Debt, generally in the form of credit accounts, was widespread, and at least one survey found that annual living expenses for an average family regularly exceeded available resources.[18]

Isaan (also rendered as *Isan* or *Isarn*) was also culturally distinct from Thailand's other regions. It was Thai-Lao in orientation, even though the population was far from homogeneous. Northeasterners thought of themselves as part of the Thai kingdom and looked to Bangkok as the locus of a Thai culture that in some respects, surveys showed, they regarded as superior to their own. Yet they retained their sense of regional identity and local pride.[19] Recognition by Northeasterners of their region as a unique entity manifested itself in the political arena. Consolidation of national control by Bangkok was only achieved during the reign of King Chulalongkorn (r. 1868–1910). This led to the imposition of central officials and brief uprisings of a millenarian nature.

The creation of a parliament following the overthrow of the absolute monarchy in 1932 presented a forum for the expression of regional concerns by members of the displaced traditional Northeastern aristocracies, as well as by other *Isaan* politicians. They quickly established a reputation as an opposition group with "leftist" leanings, a stance that led to their repression by the ruling powers after Phibun Songkhram's conservative regime established itself in April 1948. In the "Kilo 11 Incident" (March 1949), four prominent Northeastern politicians were assassinated. As Keyes summarizes:

> In the subsequent period these four men became symbols of growing sentiments shared by a large part of the northeastern populace that they were discriminated against as a whole by the Central Thai and the central government. The death of these prominent northeastern leaders was a major catalyst in the development of Isaan regional political identity and purpose for it demonstrated most dramatically the attitudes of the central government toward those who were identified with Isaan political aspirations. In addition, however, Northeasterners also began to feel that Central Thai political discrimination was but a symptom of more basic economic and cultural discrimination. In the next decade these feelings of economic, political, and cultural discrimination were fired even more as a larger number of Northeasterners had increased contact with Central Thai.[20]

Even with the threat of violence in the air, emerging Northeastern regional identity could not be stilled. Northeastern MPs "continually raised the charge of economic discrimination of the government against the Northeast."[21] In April 1958, all Northeastern MPs in the pro-government party presented a set of four demands[22] that they urged on action on within fifteen days. If these were not met, they announced that they would bolt and form a separate Northeast Party in collusion with Northeastern leftist MPs. The demands were not met, and no Isaan party resulted, but the attempt added to government fears of growing regional identity.

The fact that the radical movement in the kingdom at the time was predominantly a Northeastern product, together with the active role played by Northeastern delegates in fostering neutralist sentiments,[23] caused the ruling elite to look with jaundiced eye at regional demands. Keyes presents the situation in these terms:

> Officials in the government close to General Sarit [military commander-in-chief and later prime minister] viewed the pressures exerted primarily by Northeastern representatives, for "socialistic" programs to improve the economic position of the Northeast, for greater toleration of leftist political action within the country, and for a neutral foreign policy with grave apprehension. They were beginning to feel that if given free rein the activities of the northeastern MPs could seriously threaten the security of Thailand.

There was a growing awareness among these government leaders of the need to deal with what they considered a "northeastern problem." After Sarit inaugurated a new period of military rule in late 1958 [he was to rule until his death in December 1963] this "problem" and its "solutions" were to become a major preoccupation of the Thai government.[24]

The "Northeastern problem" was of particular concern to Thai policy-makers when considered within the context of other events in Southeast Asia. Thai foreign policy during this period was predicated largely on an analysis of how best to safeguard Thailand's security in the face of a perceived dual threat of communist aggression and subversion. The Laotian Crisis of 1959–61, which involved people with whom *Isaan* inhabitants had close affiliations, together with the growing conflict in South Vietnam, heightened fears that Northeastern political dissent was part of a larger communist-led conspiracy to detach the Northeast from the kingdom and to threaten the government. Thus Bangkok moved directly against the threat, and in the 1958–62 period those labeled as communists were suppressed.[25] In such an atmosphere many opposition figures, particularly in the Northeast, went underground and linked up with the CPT's covert apparatus.

As we have already seen, the CPT had long been active in the Northeast. The activities of the Vietnamese community have been recounted. As early as 1936, for instance, the communists, many of them Vietnamese, had paraded openly in Khon Kaen Province; and during the period 1949–52 cadre were sent by the CPT to the Northeast to proselytize. With cadre having already been sent abroad for training in the late 1950s, and with the network of the 35th PL/95th NVA Combined Command in place to provide logistics support for insurgent action, it was logical that it was the Northeast chosen for the "jungle headquarters" established in response to the Third Party Congress announcement that armed struggle was the proper strategy for liberation. Despite such preparation, the CPT's Sino-Thai elite remained relatively isolated until the political events detailed above offered up the manpower it needed to form a viable movement.

A key incident was the execution, of Krong Chandawong, a longtime Northeast activist, on 31 May 1961.[26] A former underground leader in the Northeast during the Second World War, and later a respected MP, Krong had thrice been arrested for alleged subversive activities in the years following the war. His efforts to have parliament repeal the Anti-Communist Act and to adopt a neutralist foreign policy aroused the ire of authorities, but apparently he sealed his doom when he founded the *Samaki Tham* (United in Dharma) movement, "a loose grassroots organisation to promote self-help and development among northeastern villages." Viewing the organization as a communist front, authorities had him arrested and executed, together with another Northeast activist, by a police firing squad. An estimated 200 *Samaki Tham* members were also seized, an action that had predictable consequences. Hundreds of supporters fled and joined the only viable force capable of resisting the repression, the CPT. Among these fugitives were Krong's children, one of whom, his daughter Kruankhrong, became something of a revolutionary cult figure under the alias "Rassamee."[27]

The political space created by repression, then, allowed the CPT to tap the latent grievances already present as a result of social and ecological realities.[28] To focus the resulting outburst, the CPT constructed an infrastructure following standard Leninist lines. At the apex was the seven-man Politburo (Political Bureau). It purportedly represented a 25-man Central Committee. (Insurgent movements are actually constructed from top down, not the other way around, so those in the lower organ have normally been selected by those in the higher.)

Central Committee members performed various staff functions, among the most important being overseeing the military apparatus and attempting to build a united front as called for by Maoist ideological thought. Additionally, they often served as heads of Party Provincial (*changwat*) Committees. These oversaw CPT district (*amphoe*) committees that, in turn, guided "township" (*tambol*) and village (*muban* or *ban*) party structures. The precise combination of these elements at any particular time was problematic. Villages and hamlets, of course, were particular social and physical entities, but CPT "districts" and "provinces" frequently did not correspond to government equivalents. More often than not, the standard nomenclature for identifying a particular area of CPT activity was to designate it a "zone." As such, a zone could embrace anything from a village to a province.[29]

This structure was a political entity, a counter-state. Its purpose was to further the communist goal of revolution. Robert F. Zimmerman, a US official with long experience in Thailand, has provided a good look at its basic component, the village:

> The party's greatest strength . . . lies in its elaborate organization at the village level in those areas where Communist insurgents are strongly entrenched. An excellent illustration of this organization at its best is the infrastructure that existed in Ban Nakham village, Ubon Ratchathani Province, in 1966. Although government Communist suppression operations destroyed this infrastructure, there is little reason to doubt that it remains typical of Communist practice in areas where the insurgents are in control.

The Ban Nakham village organization was headed by a village committee consisting of a chairman, two assistant chairman, and four other members, with one of the assistant chairmen and the four ordinary members responsible for directing the activities of eight specialized committees of 15–30 members dealing with such matters as youth and military affairs, political propaganda, labor and business, women's affairs, etc. This structure functioned within the village but was responsible to a "zone commander" and two assistant commanders based in the jungle.

Through this apparatus operating at the local level, the Communists have been able not only to recruit and motivate active adherents but also to mobilize sufficient popular support in the major insurgent areas to generate sources of manpower, food, shelter, and finances (in part through local tax levies), and to develop an effective intelligence network. They have also benefited from a certain amount of illicit "assistance" in the form of accommodation or even bribes offered by government officials or by private construction firms engaged in building roads into the insurgent areas. . .[30]

How extensive this infrastructure became is reported by another US official, former CIA officer Ralph W. McGehee:

Using all the index cards and files, I wrote a final report. I prepared name lists of all cell members, including their aliases, by village. In this district the list contained the names of more than 500 persons. Those 500 persons did not appear anywhere in the Agency reporting at the time. The CIA estimated there were 2,500 to 4,000 Communists in all of Thailand. But our surveys showed the Communists probably had that many adherents in Sakorn Nakorn Province alone.[31]

Although not discussed in McGehee's work, it appears he and his superiors were attempting to compare apples and oranges. The 2,500–4,000 figure would seem to be the then-current estimate of armed guerrillas, while the 500 individuals in the district in question were part of the mass base. To wit, as a village came under control of the CPT "shadow government," its mobilization included providing manpower for a militia. The best members of this body joined the actual guerrillas in the CPT's base areas, located in inaccessible areas. Thus, at any given time, the actual number of individuals involved in the movement far outnumbered those bearing arms. These arms, it must be added, according to the romantic vision of the guerrilla put forth in much literature, were to come from the government itself, captured mainly in raids and combat, but as has been noted, a significant proportion of CPT weapons and equipment came from foreign communist sources.

Captured photo of CPT combatants at a camp in the Thai South. As was typical of the era, the insurgents sought to imitate the uniforms and symbols of the People's Liberation Army (PLA) of China. (Photo: captured, Bangkok Post in Author Collection)

Nevertheless, with supplies and training from abroad used to outfit manpower thrown up by repression at home, the CPT was able to expand steadily. By the early 1970s, a majority of the provinces in the kingdom had been classified as "infiltrated," meaning some sort of CPT activity was present.[32] Still, this activity remained confined to areas outside the heartland, beyond the central plain that was the social, economic, and political locus of Thailand. Penetration there would have to wait for later events.

State Response to Insurgent Challenge[33]

As we would expect in a polity wherein coercive power had created the political space for insurgency, the Thai government during these early years responded inappropriately to the CPT challenge. True, in December 1965, the highest levels of the Thai military government moved to deal with the communist problem by ordering the formation of the Communist Suppression Operations Command (CSOC), later to become the Internal Operations Command (ISOC). And, true, they placed in charge of it a respected officer who had a background that included covert operations in Laos against the communists, Saiyud Kerdphol. But what the powers-that-be had in mind was better management of the anti-guerrilla campaign, not counter-insurgency.

Saiyud has observed:

> The RTA [Royal Thai Army] then was run by "the old school," the pre-World War II officers. They had tremendous difficulty understanding counter-insurgency, rebellion, and the fundamental causes which fed revolt. Praphas [former Deputy Prime Minister and the "muscle" behind the government which ultimately fell in 1973], for example, named CSOC the "suppression command." He could understand that the fight had to be coordinated—that's why he set up CSOC—but he wasn't talking about CPM [civil-police-military; essentially the coordinated application of all resources to the insurgent problem, as done by the British to defeat the communists in Malaya during the Emergency]. The younger generation of officers, though, at least some of them, were more attuned to reality. Among them was Prem [later Prime Minister].
>
> We understood immediately that what we were dealing with was a political problem. We applied CPM to the problems of the Northeast, yet we knew more was needed than simply a response. Coordination is the key to winning, but all must look at the problem through the same eyes. You need a common blueprint on which to base the plan.
>
> Two things were obvious: there was nothing worse than to fight the wrong way, *and* the key is the people. We had to ask ourselves, why do the people have a problem, why are they taking up arms? We did a lot of mechanical things, such as setting up Village Defence Corps and special training centers through which we could run all regular companies.
>
> The crucial point, though, more than numbers, is orientation. You have to keep analyzing a target area. You have to keep asking yourself, "What are the reasons for popular discontent? What are the problems?" Figure out the solutions, then implement and coordinate.[34]

Saiyud's conception was that CSOC would do this. To establish the nature of the problems, he did two things. First, an intelligence analysis center was set up with branches in the field. Copies of all government reports (and any other data that could be gathered up) were fed into the system, then analyzed with the aid of borrowed computer time, a novel methodology for Thailand then. This allowed typical bureaucratic misstatement and inaccuracy to be weeded out and a definitive assessment of the problem to be distributed.

Secondly, an extensive research and analysis branch began to function under the brilliant and at-times controversial scholar Somchai Rakwijit. It soon produced comprehensive assessments based on sound data. In particular, it sent researchers into the field, often alone, to conduct studies of insurgent-infested areas.

Using this data, Saiyud directed his response, a mix of civil and military measures. It was classic counter-insurgency, the sort of approach textbooks outline: identify the problem; move in with solutions using the military to shield the effort; send specially trained forces to seek out the guerrillas. In retrospect, it seems a logical enough strategy, yet it encountered considerable difficulties.

CSOC was at first given command authority only over the small CPM task forces deployed to insurgent-affected areas. Guided by a comprehensive intelligence network set up by Saiyud, these began to show promise by 1967 in uncovering and dealing with the CPT infrastructure, but when CSOC asked for more units, military opponents, jealously guarding their own turfs, demurred. Hence, authority over field units was transferred back to regional army commanders. Thereafter, the counter-insurgency program became largely ineffective. Most commanders simply did not deploy their forces in what was viewed as a secondary mission. Instead, they concentrated on political and economic concerns. When called upon actually to move against insurgent forces, they did so in military fashion, "search and destroy."

Nowhere was this more obvious than in the North. There, a number of land quarrels in Chiang Rai and Nan Provinces between Hmong tribesmen and Thai exacerbated longstanding lowlander-hill dweller tensions. December 1967 saw the beginning of a series of incidents, first in Tung Chang District of Nan Province, later in Chiang Kam and Terng Districts of Chiang Rai Province, as well as Mae Sod District of Tak Province. Others occurred in the three provinces of Petchabul, Loei, and Phitsanulok.[35] Initial Thai response was heavy-handed and succeeded primarily in making enemies. The security forces responded to ambushes with artillery and air strikes, which destroyed villages and threw still more recruits to the insurgents. A flood of refugees resulted, and the economy of a large area in the North was completely destroyed.[36] Attempts by more enlightened officials to adopt alternative means of addressing the problem were mired in red tape and lacked resources.

Realizing the inappropriateness of suppression, Saiyud fought to implement his CPM strategy. As detailed in his manuscript, *The Struggle for Thailand, Section II,*

Saiyud Kerdphol (with author) in Pua, Nan Province of Thailand, in May 1973. Saiyud was unusual for a Thai senior officer in that he fed his desire for solutions by actively seeking out those he thought might be have useful knowledge—whatever their ranks, regardless of nationality or service. (Author collection)

A Solution for the North, Saiyud saw counter-insurgency among the hill tribes as consisting of three stages. In Stage 1 development would take place in an attempt to ward off attempted subversion. This failing, Stage 2, suppression, would begin. Once Stage 2 had been handled correctly, Stage 3, rehabilitation, could occur. The key, though, as Saiyud pointed out, was the development activities of Stage 1.[37]

Saiyud's approach was not accepted by key government officials. Consequently, little came of it. "Body count" remained the order of the day throughout the 1960s. The heavy-handed (and, in many cases, ham-handed) official approach only increased the ability of the insurgents to recruit. As the number of villages destroyed grew, so, too, did the number of guerrillas. Some CPT propaganda sessions reportedly involved as many as 200 armed guerrillas. Although its strength in the North

Local patrol in Uttaradit Province, northern Thailand. Such routine security duties, when conducted in the tangled jungle terrain that covers the region, proved very useful for transitioning troops from their normal lowland environment to the strenuous demands of highland duty. (Photo: Bangkok Post in Author Collection)

was only an estimated 3,000 by 1973, the guerrilla movement managed to make life there extremely unsettled in many areas.[38]

Pointless "search and destroy" culminated in January 1972 when some 12,000 security forces personnel engaged in Operation *Phu Kwang*, the largest such exercise ever conducted in Thailand. Its aim was to dislodge several hundred Hmong based in the rugged Tri-Province area. (Vietnam had its Parrot's Beak threatening Saigon; Thailand had a Laotian equivalent bordered by three Thai provinces and pointing like a dagger toward the central Thai heartland.) The operation ended after some two months, with nothing to show for its efforts except 60 troops dead and another 200 wounded, virtually all to booby traps. Most insurgents monitored the operation from Laos, to which they had withdrawn as the logistical buildup for the large maneuver became obvious months ahead of time. Once the assault ended, they re-infiltrated into Thailand.[39]

Staging point for small unit patrols in Nan Province, northern Thailand. Vehicles were used to move troops to jump-off points and to provide bulk supplies. Harsh terrain meant tedious foot patrolling under dangerous circumstances. (Photo: Bangkok Post in Author Collection)

This remained the general pattern of events. Although many Thai appeared to comprehend the socio-economic nature of the Northern insurgency, the government response was such as to insure its failure. At the root of the problem lay the fact that the target population, the Hmong, was not comprised of ethnic Thai. Hence, its members were treated as second-class citizens by many, if not most, Thai.

There were few qualms felt in the use of force against a "non-Thai" population in revolt against the legal government. The racial attitudes carried by the average Thai soldier were difficult to overcome and frequently translated into hostile actions against the population. Suppression thus became a double-edged sword. The CPT was able to use this sword. As one former Hmong insurgent recounted:

> The communists were Miao [the Thai term for the Hmong, still much in current use], though some cadre were Thai. Some people wanted to resist them, but the army policy then was

75

that the Miao should not be trained in weapons, only development. But the communists took some young Miao and trained them to use arms. Then the BPP [Border Patrol Police] had conflict with young Miao, especially over girls. The communists took those who had conflicts with the BPP and trained them. They then sent them back to attack. The communists came and burned the school down and established themselves. Those Miao associated with foreigners or the government had to leave to seek safety.[40]

Saiyud Kerdphol talks with tribespeople in Pua, Nan Province of Thailand, in May 1973. Civic action activities are being carried out in the background. Then a Major General, Saiyud had early in his career attracted attention for his insights into insurgency and counter-insurgency. (Marks photo)

Safety, too, was a prime concern in motivating many such as Nuyua Sayang (age unknown) to join the communists: "I was just a member of the mass base. The communists said they could give us better lives. The young men believed them, but the old men didn't. Safety was the prime factor [why we joined]. People sided with whomever they thought could guard them. You just try to go on with your life."[41]

Reflecting what it was that led some young to throw in their lot with a movement committed to attacking the government, certainly a dangerous undertaking, Laopao Sasong, 40 years of age and a CPT village militia member for more than a decade before his surrender, observed: "I joined because the communist propaganda said if they liberated the country, every race would be treated equally."[42]

Here we see a variety of motives but all culminating in the individuals concerned becoming a part of the CPT counter-state. Once inducted, new members could gradually work their way up to higher positions. Yet in its infancy, the insurgency

Royal Thai Army (RTA) training exercise in cordon and search conducted in Nan Province, northern Thailand, date unknown. RTA made good use of mobile training teams to bring small unit tactics up to levels necessary for the independent work that is at the heart of dominating human terrain. (Photo: Bangkok Post in Author Collection)

followed the classic leader-follower division outlined by Scott. It was the structuring of grievance through the counter-state that channeled anger in support of the effort to make a revolution. Certainly Hmong status as a minority group influenced Thai behavior in its efforts to put down rebellion. Still, military action in the North was not dissimilar to that undertaken elsewhere in the kingdom. For the first decade of the declared insurgency, force remained the principal methodology for dealing with the CPT's political movement. It is noteworthy, however, how contingent support was for the insurgents in those areas where the CPT was active. Villager loyalty, regardless of structural conditions, was very much "up for grabs."

Significantly, most Thai, unless traumatized by specific grievances, preferred to side with the *status quo*. In fact, in 1966–67 Saiyud was instrumental in forming the Volunteer Defence Corps, effectively, village militia. These had no trouble gaining recruits and grew rapidly. Initially limited to their local areas, they eventually evolved into more mobile combat forces. As might be predicted, they were highly effective, because they knew their areas. Ultimately, they became what in English is normally rendered as "Rangers." The communists would have called them "regional forces." They were to be the units that broke the insurgency's military back.

An Alternative Approach

All of this was to come in the future. During the period under consideration, military action continued mainly to be conducted by regular forces. Nevertheless, military measures were not the whole of the government approach. Particularly in the Northeast, where the target population, although technically non-Thai was nonetheless regarded as "Thai," there were efforts, pushed through by individuals such as Saiyud, to meet the popular needs through regional development. Paradoxically, while repression was directed against those perceived as security threats and served to swell insurgent ranks, simultaneously a "hearts and minds" campaign was in effect.

Publicly, at least, Bangkok was under no illusions concerning conditions in the countryside and acknowledged that the rural masses continued to live in poverty.[43] Consequently, even before the actual outbreak of violence, a number of development programs had already been begun during the early and mid-1950s. By 1958, this approach had been broadened and included the first Community Development pilot projects. In 1960, a National Community Development Program was put into effect, consolidating many of the already existing programs, which were scattered among various departments.

According to government literature,[44] the program was designed to bring about the partnership of the Royal Thai Government and its people at the local level. Further, it aimed "to encourage the people to exercise initiative to improve their communities and ways of living through cooperative efforts on the self-help basis" and to "bring the coordinated support of the various ministries concerned to assist the villagers in carrying out their projects."[45] By the end of 1961, at least on paper, most Northeastern villages were covered by the program, even, it should be noted, as repression sent activists fleeing to the CPT for protection.

Indeed, while National Community Development was directed at villages throughout the kingdom, specific measures to deal with the Northeast were also implemented. A Northeastern Committee was created in the National Economic Development Board of the Prime Minister's Office in 1961, and an independent regional development plan was promulgated.[46] Much of the proposed USD 300 million in plan expenditures was to be provided by the US.

These development efforts in the Northeast were both reaction to events—calls for redistribution of resources—and an attempt to ward off an even more undesirable event: the outbreak of violence should grievances be left unsatisfied. Some sort of violence was, in any case, expected, since the CPT was known to be working toward that end. In the period prior to the actual outbreak of guerrilla warfare in 1965, the government continued to broaden its rural development programs, proceeding on the theory that advancing the people's economic welfare would gradually eliminate grievances thereby removing the objective conditions of poverty that could be exploited by the CPT. This effort was facilitated by the US, which had established an economic aid mission to the kingdom in 1950.[47]

The principal vehicle for American assistance in this field was the Accelerated Rural Development (ARD) scheme. Provinces selected for ARD were to be those most in need of immediate developmental help, which, in practice, meant those threatened by communist insurgency as so-designated by the National Security Council (NSC). Once a *changwad* was designated an "ARD province" by the NSC, the staff and equipment available to the governor were augmented. ARD created, trained, and equipped a local organization with the capability of planning, designing, constructing, and maintaining rural roads and other small village projects. Simultaneously, steps were taken at the national level to give the governor authority to implement village-level projects on his own initiative without constantly referring to higher authorities in Bangkok for approval.[48]

By 1969 the governors of the 24 ARD-designated provinces, most in the Northeast, had progressed from a point where they had virtually no resources with which to mount any type of development program to one where they had staffs of some 250, millions of dollars worth of equipment, and a vastly increased budget. The government had committed a cumulative total of US USD 58,824,000 to the program, supplemented by USD 49,308,000 from the US.

The way in which these funds were expended, it should be noted, reflected economic priorities. Road building and maintenance were the dominant categories. Other ARD activities included mobile medical teams, district farmer groups (cooperatives), and youth and potable water programs. Results of the ARD program as judged in 1969 were mixed. Although physically and statistically there was a great deal of progress to show, the ultimate objective was to "reduce, or even eliminate, insurgency through the development effort."[49] This did not happen.

To the contrary, American and Thai evaluations consistently noted that ARD made no meaningful difference in the target population's disposition,[50] despite the fact that the actual activities involved were generally used and appreciated. Even where a demonstrated improvement occurred in the lot of the villagers in an area, as measured by a classic indicator such as increase in per capita income, the rosy statistical picture often did not reflect the poor realities of the security situation. Only certain groups benefited from the increased contacts with market mechanisms, but examination of even those who had actually profited from development showed there was no apparent change in orientation toward the government or the communists. In fact, a Cornell University report confirmed a phenomenon already observed by some American officials: namely, that there appeared to be a strong association between rate of structural growth and incidence of insurgent activities.[51]

Thus ARD had failed to achieve a great deal toward realizing its objectives. What did emerge time and again from the official analyses of the program was that Northeasterners were loyal Thai in their orientations and were both concerned with the problems of survival and fearful of an abstract menace called "communism." They responded well to efforts to integrate them into the processes of decision-making and development, but these efforts remained so limited in scope as to have little real impact on their situation.

That the ARD program did not reach its goals was unsurprising, for it was an economic response to a political problem. It was simply one facet of a uni-dimensional Thai approach to development. That approach attempted to address the grievances that had resulted in insurgency through a strategy emphasizing economic concerns. This was as predictable as it was ineffective. What the communists were after was restructuring the existing systems of social stratification through seizing state power. That violence was their vehicle resulted from their inability to use peaceful means to accomplish their ends. They could not even hope for this, because they were frozen out of the political system. So, too, were most others who sought to change the system from within. Unless willing to be co-opted by the government, they had no choice but to sit on the sidelines or to join the insurgents. There were no other viable opposition groups.

The solution to such a structural dilemma, then, should have been political development. Yet this Bangkok could not see. The emphasis on maximization of economic growth had been inculcated in the Thai elite through a long process of exposure to and assimilation of Western development ideals. Thailand's pre-1932 absolute monarchs, particularly Mongkut and Chulalongkorn, chose to advance the kingdom by methods and in a fashion of their own choosing, but always their conception of "modern" focused on economic advances. Even after the monarchy became constitutional, there was little political development, because power devolved to the authoritarian structures of the bureaucratic polity rather than to any form of constitutive system.

Thai development notions continued to maximize economic growth to the virtual exclusion of all other forms, notably and particularly political, an emphasis was widely noted at the time in the appropriate literature.[52] Under these circumstances, the logical government course of action, when faced with unrest in an underdeveloped region such as the Northeast, would be that which was carried out: to attack the problem's economic dimensions. Examination of ARD objectives shows this to have been the government's course of action. Although political development receives mention, this aspect of the program was completely overshadowed by economic factors, such as infrastructure development. The skewing of goals was reflected in the indecisive ARD results.

The argument is frequently made, and its implications of cultural chauvinism all too often not appreciated, that Thai actions in the post-Second World War era were taken solely at the behest or instigation of American containment policy.[53] Such a view is simplistic. Certainly the US presence and influence in Thailand were significant, yet Thailand's collaboration with the US during the period represented a marriage of convenience, driven by a shared security perspective, whereby both states sought to maximize their gains. When the partnership's drawbacks came to overshadow its advantages, the Thai backed away from the more overt collaboration.

In the arena of counter-insurgency, there is no question but that Thai authorities were influenced by American and also Western (especially British) concepts, but not in the military tactical aspects so frequently highlighted in the literature (e.g.,

Royal Thai Army (RTA) M-60 machinegunner during operations in Uttaradit Province (next to Nan on map), northern Thailand. CPT built its northern theater of operations by exploiting grievances that had long festered amongst highland tribes angered over issues connected with lowlanders intruding into their traditional areas. (Photo: Bangkok Post in Author Collection)

"search and destroy"). These were almost incidental to the heart of the problem, which was misguided strategic focus.

The growth of American attitudes toward, and capacity for fighting, limited wars was a prominent feature of the Kennedy presidency.[54] It went hand-in-glove with the foreign aid rationale that "development" was to be equated with Western-style economic modernization and would result in maximization of national potential and domestic peace.[55] Owing to the historical circumstances mentioned above, the Thai accepted this orientation. To attribute such acceptance solely, or even mainly, to American insistence is, however, inaccurate. The process was far more unwitting on both sides. There were, after all, alternative counter-insurgency models available at the time, but Bangkok opted for that used by its allies, the West.

Western doctrine, though, posited three essential tasks for successful resolution of revolt: (1) military operations against the insurgents; (2) population and resources control; and (3) eliminating grievances.[56] Within an economically dominated "development" strategy, the elimination of grievances naturally emphasized providing resources and resolving economic complaints, rather than eliminating other forms of dissatisfaction, such as weaknesses of the political system. This accurately describes the role and fate of ARD, wherein goals such as "roads built" and "wells dug" quickly overshadowed the more abstract objectives, among them fostering popular participation in the political process.

Contending Ideological Visions

Such a misdirected "development" approach, coupled with the over-emphasis on military operations, allowed the CPT not only to survive but also slowly to expand. The party initially erred in emphasizing the military content of Maoism over its political aspects. It attempted to press forward with the military aspects of the campaign without paying adequate attention to construction of the counter-state, and consequently suffered setbacks. By 1969, however, it had regrouped and begun to implement a slow, deliberate construction of the foundations necessary to support its revolt. Simultaneously, an increase of support from external sources served to boost the flagging momentum of the movement.

The CPT's timing was right. As the decade of the 1970s began, Thailand found itself enmeshed in a multi-faceted structural dilemma not unlike in form that which had confronted Vietnam before the Vietnam War (Second Indochina Conflict). An economy based on extractive agriculture was ruled by a regime with only tenuous political links to the populace. The government bureaucracy, monopolizing all power, was able to crush efforts seeking formation of a viable constitutive system.

On the one hand, the bureaucratic polity remained at odds with the fledging constitutive system; on the other, those seeking to frame the particulars of the constitutive system remained at odds with each other. This ideological conflict revolved principally about the need for a "democratic" (normally interpreted by its backers as "parliamentary") or "socialist" framework. In contrast to the approach of either the government or its opponents who favored a parliamentary option, was the Maoist variant espoused by the CPT. In its pronouncements, the party regularly cited the People's Republic of China (PRC) as the appropriate model to be followed in economic and political development. The CPT's "Ten Point Program" was little more than a re-phrasing of the tenets Mao espoused during his long campaign for power in China and reflected the Maoist belief that development could take place only when the society's political structure had been altered.

As indicated in its major pronouncements, the CPT saw Thailand as a semi-feudal colony of American imperialism and thus not truly independent or free. The Americans were aided within Thailand by a variety of counter-revolutionaries (e.g., fascists, landlords, arch-feudalists [i.e., royalty]), all of whom maintained a repressive system. To establish freedom and democracy, the government had to be overthrown and in its place a "people's government" instituted. Land would be redistributed to the peasants, debts cancelled, industry sensibly developed for the benefit of the Thai people rather than of foreign and indigenous capitalists. Aside from these general notions, however, there was nothing in the "Ten Point Program" or other available literature that would have allowed the observer to make an accurate list of specific programs that the CPT planned to apply. Reports from "liberated areas" served to confirm that the CPT proceeded in a fashion to be expected within the parameters specified by the Maoist blueprint: heavy emphasis on political indoctrination accompanied by an effort to raise the standard of living.

Adopting Maoism had more fundamental pitfalls. Obviously, it had developed as a response to the unique conditions of China. The CPT took the Chinese experience and attempted to interpret Thai realities in the same fashion. Throughout its history, for example, the CPT maintained an active interest in creating various united fronts: the principal contradiction, according to the party—in imitation of the Chinese approach—was American imperialism *versus* the Thai people. Consequently, the CPT devoted considerable time and effort in its efforts to arouse the Thai people against "the imperialists." Ironically, such was to misread Thai reality and to ignore the far more urgent "contradictions," to use their own term, particularly that between the constitutive system and the bureaucratic polity (i.e., democracy or oligarchy?). This misreading was reflected in the near total lack of success the CPT was to experience in its attempt to build a viable nationwide organization, particularly a united front reflecting the demands of non-elite groups.

Similarly, the emphasis on the peasantry was an element of Maoism that seemed, on its face, appropriate in a state such as Thailand where 85% of the population was located in rural areas. Yet this orientation neglected the shift that had occurred throughout Southeast Asia, Thailand included, whereby a substantial proportion of the "rural population" actually resided in local urban centers. Furthermore, the CPT strategy ignored the fact that in Thailand there was only one true power center of consequence, Bangkok, with its four million people. (The second urban site, Chiang Mai, had but 100,000.)

Bangkok was the socio-economic-political-cultural locus of the kingdom, and, in many respects, all that went on within the kingdom served to "feed" the capital. Developments there had a profound impact on all else that went on, but the CPT chose to eschew urban struggle even as an adjunct to a rural thrust on doctrinal grounds. As events were to demonstrate, though, conditions were ultimately far riper for an urban seizure of power *à la* Moscow 1917–18 than for a Maoist people's war.

Nevertheless, despite CPT strategic miscues, as the American War in Vietnam drew to a close, the insurgent situation in Thailand grew worse.[57] By this time, the Thai government was in trouble. David K. Wyatt has written:

> By the early 1970s, the Thanom-Praphas regime faced a major security crisis. It was not simply that the army was mired in two exhausting conflicts, trying to stem a rising tide of internal insurgency while maintaining forces in Indochina. They also increasingly feared that their closest ally, the United States, was deserting them. When President Nixon moved to Vietnamize the Indochina conflict, to let "Asians fight their own battles," and to reopen diplomatic relations with the People's Republic of China, a power the Thai believed to be supporting the antigovernment insurgency in Thailand, Field Marshal Thanom's response was to attempt to cash in on a decade of development, to bolster his now-aging regime with a bid for the support of those elements of Thai society that had most benefited from economic, social, and educational change. He was to find—like King Chulalongkorn in 1873–74, or Vajiravudh in 1912, or Prajadhipok in 1932, or even like Phibun in 1957—that their response lacked both gratitude and respect.[58]

> Thailand's commitment to economic development had reaped the whirlwind. Social turmoil itself had many causes, all of which came together in the early 1970's. Among

the most salient were: a burgeoning population, cramping lifestyles and straining social services; an accelerating urbanization, which for many meant a serious decline in quality of life; a substantial growth in the number of workers as industry became more export-oriented, but a failure of wages to keep pace with inflation or services with demand; a dramatic expansion in the number of students, especially at the university level, even as the ability of the system to absorb them declined (at least in positions commensurate with their qualifications); and growing friction as the bureaucratic polity expanded, bringing to all areas its officials, its innumerable rules, and its corruption. Traditional values showed signs of strain even as the security forces, which normally stifled dissent, fragmented into contending factions divided by strategic differences on how best to deal with the myriad external and internal problems.

Demands for redress of grievances could not be dealt with in any substantive fashion, because the mechanisms of a constitutive system simply did not exist. The bureaucratic polity thus had reached a crisis point.

A wave of student demonstrations in June 1973 snowballed in October with the arrest of activists demanding greater democracy. As violence erupted, the military regime collapsed with startling rapidity. For the next three years (1973–76), a succession of democratic governments sought to come up with a viable form of popular rule. Such could not remain the case indefinitely, however. October 1973 marked another benchmark in modern Thai political history, an episode that ranked in importance with the 1932 "revolution" that ended the absolute monarchy. Unable to deal with internal structural contradictions in the face of pressure from abroad, the bureaucratic polity, as represented in the popular mind by the military, found itself unceremoniously ousted.

Still, this occurred only because the regime's coercive power, notably the armed forces, was paralyzed by internal factionalism. Divided, the services nonetheless remained intact in terms of actual strength. Given proper circumstances, observers noted, institutional cohesion might easily return—and thus the bureaucratic polity could again rise to threaten the emerging constitutive system. This quickly happened. With the chaos that naturally enough attended the search for representative government once the mechanisms of authoritarianism were displaced, bureaucratic, especially military, cohesion was bound to reappear, particularly given the divided nature of those supporting "democracy." As forces of the left and right battled to shape the constitutive system to their liking, the kingdom slid toward chaos.

Demands by the left for the mobilization of new segments in the process of interest articulation aroused fears of "mob rule" among traditional segments of the Thai polity. They, in turn, made common cause with factions of the military favoring a return to the previous manner of conducting political affairs. A coup on 6 October 1976 brought the bureaucracy again to power through a bloody assault on the perceived center of leftist influence, Thammasat University.

Like its predecessor three years previously, October 1976 was a watershed event. In every sense it was indicative of the national polarization that had resulted from the efforts of the constitutive system to rise from the smothering embrace of the bureaucratic polity. More violence had seemed imminent before a faction of the military, apparently not involved in the actual assault on Thammasat, seized control of the government and declared martial law. Yet it was a military badly divided and strongly influenced by those ideologically committed to a more pluralistic notion of politics and the more limited role of the military therein.

This was demonstrated in the rush by the armed forces to remove themselves from the actual exercise of governance by appointing as prime minister Thanin Kraiwichian, Chief Justice of the Supreme Court. This move, far from returning affairs to a state of normalcy, further contributed to national polarization. Although Thanin plunged into his work and produced a flurry of legislation, his rigid approach quickly alienated even those rightist elements that should have been his most ardent supporters.

The left did not wait to see how things developed. A number of former officials had already gone overseas in the immediate aftermath of the Thammasat bloodbath. Many other individuals, ranging from students to activist workers to politicians, now fled into the jungles or made their way to Indochina. Eventually, they were to number in their thousands. Their bitterness was great, and their estrangement from the establishment total. In the opinion of many, they represented the flower of several generations.

Here at last was the systemic crisis for which the communists had long hoped. After years of laboring in marginalized areas, unable to penetrate the heartland, the CPT finally found itself with the political space that necessarily accompanied a state of polarization. As the acknowledged premier opposition group in the kingdom, the party was ideally situated to become the key actor in shaping and directing the forces demanding change—the first requirement in forming an actual united front.

Ideologically, the CPT was prepared, because Maoist doctrine incorporated the strategy of the united front as a vehicle for welding the opposition into a cohesive body. Since the party was the only real group about which anti-government forces could coalesce, the second important task in united front formation, the conversion of partners to the communist mode of thinking, was virtually accomplished by default. Efforts at reform had clearly failed. No longer did the CPT have to deal with organized, vibrant partners who could justly demand an equal voice in policy matters. Instead, it had only to find the means to absorb and use the high quality manpower that streamed into its base areas. Ideological unanimity was the price extracted for granting sanctuary to the fugitives, who were, in any case, ripe for fresh approaches to societal revision.

New CPT Strategic Dimensions

Presented thus with new recruits from diverse backgrounds and occupations, many of whom were "progressive" in their orientation, the CPT saw a chance to replicate the popular front strategy that had culminated for Mao in his anti-Japanese united front. For more than two decades CPT propaganda had identified the American imperialists and their reactionary allies as the Thai people's great enemies. Although this message had largely fallen on deaf ears, judging from the slow progress made in recruiting ethnic Thai and in organizing the insurgency, the CPT (and many knowledgeable observers) felt the events at Thammasat University had finally revealed to all the true fascist character of the military regime and its obedience to the instructions of the Americans.

The preliminary human results of the unmasking were already inundating CPT strongholds throughout the country in the form of those fleeing the wrath of the system. Surely, the CPT figured, there would be many more such recruits. Inspired, the CPT launched an intense campaign to form a viable united front.[59] For its standard bearer the party erected the Committee for Coordinating Patriotic and Democratic Forces, the CCPDF (also translated as the Coordinating Committee for Patriotic and Democracy Loving Forces). The core of its membership and leadership came from the post-October 1976 fugitives. The task at hand was to expand this core so that it could be linked with the already existing infrastructure in the countryside.

The CPT, in other words, had an organization of leaders: It needed to mobilize their followers. To do so required that specific strategic decisions be made that could certainly not occur in a vacuum, because elements supporting reform would be attempting to conduct their own mobilization campaign. Both would contend within the same structural environment; whichever was more successful would emerge with state power.

Initially, the CPT was the force more advantageously situated to take advantage of existing political realities. The state, though still dangerous, was seemingly all but paralyzed, its decision-making in chaos. The CPT moved quickly, using the two approaches appropriate for building a front: united front from above and below.[60] In the former, the communist party formally established links with other organizations, thereby gaining the participation and services of those organizations' members. The latter strategy, in contrast, called for appealing to the rank and file of rival organizations in an effort to bring the parent bodies into the front.

An examination of CPT united front calls broadcast over VOPT[61] shows a fair mixing of these two approaches. In the year following the October 1976 coup, no less than 75 VOPT broadcasts called for a united front "to oppose the fascist warlord clique, the US imperialists' lackeys."[62] The broadcasts culminated in the 4 October 1977 announcement that the CCPDF had been formed.[63]

The campaign was notable for the degree to which it adhered to Mao's united front instructions. Broadcasts did not focus on the CPT program or its ideology, both of which were scarcely mentioned, but rather on the need of "the people who love democracy and justice" to unite against "the common enemy," the government. Emphasis was placed on shared goals and on demonstrating that people from the entire social spectrum had joined in the struggle. A particular attempt was made to appeal to Thai patriotism, and the CPT was portrayed as the defenders of the true Thai culture and of the kingdom against imperialism.[64]

Unlike previous CPT united front efforts, the CCPDF version went to some lengths to create international links. There were several reasons for this. First and foremost was the fact that the 6 October 1976 events, accompanied as they were by grisly photographs of lynched students being battered by an enraged right wing mob, created a reservoir of sympathy for "progressive forces" and left the Thai government with an unenviable negative public relations image as a repressive regime. Groups of both overseas Thai and foreigners were quickly formed throughout the world to demand the "return" of "democracy and freedom." Most members of these groups were not professed communists, but the CPT recognized that it could enlist their energies through front mechanisms.

A second reason was the lesson learned by the communists during the Vietnam War: International links could play a decisive role in hampering establishment counter-measures. (Recall that while the CPT was "Maoist," the Vietnamese and their clients, the Pathet Lao, had considerable influence due to their major support and training role.) The Thai government, so the CPT line went, was a lackey of the American imperialists and could not long survive without the support of international capitalism. While the CPT could work to disrupt the internal mechanisms of Thai capitalism, foreign friends could best assault international capitalism's stranglehold on Thailand.

The CPT, working through the CCPDF, hence created links with overseas elements opposed to both the American economic/military presence abroad and to the Thai government. This was not particularly difficult, for with the end of the war in Indochina, Thailand had replaced Vietnam as the favorite Southeast Asian target of radical organizations throughout the West and Japan. Although they were not creatures of the CCPDF, "solidarity organizations" willingly acted as its agents. Some, such as the European Coordinating Committee for Solidarity with the Thai People (ECCSTP), went through their own processes of front construction, gradually adding members and expanding their activities.[65]

The result was a fairly well developed network through which propaganda could be disseminated and whereby the CPT—always acting through the CCPDF—could "relate its struggle into [sic] a wider international community."[66] The "solidarity organizations" acted as the CPT's spokespersons, distributed material such as statements detrimental to the Thai government, and solicited donations of money and medical supplies to support the cause. Criticism of the Thai government in the solidarity press echoed the CPT's current propaganda lines. An examination of the literature published by the groups reveals several major themes: (a) the repressive nature of the Thai government and the widespread nature of the opposition to it; (b) the links between Thai and international capitalism, and the domestic effects in Thailand of these bonds; (c) the actions and statements of the CPT and CCPDF; and (d) actions and statements of various solidarity groups that supported the CCPDF.

The publications went to great lengths to emphasize the independence of the CCPDF's partners,[67] while simultaneously voicing support only for the CCPDF, of which the CPT was presented as simply one member among equals. The goal, of course, was to portray the communist insurgency in Thailand as but one center of struggle in the worldwide war against international capitalism and American imperialism. Observed the VOPT: "International organizations and justice-loving groups of people abroad have warmly and sincerely supported the struggle of the Thai people. We have friends everywhere, because we are on the correct side."[68]

Allowing for overstatement, the CPT was not without cause in seeing "friends everywhere," or at least potential friends. After all, the insurgency had just received a substantial influx of high quality manpower. Although the formal organizations of which they were members, or which they represented, were not huge, they were by no means insignificant. More importantly, each new recruit could reasonably be expected to establish, for the CPT, links with numerous other individuals who had remained behind, either openly or in hiding.

The united front had been formed to carry out this task. With its mechanisms in place and structural conditions so propitious, the party's future looked bright, so bright in fact that Morell and Samudavanija, respected analysts of the Thai scene, were moved to write: "Success for the communist movement was certainly not imminent; but its potential had been enhanced inordinately by the influx of young new leaders. To a great extent, the future of Thailand now rests in their hands."[69] Inspirational words, they were to find themselves consigned to the dust-bin of mis-judgment due to CPT strategic error.

For the time being, however, the party felt secure enough to broaden its assault on the old-regime.[70] Throughout the insurgency, the CPT had carefully avoided even the appearance of criticizing the sacrosanct royal family due to its central position in Thai culture and popular esteem. Following the events at Thammasat University, however, and the return of the military to a central role in government, albeit a more circumscribed one,[71] the party broke with its cautious attitude and vigorously attacked the monarchy. These attacks were directed against both the institution and the person of the incumbent, Bhumipol Adulyadej, the ninth king of the Chakkri dynasty, and represented a significant change of strategy. Virtually all aspects of the "old feudal order" were now fair game and denounced in favor of a proposed new society, a communist one.

The role of the monarch in support of the *status quo*, even one in considerable disarray, particularly infuriated the left. Previously, such a stance by Bhumipol would have been enough to assure all political elements that at least a measure of fair play would prevail. But in the aftermath of 6 October's bloodshed, there was bitterness among some over the king's failure to intercede to halt the violence, as he had in October 1973. That he could hardly have done so, given the rapidity of events in October 1976 as compared to October 1973, was deemed irrelevant. Among the disillusioned new recruits of the CPT, bitterness toward the king was substantial.

Consequently, it came as no surprise that in early 1977 the CPT decided to abandon its hands-off approach to the monarchy. From later broadcasts made on the VOPT, it was clear that the top insurgent leaders believed the time was ripe to attack the royal couple for their links with traditional, reactionary elements. The intent was to discredit the monarchy and thereby to weaken its position as a rally-ing-point for the government.

Changes in the International Situation and Strategic Schism

By mid-1978, then, the CPT had two principal lines that it was pursuing: (1) Thai leaders were lackeys of Western imperialism, selling out the national culturally and militarily, and had to be resisted through a united front of all concerned citizens; and (2) the Thai monarchy was collaborating in this effort and in the murder of the

Thai people. By attacking the monarchy, the CPT made clear that it had irrevocably broken with the past, and by using the Maoist mechanism of the united front, it sought to mobilize the populace against a structure deemed both repressive and non-productive. Although the attacks on the monarchy foundered on what seemed to be a still substantial level of support for the institution, the united front campaign seemed hopeful. Conditions in urban and rural areas remained turbulent and, for many, impoverished. Externally, too, the situation seemed good, with support solid from the communist states of Cambodia, China, Laos, and Vietnam,.

Suddenly, this fine situation collapsed under the weight of events in Southeast Asia.[72] Any conception of Vietnam as a war-weary nation desiring an interlude of peace was rudely shattered when Hanoi, in November 1978, signed a treaty of friendship and cooperation, which included a military pact, with the Soviet Union, and then the next month invaded Cambodia. The speed with which this *Blitzkrieg* routed Pol Pot's forces and installed a client regime in power, the Kampuchean United Front for National Salvation, was stunning to the Thai. It brought to pass Bangkok's ultimate security nightmare: regular Vietnamese divisions on the kingdom's borders.

Thus rekindled were the fears of communist expansionism that had driven official Thai foreign policy since the Second World War. Amidst the populace, too, even among prospective communist recruits, the expected onslaught of a foreign army made all but insignificant any purported threat from abstract qualities such as "capitalism" or "imperialism," as advanced by the CPT. China's thrust into Vietnam in early 1979 heightened fears that the kingdom was about to become involved in communist intramural bickering. These doubts and fears extended to within the ranks of the CPT itself. Ironically, perceived expansionism by the communist Vietnamese rather than American imperialism now seemed to pose the greatest threat to the survival of the Thai nation, and thus to the Thai revolution.

With its close ties to both China and Vietnam, the CPT leadership was caught in a dilemma of whether to support one side in its dispute with the other, or to attempt to stand aloof and hope that events would sort themselves out. Eventually, the debate involved virtually all echelons of the party.[73] The discussions were all the more intense, because they occurred even as internal disputes over strategic approach convulsed the CPT leadership. At issue was the people's war plan of using the countryside to encircle the cities.

According to an analysis written later by John McBeth,[74] the CPT leadership claimed that it recognized Maoism was only a guide to action, that there were alternative strategies that could also be used in Thailand as circumstances dictated.

In particular, the Vietnamese approach, which called for greater emphasis on a fusion of military and political, urban and rural, actions, the "war of interlocking" (see previous chapter), had brought victory in Indochina. Thus it held an attraction for many CPT cadre, especially those trained in Vietnam. It seemed to offer a more clear-cut opportunity for success. But, while the leadership might profess flexibility in strategy, in reality it proved rigid in its adherence to its version of the Maoist line.

Most fundamentally, it was unwilling to expand its very narrow definition of united front formation. To critics within the party, it seemed incapable of moving beyond form to substance. It was not enough, they argued, to recruit the disenchanted from the urban areas. These urban areas had to be mobilized in the same way as the countryside. But this the CPT Politburo saw as falling into the trap that had led to the slaughter of the Chinese Communist Party (CCP) before Mao achieved unquestioned leadership. What fused the two debates, CPT "foreign policy" and strategic approach, into an explosive whole was their link to the larger rifts within the international communist camp. Since the CPT itself was tied to both the Chinese and the Vietnamese-Lao, with the latter strongly linked to the Soviets, the Thai could not avoid being forced into a position where backing one strategy or the other, Maoist or Vietnamese, did not have foreign policy repercussions.

Similarly, efforts by Thailand, particularly under the Kriangsak administration, to establish better relations with China, Laos, and Vietnam, advanced at the expense of the CPT. That these countries would court Bangkok at all was a result of their increasing rivalry in the wake of Hanoi's victory in South Vietnam and subsequent efforts to dominate its Indochinese partners, Laos and Cambodia. The Pathet Lao had been so thoroughly controlled by the Vietnamese for years that they posed little problem, but the Khmer Rouge were an altogether different story and relied on Chinese aid to buttress their independence. Caught between the proverbial rock and a hard place, the CPT ran out of room in which to maneuver when Vietnam seized Cambodia.

Apparently, the invasion was subsequent to several years of Vietnamese attempts to gain greater influence within the CPT at the expense of the pro-Chinese Sino-Thai leadership. This effort took its most prominent form, according to McBeth's CPT sources, in a campaign by Hanoi to deal directly with the CPT's Northeast party organ, which contained a good many personnel whom the Vietnamese had trained, together with a "suggestion" that Pathet Lao personnel operate with CPT guerrillas in the Thai Northeast. Further, Hanoi apparently blocked shipments of arms from Peking that had to transit Laos.

When the CPT refused to go along with Vietnam's plans, it paid the consequences. In January 1979 the Central Committee of the Lao People's Revolutionary Party (LPRP), which took its directions from Hanoi, ordered the Thai communists to vacate their bases in Laos. Coming as it did hard on the heels of the loss, amidst the turmoil of the continued fighting along the Thai-Cambodian border, of CPT sanctuaries in Cambodia itself—from which, at the time of the Vietnamese invasion, more than half of all CPT operations were originating—this was a substantial blow.

After months of debate, a dramatic VOPT broadcast by Si Inthapanti of the CCPDF announced that the matter had been thrashed out. It offered a united front to the government to fight against "threats from Vietnam."[75] In a stinging attack, the broadcast charged that the Vietnamese, under the direction of the Soviets, were attempting to export revolution, and that any encroachment into Thailand would be resisted by the united Thai people. Further, the author continued, given the existence of the greatest threat to the kingdom since the Second World War, in the form of Vietnamese divisions on the Thai border, it was criminal for the Thai government to devote the overwhelming bulk of its resources to suppressing the revolution when it ought to be safeguarding the kingdom from external foes.

With a change of appropriate labels, this broadcast could have passed for a Maoist proclamation directed at the KMT during the anti-Japanese struggle in China. And as the KMT had done, until Chiang Kai-shek was personally pressured to do otherwise, the Thai government rejected the offer out of hand. On 11 July 1979, Yunnan-based VOPT announced that it was temporarily going off the air,[76] apparently a victim of Peking's desire for stronger links with Bangkok in the face of its own deteriorating geo-strategic position in Southeast Asia. Sources further revealed that a bitter internal battle, complete with defections of CCPDF members to the Vietnamese side and their formation of a rival communist organization, *Pak Mai*,[77] was wracking the CPT.

This became apparent when high-ranking CPT members began to defect to the government, to include, initially, two members of the CCPDF leadership, Bunyen Wothong (vice-chairman) and Thoetphum Chaidi. Others followed, notably Thirayut Boonmee. CPT Politburo member Damri Ruangsutham was captured, though he claimed "he was on a mission to see former political activist Sang Patthanothai to act as a middleman in truce talks between the CPT and the government in an effort to form a united front against the Vietnamese."[78] Soon prisoners and defectors spoke of clashes between *Pak Mai* elements and units of the established CPT.

While rival foot-soldiers were taking shots at each other in a growing turf war, the nexus of crisis remained in the inner circles of the CPT. The Sino-Vietnamese split had caused dislocation of base areas and disruption of supply lines, but it was the ideological issues that were tearing the party apart. So intense were they that plans for the Fourth Party Congress were repeatedly delayed. Meantime, events in Thai politics continued to unfold at breakneck speed.

Replacement of Kriangsak by army commander Prem Tinsulanond, a royal intimate, took place in March 1980 when the so-called "Young Turks," an influential grouping of troop commanders, withdrew their support for the former's rule. Strongly committed to military professionalism and a limited role for the military in politics, the Young Turks found themselves cast as kingmakers. In the end, "Papa" Prem, as he was known to the centurions, was to rule Thailand for the next eight years. During that period, he was to oversee a remarkable transition: parliament became a more elected body, the economy boomed, and the Thai revolution crumbled as a proper counter-insurgency strategy was implemented.

Prem, however, stumbled at first. His stand on several important issues raised Young Turk fears of corruption and power-mongering. Consequently, they rose against him on 1 April 1981. There followed a game of political hardball, with Prem demonstrating he was as adroit at his new profession as he was on the battlefield. After initially being captured by "his children," he was able to escape to the palace. It now appears the Young Turks were forced to release him in response to a direct summons from the throne for Prem to appear. Subsequently, the royal family accompanied Prem to a loyal base upcountry, from which a counter-stroke was prepared. This proved unnecessary, for the mere fact that the monarch had sided with the government doomed the coup, and it unceremoniously collapsed.[79]

The "April Fool's Coup," as it came to be known, had an important impact on the CPT debate over strategic approach. Dissidents within the party argued vigorously that if the CPT had been ready—had it mobilized within the urban areas as the alternative approach advocated—it could have provoked a civil war between the two sides. This, in turn, would have brought foreign intervention, as the protagonists requested assistance. The result would have been chaos, with the CPT there to pick up the pieces. In April, however, the dissidents pointed out, the CPT's "rural areas surround the cities" doctrine meant it had no forces whatsoever in Bangkok. Consequently, it could only watch from the sidelines.

What the dissidents wanted was to modify the Maoist strategic orientation in favor of one more relevant to Thai conditions. Rather than the simple rural-urban dichotomy, they pushed for "three strategic zones." The First Zone was to be Bangkok, the center of capitalist strength in the kingdom. There, the CPT could make use of the growing non-communist but "progressive" organizations to directly attack the system. The Second Zone was to be the rural areas where the majority of the populace resided. There, the struggle would take the form mainly of covert political organizational work (i.e., the construction of infrastructure). Finally, in the Third Zone, the jungles, the CPT main forces were to remain based and ready for strikes to support the infrastructure in the Second Zone. Within each zone, the dissident analysis continued, there were to be two "battlefronts," political and military. To arrive at the proper combination of the two, each zone was to have an independent command headquarters for policy and tactical decision making. Each zone would have equal importance in the strategic plan, and their headquarters would not have to refer all questions to the central leadership. Instead, the central organs would issue only overall policy guidance.[80]

For the Politburo, this proposal represented a dangerous splintering of authority. Battle was joined at the long delayed Fourth Party Congress, held in regional sessions throughout 1982. The dissidents demanded change, pointing out that the Maoist approach was appropriate for a huge country such as China where the focus of unrest was in the countryside and where space provided ample room for sanctuaries. Such was not the case in Thailand, where growing urbanization had shifted the political center to the cities, Bangkok in particular, and where there were few places the government could not reach with its forces. Examining the crises that had shaken the system during the decade of the 1970s, the dissidents observed, clearly pointed to the need for strategic revision. China was no longer *the* model. Vietnam, Cuba, and Nicaragua were more appropriate to what was going on in the kingdom.

Stunned by the vehemence of the attack, the Politburo countered. At the Party Congress, the old guard was reportedly able to turn back the dissidents by two votes. (Those casting ballots included Central Committee members and representatives from various districts, provinces, and zones.) The vote, however, only made matters worse, because the dissidents protested that it was rigged. Thus the split in the ranks became all the more pronounced. It was the beginning of the end for the CPT. Battered by the hostile turn of external events, as well as the proper government counter-insurgency strategy to be outlined in the next section, the membership's disillusionment was the final straw. The trickle of defections became a hemorrhage.

State Search for a New Approach[81]

In a sense, the CPT had self-destructed. This, however, was not the complete picture. Individuals were willing to leave the party only because they had somewhere to go. It was changes in the political environment that created such a haven. These were not changes that came about quickly or easily. What is of particular relevance is that they came about from within in response to deliberate decisions made by individuals who decided that structural change was necessary.

Shortly after the October 1973 events, in November, Prem Tinsulanond, then still a relatively obscure officer, was made the Deputy Commanding General of the Second Army, charged with security in the Thai Northeast. Among his many duties was responsibility for directing the Northeast region's counter-insurgency program. He took over at a time when the "COIN [counter-insurgency] effort" was disorganized and less-than-effective. That Prem, as the second-in-command, was placed in charge of his region's most significant operational endeavor spoke worlds as to institutional priorities. The military elite had more important concerns.

Yet Prem seized the opportunity. Modifying the original CPM (civil-police-military) approach of Saiyud by enhancing its political aspects, he soon began to see results. Psychological operations, persuasion, and heavy use of the civilian provincial governors and their resources constituted a marked departure from the normal emphasis on firepower. By 1975–76, the Second Army had become a model of sorts in dealing with the insurgency.

That Prem would perform in the manner he did was no surprise to those who knew him well. Observes Saiyud:

> When Prem was in charge of the Cavalry School in Bangkok, I was with army headquarters. Together, with several others, we formed a "Golf Committee." We discussed the security situation while playing golf! Prem, especially, had time to ponder the situation. Therefore, we talked a lot about how to deal with the insurgency. Prem was also very influenced by the thinking of the king and queen, who maintained a keen interest in counter-insurgency and had papers on the subject regularly prepared for them. How precisely all the elements came together, I don't know, but, obviously, a combination of things resulted in a correct approach.[82]

This approach can be characterized as development for security, with "development" understood as a socio-economic-political process. "It is the weakness of the system which allows guerrillas to grow," states Saiyud flatly. "The target, therefore, is the population, not areas or enemy forces. Problems of the system must be addressed. The popular base of the insurgents must be destroyed. Strengthen the villages first, *then* go into the jungle after the guerrillas."[83]

This Prem did, acting within his own area of control. Eight years had passed, however, from Saiyud's 1965 assignment to CSOC/ISOC until Prem's 1973 assignment to the Northeast before his philosophy could blossom full force. During the interim, those who did not share the system's view that repression was the answer to its problems had had to be content with doing whatever they could.

Once in charge, Prem could do things differently. His methodology was not unlike, in form, that used successfully in numerous other areas around the world by counter-insurgent forces. A target area was first blanketed with troops, who insured that the CPT's armed units were driven off. Then, all particulars of the population were learned and the insurgent infrastructure dismantled through systematic intelligence collection and exploitation. Civic action programs were instituted, militia units formed. Special operations in known insurgent strongholds kept the insurgent main forces at bay.

What gave substance to the form, however, was the growth of the constitutive system. Prem's forces, rather than being the law, became the administrators of the law. They could be, in effect, the embodiment of the Buddhist ideal of how things ought to have been. Democratic political space legitimated traditional demands on the system for a just order.

Prem's success attracted attention. From then on his rise was rapid. In 1976 he became the commander of the entire Second Army Region. Only two years later, in September 1978, he assumed command of the army as a whole. By February 1980 he was prime minister. His key base of support throughout was the Young Turks, those most influenced by their counter-insurgency experiences and a desire to move the military toward more professional concerns. They were joined, though, by another group, the Democratic Soldiers.[84] They were to be of equal importance.

If the Young Turks provided the brawn, the Democratic Soldiers provided the brains. Their major difference was that while the Young Turks came from the line, the Democratic Soldiers were drawn from staff officers. Further, while the Young Turks sought to impose a knight's code of honor on their institution and society, the Democratic Soldiers were more intimately involved in the business of counter-insurgency planning.

Learning from communist defectors and their own study, the Democratic Soldiers advanced "democracy," which they left quite undefined, as the key weapon against insurgency. Among their major supporters were Major General Chaovalit Yongchaiyuth, Prem's aide-de-camp, later to be head of the army and to oversee the destruction of the CPT, and Major General Harn Leenanond, head of army operations (G3), later to command the Fourth Army in the South and to destroy the CPT there as he had helped Prem to do in the Northeast while a member of the latter's staff. These two individuals were apparently the principal authors of an extraordinary document, Prime Minister (PM) Order No. 66/23 (the sixty-sixth order in the Buddhist Era Year 2523, or 1980), "The Policy for the Fight to Defeat the Communists," subsequently augmented by PM Order No. 65/25 (1982), "Plan for the Political Offensive."[85] What they set forth was a politically-driven strategy to meet the communists. Said 66/23, unequivocally: "Political factors are crucial [to the success of counter-insurgency], and military operations must be conducted essentially to support and promote political goals."[86]

The follow-up 66/25 left no doubt what Prem had in mind:

> Let the development of democracy be the guiding principle. . . We estimate that the CPT has slowed our democratic development, using weak points as propaganda subjects to deceive the people. Simultaneously, the CPT itself has pretended to give democracy to the people. What the CPT has in mind, however, is tactical democracy. . . [To meet them] all patterns of dictatorship must be destroyed.[87]

Put in other terms, if lack of "development" in an all-encompassing socio-economic-political sense was the cause of insurgency, then it was the army's task to foster that development. That such a view could come to the fore would have been impossible without the old-regime crisis that erupted with October 1973. Just as certainly, though, the old-regime crisis took the path it did because the military acted in a very particular manner. It retreated from politics, at least from the politics of the bureaucratic polity.

Prem's strategy represented a victory for those who had sought to turn the security forces toward a more viable approach for dealing with insurgency. Prem, for instance, did not alter his beliefs in response to events. He had long held them. Yet they were unable to have an impact until the political space created by the emergence of the constitutive system created an opportunity. He seized it. Sarochna has attempted to further study the precise origins of Prem's PM Order No. 66/23.[88] His findings reinforce those here. He sees two "streams" of influence, the first coming from Saiyud's CPM approach, the second from the operational experience gained by high ranking officers in the Second Army Region. The CPM experience, in turn, had two facets: (1) the emphasis on a coordinated, integrated approach combining civil and military techniques, as set forth by Saiyud in numerous speeches and publications;[89] and (2) the emphasis on political rather than military aspects, which came later. Saiyud's role in developing CPM has already been mentioned, as have the contributions of several other individuals.

Sarochna notes additional officers whom he feels were instrumental in influencing others with the approach. They were to become familiar as the insurgency was defeated: Lieutenant General Wasin Isarangkoon, operational assistant to the army chief of staff; Lieutenant General Rian Disabanjong, deputy army chief of staff; General Prayoot Charumanee, army chief of staff; and General Sanha (or Sant) Chitrapatima, deputy army commander and previously Fourth Army Region commander (the South). To this I would add what I consider an important omission, General Pichitr "Pete" Kullavanijaya, ultimately deputy supreme commander of the Royal Thai Armed Forces (Saiyud, it should be noted, became the supreme commander under Prem).

As for those important in the second "stream," the operational experience gained in the Northeast, Sarochna lists Prem and Harn, whom we have noted, as well as Major General Pathom Sermsin and Colonel Lert Kanisthanaka (the latter did not achieve the rank of the others, which he surely would have, because he was killed in an operational helicopter crash during the course of the conflict).

Considered in sum, this is a good compilation of those whose ideas were instrumental in framing the "66/23 approach." They shared a recognition that the greater the suppression, the greater the increase in CPT recruits. All were heavily influenced by their contact with villagers themselves and with their grievances. Just as importantly, their attitudes, as with the Young Turks, had been shaped by the Thai involvement in Laos and Vietnam.

Neither of these experiences has yet been adequately documented. The crucial impact of Vietnam service on the Young Turks has been noted by observers, but equally important was the clandestine effort in Laos. There, in support of the Hmong forces used by the US-led, -trained, and -equipped "Secret Army," the Thai at one point had 27 light infantry and three artillery battalions deployed.[90] What was unique about this force was that while its men were "mercenaries" (that is, recruited specially for service in the units), its cadre was comprised completely of regular Thai Army officers and noncommissioned officers.

Necessarily, the procedures of such an unconventional force would leave an impact on those who served in it, even though it was not involved in counter-insurgency *per se*. It has already been noted, for example, that Saiyud commanded the force early in its existence, and at least some of those who became Young Turks also had service with it. Additionally, Pichitr, to cite another illustration, after two years in Vietnam, spent three years in Laos. These experiences were certainly crucial in shaping the views of those men toward counter-insurgency. Continued secrecy, though, makes information difficult to come by.

A similar problem attends the influence of the key figure mentioned by Saiyud above, the king. It can scarcely be an accident that many of the individuals who emerged as instrumental in the change of Thai counter-insurgency policy, to include most conspicuously Prem himself, were close to the throne and were known to be prior to their rise to power. Yet the role the royal couple actually exercised in influencing appointments, if any, cannot be learned.[91] Nevertheless, it is clear, if we can judge by inference from the numerous meetings that important figures held at the palace and from the oblique comments of obligation made by officers, that the king, in particular, was instrumental in encouraging those who sought to replace armed suppression with political action.

More important than such detective work, for our purposes here, is the outcome. Of this there is no doubt: Prem, in concert with like-minded individuals, completely reoriented the Thai counter-insurgency approach. Asked years later what had been the principal factor that brought about change in the campaign, after the years of fruitlessly trying to convert his fellow officers, Saiyud responded simply: "Prem. What made the difference was having someone who could order support. This made all the difference in the world. We already had the ideas and the concepts. They had been in place for years."[92]

To implement these concepts, Prem took CSOC/ISOC out of its advisory role and placed it again in the operational chain of command. Not only was it given the power to direct CPM Task Forces, as had been the case initially under Saiyud, but the regional army commanders, who had always existed independently, were fully integrated into the structure. Gradually, all regular army and security force units in operational areas were likewise placed under the CPM Task Forces. To ensure correct use of these newly unified forces, greater care was given to their commanders. In short, professional considerations became paramount in determining who would receive operational assignments, a substantial change from the criteria in force under the pre-October 1973 regime.[93]

External influences played a role in strengthening this trend. The communist victory in Indochina in 1975 reinforced traditional Thai security concerns and enhanced the need for military professionalism. Numerous units that previously had had the luxury of political involvement were redeployed to the border area to meet the threat. The necessity for competence became all the more pronounced as Vietnamese and Lao incursions were repelled; additional regular forces were withdrawn from counter-insurgency tasks and placed on a conventional footing. Their place was taken by local forces (i.e., militia).

Thai State Wages People's War

Use of local forces was not a new concept in Thailand. It had been an integral part of Saiyud's counter-insurgency plans. Yet Saiyud's response had been premature. His ideas for self-defense forces and local participation were ahead of not only the bureaucracy but even the populace. Tradition-oriented Thai peasants were not yet given to defending themselves. "The villagers were more afraid of the police than the enemy," Saiyud has noted.[94] This ended with October 1973 and its aftermath. It was democratic political space that thrust popular concerns to the fore and with them the willingness to defend what was theirs.

What *was* theirs? That which was "Thai." In this formulation we begin to pull together the many loose ends that have appeared in the course of this manuscript.

Old-regime crisis emerged when the instruments of coercion were paralyzed by internal struggle. They were not, however, destroyed. Instead, through the deliberate acts of numerous individuals, the security forces were reoriented. Not only did they adopt a new, political approach to counter-insurgency, they threw their weight behind the new constitutive system. Their willingness to allow it to grow was crucial, as was the role of the king in refusing to acquiesce in sporadic efforts to change the administration by using the previous mechanism of choice, the coup. The result, regardless of the particulars, and Thai efforts to form a viable parliamentary system went through numerous configurations, with representatives chosen in diverse ways, was a reorientation of concerns away from those of the bureaucracy to those of the people. Politics, in short, came to the populace.

There is no particular point at which we may judge the people came to think of the system as "theirs." October 1973 was surely a benchmark. Just as important, though, were the events that followed, when the left and right battled for control of the emerging constitutive system. In every sense this was a campaign of the streets. The CPT, the illegal left, erred in not recognizing the need to get into the battle directly. The legal left, which was on the streets, erred in adopting foreign cultural idioms and forms.

In particular, proponents of rapid change made the mistake of interpreting their reality in terms foreign to the bulk of the population. The left saw the military as a creature of the West, rather than recognizing that its structural position was a logical consequence of Thai historical factors; and activists ascribed to it Western motives. The result was that they were quite unprepared for the reaction their actions sparked.

It was no accident that what have normally been termed "right wing pressure groups" achieved the strength they did in the post-October 1973 era. They built upon those cultural idioms salient to popular existence: "Buddhism, Nation, Monarchy." In a sense, the second of these subsumed the other two: to be a Thai was to be a Buddhist within the hierarchy that culminated in the monarch. To lose one's place in this hierarchy was to lose one's identity as a Thai.

That the CPT, as the principal opposition group, could recruit manpower comes as no surprise. Scott's analysis of the two distinct groups present within any insurgent group allows us to explain this: CPT leadership came initially from marginalized elements of the alienated (culturally and, in many cases, racially) urban elite; the manpower came from the abused peasantry. Thai peasants had historically participated in rebellion when they were pushed too far.

Yet the CPT leadership, joined by that of the legal left, seems to have little understood just how far it had strayed from Thai cultural idioms. The two groups appear to have assumed that the same conditions that had given them an alternative worldview would automatically be shared by others. They projected their individual cases onto the whole, and by so doing, they distorted Thai reality.

Supporters of the "status quo" used the years 1973–76 to rally the populace against those who would destroy their world. Though the left prided itself on its mobilization abilities, its forces soon found themselves swamped by mass mobilization carried out by the right. The Village Scouts organization alone, for example, which had a paramilitary component and which drew its membership through appeals to nationalism (defined particularly as loyalty to the monarchy and Buddhism), reached a membership of 2.5 million by mid-1978, or over 5% of the total population.[95] The CPT infrastructure could not begin to match this strength.[96] Neither was the legal left, for all its organizational skills, able to attract such numbers.

What should be noted is that the Village Scouts was but one of several such bodies, with others, such as *Nawaphol* and *Krathing Daeng* ("Red Gaur"), though fewer in numbers, far more militant. When the legal left was perceived to have taken the logical next step in its "anti-Thai" approach, threatening the monarchy by attacking the Crown Prince, the carnage of October 1976 resulted. Specifics of the episode become, in such a context, virtually incidental. The clash would have occurred eventually, at some place and time, given the shape of the emerging cultural confrontation.

It is interesting to note, in this respect, that a neo-Marxian "structural violence" analysis, as frequently advanced by some elements of the legal left, would only heighten the tension between the radicals and the masses. Violence committed by members of the bureaucracy may have been, in one sense, common, but it cannot be judged to have been pervasive. Repression threw up the manpower mobilized by the CPT, but most peasants remained outside the theater of conflict.

The rhythms of life, in other words, were in no significant manner regulated by considerations of lethal force. Neglect, rather than intrusion, was the norm. The societal fabric was kept intact by the specifics of agricultural and Buddhist practice.

At the apex, the god afar, if we may think of him as such, was the king. Men who perpetrated unjust acts, it was felt, violated his order; they did not perpetuate it. Constituism, therefore, blessed by the king, could channel nascent nativism, as well as the more immediate demands for social justice. The growth of the constitutive system, therefore, was reinforced by traditional Buddhist concepts of the just order. Leftist appeals for confrontation were foreign to this structure.

This is not an attempt to advance an argument that violence or confrontation were not a part of Thai existence. It is to say that they were not a part of the sanctioned aspect of Thai existence. Buddhism, the Nation, and the Monarchy were cultural idioms tied to the ideal order, however divorced it might have been from specific exceptions. Leftist ideology, on the other hand, built on nothing. Instead, it was seen to attack the ultimate lynchpins of Thai existence. In this sense, it virtually mobilized its own opposition. What emerged was as close to "holy war" as Buddhism allowed.

It was the CPT attacks on the monarchy that all but sealed the party's doom. There followed a mushrooming of popular mobilization by "rightist" groups. When regular forces were withdrawn to meet the external threat, their place could be taken by local forces, because there already existed a popular base on which to build. The population aroused became the population armed.

Thus were born the "Rangers." Begun while Prem was army commander, this local forces concept turned the communist methodology of infrastructure development on its head. It used locally recruited manpower, often drawn from the already existing nationalist organizations such as the Village Scouts, to operate against the insurgents, while in the villages nationalist mass organizations insured systemic loyalty. Controlled by regular army personnel, the Rangers had by the end of 1981 grown to 160 companies, or about 13,000 men,[97] more than the CPT armed strength of 12,500 at the time. So plentiful were the recruits that they were difficult

Thai "Rangers," or local forces, examine a captured CPT camp in Nan Province, northern Thailand. The Rangers experienced explosive growth once the CPT directly attacked the Thai monarchy, revered by the population. Surveys consistently showed that more than half of all rural people viewed the royal couple as divine, a reality completely missed by a materialist movement committed to Maoism. (Photo: Bangkok Post in Author Collection)

to absorb properly. Lack of control at times forced the disbandment of units, but others were recruited to take their place. Soon, the local forces structure covered all areas of the kingdom.

This development occurred with almost startling rapidity. In a sense it capped another effort, one that had paved the way for its implementation. Again, we confront the ill-understood influence of the Laotian campaign. The 1973–76 democratic interlude coincided with the winding down and, eventually, the end of the Indochina conflict. Though no systematic survey has been done, many of the returning soldiers from Laos, not being regulars who could continue in the army, were apparently absorbed into the growing right wing response to the challenge of the left. Additionally, as the government pushed to integrate all areas of the kingdom,

Form over Substance: The Communist Party of Thailand

growing numbers of ex-soldiers were hired as security forces by the construction companies charged with building strategic roads. As such, they engaged in regular combat with the insurgents.[98] Others became members of a growing effort to settle contested areas with ex-soldiers and their families.

All of these measures met with success. That CPT people's war should be buffeted by Bangkok's people's war was irony of the first order. What followed was almost anti-climactic. Because the change in government strategy coincided with the larger changes in the international situation and with the intra-party strategic debate, all elements necessary for the demise of the CPT came together simultaneously. Hard fighting remained, but as the decade of the 1980's wore on, the communists were in increasingly difficult straits.

No incident symbolized this more than the fall of their headquarters and principal base area, located in a formidable position in the Khao Khor mountain range along the Petchabun-Phitsanulok provincial border.[99] The operation, led by Pichitr Kullavanijaya, was complete by early 1982, just in time for the CPT Fourth Party Congress. Held, as noted previously, in staggered fashion in different regions, the Congress ended acrimoniously. There followed a dramatic increase in defections. What began as a trickle became a hemorrhage.

Important to the willingness of the communists to lay down their arms was the element of Prem's political strategy that held the insurgents would not be treated as prisoners but as those returning to the fold. With minimal security precautions, they were allowed to resume normal lives.[100]

In all the main operational areas, developments proceeded in similar fashion. Placing hand-picked officers in key positions, Prem kept the campaign going. In the deep South, his success in the Northeast, and Pichitr's success in the Tri-Province region, was duplicated by Harn, whose use of "politics first" was particularly effective.[101] Chaovalit, as army commander, coordinated the whole. By mid-1983, the CPT had, for all practical purposes, become a nuisance rather than a threat.[102] The insurgents returned to a different Thailand. Not only had the constitutive system created a new political environment, but Prem's administration had also paved the way for an economic boom by abandoning statist policies in favor of greater integration within the world economy.

This is not the place to consider these changes in detail.[103] What is important is that reform formalized under Prem resulted in a period of significant economic expansion that continues to the present. Rapid industrialization and urbanization spawned a whole host of problems, but ones so different in their immediate concerns to those being discussed by radicals that the CPT appeared, at best, irrelevant.[104]

106

Deep South: In May 1985, COL Chamnong Phirot, commander of Task Force 43, inspects sand-table found in CPT remnant camp in Thanto District of Yala Province, in the Thai South (where troubles have again broken out). Links with Malaysian communist remnants, who had refused to surrender following the defeat of their movement in The Emergency (1948–58), allowed the Thai communists to hold out in the South even after the CPT itself had all but collapsed. (Photo: Bangkok Post in Author Collection)

Weapons captured in the same camp. (Photo: Bangkok
Post in Author Collection)

Too late, the CPT leadership offered a compromise to its own membership. A
position paper dated 3 July 1984 was circulated entitled "Four Strategic Zones and
Five Battle Fronts."[105] It adopted the dissidents' tripartite division of the conflict
within Thailand itself, but to it was added a Fourth Zone, the international arena.
The crucial role foreign activity and support could have on events within the revolutionary country itself were thereby recognized. Similarly, the five battle fronts
built on the dissident proposal. To political and military spheres of operations were
added economic, cultural, and diplomatic. In particular the document recognized
the need to pursue non-military approaches, such as subverting newspapers and
important social groups.

As a first step, a "Mass Organization Plan"[106] concentrated on establishing links
with the three key groups needed for the construction of a new united front: farmers
(peasants), labor, and students. A plan of action was outlined in "Coordination of
Forces to Overthrow the Present Regime,"[107] a document that appeared to have
drawn on the Nicaraguan experience, wherein the party ascertained that it needed

May 1985, Thai soldier on guard duty at patrol base of 4th Company, 5th Battalion, 5th Infantry Regiment (carving on tree) during operations in Betong district of Yala Province in the Thai south. (Photo: Bangkok Post in Author Collection)

to bring together a reaction involving four groups: legal political parties, the CPT itself with its own mass organization, the Thai People's Liberation Army (TPLA), and leading "progressive" elements within the Thai armed forces.

By infiltrating legal political parties, the rationale went, the CPT could provoke a conflict between moderates and the "right wing." This would necessarily involve the progressive and "fascist" factions within the military. Hence, either wittingly or unwittingly, the result would be cooperation of the CPT and the progressive military against the ruling class, with the TPLA able to tip the scales in favor of the former.

This new approach, though it contained certain unrealistic elements, was clearly a step in the right direction. At least it sought to deal with Thai realities in a systematic fashion, rather than strategically stuffing Thailand into the Chinese mold. Nevertheless, it was too little, too late. More fundamentally, the moment of old-regime crisis had passed.

Conclusions

Thailand had "won" its battle with the insurgents of the CPT. Noteworthy as the victory was, however, particularly in light of the results in Cambodia, Laos, and Vietnam, it would be incorrect to see it as a model of a particular combination of tactical techniques. To the contrary, it was a victory for a strategic approach realized in operational art that sought ultimately to respond to Thai realities, particularly political realities.

Only the change in those realities made effective the approaches chosen. Just as certainly, though, had the various elements outlined above not been carried out, the results of the struggle could have been very different. In this sense, the counter-insurgency existed in a symbiotic relationship with its society. As Saiyud has stated above, it was the weaknesses of the Thai system that provided the opportunity for the CPT. This should not be read to mean a group of conspirators sought to take advantage of societal weakness. The system itself "threw up" the manpower that became the CPT.

Thus my explanation has leaned heavily on the unique historical particulars of Thailand. The emergence of the bureaucratic polity, the authoritarian focus of which was oriented almost exclusively toward economic development, was bound to produce a reaction. This could take the form of rebellion or insurgency.

Use of the strategic model provided by people's war, combined with the absorption of manpower produced by government abuses, allowed the CPT to grow and allowed insurgency to win out over peasant rebellion. The insurgency, seeking

In hill areas of Chiangrai Province, northern Thailand, author uses Mandarin to speak to Yao tribesmen. Yao and Mandarin are related, which allows communication. Tribesmen had reported illegal logging, which was hurting crop yields; the government was seeking to discern whether insurgents were using the activity to generate funds. (Photo: Ben Barber in Author Collection)

structural change to pursue socialist development, established itself in remote areas, working to build the sanctuaries necessary for achievement of critical mass. It then sought to expand to the lowlands, to build a viable counter-state. This proved possible in some areas, particularly the Northeast. Yet in each of its three main operational areas—the Northeast, North, and South—the party was dealing with unique circumstances that favored recruitment among marginalized individuals. Unable to penetrate the central heartland of the kingdom, it had to wait for new developments.

These came with the explosive ouster of the bureaucracy, as exemplified most prominently by the military, from power and subsequent chaotic efforts to fashion a constitutive system through implementation of parliamentary mechanisms and increased local government. Sudden allowance for interest articulation and aggregation naturally enough produced different views of how this should occur and what shape the result should have.

To that end, the forces of the left and the right, as they are termed in Western shorthand, locked in conflict. If this democratic political space was midwife to societal conflict, it also produced the salvation for the system. New military leadership emerged that carried with it a vision of counter-insurgency as counter-mobilization.

As the fate of the absolute monarchy in Thailand makes clear (it was, after all, the monarchy that attempted to "modernize" the kingdom) political mobilization is a dangerous business in the absence of institutions into which unleashed popular forces can channel their energies. In the counter-insurgency campaign, Thailand's existing cultural practices and idioms provided these. Numerous mass organizations in support of the traditional "pillars" of society—Buddhism, the nation, and monarchy—were formed. Their energy amounted, at times, to millennial fervor, as would be anticipated in a time of profound structural upheaval. In voicing their support of the "pillars," members could opt for utopia, a perfect Buddhist world, even while remaining firmly fixed in reality—support for the system that protected the pillars.

That the security forces were able to mobilize this outpouring while the communists could not resulted, of course, from the fact that the communists never really attempted to do so. Instead, their ideological worldview overpowered their strategies, an error for which Mao would have condemned them. For the essence of the united front strategy passed on by Mao called for exploitation of structural reality as the would-be revolutionaries found it. This, the government, rather than the insurgents, was able to accomplish.

"Government" is a term that must be used with some reservations, though. Prior to October 1973, a fundamental weakness of the Thai counter-insurgency campaign was that it was not a national effort but rather a task assigned to the security forces. It was entirely logical that those who led these forces responded to violence with violence. Some, to be sure, were more enlightened than others and recognized the counterproductive nature of repression, but they were neither in positions of power nor citizens of a system that could behave otherwise.

This is not to say that counter-mobilization against the insurgents could not and did not occur on a tactical scale. It did, particularly while Saiyud was given command authority through the mechanisms of CSOC/ISOC. Yet such could only be a short-term solution given the long term structural dilemma at hand: how to ask the populace to fight for "their" system when they had little direct stake in it

In 1989, Saiyud returns to former Hmong insurgent strongholds in Chiangrai Province, an area once active with CPT activity. Though he was to rise to the highest military position in the country, Saiyud never forgot former insurgents and worked hard to ensure the success of their reincorporation into society. (Marks photo)

Young novices sit with Buddhist monk in Chiangrai town of Chiangrai Province, Thailand. Buddhist cultural idioms, with the monarch structurally situated at the apex of the Thai world-order, were to prove key in marginalizing the CPT. While the communists tried to revolutionize society, reformers sought to build upon what was. (Marks photo)

113

aside from the lifestyle offered by the status quo. This became possible only when a faction of the military, represented most signally by Prem and Saiyud, became the government and could mobilize the populace behind democratic institutions.

This process further highlighted the importance of cultural idioms. The bureaucratic polity was not necessarily predatory. It was kept in check by the same cultural dicta that had in the past checked the absolute power of the monarchy. CPT efforts at mobilization could overcome this worldview and replace it with an alternative construct where the representatives of the bureaucratic polity had crossed the norms of acceptable conduct. That these transgressions never reached the level necessary to negate existing popular conservatism and latent support for the ideal order resulted from specific decisions made by numerous individuals we have encountered above.

In a phrase, they rescued "the system" from itself. Such was not preordained. Prem and Saiyud, for example, wandered in the bureaucratic wilderness for years before their moment came. Yet they were produced by the same structural configuration that "made" their opposite numbers, whether in the bureaucratic polity (rival officers) or in the developing constitutive system (the insurgents). That they saw reform as the more proper course resulted from individual choice. When the moment came to be heard, they acted. Had they given heed to opposing consul, the situation could well have been exacerbated to the point that even the CPT's mistakes would not have kept the party from becoming a key player in the drama of the constitutive system.

It follows naturally enough that the precise techniques adopted by Prem and his cohorts, while necessary, were certainly not sufficient to insure the victory of the parliamentary option in the constitutive system. The counter-insurgency methodologies implemented, from local forces to special unit operations, had been in existence, but they had never been brought into play in support of a viable political goal. Predictably enough, to do so is the only possible "approach" to insurgency.[108]

Notes

[1] The gist of this chapter originally appeared in *Maoist Insurgency since Vietnam*. It has required minimal updating.

[2] Prior to the Vietnam War era, the percentage of young men who actually followed this stipulation was estimated at 90%. By the 1990s, the figure was reported to have fallen to 55%. Still, the point should not be lost that even today, and certainly during the modern period addressed by this chapter, fully half of the male population of the kingdom yet felt compelled to follow a path of correct conduct specifically sanctioned by society. For an

interesting examination of young men's motivations for joining the *Sangha*, see Toshio Yatsushiro, *Village Organization and Leadership to Northeast Thailand* (Bangkok: USOM, 1966).

[3] A partial listing would include such significant works as Herbert Phillips, *Thai Peasant Personality: The Patterning of Interpersonal Behavior in the Village of Bang Chan* (Los Angeles: University of California Press, 1966); Howard K. Kaufman, *Bangkhuad* (Locust Valley, New York: J. J. Agustin, 1960); John De Young, *Village Life in Modern Thailand* (Berkeley: University of California Press, 1955); Michael Moerman, *Agricultural Change and Peasant Choice in a Thai Village* (Los Angeles: University of California Press, 1968); Steven Piker, *An Examination of Character and Socialization in a Thai Peasant Community* (Ann Arbor, Michigan: University Microfilms, 1964); and Yoneo Ishii, ed., *Thailand: A Rice Growing Society*, trans. Peter and Stephanie Hawkes, Monograph No. 12 (English Language Series) of Center Press of Hawaii, 1978). For further information on the "loosely structured" analysis that established the dominant paradigm for studies on Thai society, see Hans-Dieter Evers, *Loosely Structured Social Systems: Thailand in Comparative Perspective*, Cultural Report Series No. 17, Southeast Asia Studies, Yale University (New Haven, Connecticut, 1969).

[4] Fred W. Riggs (University of Hawaii), who originally set forth the theory of the bureaucratic polity, has conceptualized its opposite, the constitutive system, as those mechanisms allowing realization of the popular will.

[5] Background on the CPT can be found in Virginia Thompson and Richard Adloff, *The Left Wing in Southeast Asia* (New York: William Sloane Associates, 1950), especially Chapter 3: "Thailand (Siam)," 51–57; David A. Wilson, "Thailand and Marxism," Chapter 3 in Frank N. Trager, *Marxism in Southeast Asia* (Stanford, California: Stanford University Press, 1959), 58–101; Justus M. van der Kroef, *Communism in Southeast Asia* (Los Angeles: University of California Press, 1980), especially 17–22, 80–86, 155–63, 194–202, 271–73; Patrice de Beer, "History and Policy of the Communist Party of Thailand," *Journal of Contemporary Asia*, 8.1 (1978), 143–58; *The Road to Victory: Documents from the Communist Party of Thailand* (Chicago: Liberator Press, 1978); Ross Prizzia, "Thailand: New Social Forces and Re-Emerging Socialist Principles," *Asia Quarterly*, 1975.4, 343–65; Prizzia, *Thailand in Transition: The Role of Oppositional Forces*, Asian Studies at Hawaii No. 32, Center for Asian and Pacific Studies (Honolulu: University of Hawaii Press, 1985); Yuangrat (Pattanapongse) Wedel, *Modern Thai Radical Thought: The Siamization of Marxism and its Theoretical Problems* (Ann Arbor, Michigan: University Microfilms International, 1981), published as *Radical Thought, Thai Mind: The Development of Revolutionary Ideas in Thailand* (Bangkok: Assumption Business Administration College, 1987); Kanok Wongtrangan, *Communist Revolutionary Process: A Study of the Communist Party of*

Thailand (Ann Arbor, Michigan: University Microfilms International, 1981); and Thaddeus Flood, "The Thai Left Wing in Historical Context," *Bulletin of Concerned Asian Scholars* (April–June 1975), 55–67.

⁶ For a theoretical discussion of this distinction, see Larry E. Cable, *Conflict of Myths: The Development of American Counter-insurgency Doctrine and the Vietnam War* (New York: New York University Press, 1986).

⁷ A map may be found at p. 12 of my *Thailand: The Threatened Kingdom*, Conflict Study No. 115 (London: Institute for the Study of Conflict, January–February 1980). For further data on Vietnamese aspects of the support structure, see Office of the Deputy Chief of Staff for Intelligence (G2), US Army Pacific (USARPAC)-Intelligence Division, *The 35th PL/95th NVA Combined Command: External Support to the Thai Insurgency*, Confidential document No. AB-335-6-1-74 dated 1 June 1974. This document, now declassified, was apparently used as the basis for most press discussions on the subject of foreign (i.e., Vietnamese) aid to the Thai insurgency. Chinese support has not been examined in as much depth. The memoirs of Allied agents who infiltrated into Thailand from China during the Second World War are an important source, however. Comparing their recollections with data from sources relevant to the insurgency reveals that the communists used these same, long established routes. A summary can be found in John B. Haseman, *The Thai Resistance Movement during the Second World War*, Special Report No. 17/1978 of the Center for Southeast Asian Studies (DeKalb: Northern Illinois University, 1978), especially 71–79, 85–86. A useful map is found on p. 79.

⁸ John McBeth, "Thailand: Seeking a Strong Local Accent," *FEER*, 22 August 1980, 30–32.

⁹ "New Direction, New Blood," *FEER*, 27 July 1979, 7.

¹⁰ "CPT Secretary General in Beijing Hospital," *Bangkok Post*, 6 November 1981, 3.

¹¹ See John McBeth, "Thailand: In From the Cold (2)," *FEER*, 17 September 1982, 12–15.

¹² Thaddeus Flood.

¹³ Internal Security Operations Command (ISOC), *The Development and Organization of the CPT in Trang and Phatthalung Provinces, South Thailand*, mimeo document dated 26 December 1976; Ref. No. Z1013.

¹⁴ See Marks, "Government Policy as a Reflection of the Development Model: The Case of Accelerated Rural Development (ARD) in Northeast Thailand," *Journal of East & West Studies* (Seoul), 10.1 (1981), 59–95.

¹⁵ For details see Jere R. Behrman, "Significance of Intra-country Variations for Asian Agricultural Prospects: Central and Northeastern Thailand," *Asian Survey*, 8.3 (March 1968), 157–73; Ronald C. Y. Ng, "Some Land Use Problems of Northeast Thailand," *Modern Asian Studies*, 4.1 (1970), 23–42; and Millard F. Long, "Economic Development in Northeast

Thailand," *Asian Survey*, 6.7 (July 1966), 355–61.

[16] Even in 1968–69, 97.3% of the farmers in the Northeast were owner-operators. See Andrew Turton, "The Current Situation in the Thai Countryside," *Journal of Contemporary Asia*, 8.1 (1978), 112.

[17] Behrman cites a 1966 figure that Northeastern incomes were 65% of the national average.

[18] Kamol Janlekha, *Saraphi: (A Survey of Socio-Economic Conditions in a Rural Community in North-East Thailand* (Zurich: Geographical Publications, 1968).

[19] See Charles F. Keyes, *Isan: Regionalism in Northeast Thailand* (Ithaca, New York: Cornell University, 1967). For attitude surveys, see Somchai Rakwijit, *Village Leadership in Northeast Thailand* and *Study of Youth in Northeast Thailand* (Bangkok: Joint Thai-US Military Research and Development Center, 1971).

[20] Keyes.

[21] *Ibid*.

[22] These demands called for a short-term development project in the Northeast to deal with urgent problems and a long-term effort which would include establishment of heavy industries in the Northeast, together with an increase in educational facilities.

[23] For the context, see Marks, "Sino-Thai Relations," *Asian Affairs* (London), 5.3 (October 1974), 296–310.

[24] Keyes, 49.

[25] Donald E. Weatherbee, *The United Front in Thailand* (Columbia: University of South Carolina, 1970), 24.

[26] John McBeth, "Revolution to Evolution," *FEER*, 12 May 1983, 24–25.

[27] Although she actually was a medic rather than a guerrilla fighter as portrayed in propaganda, two of her brothers did rise to provincial level positions in the insurgent organization. (Much later they were to surrender to the government.)

[28] See Komsan Madukham, *Dong Prachao: Land of the Dead* (Bangkok: Pitakpracha, 1977) [in Thai]. This is a useful volume, one of eighteen such works that Somchai Rakwijit, Research Director for CSOC/ISOC, arranged for his personnel to produce using pen names. The authors, such as Komsan, thus had access to all available data, to include classified material.

[29] Interview with Somchai Rakwijit, former CSOC/ISOC Research Director, Bangkok, 13 May 1986. See also David Jenkins, "The Hit-Run 'Government,'" *FEER* (23 July 1973), 26–27.

[30] Robert F. Zimmerman, "Insurgency in Thailand," *Problems of Communism* (May–June 1976), 27. Additional details may be found in Justus M. van der Kroef, "Guerrilla Communism and Counter-insurgency in Thailand," *Orbis*, 17.1 (Spring 1974), 106–39 (see especially 119–22).

[31] Ralph W. McGehee, *Deadly Deceits: My 25 Years in the CIA* (New York: Sheridan Square, 1983), 109.

[32] Zimmerman, 21, observes: "There is sometimes considerable controversy both within and between various government agencies (Thai and foreign) as to where 'Communists' are or are not 'active'."

[33] Portions of this section have appeared in my "Thailand's Terror Years," *Soldier of Fortune*, 15.8 (August 1990), 30–37 (cont).

[34] Interview with Saiyud Kerdphol, former Supreme Commander of the Royal Thai Armed Forces, Phayao Province, 31 August 1987.

[35] See Saiyud Kerdphol, *Struggle for Thailand, Section II, A Solution for the North* (Bangkok, nd).

[36] Arnold Abrams and Chiang Kham, "Mountains of Discontent," *FEER* (2 July 1970), 20–22.

[37] Kerdphol, 7–11.

[38] John R. Thomson, "The Burning Mountain," *FEER* (25 April 1968), 218–20.

[39] James P. Sterba, "Thais Attack a Rebel Stronghold," *NYT*, 18 March 1972, 3; Sterba, "Thai Drive Snares Few Red Guerrillas," *NYT*, 26 March 1972, 1.

[40] Interview with Deputy Headman (name indistinct) of Ban Huasan, Phayao Province, 31 August 1987.

[41] Interview with Nuyua Sayang, farmer, Ban Huasan, Phayao Province, 31 August 1987.

[42] Interview with Laopao Sasong, farmer, Ban Huasan, Phayao Province, 31 August 1987.

[43] Community Development Program, *Summary of National Community Development Programme Thailand* (Bangkok: Department of Interior, 1961).

[44] For example, Community Development Bureau; Thanom Kittikachorn, *Trends in Community Development* (Bangkok: Department of Interior, 1964); Vichit Sukaviriya, ed., *Facts about Community Development Programs* (Bangkok: Ministry of Interior, 1966).

[45] Community Development Bureau, 1.

[46] Keyes, 56.

[47] According to D. Saharuni, *United States Aid to Thailand*, USAID mimeograph dated 6 November 1969, early programs, which averaged about USD 7 million per annum through FY 1954, consisted almost entirely of technical assistance. These were expanded in 1955, the growth reflecting increased US concern over the security and development of Southeast Asia after the French withdrawal from Indochina. In addition to technical assistance, the program turned to commodity support and major infrastructure development. Grant assistance during the period FY 1955–62 averaged approximately USD 27 million per annum.

Also during this time, the US initiated its development loan program to Thailand, which totaled USD 49.6 million through 1962 and was supplemented by over USD 26 million in long term loans by the Export-Import Bank.

[48] Saharuna, 8–9.

[49] George K. Tanham, *Trial in Thailand* (New York: Crane, Russak, 1974), 75.

[50] See, for example, Ralph E. Dakin, ed., *Security and Development in Northeast Thailand: Problems, Progress and the Roles of Amphoe, Tambol and Muban Government* (Bangkok: USOM/Thailand, 1968); USOM/Thailand, *Impact of USOM Supported Programs in Changwad Sakon Nakorn* (Bangkok: 1967). Further analysis is contained in Peter F. Bell, "Thailand's Northeast: Regional Underdevelopment, 'Insurgency', and Official Response," *Pacific Affairs*, 42.1 (Spring 1969), 47–54.

[51] Joyce Nakahara and Ronald A. Witton, *Development and Conflict in Thailand* (Ithaca, New York: Cornell University, 1971).

[52] See Norman Jacobs, *Modernization Without Development: Thailand as an Asian Case Study* (New York: Praeger, 1971); James C. Ingram, *Economic Change in Thailand 1850–1970*, revised edn. (Stanford, California: Stanford University Press, 1971); T. H. Silcock, *The Economic Development of Thai Agriculture* (Ithaca, New York: Cornell University Press, 1970); Chandra Rabibhadana, *A Proposal for a Five-Year Plan of Social Development in Thailand* (Bangkok: Thai Wattana Panich, 1973); Richard L. Hough, "Development and Security in Thailand: Lessons from Other Asian Countries," *Asian Survey*, 9.3 (March 1969), 178–87.

[53] This is a central theme, for example, in Chai-anan Samudavanija, Kusuma Snitwongse, and Suchit Bunbongkarn, *From Armed Suppression to Political Offensive: Attitudinal Transformation of Thai Military Officers since 1976* (Bangkok: Institute of Security and International Studies, Chulalongkorn University, 1990). For an alternative approach, proceeding within a larger framework of reaction to perceived threat, see Marks, "The Thai Approach to Peacemaking since World War II," *Journal of East & West Studies* (Seoul), 7.1 (April 1978), 133–55, and "An Eclectic Model of Thailand's Participation in the Vietnam War," *Peace Research* (Ontario), 11.2 (April 1979), 71–76.

[54] See Michael T. Klare, *War Without End* (New York: Vintage Books, 1972); Frances Fitzgerald, *Fire in the Lake* (Boston: Little, Brown, 1972); and David Halberstam, *The Best and the Brightest* (Greenwich, Connecticut: Fawcett Publications, 1972).

[55] Agency for International Development, *Introduction to Program Presentation to the Congress/Proposed FY 1971 Program*, nd.

[56] For a representative selection see United States Military Academy, *Revolutionary Warfare*, 6 vols. (West Point, New York: Department of Military Art and Engineering, 1967); Naval War College, *Selected Readings for Counter-insurgency Course*, 4 vols. (Newport,

Rhode Island, 1968); Robert Thompson, *Defeating Communist Insurgency* (New York: Praeger, 1966).

[57] James P. Sterba, "Thai Insurgents Seen Increasing," *NYT*, 27 March 1972, 18.

[58] David K. Wyatt, *Thailand: A Short History* (New Haven: Yale University Press, 1984), 290. This analysis culminates Wyatt's discussion on pp. 286–90, which (especially 287–88) agrees with my work, particularly "Thai Security During the 'American Era', 1960–1976," *Issues & Studies* (Taipei), 15.4 (April 1979), 61–88.

[59] For a more detailed treatment, see Marks, *The United Front in Thailand since October 1976*, No. 71 in Courrier de L'Extrême-Orient series, Centre d'Etude du Sud-Est Asiatique et de l'Extrême-Orient (Brussels), October 1979; "The Communist Party and the Strategy of the United Front in Thailand since October 1976," *Asia Quarterly* (Brussels), 1980.1, 3–18; and "The Maoist Conception of the United Front, with Special Reference to the United Front in Thailand since October 1976," *Issues & Studies* (Taipei), 16.3 (March 1980), 46–69.

[60] See Schram, *The Political Thought of Mao Tse-tung*, 64–65.

[61] VOPT broadcasts, as well as those of other Thai radio stations, were translated and made available in the US Foreign Broadcast Information Service (FBIS) *Asia & Pacific Daily Report*. FBIS is an organ of the Central Intelligence Agency (CIA). On 11 July 1979, under circumstances to be discussed in more detail below, VOPT announced that it was temporarily going off the air. Broadcasts were never resumed, although for a time a "VOPT News Service" distributed printed party pronouncements.

[62] VOPT (Clandestine) (hereafter, VOPT [C]) in Thai to Thailand 1000 GMT (1700 Thai) 7 October 1976.

[63] VOPT(C) in Thai to Thailand 1000 GMT (1700 Thai) 4 October 1977.

[64] A table of the broadcasts used in this analysis is contained in Marks, *The United Front in Thailand since October 1976*.

[65] European Coordinating Committee for Solidarity With the Thai People (ECCSTP), founded 10–12 March 1978, listed as its members: Ad Hoc Group for Democracy in Thailand (AGDT), Britain; Thailand-Gruppen (TG), Denmark; Thailand Informations- und Solidaritatskomitee (TISK), West Germany; and Comité de Solidarité avec le Peuple Thai (CSPT), France. Other typical solidarity groups, cited in *TIC News* [Thai Information Center] and *Thai Information Bulletin*: Ligue Communiste Revolutionnaire Section Française de la 4e Internationale, France; United Secretariat of the Fourth International, France; Clergy and Laity Concerned, US; Communist Labor Party, US; Communist Party (Marxist-Leninist of the United States); National Lawyers Guild, US; Friends of the Filipino People, US; Support Committee for the Chilean Resistance, US; Action Against Apartheid, National Conference Working Group, US; Socialist Party of Japan; Pacific Asia Resources Center

(PAAC), Japan; Japan Afro-Asian Writers Association; and Ad Hoc Committee for the Thai Solidarity Campaign, Japan.

[66] *TIC News*, 1.20 (1 May 1978), 1.

[67] See, for example, Helen R. Chauncey, "The Growth of the United Front," *Southeast Asia Chronicle*, No. 60 (January–February 1978), 2–9.

[68] VOPT(C) in Thai to Thailand 1000 GMT (1700 Thai) 27 September 1978.

[69] David Morell and Chai-anan Samudavanija, "Thailand's Revolutionary Insurgency: Changes in Leadership Potential," *Asian Survey*, 19.4 (April 1979), 332.

[70] A more detailed treatment can be found in Marks, "The Thai Monarchy under Siege," *Asia Quarterly* (Brussels), 1978.2, 109–41, and "The Status of the Monarchy in Thailand," *Issues & Studies* (Taipei), 13.11 (November 1977), 51–70.

[71] See Marks, "The Military and Politics in Thailand: An Analysis of the Two October Coups (1976–1977)," *Issues & Studies* (Taipei), 12.11 (November 1977), 58–90, and "October 1976 and the Role of the Military in Thai Politics," *Modern Asian Studies* (Cambridge), 14.3 (1980), 399–440.

[72] See Marks, *Thailand: The Threatened Kingdom*, especially 17–18.

[73] See John McBeth, "A Battle for Loyalty in the Jungles," *FEER* (8 June 1979), 19–21; "Thailand: Communists at the Crossroads," *FEER* (27 July 1979), 30–31; and "Insurgencies: The Ideological Crossroads," *FEER* (8 February 1980), 32–34. These were supplemented by conversations with McBeth, especially one in Manila on 22 July 1990.

[74] John McBeth, "Communism: Hazards along the Neutral Path," *FEER* (19 September 1980), 43–48. See also McBeth's earlier "In Search of a New Direction," *FEER* (10 August 1979), 30–31.

[75] VOPT(C) in Thai to Thailand 1000 GMT (1700 Thai) 7 June 1979.

[76] VOPT(C) in Thai to Thailand 1000 GMT (1700 Thai) 11 July 1979. The broadcast the previous day also stated that VOPT would be going off the air temporarily.

[77] This rival organization, *Pak Mai* (New Party), was later to be revealed as the Thai Isan Liberation Party, founded in Vientiane on 22 October 1979. See "Northern Separatists," *FEER* (4 April 1980), 7.

[78] "Critical Time for Thai Communists," *Bangkok Post*, 22 November 1981, 6.

[79] Numerous sources exist for coverage of this episode. Among the best are John McBeth, "The Coup That Never Was," *FEER* (10 April 1981), 10–15, together with accompanying articles under the general title, "Thailand's Night of the Generals." Also valuable, particularly for its discussion of the centers of power in the Thai polity, is Philip Bowring and Paisal Sricharatchanya, "Shaking the Pillars," *FEER* (19 June 1981), 38–43, as well as "The Power Wielded by a Constitutional Monarch," 53–55, and McBeth, "A Profile of the Young Turks' Camp," *FEER* (19 June 1981), 44–53.

⁸⁰ Interview with Somchai Rakwijit, former CSOC/ISOC Research Director, Bangkok, 13 May 1986.

⁸¹ Much of the material in this section, particularly that related to personalities, has been drawn from personal experience. I am also indebted to discussions, spanning, in certain cases, at least a decade and numerous locations, with: Saiyud Kerdphol, former Supreme Commander of the Royal Thai Armed Forces; Anthony "Tony" Paul, former Regional Editor (Asia) for *Reader's Digest*; John McBeth, former Thailand correspondent for *FEER*; Mike Jones, former Lieutenant Colonel, Special Air Services (SAS) and security consultant; and John Cole and Denny Lane, both former US Army attaches in Bangkok.

⁸² Interview with Saiyud Kerdphol, Phayao Province, 31 August 1987.

⁸³ *Ibid.*

⁸⁴ See Suchit Bunbongkarn.

⁸⁵ Texts with commentary may be found in Sarochna Robbamrung, *Internal Security, Kingdom of Thailand*, unpublished paper dated 11 February 1987, prepared for US Army War College. Several sources claim that Prem himself wrote 66/23; it is not a long document. I have been unable to confirm actual authorship, though it is certain the Prime Ministerial Order was the product of much discussion amongst a small circle that included the officers named.

⁸⁶ Sarochna, 2.

⁸⁷ *Ibid.*, 5.

⁸⁸ *Ibid.*

⁸⁹ These have been compiled in edited form in Saiyud Kerdphol, *The Struggle for Thailand: Counter-insurgency, 1965–1985* (Bangkok: S. Research Center, 1986). It is significant that Saiyud attributes impetus for the book, at least in part, to the late Gerry Waller. A veteran of the pre-Second World War Indian Army, Gerry was later to serve with the Malayan Police Force during the Emergency, 1948–60, and then as a consultant in Thailand for the Stanford Research Institute (SRI). He met Saiyud in 1970 and became a close confidant, thus contributing his own insights to the evolution of CPM, which itself drew inspiration from the British approach in Malaya. He died of cancer in May 1983 in Bangkok.

⁹⁰ This figure appears in John D. Blair IV, *Thailand 1984: A New Generation Prepares to Assume the Reins of Power*, unpublished paper prepared for presentation at the US Pacific Command Security Assistance Conference [site not specified], 3–7 December 1984. It is in agreement with figures provided by Saiyud Kerdphol, former commander of the force, in an interview, Honolulu, 6 December 1987.

⁹¹ *Lèse majesté* remains a serious crime in Thailand. Even the musical and films of *The King and I* continue to be banned. Convictions have demonstrated the latitude with which

the charge may be interpreted. Consequently, research dealing with the royal family's role in society remains a difficult proposition.

92 Interview with Saiyud Kerdphol, Phayao Province, 31 August 1987.

93 For these insights I am indebted to John Cole, especially his *Professionalism in the Royal Thai Army: National Defense or Political Actor? The Prem-Arthit Era*, unpublished manuscript dated 1 February 1984.

94 Interview with Saiyud Kerdphol, Bangkok, 13 May 1986.

95 This is the figure given by Marjorie A. Muecke, "The Village Scouts of Thailand," *Asian Survey*, 20.4 (April 1980), 407.

96 Anthony Paul, "The Jungle War the Communists Lost," *Reader's Digest,* Asian edition (October 1984), 2–6, gives CPT strength as 14,000 armed insurgents, with another 20,000 directly involved in support activities. No estimates ever placed the mass base in the 2.5 million range (the number who went through the Village Scouts Training Program, a one-week course).

97 Paisal Sricharatchanya, "Security: Playing the Same Game," *FEER* (18 December 1981), 15–16.

98 See, for example, Jim Coyne, "Thailand's Battle Road," *Soldier of Fortune*, 7.2 (February 1982), 37–43 (cont).

99 See Anthony Paul; John McBeth, "Thailand: The Bulldozer Invasion," *FEER* (8 May 1981), 26–28.

100 Anthony Paul has noted, in a witty piece, "Insights: Sex and the Single Insurgent," *Asiaweek* (8 April 1983), 24: "As the surrendering insurgents have flooded into the Army's 'open arms' over the past twelve months, the soldiery have been impressed by the defectors' priorities in the first hours of their new coexistence with capitalism. Said a Phitsanulok-based colonel: 'As far as I've been able to establish, a communist is someone with an overpowering interest in seafood [notably missing from the jungle diet] and sex. Did Marx say anything about this?'"

101 See Rodney Tasker, "Insurgency: A More Peaceful South," *FEER* (11 October 1984), 28–29.

102 For an excellent overview, see Anthony Paul, "Winding Down a War," *Asiaweek* (8 April 1983), 16–24.

103 Good overviews may be found in the several articles contained in Ho Kwon Ping's cover story, "Thailand Inc.," *FEER* (23 May 1980), 40–46; see also National Westminster Bank, "Thailand: An Economic Report," January 1981. A more recent analysis of the Thai economy across time, with a discussion of this increasing integration into the world economy, is Kevin Hewison, *Bankers and Bureaucrats: Capital and the Role of the State in Thailand* (New Haven: Yale University Southeast Asia Studies, Monograph Series No. 34, 1989).

[104] It is useful for my cultural argument that the structural strains created by this economic boom resulted not in the growth of radical solutions but of Buddhist religious movements outside the established hierarchy. Although I do not necessarily agree with the conclusions, a limited overview of this phenomenon may be found in Suwanna Satha-Anand, "Religious Movements in Contemporary Thailand: Buddhist Struggles for Modern Relevance," *Asian Survey*, 30.4 (April 1990), 395–408.

[105] Original in Thai; examined with the assistance of Somchai Rakwijit, Bangkok, 3 March 1987.

[106] *Ibid.*

[107] *Ibid.*

[108] This is what the French discovered in Algeria. They perfected superb techniques for decimating the insurgent infrastructure, but in the absence of a genuine strategic cause for which to fight, their concocted alternative, *Algerie Française*, proved to be only a stop-gap solution. See Peter Paret, *French Revolutionary Warfare From Indochina to Algeria: The Analysis of a Political and Military Doctrine* (New York: Praeger, 1964); also Roger Trinquier, *Modern Warfare: A French View of Counter-insurgency* (New York: Praeger, 1964). Unwilling to forever bail even as the boat filled, Charles de Gaulle pulled the plug on the French commitment. The most compelling account of both the particulars and the emotions of this episode is to be found in Jean Larteguy, *The Centurions* (New York: Avon Book Division, 1961). No such end was in store in the Thai case, because the growth of constituism provided the cause, one sanctioned by the "voices" that carried the most weight in Thai society, the king and Buddhism.

Chapter 4

Strategic Miscalculation:
The Communist Party of the Philippines

If the Communist Party of Thailand (CPT) can be said to have emphasized form over substance, the Communist Party of the Philippines (CPP) may be thought to have destroyed itself through strategic miscalculation. Thus did it decline from seemingly standing on the doors of power to its present status as one contender among many in the Philippine political spectrum. Though it remains a viable entity, which has rebounded from its disastrous decline in the late 1980s and early 1990s, the party is not at present a threat to the polity. Its greatest capabilities lie in its continuing capacity to initiate urban protest and to carry out tactical ambushes in rural areas. The former are disruptive; the latter have killed as many as roughly a dozen-and-a-half government personnel at a time, but neither is yet part of a more pronounced operational or strategic advance.

That such is the case, as will be evident below,[1] stems from the history of the movement, a history that saw the CPP ride propitious national and international circumstances to great heights, but then disintegrate because of bitter factionalism caused by differences of opinion over how to turn the strategic approach of Maoism into operational reality. This debate, which would have been debilitating on its merits, coincided with the altered strategic environment of the post-Marcos and, subsequently, post-Cold War periods, as well as a correct government approach to counter-insurgency. The CPP proved unprepared for either of these factors, and the result was that what could, in other circumstances, well have proved to be both correct form and substance, collapsed.

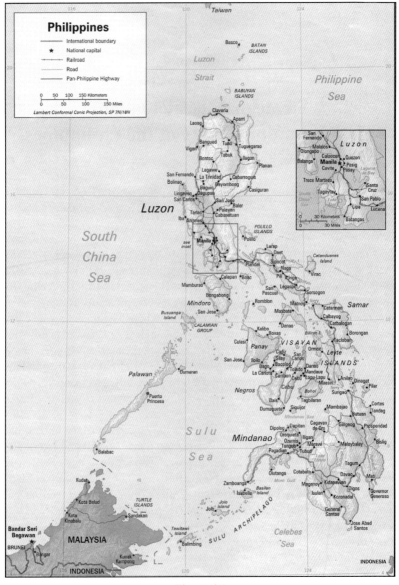

Figure 4.1

Growth of Insurgent Challenge to the Old-Regime

Communism, of course, is a political response to societal realities. The Philippines (see Figure 4.1), as is the case with most developing countries, has long suffered from an array of socio-economic problems: poverty, malnutrition, disparity of wealth, and so forth. These have interacted with the multi-faceted legacy of three and a half centuries of colonial rule (three centuries by the Spanish, the remainder by the Americans). In particular, the country has been cursed with a skewed economic structure centered about subsistence plots and the cash-generating capacities of extractive industries and export agriculture, a structure unable to absorb fully the Philippines' relatively well-educated work force. Although democratic in framework since independence, which was achieved in the immediate aftermath of the Second World War, the political system has proved incapable of addressing this reality and in assuring social justice for all. Small wonder, then, argue critics, that the country has a history of peasant revolt, the most recent episode being the present insurgency.

Still, the CPP cannot be seen as a necessary outgrowth of Philippine realities. Indeed, it would probably not have become a going concern at all had it not been for the opportunity provided by the political repression of the regime of Ferdinand Marcos.

First elected president in 1965, and again in 1969, Marcos secured his position by declaring martial law in 1972. (He would not be ousted until 1986.) At that time, he attributed his drastic action to various circumstances, among them the threat of communist insurgency, economic and social malaise (including corruption), and escalating civic violence. In return for his being allowed to exercise extraordinary emergency powers, Marcos spoke of a "democratic revolution" and a resulting "New Society." Although it was impossible to judge the veracity of his declared motives as opposed to his possible personal ambitions, Marcos was correct that at that particular juncture the Philippines was facing a difficult period.

Centuries of colonial rule had left the country an Asian hybrid, a mixture of East and West, comfortable with neither. By geography and ethnicity, the Filipinos are Asian; by culture, heritage, and orientation, they are Westerners, "brown Americans" as the sobriquet went. Economically, the Philippines had emerged from colonialism in a sorry state. Possessing in any case minimal infrastructure or industry, the islands had during the Second World War been the scene of heavy fighting and of a harsh Japanese occupation. Shortly thereafter occurred the so-called "Huk Rebellion" and the dislocation it caused in the "heartland" of Luzon. The product of these events was a weak free enterprise system heavily dependent on external sources of capital. Centered about agricultural products and extractive industry, this system benefited a small minority. Foreign capital, especially American, was instrumental in expanding the two sectors just mentioned. Americans provided 80% of all foreign investment in 1970, and US holdings that year comprised 19.5% of all Philippine assets in manufacturing, commerce, services, utilities, mining, and agriculture. Particular concentration occurred in certain industries, such as oil, where assets were 80% American-owned.

By the late 1960s even substantial foreign investment could not make up for growing structural problems. Under- and unemployment were widespread, the economy was stagnant, and there was unrest in the countryside, where land distribution was highly skewed, and among urban workers. The political process, which would have been expected to meet demands for change, for it was patterned after the American republican and federal system of democracy, was co-opted by the same narrow segment of the population that benefited from the economic arrangements.

Corruption was widespread and massive. Notably, even as government bureaucracy, both civil and military, grew, disenchantment with the political process among the politically active sector took the demand-making function out of established channels and onto the streets. Although the precise impetus for and process whereby this occurred have been attributed to a variety of factors, it is clear that the political activism prevalent worldwide, especially in the US, during the 1960s served at a minimum as a catalyst for a resurgence of nationalism with anti-systemic overtones. This movement, while by no means limited to the intelligentsia, had at its heart the universities of the Manila area. Students and instructors were soon joined by others, notably discontented workers.

Simultaneously, the communist opposition, dormant since its decimation in the 1950s by Ramon Magsaysay's counter-insurgency program, experienced a resurgence. Drawing its strength from the same nationalistic organizations of youths, intellectuals, workers, and peasants as were denouncing (and renouncing) the formal political system, a new Communist Party of the Philippines (CPP) in 1968 convened a secret conference and then announced its adherence to Maoist people's war. The CPP was actually a splinter from the older Philippine Communist Party (*Partido Komunista ng Philipinas* [PKP]) but had split with the PKP due to fundamental differences of doctrine and strategy.

As would be expected from a Maoist-oriented party, the CPP was particularly active in united front activities designed to promote communist goals legally while concealing the actual communist source and direction. Thus the pre-martial law period was marked by the appearance, even prior to the announcement of people's war, of a number of communist front organizations, ultimately linked through the mechanism of the CPP-controlled National Democratic Front (NDF). Central to the orientation of these organizations was the advancement, particularly in the pages of the *Progressive Review*, edited by Jose Maria Sison, a one-time lecturer at the University of the Philippines, of the concept of "neo-colonialism." This approach, which was not an innovation, stated that true national independence from the colonial power (the United States) did not exist, because in the neo-colonial arrangement at hand "the responsibilities for governance of a colony are transferred to the nationalist leaders but only after a process whereby the latter are tamed and integrated into the capitalist system."[2]

"Neo-colonialism" was to prove a key concept. While it was certainly a part of every Marxist lexicon, it was also a staple of radical, non-communist thought. The CPP could thus link its aspirations for power with the emerging nationalist sentiments of various aggrieved popular sectors. Furthermore, within this "neo-colonial" framework of analysis, to be a nationalist was necessarily to be opposed not only to the controlling neo-colonial power (the US) but also to its domestic "lackies" (Marcos and his supporters), who, according to the line, were nothing more than pawns who owed their positions and wealth to Washington. All components of the existing system, in fact, served to maintain the neo-colonial order and therefore were suspect and subject to attack as the situation dictated. In particular, the economic and political structures were interlocking and mutually supportive and could not be considered apart from each other. Bringing down Marcos, in other words, would only lead to a like-minded replacement; the existing socio-economic-political structure required total alteration, a revolution.

Against this background the electoral campaign of 1969 was an important turning-point. Although Marcos won re-election, the process was marked by a level of graft and expenditure staggering even by jaded Filipino standards. The embittered legal opposition turned to obstructionism, while among radicalized elements, disillusionment and discontent gave way to outright opposition. Street demonstrations became commonplace in the capital, particularly as labor elements joined the fray. Far to the south, on and about Mindanao, there was also an upsurge of violence carried out by dissident Muslims dissatisfied with their position within a Christian, mainly Catholic, society. The government responded to these challenges with repression, thus further fanning the fires of discontent. On 22 September 1972, martial law was declared by Presidential Decree 1081.

It is not necessary to review here the progress of martial law or its particular programs. What is important is that martial law, whatever its intentions, became increasingly inefficient, corrupt, and brutal. By at least the second half of the 1970s, it was clear that martial law was not living up to its "New Society" billing and that the economy was not functioning well. Furthermore, the increasing integration of the Philippines into the world-economy meant there was little immediate prospect for improvements at a time of global recession.[3] The point was not that these conditions were necessarily new or caused by martial law. Rather, they undermined the justification on which martial law had been built: that is, that it was necessary to curb political liberties if the welfare of the people was to be improved.

Such statistics and others were viewed by dissidents within the context of a massive influx of foreign investment capital into the economy,[4] and a relationship between the continued poverty and deprivation, on the one hand, and foreign capital, on the other, was widely articulated and accepted. Both foreign government and private aid, loans, and investment were viewed as props for the Marcos regime. Indeed, as time passed, this view espoused the widely believed point that, save for these capital influxes, Marcos could have been toppled. That this was not necessarily or particularly valid was beside the point; it was a critical locus of philosophy about which both outlawed and "establishment" opponents of martial law could rally.

Drawing on its Maoist blueprint, the CPP quickly recognized that the declaration of martial law provided it with a golden opportunity to make common cause with dissident non-communist elements. A directive adopted by the CPP Central Committee in October 1972 explicitly recognized the polarization that was bound to result from Marcos' move and stated that the party should capitalize on this by playing down the class basis of the broad resistance movement directed against the regime. Instead, the document summoned "all those who are interested in achieving national freedom and democracy" to join the CPP in a united front to carry on the struggle. A program for a coalition of anti-Marcos forces centered on: reestablishment of "democratic rights" for "anti-fascist forces"; nullification of "unequal treaties" with the US; bringing Marcos and his "diehard accomplices" to trial; and strengthening the armed forces of the CPP, the New People's Army (NPA).

Emphasis on building "national democracy" (also called "new democracy" or "national communism") was borrowed directly from Mao's "New Democracy" concept, but as articulated publicly by the CPP, it claimed to lean more heavily toward a genuine national coalition under a form of democratic socialism. This orientation was formalized in April 1973 when a Preparatory Commission for the National Democratic Front met and issued a "Ten Point Program" that was to be the keynote document for construction of an anti-Marcos united front. In the explanatory text accompanying the "Ten Point Program of the National Democratic Front in the Philippines," the pronouncement stated:

> There should be no monopoly of political power by any class, party or group. The degree of participation in the government by any political force should be based on its effective role and record in the revolutionary struggle and on the people's approbation... The coalition government should allow the free interplay of national and democratic forces during and off [sic] elections. Thus, a truly democratic system of representation can develop and operate to the benefit of the people. Such a government should always be subject to the will of the people.[5]

Some analysts viewed this position as a possible departure of great importance from the standard communist strategy for victory through class warfare, that the CPP was actually willing to accept a post-capitalist coalition along the lines of democratic socialism. Supporting evidence for this conclusion, in addition to the CPP's statements, was allegedly provided by observing the priority that the CPP gave to united front construction over armed struggle. Such an analysis, however, was a fundamental misreading of people's war tenets. In them it was clear that the building of a united front was not an optional tactical expedient. To the contrary, Mao stated that it was a key element of people's war.

That those who threw in their lot with the NDF chose to ignore the ultimate political consequences of their collaboration with the CPP (making a pact with the devil, if one will) reflected increasing polarization within the Philippines and the extent to which the communists were seen as the only credible anti-Marcos force. Thus the NDF grew rapidly, aided by reported human rights violations that served to radicalize even some of the Catholic clergy. The NPA also expanded substantially. By the early 1980s the communist movement, whether considered in its armed wing or as a united front, had become a vibrant, growing concern throughout the archipelago.

For his part, Marcos capped the restructuring of the formal political system by a series of maneuvers designed not only to institutionalize his rule but also to provide for a smooth transfer of power. In January 1981, a formal end to martial law was declared by Presidential Proclamation 2045. Subsequently, a plebiscite held on 7 April 1981 was used to change the British-style parliamentary form of government, itself brought in earlier to replace the American-style Presidential form, to a modified French-style system. The resulting powerful presidency was filled, of course, by Marcos in a bitterly-protested 16 June 1981 election. A 14-man Executive Council was created to provide for orderly succession.

Despite the fanfare that accompanied the alleged return to normalcy, all that had actually been done was to put an end to military tribunals and to the use of the term "martial law." The powers of the president to legislate and to order the arrest and detention of anyone considered subversive remained unchanged. Edicts issued previously under Presidential Decree 1081 drew their authority, instead, from Amendment Six to the 1973 Constitution as ratified in 1976. All martial law proclamations, orders, decrees, instructions, acts, and organizations remained intact.

These forced political changes served to invigorate the fragmented "establishment" opposition (i.e., those who prior to martial law had been in the ranks of the opposition or had been disposed toward Marcos' opponents). An attempted boycott of the presidential election drew some support but not enough to make any difference in the proceedings. Increasingly, therefore, this inability of the "establishment" opposition to find a viable means to counter Marcos meant that opponents of the regime were forced to turn to those who advocated violence as the only possible counter.

The sense of estrangement from all hope of reform often took the form of virulent anti-Americanism. In a growing number of publications, the drift of the opposition toward the left was evident, and increasingly US support was viewed as the lynchpin of Marcos' tenure in office. The CPP was able to recruit directly many such disillusioned individuals. Even those not actually co-opted gradually moved to a position where their viewpoints were scarcely distinguishable from those of the CPP. The result was that the party, with growing confidence, was able to assert the rectitude and primacy of its line: only people's war offered a means to end the Marcos dictatorship and its oppression.

In contrast, the moderate opposition consistently had the ground cut out from under it by a relentless combination of Marcos' centralization of power and Washington's consistent support for him. Unable to make headway by either violent or non-violent means, it faded. Students did return to the streets in October 1981 but were routed. Colleges themselves were forced to crack down on dissidents, expelling them. Many of the disenchanted turned to the NDF, which had room within its structure for a variety of pursuits other than direct participation in armed struggle. Those not satisfied with this approach joined the CPP/NPA.

Drift toward the violent alternative was of particular concern to the Catholic Church, which nominally embraced 85% of all Filipinos and acted as a unifying force in Philippine society. Although historically the church could be thought of as a buttress of the *status quo* in the Philippines, the same gradual change seen elsewhere in the world, particularly in Latin America, was evident: The continued growth of poverty and repression split the clergy over the extent to which direct action against the system should be used. There were calls by many clergymen for the church to denounce social injustice, and a liberation theology developed, attracting church intellectuals and radicals in the ranks.

Indeed, with the passage of time, the authorities increasingly viewed the church with suspicion, particularly in light of the fact that roughly a sixth of the 99 members of the Catholic Bishops' Conference of the Philippines (CBCP) were quite vocal in their dissatisfaction with the "church as institution" approach. They favored, instead, a more activist "church as people" stance, a strategy resisted by the head of the Catholic Church in the Philippines, the Archbishop of Manila, Cardinal Jamie Sin. Nevertheless, Sin saw his church being torn apart by the same polarization that had rent society at large, and he increasingly spoke out forcefully against oppression. In late July 1982, three senior government officials publicly denounced Sin as a "Filipino Khomeini" and claimed that he sought to replace Marcos as president.

Marcos was not oblivious to the danger. Even amidst his suspicion of some church elements, he sought to promote Catholicism as an integral part of the Filipino identity. Likewise, he tackled the communists by offering an olive branch of sorts. The PKP, though reduced to but several hundred hardcore members located principally in the Metro Manila area, was allowed a quasi-legality. After its February 1973 national congress, the PKP indicated its willingness to follow a path of "peaceful revolutionary transformation." Thus, it was not surprising in late 1981 that Marcos offered to consider legalizing communism.

Constructing the Counter-State

Foreign communists, to be sure, had been active in the country since the 1920s, but the PKP was not born until 7 November 1930. Its platform included standard Marxist fare, and its activities soon led to its proscription. It thus went underground and operated through labor fronts and the small Socialist Party of the Philippines, with which it merged in 1938 on orders from the COMINTERN in Moscow. Such work gained for the PKP a certain semi-acceptability by the close of the first decade after its formation; and, with the party's participation in the Second World War resistance against the Japanese, Philippine communism was able to make significant strides.

133

The post-war Huk Rebellion, viewed by both the government and the United States as a communist insurrection, seems now, on closer examination, to have been in many respects a peasant uprising that the PKP could exploit. The rebellion was preceded by a decade of peasant unrest in Luzon, and the *Hukbalahap* (*Hakbong Bayan Laban sa Hapon*, or "People's Army against the Japanese") itself drew its initial strength from anti-Japanese sentiment among the abused populace. After the war, it was starting to disband when peasant grievances again came to the fore. The government repression that followed allowed the PKP to link up with the movement, offering it leadership and ideological guidance. Yet it does not appear to have controlled it *per se*. While its political brains were PKP, many of its local leaders were not.

Still, the complexity of the "Huk Rebellion" was not fully appreciated at the time.[6] But this complexity was significant, because eventually the government's counter-insurgency program was able to succeed, not because of the decimation of the PKP leadership and infrastructure, which did occur to an extent, but because certain reforms satisfied peasant grievances and robbed the insurgency of its manpower, the "grievance guerrillas."[7] The peasants' grievances were actually quite moderate and consisted essentially of calls for reform of tenancy (lower rents and provision of loans), equal rights under the law, and the right to organize. There was no plan to overturn the system, the goal of the PKP. As reforms were achieved in these areas and government repression toned down, particularly under Ramon Magsaysay, the rebellion faded.

Defeat of the Huks marked the low point of Philippine communist fortunes. The PKP had been decimated, with most of its Politburo captured in October 1952. There followed slow disintegration, and by the early 1960s the movement was moribund. Nevertheless, if the movement had at the time lost its foot soldiers, it had maintained its intellectual base. The party and its efforts to overthrow the system were revived in December 1968–January 1969 when a new "reconstituted" Communist Party of the Philippines (CPP) convened a secret conference and announced its adherence to the Maoist precept of "people's war." Since the CPP was actually a splinter from the older PKP, press materials of the period often referred to the CPP as the "CPP/Marxist-Leninist" or "CPP-ML," while calling the PKP itself the CPP. With time this clumsy notation was abandoned, for the PKP faded into relative obscurity and the CPP became the only standard-bearer for armed Marxist rebellion.

In order to make revolution, there was a pressing need for "liberation forces." Even after the Huk Rebellion collapsed, low-level violence continued as some Huk

A former anti-Japanese guerrilla during the Second World War, Ramon Magsaysay (above) rose steadily in post-war politics until becoming president. Under his charismatic leadership, ably assisted by two Americans (below) whom he requested by name—"Bo" Bohannan and Ed Lansdale (respectively, at photo below)—the first effort of the communists to seize power in the Philippines was defeated. (Photos: Bohannan in Author Collection)

commanders and their protégés refused to surrender. The young Maoists of the CPP forged tenuous links with these Huk remnants, all of which were active in banditry at the time in the central Luzon area north of Manila,[8] sparking another round in the conflict, but one now consciously modeled after Chinese "people's war."[9]

"These people were our best and brightest," theorized Noel Albano during a 1988 interview. Then editor of the Manila daily *Malaya*, once a left-wing standard-bearer with close ties to the CPP, Albano continued: "They were able to revitalize the CPP, which at that point was rather stalled in ideological squabbling."[10] There followed explosive growth for the movement as the influx of high quality manpower allowed the rapid expansion of infrastructure. Grievances aplenty already existed among the masses. The party needed only to tap them.

That they were able to do this was in large part a result of Philippine geography. That is, when the same process occurred in Thailand in the aftermath of the military assault on Thammasat University in October 1976, the opposition was driven underground into the waiting arms of the communist insurgent movement and the Communist Party of Thailand disintegrated in ideological turmoil as the old guard and newcomers disagreed over strategy. In contrast, in the Philippine archipelago, each newcomer could find his own niche by achieving organizational success in the "outer islands." The decentralized nature of CPP control allowed for experimentation away from the movement's initial center of mass in Luzon. Once they were successful, these individuals could return and reinvigorate the center's strategic thinking.[11]

Such thinking, as mentioned, was Maoist in strategic design and thoroughly Leninist in operational and tactical flexibility. To grow in a hostile environment, the party adopted Mao's technique of revolutionary warfare, with the rural countryside the principal area of struggle. Using its NPA as a shield, the CPP painstakingly constructed its counter-state. To the task at hand, the party brought an organizational finesse that grew with the years. It was these skills that enabled it to harness peasant dissatisfaction and turn it from rebellion to insurgency. There was never an entire area that rose up and subsequently became linked to the CPP, although in some respects the Cordillera Liberation Army in northern Luzon's Igorot areas, a minority upheaval, might be considered in this light.[12] What normally occurred instead was far more painstaking and certainly less dramatic than the romance of the peasant rebellion.[13]

Struggle in the Villages

Contacts were first made with a community by a propaganda team normally working through acquaintances or relatives (accompanying this discussion, refer to Figure

4.2). This gave the CPP sufficient local presence to make a number of converts, who then formed the basis of sectoral Organizing Groups (OG). (All acronyms are those used by the CPP itself in its documents.) The sectors included one each for peasants (that is, men), women, and youth (later, children were added as a separate sector). These were the "sectors" used in rural OG; in urban areas they related to occupations. OG members were split into cells to compartmentalize the organizations and were indoctrinated by taking designated courses (e.g., "Special Mass Course").[14]

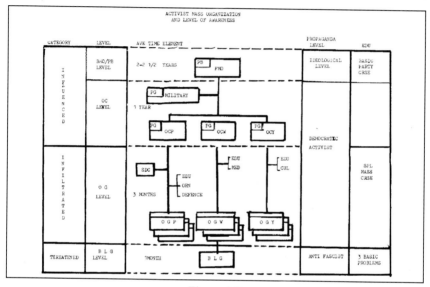

Figure 4.2

The best individuals of each OG cell became members of the higher Organizing Committees (OC), which were also sectoral. Where there could be any number of OG, though, there was but one OC per sector. OC members went through a more advanced series of courses (e.g., "Five Golden Rays," "Revolutionary Guide of Land Reform," and "Lessons for Mass Activists"). Ultimately, the best of these were themselves graduated to become Candidate Party Members and, after still further schooling, full-fledged Party Members. By this time, the hamlet (*sitio*) or village (*barangay*) concerned would be co-opted, dominated by a functioning Party Branch (PB). It was the controlling political entity, with its own legal framework and mechanisms for generation of revenue.

As villages were organized in precise sequence, graduating from the OG to OC to PB, they fielded their "local guerrilla units" (LGU), a "self-defense corps" at the lower end of the spectrum, a more comprehensively organized *yunit militia* at the upper end. The extent to which these part-time guerrillas were armed depended on the weaponry available. In October 1986, for instance, captured CPP documents claimed an "armed strength" of 5,924 on Negros, a "banner of the revolution"; but its weapons inventory for the same period was less than 900.[15]

If villages and their militias may be considered the base of a pyramid, there remained considerable structure above. Villages fell under Sections, which corresponded closely to the government's own municipalities (*municipio* or counties). These Sections controlled the village operatives and themselves answered to party Districts, which, in turn, fell under Fighting Fronts (not to be confused with political fronts, the legal or semi-legal organizations infiltrated and partially or completely controlled by the CPP). Fighting Fronts (FF) answered to Island Party Committees

Village on Samar: Patrol talks with villager in the interior of the northwest, a region with a strong CPP/NPA presence that had, during 1986, been decimated by 52nd Infantry Battalion. CPP presence in the rural areas enabled the Party to become a viable entity. (Marks photo)

(IPC), these to Regional Commissions, these to the Politburo (PB) and the Central Committee (CC).

This hierarchy may be seen in Figures 4.3, 4.4, and 4.5. Figure 4.3 begins with the Party Branch (PB) structure within the villages, moves up to the Section Committees ("Sec Com"), which themselves are grouped under District Committees (Dist Com). Districts fall under Fighting Fronts (Front). Figure 4.4 follows by illustrating a typical regional structure (i.e., Northeastern Mindanao), comprised of a variable number of Fighting Fronts. Figure 4.5 begins with the Regional Party Committees (RPC) coordinated by Commissions, all under the national leadership.

As can be seen on the Figures, while the militia of various sorts (LGU) protected the villages in the Sections, each District had its own party chain of command and District Guerrilla Unit, or DGU (approximately platoon size). Likewise, each Fighting Front had its own Front Guerrilla Unit, or FGU (approximately company size but always seeking to become as powerful as possible). Reportedly, at least two Main Guerrilla Units (MGU, intended to be of approximately battalion size) were also formed, one on Samar, the other on Luzon, but these were not true forces in being.[16]

All of the major levels (Fighting Front, Island, and Region) had available the special *Yunit Partisano* (partisan units) or "sparrows," assigned the mission of complementing rural action through urban operations and thus carrying out acts of terror, notably assassinations. Sparrows[17], together with the soldiers of the DGU, FGU, and MGU (the *yunit gerilya*), comprised the regulars of the movement, those classified as members of the NPA. This division into various categories of forces accounted over the years for the frequent confusion concerning the number of enemy facing the security forces. Not only did all of the "soldiers" not carry weapons, but there were also different categories of "soldiers." As the case of *Westmoreland vs. CBS* made clear to the American public,[18] a bean count of the enemy depended completely on which beans were chosen for inclusion in the tally. To return to the Negros case, guerrilla strength on the island in late 1986, just prior to a ceasefire with the government (discussed below), could legitimately be tallied as anywhere, in round figures, from 500 to 6,000 (see Figure 4.6). Only some 500 (499) of these were classified as "combatants," those in the guerrilla (DGU, FGU) and sparrow (partisan) units.[19] By 1980, total figures for NPA "combatants" had reached 24,000.

Regardless, the most fundamental point was that in the CPP insurgent hierarchy, everything depended on the base. The party divided all its manpower into three categories, depending on the level of individual training: organized masses, mass activists, and party members. An individual working at the OG

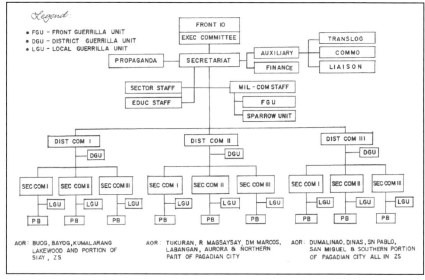

Figure 4.3

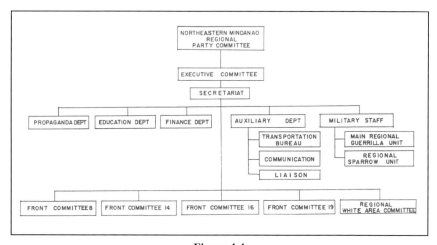

Figure 4.4

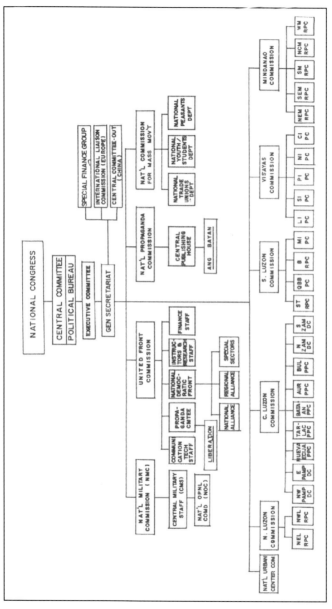

Figure 4.5

GUERRILLA STRENGTH ON NEGROS (OCT 86)

FORMATION	STRENGTH	% TOTAL	% COMBINED
YUNIT GERILYA	394	6.7	8.5
YUNIT PARTISANO	105	1.8	
YUNIT MILITIA	3,124	52.7	91.5
SELF-DEFENSE CORPS	2,301	38.8	
TOTALS	5,924	100.0	100.0

Figure 4.6

level was considered a member of the organized masses; those promoted to OC level became mass activists; and, in the end, party members. Similarly, the ranks of the NPA were filled by those recruited from militia formations. These individuals themselves were first members of the organized masses and, later, mass activists. Most NPA, therefore, were party members. This was a fairly rigid progression and only broke down when conditions dictated otherwise. Under normal circumstances, manpower for higher formations was never picked up off the streets, so to speak.

Thus occurred the systematic construction of the counter-state. This counter-state gave the CPP its staying power. Peasant grievances were certainly tapped by the CPP as it gathered momentum, yet the sheer scope and comprehensive nature of the CPP organization insured that by the time political events changed dramatically in February 1986, at which time Marcos was ousted, the movement had long since ceased to rely on those grievances for its survival. It had become an alternative political structure that purported to offer a superior existence for its members, or at least the hope of a superior existence, better than that which they could hope to achieve under the existing governance structure. It fulfilled its personnel requirements through internal promotion of individuals who had gone through an extensive socialization process. It met leadership needs through transfers as circumstances dictated. Orders issued from the center were obeyed, with severe sanctions for violations of both general policies and specific instructions. Mechanisms of funding provided sustenance.

The party's goal was always to create so-called "liberated areas," geographic entities in which life could be ordered as directed by the CPP. The NPA's purpose was to keep the government from interfering with this effort. As the CPP apparatus took hold, terror was used to prevent any dissent or infiltration. Liquidation of enemies was an important feature of the campaign.

Struggle in Urban Areas

Creation of its own "liberated areas" in the government-controlled countryside forced the CPP to grapple with the other half of the equation, the urban areas. With respect to these, it took the party longer to arrive at a correct approach, but eventually it did just that.

Initially, the CPP approached the target only in the most rigid of Maoist frameworks. True, it could see the opportunity presented by the September 1972 declaration of martial law, for it correctly ascertained that this would provide the basis for making common cause with dissident non-communist elements. By October 1972, the CPP Central Committee, in its discussions, had already decided that societal polarization was bound to result from martial law and that the party should capitalize on this by downplaying the class basis of the broad resistance movement directed against Marcos. Subsequently, the party created the NDF. When it became an organizational reality, the NDF, far from being an independent umbrella organization of anti-Marcos opponents, as it endeavored to portray itself, was but one of the principal organs of the CPP's United Front Commission, itself one of the four main divisions under the CPP's ruling Politburo and Central Committee (see Figure 4.5).

Having made this strategic move, the CPP nonetheless seemed unsure how to derive maximum benefit from the NDF and the subordinate fronts that grew up under it. The answer came with the party's realization that the human geography within which it operated had changed substantially. A key CPP document analyzed things thus: "The role of urban centers in advancing the revolutionary struggle increases. If before we concentrated 90 percent of our efforts in the CS [countryside] and only 10 percent in the UCs [urban centers], the ratio now should be perhaps 60:40."[20] From this assessment came a formal policy decision that moved united front activity from a mere orientation to an actual measure that created an urban counterpart to the rural infrastructure.

The field for operation was certainly ripe. As corruption and abuses of power by the central government increased in the early 1980s, a host of legal bodies sprang up demanding societal change. The CPP was able to infiltrate a wide variety of these groups and convert them to fronts actually controlled by members of the CPP underground. Church and student bodies were particularly vulnerable because of their extensive involvement in social action.

Infrastructure to support this campaign was every bit as extensive as that in the countryside. Outlined in detail by the CPP's "Political Program for 1983" and amplifying documents was the necessity of forming highly disciplined, clandestine cells for infiltrating "case-oriented groups," and then using their work to further party goals. Stated the "Political Program": "*Our key task for 1983 is to develop our ND forces* [National Democratic; i.e., united front; emphasis in original]. . . Solid and well-oiled UG [underground] machinery activity would make possible the advance of the OMM [open mass movement]. . . Further, we shall be able to exercise political leadership with a developed UG network."[21]

Such directions, when they were published in late 1982, did not reflect a new tack by the CPP but rather re-emphasized a policy decision made at least a year before.

Urban operative on Negros: Captured in Bacolod City in 1988, CPP member is interrogated by municipality mayor as policewoman and security personnel look on. As the demographics of the Philippines shifted, and the country became more than half urban, the Party modified its doctrine and moved combatants into the cities. (Marks photo)

One of the best illustrations of the success of the front mechanisms, in fact, had already come to light that year on Samar, which only a few years before had been the nexus of CPP activity in the archipelago. The case was also indicative of the extent to which infiltration had already progressed in some major Philippine institutions.

When the premier Social Action Center (SAC) of the Catholic Church, Paul VI SAC in Catbolagan, capital of Samar Province itself, was raided in September, documents and interrogations revealed that virtually the entire framework for social work and human rights assistance in the Visayas region, stretching across the Central Philippines, had been co-opted. Both the Paul VI SAC and the Visayas Secretariat for Social Action (VISSA) were controlled by priests working for the CPP. In a single year prior to the raid, Father Edgar Kangleon, the SAC's director, had been able, among numerous other support activities, to send 60,000 pesos (then approximately USD 15,000) to the Financial Department of the CPP's Visayas Commission by using donations intended for the poor. Additionally, by directing Kangleon to give a member of the CPP underground control over the Projects Desk, the party was able to submit and have approved its own development schemes. A significant portion of the funding was obtained through donations sent directly by cause-oriented groups overseas, mainly in Europe.[22]

Materials from the Kangleon case implicated other church groups. Among the most notable, based in the SAC, the Samar office of Task Force Detainees of the Philippines (TFDP, then simply called TFD), the organ that regularly provided documentation on alleged human rights abuses to international cause-oriented groups such as Amnesty International (AI), was headed by a Catholic nun taking CPP orders. TFDP, it was further noted, was an offshoot of the Association of Major Religious Superiors (AMRS), an important church body. Its one-time Executive Secretary, Victor Bulatao, was recruited by the CPP while serving AMRS and was also arrested in 1982 in Samar while acting in his capacity as head of the CPP's Visayas Regional United Front Group. According to the Kangleon documents, there was even a "Visayas Church Sector Consultation of the CPP," a 10-member body that included six priests and a nun.[23]

Infiltration was repeated many times in many groups. Local grievances were exploited to draw participants, but the real agenda was decided behind the scenes by the CPP.[24] By the early 1980s, the party was clearly in the driver's seat in both rural and urban areas. The inefficiency and repression of martial law allowed the CPP to operate strategically virtually at will. Key organizational changes, already reflected in the discussion of CPP structure above, had been made to take better operational advantage of this situation. At meetings of the Politburo and Central Committee, it had been decided to abandon structurally what had remained an approach still oriented toward Luzon, psychologically at least, as well as the continued effort to run operations from the center. Instead, the party leadership decided that it would set strategic policy but would oversee a decentralized movement that would allow each Island Party Committee (IPC) to take operational advantage of local conditions as it saw fit, deploying its tactical forces independently and largely managing its own generation of funds.[25]

The motivation for this change appeared to stem as much from social analysis as from strategic considerations. In particular, the party realized that the traditional areas of unrest on Luzon were not suitable for further expansion, because, for various reasons, among them economic progress and simple war-weariness, there was popular reluctance to becoming involved in "another Huk Rebellion." The result was the shift in emphasis away from Luzon to the outlying islands, notably, Samar, Negros, and Mindanao.

Samar provides a useful illustration of how the process worked itself out. Party presence apparently had begun in 1970 through the activities of a youth organization, the "Movement for a Democratic Philippines" (MDP), the followers of which were students at the University of the Eastern Philippines in Catarman. Initial recruits were reacting to the increased authoritarianism of the Marcos administration, but the movement's ranks grew to include local politicians and priests dissatisfied with the government. Many of its leaders were imprisoned when Marcos declared martial law. Subsequently, the dissidents regrouped in the fertile Catubig Valley of northern Samar, the island's so-called "food basket". Dissident groups in eastern Samar then crossed the mountain ranges to the north in an effort to control the entire area. Further augmentation of CPP manpower was received from Cebu, which had proved inhospitable for guerrilla action at that time.[26]

By 1972 the CPP had implemented its so-called "Dulo Plan," which divided Samar into six districts (*dulo*) targeted for subversion. Author of the plan, according to Philippine government sources, was Jorge Cabardo of Balangiga, eastern Samar, a dismissed cadet from the Philippine Military Academy (PMA) class of 1971. First penetration was achieved through relatives in the region southwest of Catbalogan, with the primary objective being the central interior. CPP reorganization in late 1976 divided Samar into northern and southern area commands, both still under Politburo's direct supervision. This arrangement ended with the 1980 Politburo decision to create IPCs. The Samar IPC was set up by mid-1981, as was its superior Visayas Commission (with its headquarters in Cebu). These superior organs thereafter ran the "liberation struggle" on Samar.

146

Initially, CPP expansion forces on Samar were quite small, but they were able to operate in a near-absolute vacuum of government authority. In 1973, the only security force presence on the island was a single Philippine Constabulary company of 30 to 40 personnel. They responded to the problem of subversives as one of "peace and order." The resulting official misconduct only swelled the insurgents' ranks. Using as their rallying-cry the repression of the "US-Marcos Dictatorship," the CPP, between 1974 and 1975, was able to penetrate nearly half of Samar. By 1979, Sheilah Ocampo, writing for the *Far Eastern Economic Review*, judged that the CPP controlled 85% of eastern Samar, 40% of northern Samar, and 60% of western Samar. An effective shadow government was in place by 1982, she further claimed, and the island was considered the most solid CPP stronghold.

Although other analysts thought this somewhat overstated the case, it was clear by the late 1970s that the situation on Samar was serious. Faced with what had become the most developed communist infrastructure in the country, Manila deployed no less than twelve infantry battalions to the region, a larger maneuver force than that available to the whole army at the time martial law was declared. Although the number was down to nine battalions by 1981, this was still one of the largest concentrations of military power in any sector at the time. That year, then-Brigadier Salvador Mison, regarded as one of the top Philippine combat soldiers, took charge of the island, which together with Leyte made up Regional Unified Command 8, or RUC-8.

To complete the story, Mison realized that security force misconduct and misapplication of assets served to drive manpower to the CPP. Consequently, he tightened discipline considerably. A more comprehensive approach was implemented in attacking the CPP effort. In the field, multi-battalion operations were launched to break up larger guerrilla formations. Simultaneously, to deal with the CPP proselytizing effort, adroit use was made of intelligence assets to uncover and dismantle the main communist political activities. Once key CPP organizational centers, both urban and rural, had been neutralized, the long tedious task of small unit warfare could begin. By 1985, army strength in RUC-8 was down to five battalions.

Contending Ideological Visions

Even as such military activities sought to grapple with the CPP nationwide, larger developments were afoot. Most significantly, by the early 1980s, the Philippine

147

Combat on Samar: Above, troops of Philippine Army's 52ⁿᵈ Infantry Battalion ("52 IB") move against CPP/NPA ambush in early 1986. Below, having driven NPA unit from a village in the northwest., troops respond to harassing fire. With the assignment of "Buddy" Mison to command of RUC-8, which included Samar and Leyte, the situation improved substantially. (Marks photo)

economy began to experience severe difficulties. The growth of nationalist reaction to real and imagined foreign penetration of the polity has been discussed earlier, to include the integral connections dissidents drew between the political and economic spheres. For the state, the challenge was elemental: how to modernize a basically agricultural economy so as better to provide for the population's growing needs and aspirations. What was at issue was the route to take to accomplish this: either continue in the capitalist mode or adopt a socialist course. The state chose the former and sought to emphasize export-oriented agricultural and primary-extraction development. Simultaneously, import-substitution industries were fostered to a degree compatible with free trade and fiscal prudence. This necessarily meant the increasing integration of the Philippines into the world-market, a position that left the economy vulnerable to the vicissitudes of the global economic environment. This vulnerability was compounded by internal economic mistakes and the corruption inherent to martial law.

Several sources have noted that the very areas of greatest insurgent growth coincided with those regions where the government sought to expand export-oriented agriculture and primary-extraction development. When economic needs were harnessed with the abuse inherent to the mechanisms of an authoritarian state, the result was dispossession for thousands of small landowners. As they fled to the more marginal areas geographically, they were courted by the CPP and often recruited into its infrastructure.[27]

To extreme elements, such as the CPP, the internal and external arrangements created and maintained by the acceptance of the capitalist development model were unacceptable. Instead, the CPP stated, only a communist/socialist approach offered hope for an equitable, prosperous future. Non-communist left-wing elements allowed room for some "negotiation" with respect to the precise shape a future system would take, but among the Philippine intelligentsia[28] there was widespread acceptance of the radical view that the Philippines was at least a "new-colony" of the capitalist world, especially of the US. The result was that many individuals who did not claim to be communists were nevertheless willing to throw their lot in with the CPP because of the perceived identity of world-views. In many respects, Manila was caught in a no-win situation. The obvious connection between grievances and CPP recruitment was noted, yet even the most rational and best intentioned efforts taken within the existing ideological framework often had security implications.

To cite but one particularly useful example. If the analysis above may be thought of as the strategic dilemma facing the economy within the structure of the international economy, then the tactical problem at hand was to contain the growth of the oil import bill. Oil accounted for 88% of all energy expenditures in 1980, down from 92% in 1979, but 93% of the total still had to be imported. This importation comprised fully 44% of total imports-value in 1981. With the total import figure that year put at USD 7.134 billion, this amounted to an oil bill of USD 3.15 billion. While plans called for the reduction of the oil percentage of energy expenditure to 55% by 1985, this never proved possible. One logical way in which to reduce the oil import bill, therefore, was to look to alternative energy sources, particularly the vast, largely untapped, hydroelectric potential of mountainous northern Luzon.

Studies of the Chico River Valley in southern Kalinga, a sub-province of Kalinga-Apayao, had been begun as early as 1962, but not until oil prices skyrocketed in the early 1970s did a massive hydroelectric scheme seem feasible. The largest hydroelectric project in Southeast Asia was proposed along the Chico River. While its main purpose was power generation, a secondary benefit would be the possible irrigation of some 49,000 hectares of farmland. The basic problem with the scheme was that the four dams would displace an estimated 100,000 people living in six Bontoc and ten Kalinga tribal villages. The tribesmen, who even during the American occupation practiced headhunting, lived a lifestyle that revolved around their labyrinth of mountain rice-terraces. Their entire way of life was threatened by plans to relocate them. Unsuccessful attempts to reach a peaceful compromise on the dam led to increasing violence after February 1974 when Marcos ordered the National Power Corporation to begin work on the basin project.

What followed was a textbook case of security forces alienating the population and thereby inspiring the emergence of increasingly radical leadership. Initially, the tribesmen sought to work through government and church-affiliated organizations, but when it seemed that even the government body specifically set up to protect tribal Filipinos, the Presidential Assistant on National Minorities (PANAMIN), was involved in escalating repression, and that the church groups were unable to halt a campaign of government intimidation and assassination, the tribesmen became more willing to consider offers of aid tendered by the NPA.[29]

In late 1976, the NPA, hitherto shunned by the tribesmen, penetrated the closely knit Kalinga-Bontoc tribal system. Through a process of persuasion and education, CPP operatives were able to expand their influence. Government units sent into the area, first Philippine Constabulary battalions, subsequently regular army units, inflamed the situation. By 1981, more than 100 dam-related killings had been reported, including the assassination of Macli-ing Dulag, the Kalingan tribal leader who had led his people's struggle against the dams. In the years that followed, the rebellion gained strength and ultimately became the full-fledged thorn in the government's side represented by the tribal forces of Father Balweg and his associates.

The upshot was that, in the early 1980s, the Philippines found itself with a badly deteriorating economy, spiraling debt, and worsening security problems integrally linked to the first two problems, for the economic crunch played itself out on the ground was in dramatically lower social welfare indicators. The crucial development was that the economic dislocation coincided with the dramatic decline in the efficiency of the Marcos regime brought about by nepotism, corruption, and unbridled avarice.[30] To wit, the depredations of the Marcos clique could no longer be absorbed by the badly limping economy. Since the regime could use repression to ensure that its resource needs were met, the decline could only be absorbed by the people. This drove many into the arms of the guerrillas.

State Response to Insurgent Challenge

Faced with the construction of a counter-state, Manila's response suffered from that common to governments whose mistakes and repression serve to spark revolt: it countered with further repression. Much of this, it is important to note, was carried out by the regional forces that fell midway between the police and the army organizationally, the Philippine Constabulary (PC), as well as by militia that the PC was supposed to control. Essentially a police field force that had grown out of the army itself and its involvement in the Huk Rebellion, the PC in many respects mirrored the army in organization and equipment. Its greatest disadvantage, when viewed from afar, was its regional basing posture, which allowed its men to become inefficient militarily and to involve themselves in local politics and corruption. Not all units were second-rate, certainly. A good commander meant a disciplined unit, and there were PC combat battalions that performed military roles with the army and Marine Corps, but too often problems with the populace stemming from "military" indiscipline could be traced back to the PC.

At the time martial law was declared, in fact, the army was quite small. It was quickly forced to expand dramatically, a process spawning a host of its own problems. Ironically, the impetus for this expansion was neither martial law nor the CPP insurgency but the challenge of Muslim separatism in the form of the Moro National Liberation Front (MNLF). Operating out of the southern Philippines, the MNLF posed a threat of a different sort to Manila than did the CPP. While the CPP sought the overthrow of the existing socio-economic-political system, the MNLF sought autonomy for the country's 2.5–4 million Muslims. The resulting conflict was to prove a significant drain on national resources even as the economy began to decline.

Influence of Muslim Revolt

Armed confrontation between the MNLF's military wing, the *Bangsa Moro Army* (BMA), and the Armed Forces of the Philippines (AFP) erupted after Marcos's 1972 declaration of martial law, peaked during the 1973–75 period, and remained in a state of political and military standoff after a 1977 ceasefire collapsed. Thereafter, the war was smaller than it had been in 1973–75, but it still killed thousands each year. The impact on the military was enormous, as it expanded substantially. By mid-1982, the combined total of army, Marine, and PC combat battalions numbered 70 (later 71). At the height of the fighting, most of it conventional, a single army brigade commanded by the previously mentioned Salvador Mison on Mindanao had assigned to it twelve maneuver battalions. To highlight the point again, this was a larger force than that available to the entire army in 1972. As late as 1978, in fact, nearly 80% of all available government maneuver battalions were committed against a BMA force once estimated at 30,000, later reduced to 10–12,000, rather than against the NPA. Only in 1982 were even half of the military's available maneuver assets thrown into the counter-insurgency campaign. A comparable amount of assets remained tied up with the MNLF problem.[31]

That the MNLF revolt erupted after the implementation of martial law was probably due less to any specific incident than to a justifiable belief by the MNLF that secession would be impossible to achieve peacefully through negotiation with an increasingly centralized, Christian polity. Failure to achieve military success led to the revision of the MNLF's original goal in favor of autonomy, but splits within the movement prevented the government from fully exploiting this modification. In January 1976, a truce document between Manila and the MNLF, which proposed autonomy for the Muslims in the south, was signed in Tripoli under the auspices of Libya and the Organization of the Islamic Conference. This autonomy was to be achieved "within the framework of sovereignty and territorial integrity of the Philippines."

A fundamental problem with either secession or autonomy for the Philippine Muslim population was that the "southern problem" was never the clear-cut picture of a Muslim south dominated by a Christian north that the MNLF attempted to paint. While Muslim concerns for cultural identity were in a sense justified, as were many of the specific grievances against government representatives, the Muslim population was not simply a minority, geographically and culturally distinct, amidst the then-49 million population of the Philippines. Muslims actually were a clear minority even amongst the 10–12 million people of Mindanao, known internationally as the "Muslim heartland," and the Sulu Sea area. They were a majority only in three areas: Lavao del Sur, Maguindanao, and Sultan Kuderat. They were large minorities only in the north and south of Zamboanga and Cotobato Provinces.

These realities led to the emergence of autonomy as the more convincing alternative, but the precise form such autonomy was to take, and the strategy for its achievement, led to the breakup of the MNLF. While defections hurt the MNLF, they also strengthened it, for the inability to reach an outright military victory led the mainstream MNLF leadership to take greater notice of the polarization of forces in the rest of the country. How best to take advantage of this reality sparked yet another debate, but the view that emerged held that the Muslim cause could not be won without coordination with anti-government, non-Muslim groups that had goals and ideals not fundamentally in conflict with those of the MNLF. From a position of cultural and ethnic chauvinism, the MNLF came to see itself as part of a larger struggle and to accept that a virtual prerequisite for its own long-term plans was the downfall of the authoritarian Marcos government and a return of representative government.

A logical consequence of such reasoning was cooperation with the strongest anti-government force, the CPP, although it could certainly be held that the communists' goals were in conflict with those of the Muslims. Nonetheless, "progressive" Muslim elements favored such cooperation. In time, even the more traditional leaders, who saw communism as anathema to all the Muslim religion represented, were willing to sanction some degree of tactical coordination. The general CPP approach to revolt also presented lessons that the MNLF absorbed. Thus the movement began to turn from its narrow focus on religious rebellion to the more complex business of fashioning an insurgency with an infrastructure that could survive even in "occupied" areas.

Hand-in-glove with the new doctrinal and organizational approach was a more sophisticated evaluation of Manila's vulnerability on the international front and the important role diplomatic and economic pressure could play in the conflict. Dependent as it was on Middle Eastern Muslim sources for the preponderance of its oil imports, the Philippines had to give particular ear to the advice of and pay heed to the sensitivities of its Arab suppliers. Simultaneously with this campaign, the MNLF expanded its formal contacts with the "establishment" opposition. Even as the CPP began to expand substantially in the decade of the 1980s, and the economy sputtered, the MNLF revolt remained an on-going proposition that tied up approximately half of the Philippine armed forces and served as a costly drain on scarce resources. Had the Muslims been willing to effect a joint effort with the communists, an unlikely yet possible proposition, Manila would have faced serious difficulties in responding. As it was, the dramatic expansion of the armed forces required to meet the threat of the MNLF revolt actually provided additional forces that were eventually shifted to fight the NPA.

Deterioration of the Security Forces

It would be expected, too, from all that has been said above, that "the shifting of forces" was, indeed, how the Marcos regime saw the CPP insurgency. It was not that there were few individuals who appreciated the non-military roots and dimensions of the problem. There were many. Not only had thousands of Filipinos engaged in guerrilla action during the Second World War and the Huk Rebellion, but still others had also served in Vietnam as part of the Allied effort (some individuals spanned all three conflicts[32]), both in an engineer unit deployed to South Vietnam (commanded at one point by Fidel Ramos, later AFP head and subsequently President) and as civilian advisors in the pacification scheme. These conflicts resulted in a significant reservoir of personnel familiar not only with the mechanics of guerrilla fighting but also with the non-military dimensions (e.g., civic action) of unconventional warfare. Yet it was not these individuals who were in power. Indeed, one of Marcos' first actions on declaring martial law had been to pack off as Ambassador to Thailand the veteran army commander, Raphael "Rocky" Ileto, who had refused to go along with the President's plans.[33]

Just as Ileto was pushed aside, so during the Marcos years were the upper echelons in uniform increasingly used for exercising patronage, irrespective of the needs generated by security concerns such as the CPP or MNLF revolts. The number of general officer positions was expanded, and loyal service to the president and his entourage was rewarded by promotion and stars. Professional skills, demonstrated by command and combat experience, had little to do with the process. Regulations detailing requirements of seniority and schooling were systematically ignored. Eventually, the AFP Chief of Staff position was given to Lieutenant General Fabian Ver, a former Marcos bodyguard who never commanded a troop unit in the field or went through any of the established schooling cycles.

As might be expected, such individuals as Ver often had little concern for executing the duties required by the positions they occupied. Most appeared to devote their energies to personal enrichment or to miscellaneous chores given them by the palace. Further, once having gained a plum, a loyal senior officer could be fairly sure of retaining it almost indefinitely. The palace simply extended the man each time his retirement date came due. By 1986 this "extendee" group alone numbered more than a fifth of the approximately 120 general officers. With promotion to higher ranks increasingly so-monopolized, a growing number of those with field experience were not able to achieve advancement beyond the battalion and brigade levels.

By 1986, battalions numbered 71 if all units, such as the three air force security units, were included. Most were army and infantry, assigned to fifteen brigades under five divisions. Operationally, the battalions and brigades were commanded by the twelve Regional Unified Commands (RUC) into which the country was divided. The divisions performed only at a support level. Rank-wise, RUC, division, and brigade commanders were all brigadier generals. Since general officer positions were the main objective of patronage, the brigade level was the fire-break between what, in effect, became two officer corps, a field and a patronage faction. RUC and division commanders were frequently palace favorites; brigade commanders were a mixture of combat and patronage appointees. The result was growing estrangement between combat formations, commanded in the main by those promoted for considerations of seniority and military proficiency, and the upper headquarters, populated through contacts with, and loyalty to, Marcos and Fabian Ver.

The filling of upper-level functional positions by those little capable or inclined to perform necessary military tasks led to a near-complete breakdown in the security force replacement, training, and supply systems. That the battalions could continue to function was a direct result of the efforts exerted by the field commanders. With the NCO corps essentially non-existent in a leadership sense, unit officers shouldered the burden. They were able to do so because of their technical competence, often self-taught, and professional expertise, gained through long tours in combat. Their understanding of revolutionary warfare was often surprisingly sound. This comprehension allowed them to make the most of their limited resources. Of note, too, officers outside Manila normally shared the hardships with their men. The result was generally high troop morale despite the material deprivations.

Still, bitterness toward the regime and its military clients was deep and widespread among that portion of the officer corps, the bulk, consigned to the field. Under the impact of the patronage system, normal career progression was severely disrupted, particularly once the field grades (major through colonel) had been reached. As a result, command tours were all but frozen. Battalion commands of five years in combat became the norm. One individual interviewed in 1986 had a nine-year tenure. Longer tours were on record. Exacerbating the resentment was a near-universal belief that no amount of military proficiency could defeat the insurgency in the absence of reform at the top, which the palace was unwilling to provide. Widespread knowledge of financial wrongdoing only heightened anger.

A War of Battalions

Ironically, the particulars described above, which could have played out in a number of ways, in the Philippine scenario had the impact of making the situation more difficult for the insurgents, because they strengthened the military as an opponent. While professional dissatisfaction increased as promotion stagnated, for instance, with commanders forced to serve excessive tours in the field, the inevitable result was a military in which more often than not the field units were led by veterans. Likewise, the hardships visited on the units tended to foster not disintegration but unity. Few individuals ever viewed defection as a viable option. Consequently, units hung together if for no reason other than the increased prospects of survival accompanying such a course of action. Even the lack of weapons and equipment had the perverse impact of improving the counter-insurgency, because this insured that military operations were in the main small unit actions rather than large, costly search and destroy operations. Air-mobile assaults and the like were infrequent in a country the size of all Vietnam in which no more than several dozen helicopters were operational at any one time.

Perhaps most important for cohesion, however, was the influence of the professional code maintained by the bulk of the officer corps. Domination of the security forces by graduates of the Philippine Military Academy (PMA), a virtual copy of its colonial parent at West Point, was only the most obvious element in this development. The "West Point ethos," to be sure, provided an element of institutional glue that had proved lacking in many of the developing world's armies. Just as crucial, however, was the cohesion engendered within the officer corps by the legacy stemming from the circumstances surrounding the birth of Philippine nationhood. Not only had Manila been promised independence at the time of the Japanese invasion and conquest, but the Philippine armed forces also subsequently played, with much heroism and suffering, a key role in making victory a reality. This, of course, was followed by the successful campaign against the Huks, which, even considering American assistance, was an indigenous effort, particularly under Magsaysay. The result was that the military saw itself, as opposed to the left, as

Improving the counter-insurgency: Cast adrift, with minimal resources, Philippine Army units conducted principally small unit operations that sought to dominate human terrain. They were aided immeasurably by the fact that locally recruited troops could invariably communicate with the people in whatever dialect was being spoken. (Marks photo)

the true embodiment of Filipino nationalism. Backed by a large and active cadre of service veterans, many highly decorated, the military as a corporate body was determined to survive Marcos, his cronies, and the CPP.

Such determination revealed itself in several ways. On the one hand, there was little open revolt against Manila, because non-patronage officers saw their loyalty not to the person of the commander-in-chief, which Marcos was by law, but to the constitutional reality of the office and to the military (or security forces) as an institution with a code of non-interference in "civilian" affairs. Commanders in the field continued to function, because they believed their ultimate duty was not to a regime but to a code. On the other hand, such focus on the code, openly violated by Marcos and those around him, led many "younger" non-patronage officers to form the RAM ("Reform AFP Movement"), a secret organization, dominated by PMA graduates, dedicated to reasserting professional ideals. At its forefront were field commanders who believed matters could not continue as they had been for much longer.[34]

Marcos recognized the potential for subversion of an organization such as RAM, but he was too enmeshed in his own world to give it more than passing notice. Indeed, toward the end of his rule, he seemed all but oblivious to the realities in the countryside that were turning the officer corps against him.

As the Marcos regime's efficiency and legitimacy declined, there was a commensurate increase in the extent to which armed force, as represented by the seventy-odd, individual military battalions, became the crucial foundation on which the government's survival depended. This proved significant, because in the absence of any other viable government presence, the battalions became, like so many warlords, the rulers of their domains. Consequently, it was the peculiarities, strengths or weaknesses, of any battalion that influenced the situation in its area of operations nearly as much as the socio-economic-political conditions that had given rise to the revolt. For at no time was the NPA, in any area of the archipelago, able to achieve a concentration of strength such that government forces could not appear at will. The result was that, even in those areas where the CPP had achieved local supremacy through its shadow organization, it could not develop a viable societal alternative to that which had existed previously. This had the effect of keeping the military aspects of the conflict salient, but in these the party simply could not compete with the government's greater resources, regardless of the substantial disadvantages under which the security forces operated.

Ultimately, the CPP drive, while it grew in numbers, stalled because of its inability to achieve true strategic parity. NPA units could not, even in the favorable strategic conditions provided by the corrupt Marcos regime, protect gains that had been made. The CPP, in other words, could not get the lynchpin of the regime, its armed forces, to crack. This placed the strategic campaign in the peculiar position of being heavily dependent on the most human of qualities, the leadership abilities of individual government commanders. These, by virtue of training and professional orientation, remained generally superior to those of its CPP opposition.

State Search for a New Approach

Essentially, then, it can be seen, Marcos manufactured the instrument of his own destruction. He had created the proverbial "two armies" noted by so many writers: a force in the capital for show, which played games unrelated to "the real world," and a force in the field that was in deadly earnest about its activities, a force that bore the casualties, frustrations, and hopes of the military.

With the assassination of Marcos's main rival, Benigno Aquino in August 1983 on his return to Manila, events took on a life of their own. Security force elements associated with Ver carried out the assassination; the resulting popular alienation and unrest proved irresistible. As discontent mounted, a snap election held in February 1986, conceived as a means for Marcos to demonstrate his popularity (and to please Washington), instead gave victory to the opposition led by Aquino's wife, Cory. When Marcos tried to reverse the outcome through electoral fraud, an estimated million people took to the streets of Manila and elsewhere. Early on, the masses were joined by Defense Minister Juan Ponce Enrile and PC Commander Fidel Ramos, who had reason to fear for their personal safety at Marcos's hands. The bulk of the officer corps, in any case, was ripe for defection. In his press conference, posturing during the crisis, Marcos could produce an array of patronage senior officers who publicly pronounced their support of the regime, yet neither the troops nor their real leaders, the field commanders, would follow these cronies.

When the explosion came in Manila, most battalion and brigade commanders had no loyalty to the regime. The crucial decision was that of Enrile and Ramos to back Mrs Aquino. This allowed the alienated, anti-patronage group in the officer corps to support the "reformists," as the anti-government forces became known, because it allowed them to act within the dictates of their professional code. The military rebels declared not a coup but support for what they claimed was the lawfully elected presidential candidate, Mrs Aquino. Most commanders consequently were willing to act in their corporate professional interests and did so, disobeying orders from the Marcos camp because they were "illegal." In the end, the defection of virtually all maneuver battalion and most brigade commanders to the "reformist" cause brought the regime down. Marcos's orders to move reinforcements to the capital, obeyed in some instances, were disregarded in most. Those troops that did arrive eventually defected. This kept the confrontation in Manila a relatively small and bloodless affair that could be settled by the masses in the streets. The "loyalist" facade crumbled.

For the military, this meant significant changes carried out at a rapid pace. Eventually, "Rocky" Ileto became Defense Secretary (after an initial tenure by Enrile); Ramos became AFP Chief of Staff (for a time the military referred to itself as the "New AFP" or NAFP); and Mison moved to Vice-chief of Staff. Extendees were retired quickly; leadership positions were given to combat veterans. In the first months after Marcos' ouster, some 80% of all major command positions changed hands. Training and personnel systems were revamped. The supply pipeline, freed in the main from the corrosive influence of corruption, again began to function, with considerable US assistance. Troop deployment posture was examined and modified. Most "palace guard" units in the capital were deployed to the field. Discipline and control over the militia forces was tightened. Further, the delicate process began of disarming the numerous private armies that had been allowed to flourish under Marcos.

As these military moves were carried out, the nature of the insurgency was transformed fundamentally by the "return" to democracy. A ceasefire with the CPP was declared by the government effective on 10 December and lasted for sixty days. This controversial but necessary move demonstrated once and for all that the CPP sought not reform but revolution.

Debate on the merits of entering into the ceasefire had dominated the Manila political scene for months prior to implementation. Arrayed on one side within the government had been those in favor of pursuing the peace initiative, a group including Mrs Aquino and her closest advisors, many of whom had pronounced "progressive" sympathies after years in opposition to Marcos. In the other corner were the conservative elements, typified by Defense Minister Enrile, soon to leave the administration and become an opposition senator. The conservatives opposed the truce not in principle but as it was implemented. They saw it as little more than a communist tactical ploy designed to allow the CPP to rest and regroup.

In the event, they were correct. The CPP had never had any illusions that the ceasefire would provide more than a respite. Forced onto the defensive by Marcos's sudden and unexpected ouster, the CPP saw the truce as a means to avoid being isolated from popular sentiment and to regain the initiative. Specifically, the party recognized that it had stumbled badly by refusing to participate in the 1986 election that precipitated the regime's demise. Subsequently, after decades of justifying its insurgency in terms of opposition to the "US-Marcos Dictatorship," it suddenly found itself having to explain its continued existence in a post-Marcos era dominated center-stage by a tremendously popular, democratically elected leader dedicated to the very causes of social and economic justice the communists claimed their own.

Disunity appeared in the CPP ranks, with different groups striking out independently in their search for an approach to the Aquino phenomenon. After much discussion, the CPP leadership declared that intra-party unity and future success could best be assured by giving in to the strong public sentiment for a ceasefire and exploration of reconciliation. Such a hiatus would not only avoid the party's being branded "anti-peace" but would also allow it to rectify the glaring organizational weaknesses revealed in February 1986.

The CPP, the logic went, had been unable to take advantage of rapid political developments in February 1986 because it had not sufficiently developed its urban components. Extensive though the infrastructure was in built-up areas, it was not yet a stand-alone weapon but an overwhelmingly political phenomenon designed to support party activities in the countryside rather than make an independent contribution of its own. It was particularly weak in the armed force it could muster. When the window of opportunity appeared, therefore, it could not put the trained, armed manpower on the streets as needed to assure itself a central role in developments. This was to be remedied by stepping up as much as possible urban recruitment activities by fronts and by illegal, underground organizations. When a chaotic political situation again developed, as the CPP felt it would due to the left *versus* right strains present in the Aquino government, the communists would be ready to put their own legions into the forefront of the struggle, allegedly in support of democracy against attempts to restore the dictatorship.

A ceasefire, which necessarily involved freedom of movement and unrestricted political activity, was obviously the best environment in which to carry out such a plan. The communists pragmatically supported Aquino's truce initiative, all the while dickering over technicalities so as to achieve the best terms possible. "The revolutionary movement is most capable in maximizing its gains in a generally open democratic space," noted the analysis contained in "Some Notes on the Issue of Ceasefire," the product of a policy review conducted by high-ranking CPP cadre on 5 July 1986. "We are most capable in organizing and mobilizing the people and in taking advantage of the socio-economic programs that may be set [up] by the civilian government [of Mrs Aquino]."[35]

To that end, party political workers were directed to press on with recruiting and organization efforts. The NDF was given the lead role in this. The effort to conceal ultimate CPP authority and intentions meant that ceasefire negotiations and activities were carried out by, and in the field allegedly implemented on behalf of, the NDF. The NDF even claimed that the CPP was but the leading organization of the NDF's co-equal constituent members and that the NPA was the NDF's armed forces. Such, of course, was far from the case. As already noted, the NDF had been created by the CPP in 1973, as had been the NPA some years earlier. Both took orders directly from the party leadership. But by allowing the NDF heads to appear in public—many NDF personalities were reasonably well-known personalities of various backgrounds who had crossed over to the insurgent camp in opposition to the Marcos regime—the CPP sought to foster the image it wished to project, that of the abused driven to armed revolt by societal injustice and government repression. The real leadership, the CPP hierarchy, was not forced to subject itself to public scrutiny.

As was the case with political operatives so, too, were combatants told to go about their normal duties but to avoid firefights (called "encounters" by both sides) that might endanger the ceasefire. "The struggle will continue," an 18-year old former Political Organizing Team member observed. Until his capture in early November 1986, he had been charged with recruiting villagers in northern Samar, at that time a point of emphasis in the CPP effort. He went on:

> We were directed to continue politicization even during a ceasefire so as to get a bigger group. We were told not to trust the government about ceasefire talks. Cory Aquino is still the same as Marcos. She is rich. She still belongs to the higher class. So the way she will run the government will be the same.[36]

The other prime actor in carrying out the ceasefire, the military, was aware of this strategy and felt strongly that the ultimate effect of the ceasefire would be to increase CPP capabilities. Stated "Post-Revolution [February 1986] Communist Strategy in the Philippines: Indicators and Potential," a Ministry of National Defense Document distributed to all units in August 1986:

> THE NDF/CPP/NPA have said and continue to say that although Marcos has been deposed, the warlords and the unjust colonial imperialistic structures still remain, and therefore the parliamentary/armed struggle must continue and even be intensified (in order to attain the NDF/CPP/NPA objective of having a communist government to finally "liberate" the Filipino people).[37]

In their press conferences held in Manila, NDF representatives were boldly saying as much. "Now," the document concluded, "the enemies (NDF/CPP/NPA and affiliates) are waging 'total war' [through political and military means] against President Aquino, her government, and the Filipino people."[38]

Although they could not know it at the time, the military had been far more accurate than it realized in its assessment. To recap briefly: What ruined the favorable strategic situation for the CPP was the February 1986 overthrow of Marcos's corrupt regime. In a single blow, the party was robbed of its greatest recruiting asset. Additionally, having boycotted the national election that precipitated the "Edsa Revolution," the CPP was not a player in the mass uprising. Political events were developing at such a rate that they outran the party's ability to react. To get into the game, argued a group within the CPP, required "rectification" of past errors, specifically the failure to exploit fully the opportunities for mass organizing afforded by "democratic space." Thus resulted the 60-day ceasefire that began in December 1986. Able to regroup unhindered as representatives of its leadership, in their NDF guise, met with the government and appeared on TV talk-shows, the CPP emerged from the ceasefire greatly strengthened; in early 1987 government order-of-battle figures put the NPA at its high, 25,200 combatants. At this point, however, it misread the situation and blundered into "total war."

Colonel George Vallejera recounted some time later, while serving as a division operations officer on Negros:

What happened was that the communists made a fundamental error. They underestimated the situation. Because they were able to grow 100 percent in the immediate aftermath of February 1986, they thought their moment had come. They therefore pushed for advantage. They began to experiment with more aggressive tactics, in particular in Bicol [in the extreme south of Luzon Island]. But they hadn't thought the business through thoroughly. What resulted was that they caused all sorts of problems for the people. And the people reacted very negatively. Who gets hurt if infrastructure is destroyed? Who gets hurt if an area is cut off from Manila? The people turned on them [the communists]. We had a dramatic increase in intelligence. It has never stopped.

Now there is an internal struggle in the CPP over what strategy to follow. The 'hardliners,' those who favor the more aggressive stance, appear to have the upper hand over the 'moderates,' those who want to keep organizing. The hardliners look at the examples of Vietnam and Nicaragua, and they think that they have reached strategic stalemate, the phase of [Maoist] insurgency when the guerrillas can battle the government on its

163

own terms and protect "liberated" territory. But they're not even close, so their tactics are not appropriate to the strategic situation.[39]

Tactics appropriate to the situation: George Vallejera, eventually a brigadier general, was one of the Philippine Army's (PA) finest field soldiers. He and his fellow officers were able to combine astute analysis of the insurgents with appropriate operational implementation, thus to provide the shield behind which democracy was restored. (Marks photo)

Unintentionally, the CPP "moderates" attempted to make the same argument as Colonel Vallejera. Rather than a heightened military posture, they argued, "democratic space" provided the ideal medium for continued clandestine organizing and use of fronts. Numerous purges resulted. The grim fallout was to be found in mass graves discovered in many areas by security forces and villagers. In the end, the hardliners were victorious. Their ascendance brought about a more active CPP military posture. Captured CPP directives called for emphasis on "regularization" (i.e., creating standardized units), forming larger formations, upping the tempo of military operations, arming soldiers with heavy weapons, increased front activity, greater use of mines and booby traps, and greater use of sparrow squads for assassinations. Further, the CPP wanted to hold territory through formation of "fighting villages." This last directive was part of a larger CPP campaign to achieve international recognition and belligerent status for its combatants.

Upping the military tempo would have been a mistake on its own terms. NPA formations were nowhere near the point where they could stand and go toe-to-toe with the Philippine military. More fundamentally, however, the Achilles heel in such an approach was that it pushed to the fore military considerations in what was, after all, a political war.

The reintroduction of politics into Philippine life was what made this CPP shift such a blunder. In the years following February 1986, elections, so long delayed or rigged by Marcos, were held at all levels, to include municipality (county) and village. The result was that throughout the country there existed mechanisms for expressing the popular will. Imperfect though they were, these began to shape the socio-economic environment by addressing longstanding development concerns and demands for social justice. They could do this due to the federal structure of the nation, which devolved authority to an extent unusual for a developing country. More important than immediate results was the feeling among the populace that non-violent avenues were available for interest articulation and realization. The CPP's ability to appeal to economic and political dissatisfaction was thus dealt a severe blow. Coming as it did when the party was pushing its hard-line strategy, enforced by liquidations of recalcitrant CPP elements throughout the archipelago, this development led to an increased flow of surrenders. In interviews with them, analysts were often struck by their classic "grievance guerrilla" profiles. They had given up precisely because the hard-line approach contradicted their concern for social justice.[40]

One major labor organizer on Negros, Manuel Jurada or "Bunny," a CPP member with District Secretary rank, put this in perspective when he spoke of direct, face-to-face orders delivered by the ranking CPP men on Negros (one a former priest, Francisco Fernandez) to stop engaging in union activities that would better the lot of the workers. "Bunny" was admonished that sharpening the contradictions was what he was supposed to be about, not helping the system perpetuate itself through reform. Noted "Bunny," then aged 39:

> Whenever there is a problem [between the workers and the landlords], we're not supposed to talk but to intensify the struggle through strikes, economic sabotage, and so on. If there is an intensification of mass action, it is complemented by armed struggle. That's what the CPP wants to happen. The higher organ wants people to be engaged in mass action so that attention will be directed from the countryside to the urban areas.[41]

Such a CPP line was hardly new to students of the movement, but for "Bunny" it was a revelation of gut-wrenching proportions: If social justice was not the issue, what was? The answer, as those who followed the CPP knew, was that the party was after the communist version of social justice. And that involved doing whatever was necessary tactically to gain strategic victory, defined as communist political power. Old Lenin, to be sure, but new for "Bunny." He surrendered.

Philippine State Wages People's War

Ironically, the CPP turn toward increased violence came even as the government embraced the primacy of political factors. Beginning in 1988 but adopted formally in 1989 with OPLAN (operations plan) *Lambat Betag* ("Net Trap"), the Philippine military moved from a "search-and-destroy" philosophy to one dominated by the identification and destruction of the CPP counter-state. This was a fundamental reorientation of strategy and married a correct military approach with popular support for the revitalized political structure even as the CPP adopted an incorrect military approach amidst a loss of political legitimacy. The results were devastating for the party. As early as 1990, the communists found themselves unable to replace lost manpower or to generate a viable approach capable of dealing with "democratic space." In the four-plus years that followed the ouster of Marcos, the party, by its own count, contracted from 73 to 56 Fighting Fronts. In some areas, such as Negros, CPP documents revealed a 50% loss of "mass base." Key CPP/NDF/NPA leaders were captured with such regularity that the Politburo and Central Committee went deep underground, even declining to give their customary briefings to the foreign press.

This switch by the government, of course, had not "just happened." Rather, it was a direct outgrowth of the wholesale change in personalities that followed Marcos's departure. As field commanders moved into planning positions, they sought a new direction. Crucial to the process were the ideas of Victor Corpus, PMA '67. In 1970, as a junior officer in an elite PC unit, he had created a sensation by defecting to the CPP. There he was instrumental in making the fledging NPA a going concern. Six years later, however, disillusioned with the party, he returned to the government fold, only to be imprisoned for ten years. Released when Marcos was ousted from power in February 1986, and later reinstated in the military as a lieutenant colonel, he became the central force in radically re-orienting Philippine counter-insurgency away from its emphasis on military operations. Instead, the weight of effort went to socio-economic-political development.

166

Re-orientation began with Corpuz' assignment, after his release, as a consultant to a Ministry of National Defense counter-insurgency study group that included a number of key RAM members. Later, in October 1987, with RAM in disarray following its abortive coup efforts against what it perceived to be a bumbling, hapless Aquino government, he moved to the Combat Research Division of AFP Operations (J3). Working for Colonel Clemente Moriano, Corpuz and a number of other officers, on a team tasked with formulating strategic ideas, went around the country trading ideas with commanders and subordinates. In many areas, such as that of the 4th Infantry Division on Mindanao, they found a version of what they had in mind already being used. There, a relatively low-ranking officer, Captain Alex Congman, was credited with implementing a "Special Operations Team" (SOT) concept that reverse engineered the CPP's infrastructure. That is, government SOTs performed the same function as the CPP's armed propaganda units, followed by the counter-mobilization of the target area in support of the government. And on Negros, Brigadier-General Rene Cardones, who assumed command of that embattled island shortly after Marcos's fall, had by mid-1988 moved this counter-mobilization approach to perhaps its most developed form of any area in the Philippines.[42] That the people could be counter-mobilized, of course, was because the political environment had changed for the better. Thus it was the government that represented social justice rather than the CPP. Congman's simple concept had grown ultimately into a broader "triad strategy" adopted by the entire army. It gave equal importance to military operations, intelligence, and civic action within an overarching development effort by elected officials. This "triad strategy" was worked into a final campaign plan, a "war of quick decision," that was presented by the Corpuz study group in April 1988 to a commanders' conference.[43]

At first, the plan, which called for intensive anti-infrastructure operations against a prioritized list of CPP Fighting Fronts, an oil-spot technique waged at the operational level, met with a lukewarm response. Rotation to the Chief of Operations (J3) position, however, of Brigadier-General Lisandro Abadia tipped the scales in its favor. For it had been under Abadia that the SOT concept had originally been given a chance to prove itself. The result was that the new *Lambat Betag* was completed by late 1988. The following year, 1989, was in effect to be a trial run for the plan, a preparatory phase during which SOTs and other anti-infrastructure personnel were tested, but the AFP decided the situation warranted immediate implementation. As noted above, the results were rapid and dramatic, more so because Abadia eventually became army head. As Corpuz later said in an interview: "If we can maintain the democratic system the Communist Party of the Philippines is indeed a spent force."[44]

It is noteworthy that the Filipinos had, in a sense, reinvented the wheel. Their approach incorporated those elements that other successful counter-insurgencies had found necessary for victory, yet they had been arrived at independent of foreign advice or assistance. The American presence, for example, so often portrayed by both the Western media and the CPP as crucial to Manila, was actually most important in a material and financial sense. It added very little doctrinally. In terms of intelligence, too, the major American contribution was technical, particularly in interception of CPP signals and the breaking of codes, rather than operational.

Observed Corpuz:

> We drew mostly on my experience. We didn't refer to any books. We had read the US manuals on low intensity conflict, but we blamed those manuals for introducing COIN [counter-insurgency] doctrines that only aggravated the situation. They apply conventional methods to an unconventional situation. In particular, traditional civic action is a mere palliative. It does not go to the root causes of the problem, to the lack of democracy.[45]

Operationally, getting to the "root causes of the problem" translated into the formula "clear, hold, consolidate, and develop." To reclaim an area, the government moved in with its troops (again, the battalion formed the basic building block) and destroyed or drove out resident NPA units. Overwhelming force was mustered to ensure that this was invariably the case. Once this had been done, the government battalion concerned remained in control of the area while it uncovered and dismantled the communist counter-state. Simultaneously, a government intelligence net was set up, and citizens were organized into militias to defend the area. Each militia detachment guarded its village and outlying hamlets and was controlled by several regular government soldiers. Eventually, when security had been reestablished, government officials could come in to supervise normal functions and development efforts. The militia continued to perform security and patrol duties throughout and day and night, working in shifts. Just in case the communists tried to return in force, part of every battalion was kept at all times in reserve as a strike force. Finally, Special Forces control teams took over handling the militia, and the battalion moved on to the next area to be won back.

Central to the approach was providing the security that allowed elected government to function and to address socio-economic concerns. Most of the counter-state could be rendered impotent simply by exposure, precisely because "grievance guerrillas" were at the heart of the CPP movement and responded to decent treatment within the context of the new political and economic environment. The shift in popular attitude was palpable. With it came a decrease in the difficulty government agents had in penetrating the CPP apparatus. The CPP responded with bloody purges to weed out alleged infiltrators. This only drove still more of its members to surrender.

Most important, cutting off the CPP from its mass base was far more than simply a mechanical exercise in neutralizing the movement's infrastructure. In the absence of reform, to eliminate the fundamental grievances that had driven individuals to seek redress through armed struggle, new cells would have constantly sprung up. Traditional "civic action" (digging wells, providing medical treatment, and so forth) was but a band-aid, as Corpuz noted. Root causes had to be attacked. The only way this could occur was if there were mechanisms that allowed the population a role in their own lives. Democracy was one of the best such mechanisms.

Clear, hold, consolidate, and develop: A battalion commander on Negros in 1988 speaks to assembled villagers concerning mechanics of local democracy. SOT members are evident in the crowd. Military provision of a shield behind which local government could function was the decisive element in decimation of the CPP. Its mass base deserted in droves. (Marks photo)

The result was that in the decade's closing years the government, as represented by the military working with civilian authority, was moving to "eliminate the grievances" even as the CPP opted for gun-slinging. As a growing number of individuals returned to areas of greater government presence, they flowed into the militia for self-protection. This was a turning-point. So often portrayed in foreign activist media as little more than thugs and the dregs of society, the militia became the ultimate Maoist nightmare: the people numerous and armed. Evidence of the degree to which the CPP was feeling the bite of this trend could be seen in its stepped up domestic and international campaigns to paint the Philippine government, and especially the militia, as guilty of widespread human rights violations. Extra-legal killings were certainly carried out by government supporters, but best evidence showed such activities to pale in numbers when compared to the institutionalized violence of the CPP (the left's "structural violence" argument turned on its head). The government recognized that control over militia activities was critical to prevent the abuses that figured prominently in frequent criticism of the Marcos-era counter-insurgency

The people numerous and armed: Local patrol on Negros. CPP miscalculation caused the people to rise up against the Party's terror. Particularly startling was that large proportions of the government's local forces were comprised of former members of the CPP counter-state, who now sought to protect themselves from their former comrades. (Marks photo)

effort. Obviously, such control was achieved in the main. On the communist side, with its heightened emphasis on violence, it was not. Everywhere, refugees, asked why they had "come in," answered with two responses: "We can no longer take the [CPP's] taxes. We can no longer take the [CPP's] violence."[46] There was the CPP's miscalculation in a nutshell. Its strategy of increased exploitation of the people and violence ignored the desire for justice that had been the fundamental driving force at the heart of the Philippine insurgency, the force that had allowed a committed communist leadership to recruit non-ideological peasant manpower. The return of the political process to the Philippine people allowed justice to be pursued and made the exercise of politics itself the ultimate government weapon.

Terror and the Counter-State

Ironically, even as the CPP contracted, with its Fighting Fronts, for instance, declining from more than 70 to less than 50 as the 1990s began,[47] violence continued. This was predictable. Two forces were at work: one, bureaucratic process; the other, tactical. Bureaucratically, with the firm establishment of sparrows as regular components of the CPP/NPA's structure, assassinations became a normal operation. Consequently, numbers of victims jumped as the units became better established. Tactically, as the CPP came under government pressure, there emerged the need to deal more forcefully with those who would endanger the counter-state.

These realities highlighted, as in the Thai case, the importance of scale and the changing relationship between the elements of terror, recruitment, and infrastructure. The Philippines was sufficiently large and diverse to have innumerable "marginal" areas in which subversive political activity could operate with minimal fear of government intervention. For a good part of its existence, therefore, the CPP was often able to expand its political sway mainly through persuasion. The counter-state was, in a very real, the only political game in town: "political space" complemented physical space. If areas were not already physically isolated from Manila's writ, they were bound to be politically estranged by their hostility to the repression and corruption that flourished during the Marcos era. The CPP was able to mobilize manpower by emphasizing resistance to oppression.

Nevertheless, the very incompetence of the Marcos regime, which made repression haphazard and not particularly universal, left vulnerable a CPP stance largely based on opposition. Even before the actual re-establishment of democratic process, therefore, political space became far more restricted, as an increasing number of

171

contenders jostled one another in advancing their claims to political support. The moment inevitably came, in area after area, when further CPP expansion, as well as the consolidation of those gains already made, could take place only in the face of opposition. Increasingly, the CPP leadership, once it was no longer the only viable option for those who sought to engage in politics, found itself judged and opposed for the shortcomings of its communist agenda. Yet as a clandestine, proscribed political body, the party could respond in but one fashion to those who questioned it: with violence. This was inevitable, for the counter-state could not allow resistance or uncertain commitment if it was to survive, much less flourish.

In striking out, however, the CPP made the fateful transition from messenger to message. The mechanisms of organization, of the counter-state, shifted from being a tool to being an end unto themselves. Put simply, an alternative body, the CPP, had come into existence. Those who joined it no longer did so purely, or even in the main, in response to grievances, but instead for a more complex mixture of motives. These ranged from desire for advancement to fear.

Terror played an important role. Those who tried to resist, or were simply unwilling to cooperate, disappeared. How widespread such practices were remains a matter not fully explored, but it seems clear that the scope of CPP terror was substantial. *Time* magazine correspondent Ross H. Munro threw the issue on the table in 1985 with his "The New Khmer Rouge" in the December issue of *Commentary*.[48] There, he set forth in some detail the extent to which terror had become an integral part of the CPP/NPA/NDF campaign. This did not surprise security analysts, but the price came as a shock to those accustomed to seeing the NPA as "Nice People Around," as they were ostensibly called by villagers. The debate that followed was useful, because it stripped away many of the Robin Hood myths that had grown up around the NPA.

Intimidation and coercion are inherent in any armed campaign to seize power. The Philippine communists were no exception. A CPP document examined[49] shortly after it was captured in February 1986 in Northern Samar Province serves to illustrate this. It included a table listing the number of "counter-revolutionaries" executed in the Northern Fighting Front in Samar during 1985. They totaled 62, all civilians. Another table listed 17 sparrow assassinations, for a total of 79 civilian murders in only a lightly populated third of Samar Island. By contrast, government reports for the same period listed only 85 deaths among security force personnel for all of Samar and Leyte, which were under the single military RUC-8.[50] Obviously, the CPP was devoting more time to killing civilians than to attacking the military and police.

Even more detailed CPP records had been captured in mid-1985 on Leyte Island.[51] In the first half of the year, 60 Filipinos, mainly suspected informers, were listed by name as having been killed in the Southern Leyte Fighting Front, one of the two CPP fronts on the island. Another 129 people were listed as liquidation targets. Most of the condemned were ordinary villagers. In macabre fashion, the operations to kill both these people and suspected spies within the party were codenamed *Linis*, meaning "clean" or "cleanse."

What is striking in these figures is not the numbers *per se* but rather the comparative scale. Assassinations were driving the movement. Also significant was the dominance, in the 1985 figures, of liquidations carried out by regular insurgent personnel as opposed to sparrow squads. For in 1985 sparrows were still a relatively untested innovation. As the sparrows became more established, their proportion of liquidations rose.

Statistics to shed more light on this particular aspect of the struggle were hard to come by, because it was difficult to determine precisely which NPA units were responsible for particular assassinations. It could be established, however, judging by the manner of death, that a high proportion of security force casualties in the post-Marcos era were due to attempted assassinations. Nevertheless, no matter how the numbers were crunched, the fact remained that "counter-revolutionary" civilians continued to be the principal CPP targets. Police records and captured documents examined in 1988, for example, revealed that 128 persons had been assassinated on Negros during the first half of that year. Only 28 of these were members of the security forces (11 soldiers, 5 policemen, and 12 militiamen). The other hundred were civilians. Total security force deaths due to combat operations were 95 (34 army, 8 police, and 53 militia).[52]

This reality ultimately backfired on the CPP. As its terror reached unbearable proportions, the masses began to turn away from the party, even in some of its previously most solidly held areas. The result was that many, when offered the opportunity, joined the government militia. Terror had clearly overreached itself.

In this respect, it must again be emphasized that all things are relative. Terror succeeds not because of the numbers it mows down but because of the fear it engenders. The reverse is also true in causing the populace to feel that enough is enough. Consider the discussion in early December 1988 with Honeylee Pama aka "Ibon," aged 26, head of the Educational Staff for the CPP's District 2 on Negros (see Figure 4.7). Captured during an encounter with government forces, the unexpected end of her career as a party member came when she was already wavering in her ideological faith. "It was the killings," she stated, which had shaken her commitment to the movement. When asked how many people she knew about who had been liquidated, she said about ten. When I protested that ten people killed in her district (Negros was divided into seven such roughly equivalent CPP areas) hardly seemed like a lot, she responded emphatically, "That's a lot to me!"[53]

Similarly, a platoon political officer, 27-year old Panangganan Feliciano aka "Katagar," who worked in District 1, responded, when asked what had motivated him to surrender:

> We can no longer keep on killing people whom we don't even know. For what reasons? . . . We kill *Alsa Masa* [militia], suspected informers, local officials—for example, a mayor who enforces the program·of the government—police, soldiers. At first we were told to kill just erring civilians and abusive personalities. Now there is even a CPP/NPA program to hold up commercial vehicles and business establishments. We [my platoon] didn't like this, so we didn't do it.[54]

Both these young people were making overwhelming points. Several years later, in 1990, in the newly recaptured CHICKS region of Negros previously the CPP stronghold on the island, roughly the areas comprised of Districts 1 and 2 in Figure 4.7, I encountered an even more vivid illustration. (The name CHICKS is an acronym formed by the first letters of the major town names in the area). I was attempting to ascertain why so many people had joined the government militia. At the time, it outnumbered the regulars in the region by better than 2:1 (and by nearly 4:1 when Negros as a whole was considered). Whatever the particulars of each individual's tale, the common denominator was the inability to live any longer with CPP terror. Of more than a dozen individuals interviewed in detail, every one could give, by name, at least five personal acquaintances who had been liquidated. A majority had witnessed at least some of the killings they listed.

While questioning the individuals and noting the names they gave, I endeavored to cross-check the identities. Otherwise, all I had was a list of unknown validity. Who were these people who were killed? Why did their deaths have such an impact on the populace? It soon became clear. Asked why he had joined the militia, Tachio Tabano, aged 19, a peasant who was one of 11 siblings, responded: "The communists took my father away, claiming he was a counter-revolutionary. I will avenge the death of my father. We were a very close family."[55] Relatives, friends, acquaintances . . . at times there seemed to be no end to such stories. I asked a relatively high-ranking former CPP official about the coincidence of his surname with that of one of the victims he named. Did he know him? Yes, he answered. I

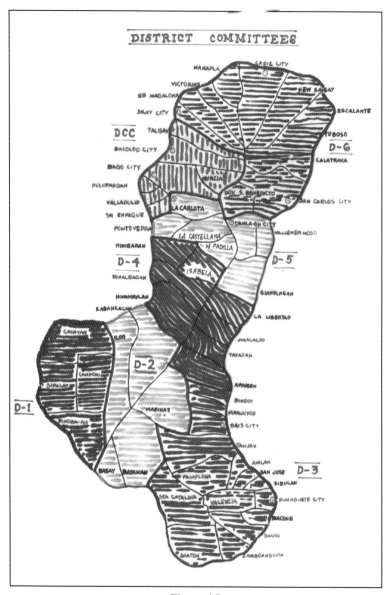

Figure 4.7

did not push the point. Later, a contact pointed out that the executed man was the party official's brother.

This former cadre was clearly troubled by what he had witnessed:

> The communists killed six people I knew. The NPA unit did it; I was not consulted. Out of the six, two were tried by the higher organs. Of these, I was informed. I saw all six killed, shot. One was accused of supporting the military, but I know this was not true. Others were accused of being thieves, robbers, but actually they were not. False accusations were made as a result of quarrels. If you've been accused of *counter-revolution*, they don't check. I wanted these atrocities to end. They had no pity. They were killing us without mercy. The government system is better. I joined CAFGU [the militia] to keep these people from returning. That is their main objective.[56]

As though speaking for the whole community, William Labrador, aged 48, a farmer with "one week of Grade 1 education" and a single child, stated:

> Under the communists, I could not do other work to support my family. I was only a robot. The communists told us what work we could do. If you're not cooperative, they kill you. Also, anyone caught close to the military is suspected of being an agent or a sympathizer of the military [and killed]. There was no court. It was completely arbitrary. I actually saw three people stabbed to death by the [CPP] district leader. I saw this. I pitied them. But we could do nothing, because we had no arms.[57]

Even as we spoke, it was clear that this situation had changed. About us clustered numerous individuals with weapons, each with a similar tale. Labrador's views were doubly potent, because he, as with many others of the militia, had previously been a member of the CPP's clandestine apparatus. Obviously, the worst nightmare of the CPP "people's war" had come to pass. The people had obtained weapons and had risen up—on the government side. There was considerable irony at work here. Marcos had made the mistake of stifling the political system even as government repression had increased. This produced a popular backlash that the CPP had been able to exploit. Yet for all the talk of Marcos regime "salvaging" (death squad activity) and filling "mass graves" (of government opponents) and maintaining a veritable *gulag* (of anti-government detainees), no startling revelations or discoveries emerged in the years following the restoration of democracy (or have since). Indeed, *all* of the mass graves uncovered turned out to be the work of the CPP purging its own ranks.[58]

This is not to say that government repression did not exist. It did. It is to say, however, that it was not of such magnitude in and of itself to stir the masses to action in the absence of political outlets for expression of grievances. Once these outlets were restored and government abuses curtailed, the CPP found that its own terror, which previously could be excused as due to the exigencies of the situation, was intolerable to the populace.

CPP Down for the Count

With hindsight it is possible to recognize the CPP's miscalculation. Less clear, however, is why the situation came to pass. Why, in other words, did the CPP opt for a strategy that seemed sure to backfire? Why did the ideologues, those favoring the armed approach, win out? Earlier, Noel Albano observed the way in which repression drove the "best and the brightest" of Filipino youth into the CPP's arms. The importance of Philippine geography was also highlighted, for it allowed a decentralization within which newcomers could each find his platform by achieving organizational success in the "outer islands." These same individuals could then come back and reinvigorate the center's strategic thinking. With the assassination of Benigno Aquino, however, a revitalized "legal opposition" of sorts developed abroad and in the Philippines. This, combined with the oft-documented change in attitudes on the part of the students of the 1980s, an emphasis away from activism and toward intra-systemic career concerns (a worldwide phenomenon, just as the student activism of the late 1960s and early 1970s was), meant that the bulk of politically motivated young people articulated their political demands in forums other than the CPP.

This trend was consummated by the ouster of Marcos and the regeneration of the Philippine political process, flawed though it might appear. Further, the removal of the visible "anti-Marcos" catalyst caused many would-be activists to return to their books and such. This was clearly visible in the leadership ranks of students protests in the late 1980s, where the traditional University of the Philippines (UP) dominance gave way to individuals from smaller campuses, individuals who simply did not have the organizational skills and broad outlook that was developed through activist work on the massive UP campuses. The result was that beginning in 1983 the CPP began to receive little "new blood" from the most vibrant intellectual sector of Philippine society. Instead, its new leaders came from within the movement or from particular sectors, such as the clergy, which had been influenced by unique factors. Predictably, intellectual stagnation set in, the results of which could be seen in the lack of CPP strategic vision.[59]

In contrast, government leadership ranks were revitalized. The changeover within the civilian administration requires no comment; that within the military has been recognized several times. Thus there developed a situation of "new blood" facing "old," if the conflict could be seen, at least in part, from such an angle. What kept the positive trend from becoming more pronounced during Mrs Aquino's six-year tenure was the lack of government unity of effort. It took the military three years after February 1986 to come to an institutionally agreed on consensus on the conflict's nature. Further, impatient at the pace of reform, military elements, led by RAM members, made half a dozen coup attempts. It could be said that the central government in Manila never did reach an understanding of "counter-insurgency."

Fortunately for Manila, in the provinces the federal nature of the political system allowed the military to work, closely and normally harmoniously, with the civil authorities. This trend was solidified as local pressures on the center led to a greater devolution of funding prerogatives, thereby making greater resources for the "develop" phase of *Lambat Betag*. Unable to deal with the government threat on the ground, the CPP attempted to undermine it through propaganda, particularly emphasis on alleged human rights violations. Domestically, the party was still able to get help from sympathetic members of cause-oriented groups. Internationally, too, solidarity groups gave not only moral backing but also financial resources. The NDF located its headquarters in the Netherlands, the better to exploit the tendency of so many international cause-oriented groups to think little but ill of a Third World government such as that of the Philippines. Prime NDF goal, and that of its fellow travelers, was to get foreign aid to Manila cut off. All that was needed, they analyzed, was enough "information" that would portray the government in the worst possible light.

Certainly this was not hard to come by. The post-Marcos Philippine government could not objectively be judged as repressive, but it was terribly inefficient.[60] Consequently, there was no shortage of heartrending human "drama of survival" to stir up condemnation. So as to leave nothing to chance, explicit instructions went out from the CPP Politburo outlining the use of certain schemes, such as "the Evacuation," as tactical ploys. In this latter maneuver, detailed plans were prepared in advance for the "flight" of refugees from areas of government operations. Rallying points were designated, demands were rehearsed, and control personnel were assigned to ensure there were no backsliders. As soon as government troops began a maneuver, an evacuation or another human rights ploy would be launched, just as would any weapons system. The point, of course, was to attempt to disrupt government operations, while simultaneously gaining as much propaganda mileage as possible.

Unfortunately for the CPP, no combination of approaches proved able to blunt the government effort. By 1993 its Fighting Fronts had declined to 42. Even the NDF found itself stymied in its efforts to continue the struggle by co-opting participants in the open political process.

There has also always been the problem for the CPP that, despite its acknowledged organizational finesse, it is operating in the Philippines. Hence, Philippine societal particulars resulted in a movement at once clandestine yet remarkably open, subject not only to penetration by government agents but also to "retirement" by its members. When a Filipino guerrilla decided he had had enough, he simply left the fight. Increasing pressure from church and family has caused growing numbers of rebels to opt out of the struggle and would-be guerrillas to look elsewhere for the redress of grievances. The result was the virtual inclusion of the CPP as a legitimate-but-illegitimate element of the societal calculus, even if a misguided and frowned upon one. CPP leaders aired their views, hopes, and dreams, and even their dirty laundry, nearly as publicly as any Philippine politician.

In the field, of course, people continued to die. In Manila, the Alex Boncayao Brigade, a separate sparrow unit that operated semi-independently, assassinated approximately sixty soldiers, police, and civilians in the first five months of 1991 alone. Yet "the war" remained one of relative scale. As normalcy began to return to numerous, widespread areas, it was unsurprising that quiet optimism surrounded the work of the Ramos-appointed National Unification Commission (NUC). Headed by law professor Haydee Yorac, it was charged with drawing up a comprehensive package for reconciliation acceptable to all. A group calling itself "Warriors for Peace," with members drawn from both former AFP and CPP personnel, even went about the hinterland preaching harmony and peaceful resolution of conflict.

Attempting to play the spoiler was CPP founder and current self-proclaimed party head, Jose Maria Sison. Imprisoned for a decade during the Marcos regime (he had been captured in 1977) but freed in the amnesty that accompanied the return to democracy, "Joma" quickly resumed his activities, setting up shop with a number of other released CPP personnel in the Netherlands. He did not attempt formally to reassert control of the party, however, until the 10th Plenum of the Central Committee in July 1992. His move was prompted by what he saw as a dangerous drift from the correct Maoist "people's war" approach of encircling the cities from the countryside to a strategy favoring a mix of techniques inspired by other approaches, notably the Vietnamese and Nicaraguan. These, Sison denounced in a key document, dated 26 December 1991, *Reaffirm Our Basic Principles and Rectify Our Errors*.[61] He called instead for CPP members to "reaffirm their basic principles."

Thereafter, those who supported Sison were known as the "Reaffirmists" (RAs), those opposed as the Rejectionists (RJs). The most important figures amongst the latter were: the CPP "Secretary General" on the scene in the Philippines, Ricardo Reyes, who had come from the Mindanao Commission; the head of the Visayas Commission, Arturo Tabara; and another key Mindanao Commission figure, Rolando Kintanar. Their support base was not only that predicted by their organizational backgrounds, the Visayas and Mindanao, but also the important NDF organs of the Manila-Rizal Regional Committee. Sison, claiming the CPP leadership, launched a "rectification" campaign, and "renegade" regional headquarters were ordered to stand down.

These elements would have none of it. Pointing out that Sison had been elected by a "quorum" of just 8 of 44 Central Committee members, they deemed his elevation illegitimate and gave their loyalty to Ricardo Reyes. The split quickly grew into a breach, with Sison's support centered on those Luzon areas outside of Manila. Significantly, it was in these areas controlled by the RJs (Manila, the Visayas, and Mindanao) that most CPP strength lay.[62]

As befit the peculiar position of the CPP within the Philippine political structure at the time, neither side was reluctant to publicize its side of the issue. Perhaps predictably, the renegades were the more candid of the two. In a remarkable interview given in January 1993, Reyes observed:

> We had not even reached [strategic] stalemate after 20 years. A whole generation has aged. . . It looks like it is difficult to win. [We must ask ourselves] Why don't the people sympathize with us and [why] can't we capture the imagination of the younger generation? . . . There is that waning appeal, reflected very clearly in the data. Fewer and fewer are joining the New People's Army, fewer and fewer are joining the underground, especially the best and the brightest of the generations that followed in the 80s and 90s. . . That is fatal for a revolutionary movement, if you fail to inspire the young . . . and so we say, "Let us reexamine the strategy of encircling the cities from the countryside" . . . We even told him [Sison], "The flaw in your analysis is fundamental."[63]

Driving the debate, of course, were aspects of Marxist doctrine, specifically whether to interpret the Philippines as still "feudal," as Sison did, using the Maoist blueprint, or as a more developed form, as the renegades posited. In particular, pointed out the Reyes faction, the Philippines was no longer even predominantly rural, since a majority of the population, even in rural areas, lived in urban areas. And an increasing proportion earned its livelihood through multiple incomes, negating considerations of class consciousness and solidarity. In practical terms, the conclusion of the RJs was that the CPP's proper strategy should remain a dual urban-rural approach closer to that of the Sandinistas in their overthrow of Nicaragua's Antonio Somoza than to that of the Maoists in their seizure of China.

Ben Reid has accurately assessed the important operational issues involved:

> ...on more substantial matters the RJs were strongly critical of Sison's claims on insurrectionism, "premature regularization" and "urban basing." The Standing Group of the Visayas Commission argued that Sison's summing up of the experiences of the protracted people's war 'proceeds from a subjective assumption of a "left deviation" from the general strategy of protracted people's war... They denied that a singular trend to insurrectionism existed and instead what Sison refers to are numerous experiments conducted in the framework of protracted people's war. Moreover the Standing Group of the Visayas Commission claimed that the strategy of breaking down existing large military formations into small units would have made them even more vulnerable to attack by the Armed Forces of the Philippines... In an anonymous document a former leader of the Minacom [Mindanao Commission] added to this by stating that the particular tactics employed in Mindanao were products of highly specific circumstances and disputed that they had been exported to the national party centre [sic] by some means... Instead, they point out that the policies of the Strategic Counter Offensive and regular mobile warfare originated from the party centre [sic] rather than an outside 'insurrectionist' tendency... The same critic was also appalled by Sison's tendency to belittle the experiences of urban mass movement pioneered in Davao such as the *welga ng bayan* (people's strikes)... The MRRC [Manila-Rizal Regional Committee] challenged Liwanag [Sison] to substantiate his claims with reference to the Marxist understanding of insurrection. Another major concern of the MRRC was to repudiate claims of "urban basing." They pointed out that mass work in the urban areas had its "own dynamic" that required the devoting of cadres to mass organisations rather than being transferred to guerrilla fronts[64]

There followed, in 1993, formal proclamations of "autonomy" by the party organs opposed to Sison. These soon coalesced into two groupings. One had as its strength various organs of the NDF; the other in the party bodies of the capital region, which looked to the MRRC under Filemon "Popoy" Lagman, linked with the Visayas Commission headed by Arturo Tabara. The latter, however, was captured in 1994, along with virtually the entire breakaway leadership, thus adding further to the disintegration.

As the CPP tore itself apart organizationally, it collapsed in the field. Long listed in CPP documents as "the banners of the revolution," the most heavily communist-infiltrated islands, Negros and Samar in the Visayas, those on which the CPP once envisaged making a "last stand" if ever necessary, witnessed a virtual collapse of the insurgent infrastructure. By 1993, more than 80% of the mass base had defected, and NPA forces on the island were down to a single platoon. While the improvement of the situation on Negros came only after some years of intense operations, the Samar turnabout was largely bloodless, fallout from the continued evolution of the larger strategic dynamic. The security forces' greatest weapon was not the rifle but political warfare.

It was at this point, however, that the Philippines stumbled. Turning its attention to pressing matters of political and economic development put on hold in order to deal with the communists, the polity downgraded the threat to one of "law and order" rather than counter-insurgency. A fierce fight for the presidency in 1992 saw Fidel Ramos succeed Cory Aquino. The former's first order of business was economic development.[65] Although order-of-battle figures stated that the NPA, early in the Ramos tenure, still had 12,000 combatants in the field, this figure collapsed by 1994 to just over 6,000. Some sources put the number at fewer than 4,000. Consequently, emergency legislation was terminated, the CPP was declared a legal entity, and the Philippine National Police (PNP) were given total counter-insurgency responsibilities in 21 of the 74 provinces and several other smaller areas nationwide. Government figures listed the PNP as responsible for security in 30,000 villages as opposed to the 12,000 that remained the AFP's responsibility. Plans were well underway to turn over the entire counter-insurgency mission to the PNP as called for by law.[66]

In fact, it was only under a formal extension of authority, granted on PNP request due to the extraordinary circumstances yet prevailing in many areas, that the AFP continued to exercise primary counter-insurgency responsibility. Nevertheless, the law that had phased out the former Philippine Constabulary (PC) and merged its personnel with either the PNP or armed forces (virtually all personnel in the PC's numerous companies chose to become policemen rather than servicemen) stipulated that counter-insurgency would become a PNP task at the end of 1992. To carry out the cutting-edge functions hitherto done by the military, a police Special Action Force was formed, manned in large part by former PC members. The AFP's continued leading role hence operated on a year-to-year extension, with the military endeavoring to switch its focus to force modernization and the more conventional task of external defense. So changed was the overall security environment that some

Philippine Congressmen began to call for the abolition of the critical militia, the Citizen Armed Forces Geographical Units (CAFGU). Though the institution was not abolished, numbers in the "Regular CAFGU" were cut sharply, and the "strike force" capability embodied in the "Special CAFGU" was eliminated.

All of this, it should be further noted, coincided with the Philippine Senate's failure to ratify the Philippine American Cooperation Treaty of 1991 (PACT) and the consequent departure of the American presence. Overlooked in the Filipino rush to assert national prerogatives was the critical role the US had come to play in the country's defense posture, quite apart from the important American investment position. Put simply, during the critical years of the internal war, Washington had become the source of virtually "everything" with respect to the security forces save their pay and allowances. The resulting US departure left the Philippines in an extraordinarily vulnerable position, so that neither operations tempo nor force modernization could proceed apace.[67]

There was considerable irony that this occurred under the administration of the man who had been the armed forces head when the CPP was broken, Fidel Ramos. As president, he seemed to have seriously misjudged CPP resiliency. In a fundamental error, *Lambat Betag*, the campaign plan under which CPP/NPA fighting fronts were prioritized and systematically neutralized, was terminated in 1995. Yet the PNP, as with the PC before it, was quite incapable of assuming the counter-insurgency role.

In a prescient analysis offered in mid-1996, George Vallejera, by then a Brigadier-General, used Negros as an illustration to describe the flaws in Manila's revised approach:

Negros is not really pacified. This is a big problem. We have not really completed the eradication [of the insurgents]. We have an enemy capable of recovering given the proper environment, the proper atmosphere. We can not allow him to recover. Yet there has been pressure, for example, to disband CAFGU. We are in consolidation [phase], which will take some time. We need massive development of the area. Reconstruction has not yet been completed. So the situation in Negros is as it was when we turned it over [to the PNP, 1994]. We need to get presence in the remote *barangay* [villages], or the enemy will reconstitute there, especially in areas where we had a presence. It took us time to get to where we were. They are reconstituting gradually on Negros Island.[68]

Perhaps no event better illustrated the overall drift that had set in within the security forces than the stunning defection to the CPP, in October 1995, of BG

Raymundo Jarque. Until his forced retirement in April 1994, Jarque had been the Commanding General (CG) of the Southern Luzon Command and one of the military's premier counter-insurgency soldiers. It had been during his tenure as CG 3rd Division that the CPP position on Negros had been destroyed. Yet it was during that tour that Jarque's evenhanded, "hearts and minds" enforcement of the law had created a vendetta with local powers, who manipulated the legal system to destroy his career and ultimately confront him with possible disgrace and incarceration. Desperate, he turned to the CPP and entered its remaining forces on Negros.[69]

There, he did well. He joined the main line faction that supported Sison, rather than the breakaway group. The latter had linked up with the Alex Boncayao Brigade from Manila to form the Revolutionary Proletarian Army (RPA). Though initially possessing some 500 combatants, the RPA was gradually whittled down to but 100,[70] even as the CPP/NPA body grew from its platoon to approximately 100 combatants.

Stunning defection to the CPP: In October 1995, Raymundo Jarque, one of the army's finest field commanders, took his fight against corruption to the extreme by defecting to the CPP. He was later to return to the fold. (Marks photo)

This it was able to do as counter-insurgency responsibilities had been turned over to the PNP in 1994, and it had not been able to duplicate army success. In the void, the CPP stuck to basics, working to recruit "grievance guerrillas," who continued to be produced by the structural deficiencies of Filipino society. For Negros, as with any number of other areas in the Philippines, found itself passed by that prosperity which did come with Ramos' focus on development. Thus, when sugar prices in 1995 suffered another in a regular series of collapses, recruits were again available, the more so as the same corruption and power-mongering that had alienated Jarque himself had gradually returned as normalcy was restored. Jarque's presence, of course, served further to advertise the CPP as a force for "social justice," as Jarque, a Visayan, remained tremendously popular in the region.[71]

Revival of the CPP

This process occurred throughout the Philippines. Following the techniques discussed in this chapter, the CPP patiently mobilized marginalized individuals into the mass base, returned Fighting Fronts to the order-of-battle, and formed guerrilla units. Assassination remained a potent weapon,[72] and "revolutionary taxation" (kidnapping and extortion) assumed a greater proportion of the CPP funding effort than had hitherto been the case. There was a steady rise in NPA numbers during the latter half of the 1990s. Although the Ramos administration had scored a signal success in forging an historic accord with the MNLF in June 1996, getting it to forego its independence struggle in exchange for regional autonomy, an unrepentant MNLF splinter, the Moro Islamic Liberation Front (MILF), which had split from the MNLF in 1978, continued the struggle in the south. It was soon joined by an even more radical splinter, Abu Sayyaf (frequently referred to as the Abu Sayyaf Group or ASG). Unlike its MNLF parent, MILF entered into an alliance of convenience with the CPP. The result, in a throwback to the Marcos era, was a transfer of still further military units from anti-CPP to anti-Muslim separatist operations.

By the time Ramos's single six-year term as president was up in 1998, his place to be taken by his vice-president, former actor Joseph Estrada, the CPP was in reasonable shape. Its debilitating fragmentation had been arrested, as the RJs found themselves unable to overcome the institutional inertia from which the RAs benefited. That is, in control of the major organs of CPP power, Sison and RA his supporters maintained their legitimacy as the "true" CPP. Although Sison's strategic approach could arguably be assessed as flawed, the tried operational and tactical approaches of the party restored its position in some areas.

A Philippine intelligence document observed:

> By the first semester of 1999, LCM [Local Communist Movement; i.e.,those forces of all factions] strength had increased to 9,460. Its high-powered firearms were tallied at 6,040, while the number of guerrilla fronts totaled seventy (70), which is almost equal to the number of guerrilla fronts when the LCM was at its peak in 1987. Some LCM party documents even claimed that their guerrilla fronts total eighty-one (81).[73]

Although the increase of Fighting Fronts alone was not an indicator of enhanced CPP strength, fronts being of widely differing compositions (as per earlier discussions in this chapter), their spread, particularly their return to areas of historical CPP activity, such as Negros and Samar, did serve to highlight the general trend. By early 2001, Philippine order-of-battle figures placed NPA combatants at approximately 13,000.[74]

To its credit, the Ramos administration was not oblivious to these trends, and even prior to the end of its term, preparations were underway for a reassessment of approach. When Estrada assumed office, he was quickly able to issue Presidential Memorandum Order No. 88, dated 21 January 1999, which adopted a "Strategy of Total Approach" for dealing with the various insurgent movements. A key figure in the strategy's preparation was again Victor Corpuz, who eventually was to become Chief, Intelligence Service, AFP.[75] In its facets, the "total approach" was a sophisticated plan that incorporated the previous successful elements of *Lambat Betag* but emphasized further the necessity for coordination of all government agencies, with the armed forces providing but the shield for a multifaceted attack on the "roots" of insurgency.[76]

Considerable developments on the ground followed. Estrada showed no hesitation in using the power of the state to move against "subversives." By April 2000, regular fighting had resumed with the separatists of the MILF and the Islamists of the ASG. This involved some fairly large operations and force deployments.[77] On the other security front, long-stalled "peace talks" with the CPP, launched during the Aquino administration, were called off in 1999. Operations against the group, though, in contrast to the anti-Muslim separatist effort, proceeded in a more deliberate, measured manner as appropriate to dealing with a movement that had again placed emphasis on construction of infrastructure. Such had not proved an easy task for the CPP. Regardless of its resurgence in combatant strength, the factional enmity remained and took the form of continued internecine violence. Some figures who fell were noteworthy: former priest Conrado Balweg, who had renounced communism and entered mainstream politics, was assassinated on 31 December 1999,[78] and Filemon "Popoy Lagman," who had become an above-ground fixture of labor politics in Manila, was shot on 6 February 2001.[79]

The CPP lack of unity was matched by the government. Increasing doubts as to the suitability of Estrada as president led to messy impeachment proceedings in the final months of 2000. These culminated in "Edsa II," a popular outpouring, reminiscent of February 1986, which saw Vice-president Gloria Macapagal Arroyo ("GMA," as the press instantly dubbed her) assume power. As in Edsa I, military support was the key factor, with a carefully worded Supreme Court decision merely adding the trappings of legality.[80] On 20 January 2001, the 53-year old "GMA" assumed the presidency, a position once held by her father, Diosdado Macapagal (1958–66). There followed the predictable "reaching out" to those alienated from the system. Estrada's "all out war" against the MILF was suspended in February in favor of negotiations. Similar efforts were made to engage the CPP in dialogue; talks resumed in April but led to no tangible results. Major sticking-points were the CPP/NPA/NDF's demands that all "political prisoners" be released and that the movement, in effect, be granted belligerency status (a longstanding CPP goal).[81]

Consequently, under "GMA," the security situation continued in much the same mode as it had under her predecessor. Proselytizing, assassinations, revolutionary taxation (extortion and kidnapping for ransom), and sharp guerrilla actions characterized the CPP/NPA effort. Most actions were small, with casualties small, but they were steady and could escalate with dramatic suddenness. An attack on a small detachment in Samar Province on 11 February 2001, for instance, saw seven soldiers killed, five wounded;[82] and a mid-November ambush in Davao Oriental Province left a reported eighteen army dead and six wounded.[83] In contrast, although united front activity under NDF auspices was continual, it simply could not muster the influence of earlier efforts. Left-wing apologists held sway in some sectors of the labor movement, but the only way in which they were able to gain real influence was by carving out an independent sphere. A CPP connection remained a definite liability.

In the background was the former colonial power, the United States. China's expansion into the South China Sea, in particular, bringing home Manila's vulnerability, combined with the continued deterioration of the arms and equipment of the armed forces, had already caused the Philippine Senate, in 1999, to approve a Visiting Forces Agreement (VFA) that allowed exercises with US forces to resume.[84] Yet nationalist positions remained hostile and did all possible to block a renewed

American role in Philippine defense. A prominent illustration involved efforts to prosecute members of a SEAL unit for the deaths of two Filipino boys, in August 2000 on Cebu, while scavenging at a firing range jointly used by American and Filipino forces. Although the case was settled by a cash payment to the families involved, critics continued efforts to use it and other arguments against Washington.[85]

The CPP, which had used the signing of the VFA as its excuse for terminating "peace talks," wedded its position to the protest effort. Unlike the heyday of the insurgency, however, there appeared to be no actual targeting of Americans. For instance, a US citizen living in Negros Oriental Province, where he was a longtime resident, related an incident in March 2000 in which an NPA unit held his family and ransacked his house, while he was away, seizing a 22-caliber pistol and a hunting rifle but harming no one.[86] Similarly, an "ambush" of US military personnel hiking in the Mount Pinatubo vicinity in June 2001 appeared in retrospect to have been a chance encounter between the hiking party and an NPA unit that sought to relieve the Filipino escort of its firearms.[87]

The events of 11 September 2001 in New York City were eventually to alter considerably the US position *vis-à-vis* Philippine defense. Negotiations with the MILF had borne fruit in August 2001, with a ceasefire agreement;[88] but this had been more than unbalanced by the renewed revolt of former MNLF leader Nur Misuari and several hundred followers in November 2001.[89] ASG's continued depredations and apparent links with Al-Qaeda[90] led to direct US commitment of forces in a "joint exercise" directed at ASG hideouts on Basilan Island.[91] Seizing the opportunity, the CPP, acting principally through the NDF, worked to mobilize and then exploit nationalist and anti-US sentiment. This, while involving much noise, lacked substance, as polls showed Filipinos overwhelmingly supporting the American presence.[92]

Conclusions

Strategically, the CPP has not recovered from its loss of "communism" as a viable goal. The Cold War's end has played itself out against the generally high global awareness of the Filipino population to leave the party adrift, an ideological dinosaur in a changed world. Operationally, the CPP has not recovered from the loss of the "US-Marcos dictatorship" as the crucial link between local grievances and the proffered communist rectification. Grievances remain, the Filipino polity is yet imperfect; but the dominant belief is that peaceful options remain for improving life's chances. Tactically, the CPP/NPP/NDF has been able to advance in specific locales, particularly those where it has long been active. It can inflict harm, particularly when the government and its security forces are preoccupied. It has not been able to parlay this into anything more.

As an entity, the CPP has "reaffirmed" its Maoist approach and re-established unity. It has done so at much cost. There are considerable doubts as to whether Sison's reading of the approach is correct. Reduced to its essence, Sison's argument is that guerrilla action must continue until the populace is adequately politicized. This means that formation of "regularized" units must be delayed indefinitely to avoid the combatants becoming cut off from the populace. Further, "other" forms of action, such as urban mobilization (particularly through united front action) or "partisan warfare" (assassinations by sparrows), must be kept in check lest they detract from the rural thrust of Maoist strategy. The dilemma is in knowing when an

US-Marcos Dictatorship: Author at conclusion of patrol in northwest Samar. CPP erred in judging as the center of gravity of the conflict the Philippine relationship with the former colonial power, Washington. Though US presence was important, particularly in the funding of the war, it was Filipinos who made and implemented all decisions. (Marks photo)

adequate level has been reached in rural organizing for necessary shifts in military and political forms to occur. Thus far the only sure judge has been not success or failure on the ground but rather Sison's word. The CPT unsuccessfully dealt with this conundrum in the previous chapter. The issue was to surface again in the future within other insurgencies seeking to follow people's war. The upshot is that even where there is general agreement on a strategic approach (e.g., Maoism), implementing it throws up a host of operational and tactical issues. What is significant about the high level of success achieved by the CPP during the 1980s, until several years after Marcos' ouster, was that the operational and tactical flexibility, highlighted in my text above, was achieved in Sison's absence and is now denounced by him as "deviation" from the correct line. This has left the CPP unable to create more than "noise" even when faced with momentary crises of the Philippine state.[93]

Notes

[1] Much of the early discussion below has appeared in various publications, to include my *Maoist Insurgency since Vietnam*. The contents of that work, however, were submitted in 1995. Continuing developments have required additional analysis.

[2] "Theoretical and Practical Problems for Contemporary Radicalism," *Progressive Review* (Manila), 1.1 (May–June 1963), 5.

[3] For a more detailed discussion of these points, see Benedict J. Kerkvliet, "Martial Law in a Nueva Ecija Village, the Philippines," *Bulletin of Concerned Asian Scholars*, 14 (October–December 1982), 2–19. See also Kerkvliet's later work, "Understanding Politics in a Nueva Ecija Rural Community," in Kerkvliet and Resil Mojares, eds., *From Marcos to Aquino: Local Perspectives on Political Transition in the Philippines* (Quezon City: Ateneo de Manila University Press, 1991).

[4] One illustration should suffice here. During the 1946–72 period the World Bank was only minimally involved in the Philippines. It loaned the government a total of some USD 300 million. In contrast, once martial law was in place, involvement mushroomed; 1980 loans alone were USD 398 million.

[5] See Union of Democratic Filipinos (KDP) and the International Association of Filipino Patriots (IAFP), *Ten-Point Program of the National Democratic Front in the Philippines* (Oakland: International Association of Filipino Patriots [IAFP], 1978).

[6] Acknowledged as the benchmark work on the conflict is Benedict J. Kerkvliet, *The Huk Rebellion: A Study Peasant Revolt in the Philippines* (Berkeley: University of California Press, 1977). Many other references exist. Useful are Lawrence M. Greenberg, *The*

Hukbalahap Insurrection: A Case Study of a Successful Anti-Insurgency Operation in the Philippines, 1946–1955 (Washington, DC: US Army Center of Military History, 1987) and a symposium published as "The Huks in Retrospect: A Failed Bid for Power," *Solidarity*, 102 (1985), 64–103.

[7] An excellent overview of the campaign specifics can be found in Charles T. R. Bohannan and Napoleon D. Valeriano, *Counter-Guerrilla Operations: The Philippine Experience* (New York: Praeger, 1962). Bohannan was the junior half of the legendary Lansdale/Bohannan advisory team that worked closely with Magsaysay to implement what has come to be regarded as a classic counter-insurgency campaign. Valeriano, as a relatively junior officer, became, in the course of the struggle, an important field commander.

[8] The best work for particulars of this linkup is Eduardo Lachica, *Huk: Philippine Agrarian Society in Revolt* (Manila: Solidaridad Publishing House, 1971). Reprinted therein (283–301) is the complete text of the important CPP document "Programme for a People's Democratic Revolution." See also Marks, "From Huks to the New People's Army," *Soldier of Fortune*, 14.2 (February 1989), 26–27 (sidebar).

[9] Key theoretical work of the party is Amado Guerrero ("Beloved Warrior"), *Philippine Society and Revolution: Specific Characteristics of Our People's War*. Written under a pseudonym by Jose Maria Sison, founder and several times head of the CPP, it borrows heavily not only from Mao but also from D. N. Aidit, at that time Chairman of the Indonesian Communist Party.

[10] Interview with author, 30 December 1988, Manila.

[11] I discuss this issue in greater depth in a sidebar, "CPP Leadership Problems," to my "Political Body Count: Philippine Army Tallies Converts, Not Corpses," *Soldier of Fortune*, 14.6 (June 1989), 32–39 (cont.).

[12] This observation touches, albeit briefly, on the issue noted in the previous chapter: the precise relationship between peasant rebellion and insurgency. My research has led me, much like Douglas Pike in his work on the Viet Cong, to emphasize the importance of the counter-state (the insurgent infrastructure) and the bureaucratic process within which it naturally enmeshes its adherents (terror is an inherent component of this process). A contrasting view, such as most eloquently advanced by Kerkvliet, would emphasize those perceived injustices that mobilize insurgent manpower and would see infrastructure and elite control as both contingent and tenuous. On the Igorot issue specifically, see Marks, "The Igorots of the Philippines," Chapter 21 in Michael Tobias, ed., *Mountain People* (Norman: University of Oklahoma Press, 1986), 158–63.

[13] I have dealt with this subject explicitly in "Insurgency Redefined," *FEER* (25 October 1990), 20–21, and "Small Victory in a Big War: Philippine Army Routs Communists on Negros," *Soldier of Fortune*, 16.2 (February 1991), 30–35 (cont.).

[14] My understanding of CPP infrastructure has been gained in nearly three decades of regular field work.

[15] S-2 (Intelligence), 301st Infantry Brigade, Philippine Army, using captured documents and interrogations, carried the CPP/NPA's weapons inventory on Negros at the time as 621 high-powered firearms (HPF; i.e., assault rifles), 83 long-barreled weapons (i.e., older rifles), 153 short-barreled handguns (i.e., pistols), 18 cal. 30.06 (i.e., shotguns), 3 Japanese rifles cal. 27 (from the Second World War), and a machine-pistol, or a total of 879 weapons.

[16] Captured CPP documents refer to instances when these regional main forces functioned as tactical entities. For example, CPP document in Tagalog captured 29 March 1988, "Visayas Report," discussion of special meeting of the CPP Politburo (24 January 1988), claimed the Samar battalion had three companies of 120 men each, equipped with a total of 316 HPR [high-powered rifles] (i.e., assault rifles), several machineguns, and a single mortar. Philippine intelligence personnel noted that the unit functioned in decentralized fashion, with a single account from the field of the battalion's constituent guerrilla units operating together. The "Visayas Report" itself notes only: "There are times when the unit is concentrated in a battalion or bigger formation."

[17] The term is taken directly from the Chinese label for similar forces. Predictably, the Vietnamese developed these forces to a degree that has been matched only by FMLN (*Frente Faribundo Marti de Liberacion Nacional* or Faribundo Marti Liberation Front) insurgent forces in El Salvador. For discussion of the FMLN version of people's war, see David E. Spencer and Jose Angel Moroni Bracamonte, *Strategy and Tactics of the Salvadoran FMLN Guerrillas* (Westport, Connecticut: Praeger, 1995); for the sappers, Spencer, *From Vietnam to El Salvador: The Saga of the FMLN Sappers and Other Guerrilla Special Forces in Latin America* (Westport: Praeger, 1996).

[18] Central works in laying out the issues are both by the key figure involved in the effort to include the support structure and militia in the order-of-battle, former CIA analyst Sam Adams: "Vietnam Cover-up: Playing With the Numbers—Statistics on Viet Cong Strength Ignored by the CIA," *Harper's*, May 1975, 41–45; and *War of Numbers: An Intelligence Memoir* (South Royalton, VT: Steerforth Press, 1995). The post-war legal action began when CBS, the television network, charged in a documentary (that featured prominently Sam Adams) that the military authorities, rather than being motivated by a desire to avoid confusion and misstatement, were instead seeking to mislead their political masters. General William Westmoreland, commander during the period in question, pursued legal action that, among other things, generated considerable useful data of relevance to our discussion of the Colombian case. See e.g. Bob Brewin and Sydney Shaw, *Vietnam on Trial: Westmoreland vs. CBS* (NY: Atheneum, 1987); Don Kowet, *A Matter of Honor: General William C. Westmoreland Versus CBS* (NY: Macmillan, 1984). Quite apart from the trial, Adams, though

remaining a "must read" on any Vietnam bibliography, has been effectively debunked on both matters of military motive and as to order-of-battle particulars. See James J. Wirtz, "Intelligence to Please? The Order of Battle Controversy During the Vietnam War," *Political Science Quarterly*, 106 (Summer 1991), 239–63, reprinted in Wirtz and James K. Johnson, *Strategic Intelligence* (Los Angeles: Roxbury, 2004), 183–97.

[19] Figures derived from exploitation of CPP documents and prisoners by 301st Infantry Brigade, Philippine Army, Negros; obtained 3 August 1988 through interview.

[20] Notebook of Victor Gerardo Bulatao y Jayme, Secretary of the Regional United Front Group (RUFG), Samar, captured March 1982.

[21] See Marks, "Don't Discount the Philippine Communists," *AWSJ*, 28 April 1986, 6.

[22] Foreign funding, though not large, has been present and important throughout the insurgency. The most comprehensive public effort to examine it took place as part of the "Workshop on Philippine Communism," held 2–8 July 1988, Marina Mandarin, Singapore; jointly sponsored by Information & Resource Bureau (Singapore), Strategic Institute for Southeast Asia (Tokyo), Institute of Asian Studies, Chulalongkorn University (Bangkok), and Naval War College Foundation (Newport, Rhode Island).

[23] Numerous documents relating to the Kangleon case are contained in the amnesty file of the principal figures involved. See Headquarters, Eastern Command, AFP (Camp Lukban, Catbalogan, Samar), "Amnesty Papers of Fr. Edgar Kangleon, Antonio Asistio, Juanito Delamida."

[24] I have discussed this case previously in *AWSJ* (see note 21 above) and in "Communist Insurgency in the Philippines: How and Why it Happened," *Gung-Ho*, 7.57 (March 1987), 40–45. See MIG 8, RUC 8 file, "Investigation Report on Salvador P. Acebuche" (numerous documents).

[25] To my knowledge, no open source work attempts to deal in detail with the scope and mechanisms of CPP funding. Obviously, the party maintained an extensive network for generating the revenue necessary to support its far-flung forces. In fact, "revolutionary taxation," as will be discussed briefly later in the text, eventually proved to be one issue prompting a popular backlash against the CPP. The 6-month cash-flow for a typical Fighting Front in Panay is contained in "Six (6) Months Program of the Northern Front Party Committee (NFPC) PIRPC [Panay Island Regional Party Committee] FM: January 87 to June 87":

Income
DC 1 [District Committee 1].........................13,004.65 pesos
DC 2...42,563.05 p
DC 3...8,264.00 p

```
EO [Economic Office]...................................................................... 1,817.00 p
FWAC [Front White Area Committee]........................................65,000.00 p
FPU [Front [Partisan Unit]............................................................ 4,067.00 p
KT-FRENTE [Front Executive Committee ...............................44,724.00 p
     Total.......................................................................................179,440.20 p
Expense ............................................................................. 177,865.20 p
                                                                                                + 1,575.00 p
```

If we use a conversion factor of USD 1 = 20.5 pesos, the six-month income figure of 179,440.20 is approximately USD 8,753, or USD 17,506 per annum, assuming the second half of the year was as profitable as the first. The CPP fielded at least 73 Fighting Fronts at the time, so a straight calculation (USD 17,506 x 73) would result in a figure of USD 1,277,964 nationwide for the Fighting Fronts alone. This figure is certainly too low. Panay would hardly seem to be the place to find a particularly wealthy Fighting Front. The resources are not there to support it, especially not in the NFPC area. Another document, for example, "Summary of Finances NFF [Northern Fighting Front, Samar] For the Period September–December 1985 Inclusive," reflects an income of 122,868.52 pesos (versus expenses of 121,683.80 p) for just those three months, or approximately USD 5,994. Converted to an annual figure: USD 23,974, substantially higher than the annual figure for the NFPC/PIRPC. It would be logical to conclude, then, that published estimates that placed the CPP's annual budget at anywhere from USD 2–7 million were well within the realm of possibility. For comparative purposes, it may be noted that the quarterly operating allowance for a government battalion on Samar at the time was 50,000 pesos (or 200,000 pesos per annum, which was approximately USD 9,756). Pay and allowances, of course, would be fixed costs not reflected in this figure, which is primarily for food and such. It may be further observed that a single tire for a *Commando* armored car then cost 40,000 pesos!

[26] See Marks, "Cease-Fire Maneuvers: Staying One Step Ahead of the NPA," *Soldier of Fortune*, 12.5 (May 1987), 48–55 (cont.).

[27] See Kerkvliet, "Patterns of Philippine Resistance and Rebellion" and Gary Hawes, "Theories of Peasant Revolution: A Critique and Contribution From the Philippines," *World Politics*, 17.2 (January 1990), 261–98. This latter source must be used with caution; many of its particulars are accurate yet it reaches conclusions that were demonstrably inaccurate even as it was being written.

[28] Little commented on in the literature but significant is the degree to which the shape and spectrum of political views in the Philippines could in many respects pass for a double of that in the United States. The result is that the world view of the American anti-Vietnam War movement, an elite-dominated phenomenon, may be found in that wing of Filipino politics

that sees itself as "progressive" (ergo, its profoundly anti-systemic outlook and infatuation with what might be called, to borrow a phrase, "coercive Utopianism").

[29] For background see Sheila Ocampo, "The Battle for Chico River," *FEER*, 20 October 1978, 32–4. Also useful is John Lindsey Foggle, "The Rice Terrace Farmers of the Philippines: A Mountain People's Struggle for Survival in a Developing Nation and the World," unpublished manuscript, 1979.

[30] See David Wurfel, *Filipino Politics: Development and Decay* (Ithaca, New York: Cornell University Press, 1988).

[31] Background data on the MNLF conflict may be found in W. K. Che Man, *Muslim Separatism: The Moros of Southern Philippines and the Malays of Southern Thailand* (Manila: Ateneo de Manila University Press, 1990); and T. J. S. George, *Revolt in Mindunao: The Rise of Islam in Philippine Politics* (Kuala Lumpur: Oxford University Press, 1980).

[32] A fascinating biography by one such individual is Edmundo G. Navarro, *Bed of Nails* (Manila: Personal imprint, 1988).

[33] Interview with author, 13 August 1986, Manila. Ironically, the exile may have been to Ileto's advantage, for in Thailand he became close friends with Saiyud Kerdphol. According to Ileto, they discussed counter-insurgency frequently.

[34] No definitive work exists on RAM. Useful background is in Rodney Tasker, "The Hidden Hand: A Military Reform Movement Takes Hold," *FEER* (1 August 1985), 10–13, and Michael Richardson, "Military Reform in the Philippines?" *Pacific Defence Reporter* (Australia), 12.8 (February 1986), 11–12. See also the appropriate chapters in the later works: Criselda Yabes, *The Boys From the Barracks: The Philippine Military After EDSA* (Manila: Anvil Publishing, 1991); and Alfred W. McCoy, *Closer Than Brothers: Manhood at the Philippine Military Academy* (Manila: Anvil Publishing, 1999, rpt. Yale University Press).

[35] Joint Meeting-Discussion of [CPP] National Urban Commission and the United Front Commission, "Some Notes on the Issue of Ceasefire," dated 5 July 1986.

[36] Interview with author, 14 December 1986, Samar.

[37] Office of the Assistant Secretary for Plans and Programs, Ministry of National Defense (Camp General Emilio Aguinaldo, Quezon City), "Post-Revolution Communist Strategy in the Philippines: Indicators and Potentials," dated 22 August 1986.

[38] *Ibid.*

[39] Interview with author, 1 August 1988, Panay. See Marks, "Victory on Panay: Red Tide Recedes From Philippine Communist Stronghold," *Soldier of Fortune*, 14.2 (February 1989), 40–47 (cont).

[40] For additional context, see Marks, "All Eyes on Negros in Philippine Insurgency," paper presented to panel on "The Militarization of Ethnic Conflict," International Studies Association Annual Meeting, London, 29 March 1989.

[41] Interview with author, 4 August 1988, Negros.

[42] See Marks, "Political Body Count" (see note 11 above) and "Sea Change in Negros," *East West*, 8.3 (Spring 1989), 24–29. Particularly interesting are the several letters to the editor of *East West* (condemning my analysis of the situation on Negros) and my response; see the "Letters" section of the 8.4 (Summer) number. The subject is discussed further in Marks, "The NPA Misfires in the Philippines," *AWSJ* (31 January 1989), 6, as well as in Marks, "Manila Starts to Win Hearts and Minds," *Christian Science Monitor*, 18 April 1989, 19.

[43] The mechanics of the plan, minus its operational aspects, may be found in Victor Corpus, *Silent War* (Manila: VNC Enterprises, 1989).

[44] Interview, 22 July 1990, Manila.

[45] *Ibid.*

[46] Although I heard virtually these words from numerous refugees during interviews conducted on Negros, July–August and December 1988, I was most taken with the passion and eloquence of Annalyn Salcedo, aged 23, whom I encountered 5 August 1988 on Negros. Former Chairman of the OC Women's Sector in her village, she had eventually reached Party Member status before surrendering to the government in early 1988. A further point of significance: when pressed to explain the level of CPP taxation, which they found unbearable, peasants would cite figures on the order of a single peso per week. It was a seemingly paltry amount but not in the village world.

[47] I explore this subject in greater detail in several works: "Guerrillas in the Midst of Defeat," *AWSJ*, 26 July 1990, 6; "Deadlock in the Philippines," *National Review*, 15 October 1990, 30–32; and "Small Victory in a Big War: Philippine Army Routs Communists on Negros," *Soldier of Fortune*, 16.2 (February 1991), 30–35 (cont.).

[48] Ross H. Munro, "The New Khmer Rouge," *Commentary*, 80.6 (December 1985), 19–38.

[49] Northern Fighting Front [Samar], "*Pagturutimbang san Armando nga Pakig-away sa Probinsiya (1984–1985)*" [Waray: "Comparison of Relative Strengths of Armed Groups in the Province (1984–1985)"], dated 14 December 1985, captured 17 February 1986 in the CPP's Far North West District, Samar. I discussed the contents at the time in "Island Fighting: 52 IB Tracks Elusive NPA," *Soldier of Fortune*, 11.7 (July 1986), 38–45, as well as the *AWSJ* and *Gung-Ho* (see note 24 above).

[50] Figure compiled from monthly status reports submitted by units assigned to Regional Unified Command 8 (RUC-8).

[51] This document is also discussed in the press articles cited in n. 49 above.

[52] Assassination deaths were tallied for 1 January–30 July 1988 by intelligence personnel of 301st Infantry Brigade, Philippine Army. Accompanying documents provided the combat

deaths, which may be expanded to include 206 civilians versus 218 CPP/NPA. Wounded of all government categories totaled 147 versus 110 CPP/NPA.

[53] Interview with author, 26 December 1988, Negros. She had been captured on 23 November 1988.

[54] Interview with author, 4 August 1988, Negros. Political Officer of Platoon "Nissan," one of the four such units comprising the FGU then operating in District 1 of Negros. He surrendered on 5 June 1988.

[55] Interview with author, 16 July 1990, Negros.

[56] Interview with author, anonymity requested, 16 July 1990, Negros.

[57] Interview with author, 16 July 1990, Negros.

[58] See, for example, "Philippines Finds Mass Graves," *International Herald Tribune*, 9 February 2000, 5.

[59] Again, I am indebted for my understanding of this subject to a discussion with Noel Albano, 30 December 1988, Manila.

[60] For a negative assessment of the Aquino years, see Robert H. Reid and Eileen Guerrero, *Corazon Aquino and the Brushfire Revolution* (Baton Rouge: Louisiana State University Press, 1995). A review of the book, useful for the information it provides, is Michael Leifer, "More Imelda than Teresa," *Times Literary Supplement* (London), 18 April 1997, 26.

[61] The document was ostensibly authored by Armando Liwanag ("Military Light"), but this was actually Sison using his latest alias.

[62] Best sources on the particulars involved are Ben Reid, *Philippine Left: Political Crisis and Social Change* (Manila: Journal of Contemporary Asia Publishers, 2000), and Joel Rocamora, *Breaking Through: The Struggle Within the Communist Party of the Philippines* (Pasig City [Manila]: Anvil Publishing, 1994. Significantly, both works are highly recommended by analysts of Philippine government intelligence organs as per Interviews, 13 March 2001, Manila. Another solid recent work, but one seriously underestimating the central role of terror in CPP processes, is Kathleen Weekley, *The Communist Party of the Philippines: A Story of its Theory and Practice* (Quezon City: University of the Philippines Press, 2001).

[63] Interview conducted by Ricardo Reyes, *Manila Chronicle*, 19 January 1993, 5. See Marks, "Philippine Counter-insurgency Shows Results," *Low Intensity Conflict International*, 1.6 (April 1993), 1–3.

[64] Reid, 45.

[65] See Paul D. Hutchcroft, *The Philippines at the Crossroads: Sustaining Economic and Political Reform* (New York: Asia Society, 1996), as well as Marcus Noland, "The Philippines in the Asian Financial Crisis: How the Sick Man Avoided Pneumonia," *Asian Survey*, 40.3 (May–June 2000), 401–12.

[66] Among the most useful accounts of the CPP's decline, described here, are Christine F. Herrera, "Guerrillas in the Mist: Another Group Breaks Away From the Communist Party of the Philippines, Pushing Unity in the Revolution—and Peace—Further Away," *Philippines Free Press*, 31 July 1993, 4–5, accompanied by Jarius Bondoc, "The CCP Split: Sison Had it Coming," 6–7 (concluded 26), and "Interview: 'The Sad Experience in Party Splits is that Both Sides Suffer as a Result'—Satur Ocampo," 7; Antonio Lopez, "Inside Story: Running a Revolution—The Life and Times of the Philippines' Most Formidable Guerrilla Chief," *Asiaweek*, 9 March 1994, 28–41 (cover: "Why We Lost the War: The Philippines' Rebel Chieftain Tells His Story—Rodolfo Salas"); and Denis Warner, "Philippines: NPA No Longer Major Threat," *Asia-Pacific Defence Review 1994 Annual Reference Edition*, 47–48. It is useful to compare the events discussed with the three most commonly cited American works on the insurgency, all possessing strengths yet also flawed, and hence victims, as per their generally optimistic conclusions concerning the CPP's future, of spectacularly bad timing in release dates: William Chapman, *Inside the Philippine Revolution: The New People's Army and its Struggle for Power* (New York: Norton, 1987); Richard J. Kessler, *Rebellion and Repression in the Philippines* (New Haven: Yale University Press, 1989); and Gregg R. Jones, *Red Revolution: Inside the Philippine Guerrilla Movement* (Boulder, Colorado: Westview Press, 1989).

[67] The judgement concerning the US role is my own, based on discussions with US advisory personnel and Filipino commanders during field visits. An early effort to quantify the already substantial importance of US assistance can be found in Marks, "An Analysis of the Brunner and Brewer Model of Political Development as Applied to the Philippines," *Philippine Political Science Journal* (Manila), Nos. 5– 6 (June and December 1977), 181–211. For the parameters and difficulties of Filipino force development, see Renato Cruz de Castro, "Adjusting to the post-US Bases Era: The Ordeal of the Philippine Military's Modernization Program," *Armed Forces & Society*, 26.1 (Fall 1999), 119–38; and Patrice Franko, "Defense Decision-making and Accountability Structures in the Philippines," *Low Intensity Conflict & Law Enforcement*, 8.1 (Spring 1999), 57–86.

[68] Interview with author, 17 August 1996, Negros.

[69] Useful background and Jarque's statement issued at the time may be found in Cynthia D. Balana, "'Frolics' of Class '61 Sobers Up," *Philippine Daily Inquirer* (Manila), 11 October 1995, 1, 7.

[70] Although he does not discuss the point, evidence of decline is clearly visible in the 1999 visit paid to the faction by Robert Young Pelton for the Discovery Channel. For a written discussion of what appeared visually, see "In a Dangerous Place: Negros," in Robert Young Pelton, *The World's Most Dangerous Places*, 4th edn. (New York : HarperResource, 2000), 776–78.

[71] See Jamie Espina, "String of Crises Allowed Left to Stage Remarkable Recovery," *Today* (Manila), 1 March 1998, np (clipping).

[72] On 13 June 1996 in Manila, for example, retired army Colonel Rolando Abadilla, an important intelligence operative during the Marcos era, was assassinated by the Alex Boncayao Brigade as he sat in his car during heavy traffic.

[73] *National Peace & Development Plan*, Annex A, Para 12 (n. p.). No publications data, but apparently issued January 2000.

[74] Interview with LTC Sammy Narbuada, Intelligence Service, AFP, 13 March 2001, Manila.

[75] As might be expected given Corpuz' background, this appointment did not sit well with some elements within the military. Nevertheless, it stuck, with Corpuz assuming office 23 January 2001. See "Former Red Cadre Intelligence Chief," *Business World* (Manila), 24 January 2001, 12. Although modest and restrained by nature, staying out of the limelight, Corpuz is quite aware of the importance of his role in shaping the counters to the CPP. I base this on my discussions with him, especially: Interview, 13 March 2001, Manila.

[76] See, for example, *National Peace & Development Plan*, Power Point Briefing for presentation to all levels of Philippine government, January 1999, and *Internal Security Operations*, Power Point Briefing, Intelligence Service, AFP, January 1999.

[77] See, for example, Hugh Williamson, "Manila Struggles to Regain Control—Heady Mix of Guns, Clans, Secession and Religion Poses Problems Afresh in Southern Philippines," *Financial Times*, 29–30 April 2000, 4.

[78] See Vincent Cabrez, "Balweg: Beyond the Symbol and Myth," *Philippine Daily Inquirer* (Manila), 3 January 2001, A12. Though the government charged some fourteen individuals in connection with the murder, citing non-political motives, Cabrez writes flatly: "Balweg's brother Jovencio, leader of an NPA unit operating in Abra [Balweg's home province], owned responsibility for the murder on orders from top communist rebels in the region."

[79] See Philip C. Tubeza, Andrea Trinidad-Echavez, and Dave Veridiano, "'Ka Popoy' Shot Dead Inside UP," *Philippine Daily Inquirer* (Manila), 7 February 2001, A1; and the accompanying "backgrounder": PDI Research, "The Man Who Called for Revolt on Ayala," A1. The latter contains a number of insightful passages, among them: "Lagman led the breakaway from the CPP in 1991 due to differences with founding CPP chair, Jose Ma. Sison, on the question of strategy of guerrilla war and the analysis of Philippine society as semi-feudal and semi-colonial. Lagman advocated a shift to the workers movement, combining parliamentary and extra-parliamentary means and a 'strategy of a workers uprising toward a socialist revolution.' . . . Today the RJ group is said to be hopelessly split into three. Among the splinters, Lagman at the time of his death was said to be the only one to hold a truly urban mass following. The rest are said to be 'paper tigers' which do not

have countryside fronts or bases." Also useful is Dan Mariano, "Opinion Today—Popoy Lagman: A Revolutionary Life," *Today*, 8 February 2001, 9.

[80] A wealth of material exists on the transition. See, for example, Sandra Burton, "People Power Redux," *Time* (Asian edn.) (29 January 2001), 14–19; with the accompanying Anthony Spaeth, "Glory, Gloria!", 20–21, and Spaeth, "Oops, We Did It Again: Ousting Presidents by Revolution Has Become a Bad National Habit," 22.

[81] Useful for its discussion of the issues on the table concerning both the CPP and MILF is Ruffy L. Villanueva, Cheryll D. Fiel, and Michael F. Leonen, "Talks With Reds, MILF Seen Soon," *Business World* (Manila), 12 February 2001, 10. See also Doug Mellgren. "Philippine Peace Talks Resume," AP-NY-04-27-01 0638EDT.

[82] The attack was against an 18-man detachment of A Company, 34 IB (34th Infantry Battalion, an 8th Division unit) based at *Barangay* Babaclayon, San Jose de Buan (northeast of Catbalogan, Samar). Arms lost reportedly included eight M-16 and seven M-14 rifles, as well as an M-60 machinegun. To my knowledge, this was the largest such loss on Samar in more than fifteen years. In October 1986, the NPA sprung a major ambush, in the vicinity of Barangay Baysag, near Rosario in northwestern Samar, on a 52 IB element responding to an ambush. Army casualties then were ten dead and nineteen wounded.

[83] This apparently was the single largest military combat loss to NPA action in at least a decade. It came during a three-day period when NPA attacks left at least thirty-three people dead and seven wounded throughout the country. See AP dispatch of 21 November 2001 (Manila); rpt. in "Rebels Kill 33 in Manila," *Kathmandu Post* (Nepal), 22 November 2001, 6.

[84] "See, for example, "Manila and US Renew Military Tie: Pact on Joint Exercises is Initialed," *International Herald Tribune*, 15 January 1998, 4; "Manila Favors US Military Pact: Philippines Senate Endorses Measure to Preserve Alliance," *Honolulu Advertiser*, 26 May 1999, A3; Tony Tassell, "Manila Agrees US Defence Deal," *Financial Times*, 28 May 1999, 6; "US-Philippines Pact a Good Deal for Both," *Honolulu Advertiser*, 1 June 1999, A6; "US, Philippines Planning Exercises: Pact Allows Joint Military Training," *Honolulu Advertiser*, 25 June 1999, A3; George Gedda, "China Threat Sends Manila Back to US," *Honolulu Star-Bulletin*, 6 July 1999, A-9.

[85] See David Allen, "Philippines May Charge SEALs with Homicide," *Pacific Stars and Stripes*, 7 January 2001, 3; "Cebu VFA Bomb Explosion Case is Settled Out of Court," *Manila Bulletin*, 4 February 2001, N-1; Jhunnex Napallacan and Tonton Antogop, "Parents of 2 Boys Killed in Cebu Blast Given P1.5M," *Philippine Daily Inquirer* (Manila), 15 February 2001, A12; "Lawyer Admits Getting Money From Toledo Blast Victims' Kin," *The Philippine Star* (Manila), 20 February 2001, 13; Connie Fernandez, "Senator Demands New Probe of War Games Deaths," *Philippine Daily Inquirer* (Manila), 20 February 2001,

A12; and "Serge, Gringo Call For 'Deeper' Probe Into VFA," *Today*, 23 February 2001, 3. As reflected in several of the headlines, it was noteworthy that a major voice calling for action against US personnel and "clarification" of the VFA was former RAM leader, Senator Gregorio Honasan. During his time of service, he had been close to any number of US personnel, with one such American withdrawn at Manila's request after he played an important role, through persuasion, in ending the most serious of RAM's coup attempts.

[86] Interview with author, anonymity requested, 14 March 2001, Manila.

[87] See, for example, Reuters dispatches: "Philippine Gunmen Ambush US Sailors; One Missing" (5 June 2001), and "Navy Officer Missing in Philippines After Ambush" (5 June 2001); as well as AP (6 June 2001) "Missing Lt. Shows Up in Philippines."

[88] See, for example, Sean Yoong, "Philippines, Rebels Agree to Cease-Fire," *Honolulu Star-Bulletin*, 7 August 2001, A11; and Deidre Sheehan, "Philippines: A Price for Peace—It Will Take More Than Brave Talk and Promises for Manila to Win a Lasting End to Revolt on Mindanao," *FEER* (30 August 2001), 17.

[89] See, for example, "Terrorism in the Philippines: The Jolo Conundrum—A Surprise Attack Upsets President Arroyo's Peace Moves," *The Economist* (24 November 2001), 40.

[90] Published evidence has been sparse. For a general discussion, see Rohan Gunaratna, "Al-Qaeda: The Asian Connection," *Jane's Intelligence Review* (January 2002), internet version. Much greater but unsourced detail may be found in Rick Parker, *Islamic Insurgency in the Philippines Primer* (Honolulu: CINCPAC Virtual Information Center, 24 March 2000).

[91] Useful background may be found in Deidre Sheehan and David Plott, "Philippines: A War Grows—A Widening War against Terrorism Brings Together the Military Interests of the US and Philippines," *FEER* (11 October 2001), 24; Mark Landler, "Global Network: US Advisers May Aid Philippine Anti-terror Effort, *NYT*, 11 October 2001, B4; for more recent data see Steve Vogel, "US Expands War against Terrorism to Philippines," *Honolulu Advertiser* [*Washington Post* original], 16 January 2002, A2.

[92] An illustrative sampling: Roel Landingin, "Mixed Feelings Over US Troops," *Financial Times*, 18 January 2002, 3; James Brooke, "Unease Grows in Philippines on US Forces," *NYT*, 19 January 2002, internet version; Oliver Teves, "Poverty, not Terror, may be Top Philippine Challenge," *Honolulu Advertiser*, 20 January 2002, A24, with accompanying Teves piece, "US Base Camp set up in Basilan Island Jungle," A24; and Pat Roque, "Anti-US Feelings in Philippines Rise," *Honolulu Advertiser*, 21 January 2002, A3.

[93] This is not to deny the steady advance on the ground. A count, from October 2001, placed the number of CPP-influenced *barangay* at 1,504 compared to 1,279 in 2000, with the number of fighting fronts up to 99 (*Philippine Star* [Manila], 17 October 2001; extracted and provided in e-mail communication to author). As mentioned previously, the figures

themselves reveal little, particularly the dramatic increase in the number of fronts compared to the high point of the movement, when there were just more than 70. What is of concern to the Philippines, particularly those charged with monitoring and dealing with internal threats, is the potential for a resurrection of the CPP as a major problem—particularly if the security forces should find themselves preoccupied as they were by the first Muslim crisis in the 1970s and early 1980s. Continued political instability and economic problems have led to a gradual deterioration of Philippine coercive power, especially arms and equipment, and it is possible to forecast scenarios where a combination of circumstances could leave Manila exposed to dramatic action by the CPP/NPA/NDF. Even if unsuccessful, this could be highly destructive and destabilizing.

Chapter 5

New World Order Meets Old: Insurgency in Sri Lanka

The insurgencies considered thus far have had much in common with the original Chinese case. Differences, however, should also be apparent, particularly the salient role played by minority actors. In the Thai case, the CPT insurgency would not have become a going concern without an ability to appeal to regional and ethnic alienation. In the Philippine case, the CPP gained its greatest strength not in the Tagalog-speaking areas of historic unrest but in peripheral areas of dissimilar language and even customs. In Sri Lanka, too, these threads appear.

What is unique about the Sri Lankan case is the degree to which all the subjective and ideological elements were present. The result is a unique laboratory of sorts for an understanding of just how insurgencies draw on the elements of people's war, either directly or indirectly.

This case is complicated, because several major outbreaks must be considered: a predominantly Sinhalese, island-wide (Tamil areas excluded) uprising that twice aimed at toppling the government and instituting a Maoist regime, and the present widespread violence in areas of Tamil settlement that pits a Tamil minority-fraction against the majority Sinhalese in a quest for an independent Marxist state. Seemingly dissimilar in character, separated at times temporally and spatially, these episodes were actually connected in a causal sense. They can be considered structurally as facets of a larger, old-regime crisis within a revolutionary situation.

A less likely setting for not one but several major outbreaks of rebellion could scarcely be imagined than Sri Lanka (see Figure 5.1). Visually stunning and blessed with a temperate climate and a relative abundance of resources, Sri Lanka has the ambience of a South Seas island, despite its propinquity to the poverty and "ordered

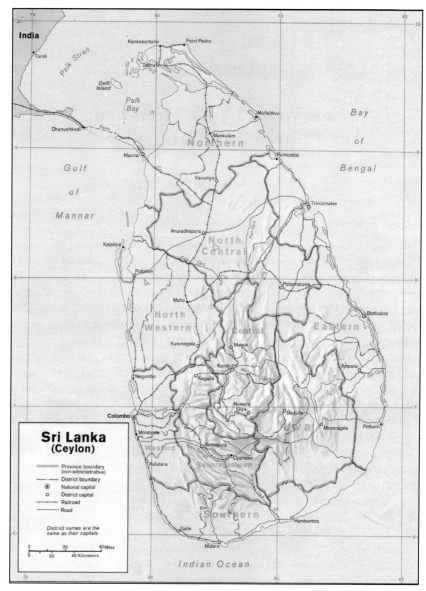

Figure 5.1

chaos" of India.[1] When independence was granted by Britain in 1948, after four centuries of colonial domination—the Portuguese, 1517–1638, and the Dutch, 1638–1796, had also been the island's overlords—the transfer of power was relatively peaceful. This was in stark contrast to the communal violence marking the birth of India and Pakistan. Indeed, Sri Lanka's majority Sinhalese, three-quarters of the population (15.2 million in the 1981 census), and the principal minority, the Tamils (approximately one-fifth of the total) seemingly had achieved an arrangement of mutual benefit based on participation in a secular, democratic state.

Growth of Tamil Opposition to the Old-Regime

In reality, the two populations were divided by a widening rift caused by differences of race, language, culture, and religion.[2] The Sinhalese claimed descent from the Aryans of northern India, spoke Sinhala, and were overwhelmingly Buddhist. The Tamils, linked to the Dravidian stock of south India, spoke Tamil, and were primarily Hindu, with some Christian influence.

The Tamils were further split into two major groups, Ceylon Tamils and Indian Tamils. The Ceylon Tamils, now generally referred to as Sri Lankan Tamils, had established themselves in the northern and eastern parts of the island just centuries after the Sinhalese had arrived. This was especially true in the northern area of Jaffna, where the Tamils had a small but flourishing kingdom. The Indian Tamils, in contrast, were brought over during the British era by plantation owners to work

Tamils and Sinhalese: (left) Tamil youth in 1987, released from detention camps where they had been held for suspected insurgent involvement. (right) Sinhalese businessman Patrick Amarasinghe, eventually chairman of Sri Lanka's combined chambers of commerce umbrella organization, with relatives in Colombo. Though calling themselves "races," Tamils and Sinhalese are actually distinct communities. (Marks photos)

205

on the estates, mainly those producing (from 1867) some of the world's finest tea. Differences between the two Tamil groups, combined with the fact that the new immigrants were settled in the hill areas of the south rather than in the north, prevented close links.

While Sinhalese-Tamil differences had been present before the end of colonial rule,[3] only after independence did they became intense. The immediate cause lay in the maneuvering by the major Sinhalese political parties to wrap themselves in the mantle of Sinhalese nationalism.

Its Tamil pockets aside, pre-colonial Sri Lanka was a Buddhist society of considerable vitality, one that had an enormous cultural and religious influence on several areas in the region, particularly Southeast Asia.[4] There was limited exchange with the much smaller Tamil areas. Although the Portuguese and Dutch colonial governments had succeeded in securing the coastline and a few inland areas, not until the British seizure of Kandy in 1816 was the entire island under one central administration. Hence, when the British departed, a return to "independence" meant different things to the Sinhalese and Tamils, the Ceylon Tamils in particular. For the Sinhalese, the "Land of the Buddha" was again free from foreign domination; to Ceylon Tamils, the independence that existed prior to colonialism was lost to a unified Sri Lankan state. Therein lay the roots of separatism.

The parliamentary framework meant that only Sinhalese parties could realistically hope to achieve power, and each election seemed to bring more strident assertions of Sinhalese nationalism by rival Sinhalese factions jockeying for position. The need for a salient issue with which to attack the party in power was pronounced, and symbolic appeals to race, religion, and destiny (a chosen people guarding the true faith in its island citadel) served the purpose well.[5] The electorate regularly turned the incumbent party out of office in every election beginning with 1956.

The Tamils, who under the British had taken full advantage of the opportunities afforded minorities by colonial rule and favoritism—and had thus gained dominance in the professions and commerce—increasingly found themselves the victims of discriminatory affirmative action schemes designed to favor the Sinhalese majority. A key juncture in this process was the designation of Buddhism and Sinhala as the official state religion and language, respectively, in 1956. There followed nationalization of all schools in December 1960, which deprived the Tamils of unrestricted access to a major means of social mobility. Instruction in Sinhala became mandatory, and in March 1964 compulsory retirement began of all civil servants unable to work in that medium.

The growth of Sinhalese chauvinism had an added dimension, because symbolic appeals to Sinhalese Buddhist sentiments were inextricably enmeshed with promises of material gains for the underprivileged classes, particularly the Sinhalese rural masses who comprised some three-quarters of the population if the Tamils were excluded. Thus two major political tendencies of considerable, continuing force developed: "the drive for recognition and recompense by the Sinhalese Buddhist majority, and the egalitarian demands of the economically underprivileged strata of society."[6] These egalitarian demands were represented principally by the non-Marxist socialism of the Sri Lanka Freedom Party (SLFP), which during the pre-1971 time period dethroned the more free market-oriented United National Party (UNP) in the elections of 1956, July 1960, and 1970. (The UNP was victorious in 1947, March 1960, and 1965.)

Growth of Maoist Insurgent Challenge to the Old-Regime

Such regular substitution of ideologically-opposed major parties would seemingly provide ample opportunity for the expression of growing egalitarian demands. That such did not prove the case was a result of the essential unity of the Sri Lankan elite. The UNP and SLFP, despite their professed dissimilarity, were inextricably linked structurally by bonds of family, caste, and Westernized culture and education.[7] This was also the case with the logical standard-bearers for the underprivileged masses, the avowedly revolutionary parties of Marxist persuasion. They were further neutralized by their incessant intramural battles over doctrinal matters (e.g., Leninism versus Trotskyism) and world communist orientation (e.g., pro-Moscow versus pro-Peking).[8]

A period of intense schism during 1963–64 resulted in the formation of several ultra-left parties, among them the Communist Party (pro-Peking) or CP(P). Even these, however, were not radical enough for some. An internal crisis and split in the CP(P) during 1964 led to the May 1965 formation of an internal CP(P) revitalization movement. At first this group was not constituted as an actual party, but it became an independent body toward the end of 1969 under the name *Janatha Vimukthi Peramuna* (JVP or "People's Liberation Front").[9] Avowedly Maoist, it adopted a Leninist structure, using a cellular base on which to pyramid local, regional, and district committees, together with a 25-member Central Committee and 12-man Politburo.[10]

Under the leadership of youthful Rohana Wijeweera, the professed JVP goal was "to make a revolution." To this end an elaborate ideology was developed and incorporated into "five lessons" used at indoctrination sessions.[11] Most such work, in keeping with the JVP's Maoist orientation, was conducted in the rural areas. The formal decision to emphasize the peasantry was reportedly made as early as 1966, with the target broadened to all rural classes in 1968. A particularly fertile group for recruitment proved to be rural youth. Rapid population growth, an expansion of education that far outstripped employment opportunities, and an inability to influence or participate in the mechanisms of power, all served to alienate and marginalize many young people. Given Sri Lanka's demographics and the particulars of island life as previously noted, this set of circumstances, while island-wide, was felt by Sinhalese youth in particular. Thus they formed the prime JVP converts.

There remains uncertainty as to Wijeweera's precise intentions and plans. In any case, the JVP, a child of left-wing schism, was hardly monolithic. The leadership around Wijeweera was comprised of multiple factions. Bodies of new recruits, after splitting off from one of the older Marxist parties or its youth organizations, would normally, on joining the JVP, keep their individual identities and leadership hierarchy. To make direction still more complex, even the JVP's elite echelon was divided by personality clashes, with the attendant disruptive impact on the unity of the membership.

The result has been a very incomplete picture of what actually occurred in the crucial period from late 1969 to the outbreak of insurrection in April 1971. In the most common view of the 1971 events,[12] the JVP was forced to take precipitous action, thereby blunting the effectiveness of its campaign. When the authorities learned in February of the plans for revolt, the JVP leadership made the decision "to arm the masses." This prompted increased police counter-measures. Government pressure, in turn, led to demands from the JVP rank-and-file for dramatic and audacious action. On 6 March, the US Embassy was bombed during a demonstration.[13] The armed forces were deployed throughout the island the next day, and on 13 March Wijeweera was arrested. The following week brought discoveries of hidden arms and explosives. Finally, a declaration of emergency was put into effect. Arrests of JVP members began in earnest.

A small group of JVP leaders reportedly met on 2 April to analyze the situation. They resolved to carry through with their plans by rising up on 5 April 1971. Many felt the time was not right for such action, but once the insurrection exploded, they, too, joined in. Violence was general throughout much of the Sinhalese-majority areas of Sri Lanka. Halliday provides a detailed narrative,[14] the major points of which have been gathered together by Alexander as follows:[15]

On the night of 5–6 April, three weeks after the declaration of the State of Emergency, police stations in different parts of the island were assaulted by JVP cadres in groups of 25 to 30. . . The aim of this first attack seems to have been to capture a stock of modern arms, and to consolidate in a liberated region of the interior, blocking communication across the island and providing a base for a second offensive.

On the first night several police stations fell, and the government soon evacuated several more: at the height of the insurrection some 90 and 100 police stations had been abandoned or had fallen to the JVP [pp. 196–7] . . . the bulk of the fighting was performed by units of armed youth, often including many members in their teens (p. 198). . . By the end of May, after extremely fierce fighting and continual deployments by the JVP, the government had temporarily driven the insurgent groups back into the upland forests and re-established its control of the rural interior [p. 200] . . . A few small groups continued to survive in the remoter jungles, but they posed no threat to the regime [p. 207]. . . The insurrection was an ambitious and highly organized attempt to seize State power [p. 214] . . .

In putting down the insurrection, the SLFP government was able to turn to an array of international sources for arms and material that were crucial given the ill-prepared state of the security forces at the onset of the fighting. Colombo's non-aligned foreign policy resulted in shipments being received from donors in both the East and West blocs. While major fighting ended after several months, it remained dangerous, until the end of 1971, for individuals to travel in certain areas, particularly in the North Central Province.[16] Nevertheless, the insurgents' tactical ineptitude allowed security forces to gain the upper hand in a suppression campaign marked by a high degree of brutality and great loss of life and property. Government competence in this operation was minimal, but the opposition was even worse.

Data gathered on those detained has provided statistics on some 12,000 insurgents or sympathizers of the 18,000 people who are estimated to have been held at one time or another. Analysis reveals that the detainees were overwhelmingly rural, male, Sinhalese youth less than 30 years of age (more than three-quarters were in the narrow 16–25 age bracket). Most were educated (less than 20% had only primary or no schooling);most held irregular, poorly paid, or low status jobs in the rural sector. Caste affiliation was mixed, although there caste representation was strong in particular areas. Many rank-and-file members apparently came from a "land army" formed in 1967 to provide employment in conservation and reclamation activities for unemployed youths (it was disbanded in 1970), but overall there was no common group-of-origin.[17]

These characteristics and related data have been summarized by Alles in a set of conclusions with which most sources are in general agreement:[18]

(a) That the movement had its origins in the rural sector particularly among the educated unemployed youth;

(b) That the system of education imparted in the rural schools provided a preponderance of students prepared for courses in the arts;

(c) That a class distinction has been created as a result of the educational system, between English-educated students from the urban schools, who predominated in the courses in science, medicine, engineering, agriculture and veterinary science, and the students from the rural schools who followed courses in the social sciences and the humanities;

(d) That as a result of this indiscriminate system of education job opportunities for the educated youth of the rural sector were scarce and unemployment and under-employment predominated in this sector;

(e) That the JVP leadership made use of the educated youth of the rural sector, who constituted a majority of the insurgents, to alter the structure of society and establish a socialist society; and

(f) That caste considerations were not a determining factor in the insurgency.

Constructing the JVP Counter-State

An ideologically driven effort by a Maoist insurgency "to make a revolution" was crushed. In previous chapters, it is at this point in the narrative that we would consider the growth of the counter-state. In the Sri Lankan case, the end came so precipitously that such an approach might seem presumptuous. Yet the JVP case offers an opportunity to explore the role played by subjective and objective elements, between ideological redress as advanced by the leadership and the more mundane grievances of followers.

An essential starting-point would be the nature of the Sri Lankan state at independence in 1948. The symbolic importance attached to participation in the electoral process was high, a reflection of anti-colonial nationalism, but the choice afforded the voters was uni-dimensional. The place of the departed British rulers had merely been taken by an indigenous, Western-educated, English-speaking elite with tenuous ties to the countryside and masses. The nationalized estate sector gave this elite an independent resource base where the main crop, tea, was grown primarily by what amounted to indentured labor, the Indian Tamils. Regardless of the ideological persuasions of particular parties, the elite was structurally one ruling class, the national component of the original landed aristocracy or gentry (*pelantiya*),[19] which had used its former position to withdraw from direct involvement in agricultural production and to enter a variety of other areas, most importantly colonial government service.

The gentry solidified its position through marriage, kin, and school ties, thereby achieving almost complete control over all aspects of the polity. Since entry into the gentry through land acquisition had essentially ceased by 1920, when most areas of lowland Sri Lanka were occupied by rice-lands and plantations (tea, rubber, and coconut),[20] elite regeneration was accomplished through participating in the administration and the mechanisms of exclusive Western education. This position was further solidified by the dependence of state finances principally on the three major plantation export crops just mentioned. Of these tea was paramount, contributing more than half of all foreign exchange earnings. Tea, of course, was cultivated almost exclusively by Tamils who were Indian nationals, denied citizenship, and effectively prevented from leaving the plantations.[21]

With its own regenerative mechanisms, interests, and financial base, the state thus existed atop an economy that lacked diversity and had not developed substantially under colonialism. Nearly all economic activity remained within traditional village confines. Initially, the key psychological preoccupation of all classes and groups was attaining independence. Once the initial glow had worn off, other concerns became more salient. These were primarily symbolic, the return of the Sinhalese people and Buddhism to their "rightful place," and economic. In particular, the growth of the market economy, a process that accelerated after 1945, led to the substantial strengthening of the Sinhala-speaking rural capitalist class (*mudalali*).[22]

This class, however, found its livelihood increasingly threatened by a variety of state policies aimed at either nationalizing or exercising control over the activities normally engaged in by the *mudalali*. Concurrently, there was accelerating marginalization of rural cultivators as smallholders were forced into sharecropping by escalating costs of production, and sharecroppers themselves were replaced by the employment of wage labor to facilitate large scale commercial production.[23] Already by the late 1960s, at least a third of the peasantry had become landless, working either as sharecroppers or wage labor.

Additionally, roughly half of the rural population did not participate directly in agricultural production but was involved in handicraft and other activities. Unemployment and under-employment were rampant. In the decade after 1960, official figures for unemployment, which understated the actual situation, more than doubled. This trend was given impetus by a mushrooming population. In the same decade just mentioned, the country's inhabitants, in a space the size of West Virginia or Ireland, increased by 20.5%, or 2.3% annually.[24]

Structurally, then, Sri Lanka in the years after independence was characterized by a state controlled by national gentry members who had moved into administration and were no longer dependent on landed wealth extracted from the indigenous (i.e., Sinhalese) rural labor force. They had access instead to the foreign exchange generated, in particular, by the plantations; this further generated primarily by a class of non-indigenous virtual serfs, the Indian Tamils. Local gentry who were not able to move into the ranks of the ruling class continued to be directly involved in surplus extraction in the countryside but retained links with the national gentry through ties of caste, kin, and education. Arrayed as possible opposition was a growing *mudalali* class, which saw its position threatened by state policies, and an increasingly marginalized peasantry/rural population that was dramatically growing in numbers. There was also a small urban proletariat, many members of which retained links with their old villages.

A crisis in the Sri Lankan old-regime was brought about by several factors. Politically, the mechanisms of electoral politics required that national gentry factions reach out for allies to ensure their control over the power structure and national resources. In the years immediately following independence, elite parties built the needed alliances through appeals to Sinhalese chauvinism. This development, however, as we shall see, had the effect of arousing the self-defense impulse of the Ceylon Tamils, for whom independence had meant essentially no more than a change of masters. Nevertheless, the Tamil reaction was initially comparatively minor in terms of the troubles it posed for the state, certainly of less moment than the possible consequences of ignoring the aroused chauvinist sentiments of the Sinhalese majority.

Thus all major Sinhalese political parties to some extent sought to play on symbols that would arouse chauvinism. The SLFP, first off the mark, was able to parlay its advocacy of Sinhala and Buddhist primacy into victory in the 1956 election, but the UNP was not to be outdone and added its own symbolic appeals. With all elite factions adopting a chauvinist approach, distinguished only by degree, the need for additional discriminators became pronounced. The result was increased ideological differentiation of the elite, with the SLFP emphasizing socialism, the UNP the free market.

Considerable antagonism developed between them. Fiery rhetoric, filled with promises of sweeping structural changes to benefit the masses, became the order of the day. Despite the essential structural unity of the national gentry, then, the doors had been opened for the ideological split of the ruling elite into mutually antagonistic left and right. The Marxist parties and their successive splits were illustrative of the consequences attendant to the process, as extreme grew from extreme, the JVP being the final product.

This development of ideological positions—and particularly of a major party, the SLFP, publicly and stridently advocating redistributive policies—became of even greater significance due to the economic dimension of old-regime crisis. This was brought about by several developments, one a result of Colombo's position in the world economy, the other internally generated.

Hit by declining prices for its agricultural exports in the decade prior to 1971, especially those for tea, Sri Lanka saw its foreign exchange earnings fall sharply and its foreign borrowings consequently rise dramatically to maintain development and imports, notably rice. That the island was no longer self-sufficient in so basic a staple was due to the colonial-dictated emphasis on monoculture.[25] Economic difficulties reached crisis proportions because of Sri Lanka's inability to absorb its rapidly expanding population productively. Programs derived from the Western development model, such as the expansion of schooling, only exacerbated matters, because newly-educated and more politically aware individuals found their expected avenues to advancement all but non-existent.

The combination of political and economic factors placed the state under severe structural strain. Arousal of Sinhalese chauvinism by symbolic appeal had alienated an important sector of the population, the Tamils, and simultaneously unleashed ideological forces that served to split elite ranks. From this weakened position, the state was called on to cope with a resource crisis at precisely the interval during which the effects of market intrusion were becoming pronounced. The state made matters worse by attempting to further its extraction of surplus through increased nationalization and economic controls, a trend involving both SLFP and UNP governments and particularly affecting activities pursued by the *mudalali*.

Mudalali dissatisfaction increasingly was directed at the most available target, the local gentry. They were joined in their hostility by other marginalized elements of the countryside. Although half the land remained in the hands of smallholders, the largest single group in the rural areas was comprised of wage laborers, a "rural proletariat." Another large, rapidly growing group was the unemployed, or those JVP leader Wijeweera characterized as "waiting to enter the rural proletariat."[26]

It should be emphasized again that distinguishing characteristics of the gentry, especially those who had become the national elite, were their Western-style education and ability to use English. Dissimilarly, the marginalized groups discussed above were overwhelmingly educated in rural, Sinhala language schools and fluent in that tongue alone. Class considerations, therefore, were inevitably and inadvertently mobilized in the nationalist response to the elite's symbolic (and increasingly chauvinist) exhortations. Once mobilized, such passions were difficult to control. Demands for increased Sinhalese participation (i.e., that of the Sinhala-speaking, rural-educated, Buddhist rural classes) in the country's socio-economic-political life necessarily involved an attack on the existing structural arrangements that guaranteed elite dominance. Increased consciousness fostered by education and the ideological appeals of dissident elite factions led to a growing awareness of the structural constraints on individual and group mobility, hence to mounting demands for change.

By 1971, the old-regime had reached a state of crisis because of internal and external pressures. Significantly, the coercive structure was quite weak. At a time when the population was more than 12.5 million,[27] there were only 10,605 policemen assigned to 41 small offices and 266 police stations, of which 172 were staffed by 20 or fewer officers. Armament was inadequate and often antiquated; ammunition was in short supply. The military was in a similar state: small, poorly armed and trained, and lacking combat experience. Authorized strength for the army was 6,578; of the navy, 1,718; and of the air force, 1,397.[28] Fiscal constraints did not allow substantially augmenting these numbers. Further, the elite was wary lest too strong a security establishment turn on its masters. The officer corps was in its upper ranks drawn largely from the gentry, but lower officer grades and "other ranks" (i.e., enlisted personnel) were principally from the rural classes. With the national elite itself split ideologically, loyalty and control of the entire apparatus could not be guaranteed. An abortive coup in 1960 had made this point clear and had led to the institution of a system of vouchers whereby potential officers had to obtain the recommendation of a serving member of Parliament. Predictably, such a system had only further degraded the capabilities of the security forces.

As outlined already, the 1971 scenario that has been generally accepted holds that at this point in time the JVP, which already had plans to engage in revolutionary action to overthrow the existing system, was pushed into hasty action by the exposure of its plans and consequent government repression. Hampered by tactical errors and inadequate armament, the effort failed. It could thus be argued that what occurred was an isolated instance of voluntarism rather than a true revolutionary conjuncture. Work by Alexander,[29] however, parts of which have already been used to inform the analysis here, casts doubt on the commonly held view of the 1971 insurgency. He argues convincingly that the role of the JVP (as an organization) has been greatly overestimated.[30] From his reconstruction of events, Alexander writes that what actually occurred was widespread rural class upheaval resulting from the processes and developments previously discussed here.

Disorganized because of the state of crisis in which it found itself, and incapable of deploying effective coercion, the old-regime was wracked by rural, local uprisings on a national scale, with areas of heavy Tamil population not participating for obvious reasons. The JVP was involved in these uprisings and even provided much of the leadership once they got underway, but the actual occurrences were apparently largely spontaneous responses to the perceived destruction of the already strained security apparatus. As reports of the initial attacks by JVP members on police stations spread, the marginalized groups rose up, excited further by local grievances, and launched new assaults. The framework of coercion was disoriented to the extent that what apparently were attacks on just five police stations—not the nationwide, coordinated assault later raised to 93—prompted the hasty evacuation of an additional 43 posts "for strategic purposes."

"It was this action," claims Alexander, "not the success of insurgent attacks, that deprived the government of control of much of the Sinhalese countryside."[31] The coercive apparatus was in such weak condition that widespread yet unsophisticated insurgent action caused roughly a third of the state's outposts in rural areas to fall or be abandoned outright. From available data and Alexander's comments, it appears that representatives of the *mudalali* assumed leadership roles or even did much of the fighting, perhaps more in the south but apparently in the other areas, as well. Additional groups rallied to them, most importantly the rural proletariat and the "potential rural proletariat."

A plurality of the upper insurgent leadership brought before the Criminal Justice Commission for trial after the insurrection (41 persons) were identified as of the *karava* caste (traditionally associated with fishing but no longer so restricted) from southern coastal regions. *Karava* areas were longstanding strongholds of the radical left in Sri Lankan politics. Further, the south in general was a prime source of *mudalali* activity because of its early exposure to the market economy (i.e., capitalism). The sketchy biographical data on the 41 leaders published to date does not allow actual comparison of class and caste, but it would appear that what might pass for a caste dimension in the insurgency was actually one tied up with class. This was certainly the case for data on the rank-and-file. As might be expected, more than half of those detained identified themselves as *goyiyama*, the majority Sri Lankan caste, with a traditional occupation of farming.

215

The JVP, in other words, was in much the relationship that we would expect from Scott's framework, with the added stipulation that the very speed of the popular explosion meant the Maoists had to race to assume leadership positions. Their own organizational effort had not yet put them in a position to fully control what was happening.

Why did the uprising fail? A key factor was weaknesses in revolutionary party ideology and, consequently, strategy and organization. Ideologically, the Maoist doctrinal roots of the JVP led it to focus on the countryside and a failure to cultivate links with possible urban allies (as with the CPT case in Thailand). There was but limited united front or international activity, no political warfare of which to speak. Furthermore, the JVP's conception of the capitalist foe was strongly colored by Sri Lanka's colonial experience and its continuing neo-colonial relationship with the world economy. Hence, the societal issue at hand was seen as one largely of the Sinhalese masses rising up against exploitation. The result was that JVP dogma took on a strong flavor of Sinhalese chauvinism in the rural areas themselves, even if national insurgent leaders did not specifically advocate such an orientation. This immediately eliminated a further source of possible support, an ethnic united front of sorts with radical Tamils.

Just as damaging as the restrictions on its possible mass base was JVP leader Wijeweera's conception of the revolution as a massive, one-day uprising that would sweep away the old-regime, similar to the Vietnamese conception of the popular uprising. While the JVP was organized on Leninist lines, there was no well-thought-out plan of action. Neither was there a concerted effort to enforce discipline in what remained far more a loose movement than a disciplined party. The administrative and organizational tasks for a protracted people's war were simply not carried out, because it was believed, based on the JVP's analysis of the Sri Lankan polity, that such an approach was not needed. Even tactical battle drill was rudimentary.

Inevitably, when the structural opportunity for revolutionary war presented itself, neither the JVP nor any other group had the requisite organization or resources to seize the moment. Since no rival revolutionary body was thrown up by the rural explosions themselves, however, the JVP was in a position to dominate the rebellion as it developed (one thinks of the relationship between the PKP and the *Huks* in the Philippines). Even with the fundamental ideological and organizational flaws that rendered it both strategically and tactically weakened, for the JVP, the moment was right. The government staggered badly in absorbing what has since been shown to have been, in objective terms, a rather lightweight punch.

The resources that would have been needed to topple the state appear minimal. Lightly armed, poorly organized, and barely tactically competent, the rebels nonetheless rocked the nation. Indeed, only after the widespread rebellion sputtered for want of effective leadership was the state able to recover, seek external assistance, and finally crush the uprising. The need for external assistance is itself further evidence that a serious situation beyond elite control had developed. The state was able to weather the storm with assistance from the very world-system that had generated the economic crisis that played such a pronounced role in weakening the established order. It provided such assistance for ideological reasons: the need for both East and West blocs to woo an important non-aligned actor.

Growth of Tamil Insurgency and Counter-State

As the situation in Sri Lanka returned to normal, the government continued its symbolic appeals as a means to mollify the discontented rural areas. This alienated further the Ceylon Tamils, who began to seek means to resist. The Indian Tamils remained more concerned with issues of citizenship, minimum wages, and improving basic education and health facilities on plantations.

To press for redress of Tamil grievances, a Tamil United Front (TUF)—later adding "Liberation" to become TULF—was formed in 1972, comprised of legal advocacy organizations. TULF was oriented towards autonomy, while a leftist-inspired Tamil Students Federation (TSF) called for more radical solutions, such as independence. Predictably, as TSF produced radical splinters at home, radical organizations also began to form amongst militant Tamil students abroad. These were significant, because they were strongly influenced by Marxism and found in its vocabulary, analytical categories, and explanatory framework a viable explanation for the Tamil situation. Their solution to their "oppression" was to call for "liberation," that is, the formation of a separate socialist or Marxist Tamil state, *Tamil Eelam* (see Figure 5.2). Membership numbers were small. The Tamil people, whatever their plight, did not readily give their support to "coffee house revolutionaries."

Without a mass base, these militants could do little more than to plan future terror actions. Police and intelligence documents speak of small, isolated groups of a half-dozen or so would-be liberationists meeting in forest gatherings in Sri Lanka to plot their moves. Actions that occurred, bombings and small-scale attacks upon government supporters and police pickets, were irritating but dismissed as the logical consequence of radicalism.

Figure 5.2: Though disagreeing on strategy, operational art, and even tactics, the Tamil insurgent groups were united in their demand for an independent Tamil homeland. All major groups claimed that it needed to be both ethnically Tamil and socialist. (LTTE graphic in Author Collection)

There was method to the upstart schemes, though. By 1975, government interrogations showed, the Eelam Revolutionary Organisation of Students (EROS), the initial overseas student group seeking *Eelam*, had made its first contacts with the Palestine Liberation Organisation (PLO) through PLO representatives in London. Shortly thereafter, EROS began to send personnel to the Middle East for training. That the PLO was itself not Marxist did not prove a stumbling block, as the issue was framed as one of "liberation from oppression" as opposed to social revolution. Indeed, as the connection matured in the years that followed, another Marxist group (see below), People's Liberation Organisation of Thamileelam (PLOT), forged strong links with George Habash's PLO Marxist splinter, the Popular Front for the Liberation of Palestine (PFLP).

Simultaneously, at home, a proliferation of very small (as few as four individuals), aggressive "liberation groups" took place. Seeking to respond to growing state marginalization of Tamils, especially the requirement of Sinhala proficiency for governmental and educational attainment, alienated Tamil youth lashed out. Assassination attempts against government officials had begun as early as September 1970; bomb-making triggered several accidental explosions in workshops in both 1971 and 1972. An early, prominent militant, Ponnudarai Sivakumaran of the Tamil New Tigers (TNT), rather than accept capture, killed himself by swallowing cyanide on 5 June 1974, after being cornered during an attempted bank robbery. The methodology came to be the premier symbol of commitment associated with the TNT's successor organization, announced on 5 May 1976, the Liberation Tigers of Tamil Eelam (LTTE). Its leader was Velupillai Prabhakaran (b. 26 November 1954), who had participated personally in the TNT's major actions, to include the 27 July 1975 assassination of the Jaffna Mayor, Alfred Duriappah, an SLFP member.

Even as such actions escalated—carried out by what was estimated at no more than 50 militants[32]—the Tamil majority remained overtly committed to resolution of grievances within the parliamentary framework. Yet an escalating series of violent episodes—attacks on the police, seizure of weapons of all types from individuals and government offices, robberies of banks and individuals, thefts of chemicals from schools and explosives from "factories," and attempts to assassinate those seen as "traitors"—led to harsh police actions against alleged militant sympathizers and, ultimately, in August 1977, to the commitment of an army battalion (four companies). Repression set in motion both an inexorable escalation of violence and mushrooming popular support (for "the boys," as the militants were increasingly called) driven by the imperative of self-defense. On 19 May 1978, parliament passed a "Proscription of Liberation Tigers of Tamil Eelam and Other Similar

Organisations,"[33] followed on 19 July 1979 by a more comprehensive "Prevention of Terrorism Act" (PTA). For all practical purposes, Sri Lanka remained under a state of emergency for the decade and a half that followed.

Such legislation had no impact upon the situation. The first attack on the army occurred on 15 October 1981, by which time 9 of 16 police stations in Jaffna were reported closed. The peninsula had become the embryonic counter-state. Parliament amended PTA on 11 March 1982 to empower the Minister of Justice to detain suspected terrorists for up to 18 months without a remand order from a magistrate. By this time, the political ground had shifted substantially. Their inability to impact the situation discredited the TULF leadership, with radical elements increasingly dominant as the voice of the Tamil cause. This voice was fragmented, to be sure; even LTTE, which had the strong leadership provided by Prabhakaran, split into a number of factions which engaged in internecine warfare. Particularly important was the departure of Kadirgamapillai Nallainathan, or, as he was more widely known, Uma Maheshwaran, who became the leader of PLOT. Yet all groups shared a commitment to terrorism as a method of action as opposed to a logic of action. Their violence was intended to spur mass mobilization, not as an end unto itself.

Sri Lanka, however, could see only "terrorism," by which it meant terrorism as a logic for action—terror committed by isolated actors with, at best, a support base, certainly not the mass base associated with a counter-state. The main arm for combating the threat remained the police, now grown to 12,000 but still armed, equipped, and deployed for a traditional "watcher" role that could best be termed "presence." Though its Criminal Investigation Division (CID) had within it some highly skilled individuals, these were few and concentrated in the capital, Colombo. The force was overwhelmingly Sinhalese. Forced gradually to abandon their exposed stations, the police gave up what security presence they had, allowing the militants to dominate further the population and to expand the counter-state. Committing the military, the only remaining card left for the state to play, had not done much to rectify the situation, because it did not have the capabilities for anti-militant action necessary to stop the terror campaign. Indeed, the army's total ground strength was effectively contained in five infantry battalions of 500–600 men each. The air force and navy were small and not structured as combat forces. The capability for intelligence gathering and surgical application of force was all but lacking.

At this early stage, the militants were still vulnerable and hopelessly divided by issues of ideology and approach. Prabhakaran, for instance, was thoroughly Guevarist and saw armed action ("guerrilla action") as the key to popular mobilization.[34]

Increasingly, the sheer ruthlessness of his will came to dominate the Tamil struggle. Rival groups, as we shall see below, were methodically, systematically wiped out. When Prabhakaran and his fellows could be numbered but in scores, there was an opening for the state. CID had considerable knowledge of the threat but no means to act in an appropriate manner. Response had to be left to the police, who increasingly were unable to defend themselves, much less arrest suspects, or the military, which proved a very blunt instrument indeed. This left action to individual initiative, of which there was a surprising amount, but when casualties began to claim these men or they were marginalized by political concerns, there simply was no second line.

Events, in any case, had taken on a life of their own. On 15 July 1983, Charles Anton, LTTE "military wing" commander, was killed in a firefight with Sri Lankan military personnel in Jaffna. In retaliation, on 23 July, again in Jaffna, an ambush executed by an LTTE element left 13 soldiers dead. Their subsequent funeral in Colombo ignited widespread rioting and looting directed against Tamils. At least 400 persons were killed and 100,000 left homeless; another 200–250,000 fled to India. Police stood by, and in many cases members of the armed forces participated in the violence.

This spasm of communal terror served to traumatize the Tamil community and provided LTTE with an influx of new manpower. Thus the ascendancy of radical leadership in the struggle for *Tamil Eelam* was complete. Even TULF expressed no confidence in the government's efforts to resolve communal difficulties. Only the radical option remained. That option, to be clear, was Marxist-Leninist, as stated directly by the leadership of all the major groups fighting for *Tamil Eelam*.

Ironically, at the time of the July 1983 upheaval, the would-be insurgents, even if united, could probably not have mustered 200 men in as many as 42 different groups. Members and their activities were generally well known to Sri Lankan intelligence. Thereafter, their strength grew quickly, reaching eventually an estimated 10,000. In the combat that followed, Sri Lanka's small security forces proved woefully inadequate for grappling with the complexities of counter-insurgency. Brutalization of the Tamil populace only created further insurgent recruits.

"Terrorists," in other words, as the authorities called them, had been provided with a mass base by the imperfections of Sri Lankan society. By co-opting the rebellion of Tamil youth that followed the July 1983 upheaval, the "terrorists" were able to become *bona fide* insurgents. The situation was soon out of control. Government writ was effectively lost in Jaffna, the area of most dense Tamil settlement. In other areas of heavy Tamil concentration, the Northern and Eastern Provinces, the security forces barely held their own. The conflict even touched

Sinhalese majority areas, a development starkly illustrated in a May 1985 attack on the Buddhist holy city of Anuradhapura in the North Central Province that left nearly 180 pilgrims massacred.[35]

Under pressure from its 55 million-strong Tamil Nadu state in the south, India, fearful lest it be forced to bear the burden of masses of refugees and already unhappy at what it perceived to be the pro-Western foreign policy orientation of Sri Lankan UNP President Junius R. Jayewardene's government, began a program of covert assistance to the insurgents (carried out by its equivalent of the CIA, the Research and Analysis wing, or RAW) and turned a blind eye to their growing presence in its own state of Tamil Nadu. This all but destroyed relations between Colombo and New Delhi.

The assassination of Indian Prime Minister Indira Gandhi in October 1984—at the hands of Sikh bodyguards caught up in the backlash that followed New Delhi's Operation *Bluestar* against terrorists based in Sikhdom's holiest shrine, the Golden Temple of Amritsar[36]—brought to power her surviving son, Rajiv. He promptly carried out a sea change in policy. Lengthy discussions were held with Sri Lankan policy makers to arrive at an approach to the "Tamil problem" acceptable to both Colombo and New Delhi; the insurgents were informed that India would not accept an independent Tamil state at its back door; their efforts to move men and supplies across the Palk Strait were interrupted; and the most active insurgent base camps in India were scaled back. On 18 June 1985, it was announced that Colombo agreed to a "cessation of hostilities" and their first face-to-face discussions in an effort to frame a political solution to the conflict.

Rajiv Gandhi's reversal of his mother's stance toward the insurgents was prompted by recognition of the obvious contradiction contained in supporting separatism within a democratic neighbor even while attempting to combat various domestic separatist movements. Tamil separatism was viewed as especially danger-ous, because it had remained a problem in the Indian south ever since the peak of the *Dravida Munnetra Kazhagham* (DMK)-led campaign for a separate Tamil entity. When he took office, Rajiv Ghandi found that the presence in Tamil Nadu of the Sri Lankan insurgents had served to revive anti-Hindi sentiments and latent Tamil chauvinism. The DMK, which had been the state assembly opposition to the ruling "*Anna* DMK" (AIADMK), an offshoot of the old movement, was waging a vigorous campaign to arouse such sentiments and to derive political advantage from them. Thus he moved vigorously to foster a solution.

Despite his efforts, however, five months of desultory talks in Thimpu, the capital of Bhutan, and a truce that never really took hold led to little of substance. That this was the result never seemed in doubt to informed observers. For there was another side to the situation most germane to the issues under consideration here. While the conflict certainly revolved around Tamil efforts to redress perceived and real wrongs suffered at the hands of the Sinhalese, all major insurgent groups claimed to be Marxist-Leninist and to be inspired by prominent insurgent approaches, such as that of Mao.

They were pressing, then, they stated, for goals that extended beyond mere "liberation" in an ethnic sense. This aspect of the insurgency received little attention, despite the fact that access to insurgent groups and their literature was fairly easy. Its significance was made plain in discussions with insurgent leadership figures: even a government offer of a considerable amount of autonomy would in the end not have been enough to induce the insurgents to give up their struggle.[37] They, regardless of group, avowed their intent to pursue Marxist revolution. This they stated explicitly—privately, publicly, and in their literature. Wrote Anton Stanislav Balasingham, leading theoretician for LTTE: "The political objective of our movement is to advance the national struggle along with the class struggle, or rather, our fundamental objective is national emancipation and socialist transformation of our social formation."[38]

Examining the insurgent movement in detail revealed an alphabet soup of initials. The dozens of different groups, however, were dominated by a "big five": Liberation Tigers of Tamil Eelam (LTTE); People's Liberation Organization of Thamileelam (PLOT, also frequently rendered as PLOTE in the Western press, a variance caused by use of *Tamil Eelam* rather than *Thamileelam* as adopted by the group itself in its formal communications); Tamil Eelam Liberation Organisation (TELO); Eelam People's Revolutionary Liberation Front (EPRLF); and Eelam Revolutionary Organisation (EROS). PLOT aside, these groups agreed in April 1985 to end their constant bickering and ambushes of each other in order to form an Eelam National Liberation Front (ENLF). Subsequently, they sought international recognition along the lines pioneered by the PLO. PLOT remained allied with several smaller Marxist groups—Tamil Eelam Liberation Army (TELA), the Senthil faction of the Tamil Eelam Liberation Front (TELF), Tamil Eelam Republican Army (TERA), and National Liberation Front of Tamileelam (NLFT).

Of these, LTTE and PLOT were the leading organizations. The animosity between their leaders, Velupillai Prabhakaran and Uma Maheswaran, respectively, became more pronounced,[39] as did differences of approach. LTTE was the more ruthless and used terror routinely against both the Sinhalese (e.g., it was responsible for the massacre in Anuradhapura) and Tamils. Specially targeted were Tamils who

223

LTTE and PLOT dominated: Shown in mug shots following detention in the early 1980s, Velupillai Prabhakaran of LTTE (left) and Uma Maheswaran of PLOT (right) were separated by age, temperament, and social mores. Ultimately, Prabhakaran, as he attempted to do with all rivals, would have Uma assassinated. (Photo: Sri Lankan security forces in Author Collection)

sought non-violent solution to the issues wracking the polity. Other Tamil insurgent groups were also frequent targets. Both groups sent personnel for training in the Middle East.

Non-Marxist separatist groups gradually were incorporated by the Marxists, either through persuasion or coercion. An extensive network of bases was set up in Tamil Nadu. In Sri Lanka itself, all groups (as monitored by Sri Lankan intelligence) attempted to construct counter-states. The degree to which this was actually done depended on: first, the group (e.g., PLOT, being more sophisticated in its Marxism than, say, LTTE, was more systematic in its efforts than not only LTTE but also the other *Eelam* groups); second, the area (e.g., Jaffna was more secure, so LTTE, which dominated there, did not find it necessary to construct more than support activities); and, third, the government response (e.g., it was much more difficult for the *Eelam* groups to construct clandestine infrastructure in the East, where there was a strong government presence, than in the North).

In this they were further aided by enhanced Indian support. In response to domestic pressures that it resist Colombo's alleged "genocide" against the Sri Lankan Tamils (the Tamil Nadu state government itself even began to assist the guerrillas), the minimal RAW effort was expanded dramatically and also brought into the fold the other insurgent groups not already under its tutelage, most notably LTTE. RAW was assisted by other Indian intelligence agencies, such as the National Intelligence Bureau (NIB), and paramilitary bodies (such as the Indo-Tibetan Border Force, ITBF). Indian officials, at the time, stated privately that their intent was to give the Tamil community a "self-defense" capability. It was all too predictable, however, that such an effort, once set in motion, would rapidly escalate beyond India's control.

While rebel manpower was indeed thrown up by the trauma of July 1983, the *Eelam* movement leadership came from the original pre-July 1983 Marxist groups. Key figures of all major formations remained those individuals whose designs were much larger than mere "self-defense." They were after "liberation" in its Marxist sense. Attempts to discern whether groups were "really Marxist" (an exercise favored by the Indian High Commission in Colombo during the term of J. N. Dixit[40]) were pointless: the insurgents considered themselves Marxist and drew from Marxist models their strategic analysis of the situation, tactical use of

Grievance guerrillas: LTTE members pose at a safe house in 1987. Tamil combatants knew little if anything about the group's ideology and had joined for more immediate reasons, such as defense of community. They were to become increasingly more focused as the decades passed. (Marks photo)

clandestine mechanisms, and ideological phraseology. They studied people's war documents intensely. To ensure that the "grievance guerrillas" shared their aims and analysis of the situation, the leadership allocated large portions of the daily training schedule to Marxist ideological indoctrination. In such sessions, as well as in their public and private pronouncements, the rebels spoke of their fight for *Tamil Eelam* as involving two struggles, liberation from the Sinhalese and from capitalism.[41]

India was not interested in the political ideology of the groups involved. Two of the "most Marxist" groups, PLOT and TELO, were the initial recipients of its largess. These groups, according to Sri Lankan intelligence, were in contact with breakaway factions of the JVP, which continued to exist despite its decimation. The JVP itself had increasingly sought to benefit from Sinhalese chauvinism. Yet this was precisely the point: The shared goal of the JVP breakaways and the *Eelam* adherents was to engage in a people's war using guerrilla tactics (a military technique) to carry through a social revolution (a political aim) that would lead to installing allied Tamil and Sinhalese Marxist regimes. Such goals were so much youthful chatter as far as RAW was concerned: it ignored them.

As normally the case with clandestine bodies, it was difficult to come up with meaningful strength figures for the insurgent groups. It has already been noted that the guerrillas were unable to increase their numbers substantially until after the July 1983 riots radicalized large sectors of the Tamil community, especially the youth, and provided abundant, motivated manpower. Sri Lankan military intelligence sources, in fact, noted that in 1975 they carried the number of hardcore insurgents as twenty-five. One year after July 1983, this figure had mushroomed to 5,000 and was subsequently put as high as 10,000, although many of the latter figure were not armed.

The significance of the number, whether 5,000 or 10,000, lay in the fact that, until Sri Lanka could mobilize its manpower pool, the combined insurgents very nearly matched the strength of the security forces. Thus they stood a chance if properly armed, trained, and coordinated of putting the latter on the ropes. That they were unable to do so owed far more to their own internal problems than it did to government capacity.

Until the formation of ENLF in April 1985, the insurgents engaged in little cooperation and coordination. PLOT remained outside the group, its representatives and those of LTTE having again, in March, engaged in gunplay to argue their points. Personal differences seemed much to the heart of the matter as opposed to matters of substance. All major groups remained Marxist-Leninist (more on this choice of terminology below), with a vague conception of people's war as their model for making revolution. Likewise, they were all firmly committed to *Tamil Eelam* in the belief that liberation could come only through both an independent Tamil state and the use of Marxist ideology to transform the relations of production. "Our total strategy," noted A. S. Balasingham of LTTE, "integrates both nationalism and socialism into a revolutionary project aimed at liberating our people both from national oppression and from the exploitation of man by man."[42]

Organizationally, insurgent groups utilized the standard Leninist constructs, with Politburos, Central Committees, and the like, but they did not always establish a party element separate from the guerrilla forces themselves. This was particularly true of LTTE, which, despite the prominent role accorded to Balasingham, nominally the group's second figure, remained the organization least committed to self-conception an irrevocable as a Marxist insurgency. This was in direct contradiction to the others of the "Big Five," PLOT, TELO, EPRLF, and EROS.

To return now to the "Marxist" characterization of the groups, it seems clear that the dimension of ethnic turmoil, spawned as it was by socio-economic-political contradictions, led to the original discontent, or "alienation," to use their own Marxist terminology. The insurgents' ideological framework was created as they groped for explanations of the repression they felt was bent on the annihilation of their people. The result was quite an eclectic body of thought, with desires for justice paramount for many of the rank-and-file, but decidedly secondary among the leadership to "deeper" considerations of the necessity for liberation from Sri Lankan capitalism and global imperialism. Since most insurgent supporters were not even necessarily in favor of *Tamil Eelam* at this point, in the separatist sense, much less the Marxist connotations held by the leadership, the groups did not make a point of pushing forward their ideological views in public debate.[43]

Most illustrative of the insurgent stance was the explanation offered by a PLOT Politburo member in 1984 when he repeatedly made the point that the insurgents were "Marxist thinkers" as opposed to "Marxists" or communists. He and his "comrades," he explained, attempted to use Marxist principles and methodologies of all varieties (Marx, Lenin, Mao, and the Sandinistas were mentioned) to arrive at an analytical framework appropriate for the Tamil situation. As such, the insurgents were inspired by, trained with, and were willing to fight for other radical causes, especially against "American imperialism." All this was a learning experience as the particulars of a unique "Tamil communism" evolved. [44]

PLOT, as evidenced in the chain of thought above, displayed considerable flexibility in its evolution of this "Tamil communism." Other ENLF members were more limited in the scope and depth of their analysis. PLOT's analysis of the situation held that the key ally of the government was Sinhalese anti-Tamil sentiment, or chauvinism. Indiscriminate attacks that served to fan such sentiments were ultimately counterproductive, PLOT maintained, because they turned what was fundamentally a political conflict, being waged against world imperialism (i.e., international capitalism) and its Colombo offshoot, into an ethnic battle. This was disastrous, the analysis continued, as there was little chance of an independent Tamil state emerging in the face of an omnipresent Sinhalese hostility. Common cause had to be made, the reasoning concluded, with the radical Sinhalese left to overthrow the Colombo government through joint revolutionary action. Under a Marxist regime, the communal problem could be solved in a way mutually agreeable to both ethnic groups.

ENLF, on the other hand, dominated by LTTE, was more colored in its approach by its ethnic roots. LTTE, in particular, was more oriented toward what it saw as the essence of the struggle, the effort to drive the Sinhalese, blinded though they might be by bourgeoisie leadership, from the "traditional Tamil homelands." Prabhakaran himself was particularly less concerned with the insurgency's purported niche in the global struggle, Balasingham's pronouncements notwithstanding.[45] The crucial element, LTTE believed, before all others, was to carry the fight to the enemy through combat operations, thereby liberating *Tamil Eelam* from "Sinhalese fascism." Ideological development and organizational particulars of the future Marxist state would follow.

Tactically, this difference resulted in LTTE (taking ENLF along) being the most active of the insurgent groups in actual fighting. Even when truces were declared during efforts at negotiation, LTTE continued its attacks, especially against fellow Tamil insurgents viewed as insufficiently committed to the tactical use of talks to further strategic gains. It was LTTE, too, that perpetuated regular massacres of Sinhalese civilians in retaliation for atrocities, alleged and real, committed against Tamils.

It was not surprising, then, that LTTE used terror extensively, especially the killing, often after torture, of those denounced as informants, traitors, or backsliders. Those so executed were frequently left tied or hanging from lamp-posts, spawning the common use of the term "lamp-post killings" or "lamp-post victim" to describe such episodes. These increased in frequency as the conflict advanced, as did bombings and related efforts to inflict damage to human targets and the physical infrastructure, such as the rail system. Far from any attempt to avoid casualties, there was an effort to maximize those affected. PLOT and the other groups (such as those within ENLF) also used terror—and internal purges were a staple of all groups—but PLOT's killings were far more selective and designed to attack the "enemy within." There was an effort to avoid actions that would likely result in reprisals against Tamil civilians, and Sinhalese civilians normally were not indiscriminately attacked.

Initially, following July 1983, the insurgent response to the situation had the character of the French *maquis* during the Second World War, guerrillas operating with popular support against an enemy force occupying the homeland. The goal was simply to strike back. Gradually, as ideological concerns began to play a greater role, the construction of embryonic counter-states became salient. This was an important indicator of the shading of separatist rebellion into insurgency. The goal had become people's war in the Maoist sense, for the purpose of liberation. *Tamil Eelam* had become more than a call for a piece of territory. It was a plan for structural transformation.

State Response to Tamil Insurgent Challenge

While an insurgency is normally more dangerous to a government than rebellion, the immediate problems for the authorities are much the same: coping with the military attacks of an armed uprising. By early 1984, therefore, the Sri Lankan military, which previously had been able to avoid all but minimal involvement in the "counter-terrorist" campaign, centered in the north, found itself faced with the need to engage in counter-insurgency. This, it was ill-prepared to carry out.

The defense establishment had grown as a result of the 1971 JVP insurgency, but it remained one befitting the island's small size: a 14,000-man army (12,000 regulars and 2,000 reserves, or "volunteers," on active duty); a 3,500-man air force flying a motley collection of small, fixed-wing aircraft and helicopters; a navy of 3,500 men that crewed 32 small craft; and a police force of roughly 12,000 assigned to small stations throughout the country. Fewer than 5% of the soldiers were Tamil, less than 3% of the officers. Personnel in all services were poorly trained. Units did not operate as such, the only reservoir of combat experience lay in older personnel who had participated in the suppression of the 1971 insurgency. Discipline was a problem, and the government was forced to move vigorously just before the nationwide riots to punish abuses, disbanding an entire battalion for indiscipline.[46]

Army combat power thus was centered in a mere four infantry battalions, all of which were under their designated 730-man strengths and stationed in company-size cantonments throughout the country.[47] Each line battalion was theoretically the first

Limited manpower: Sri Lanka was completely unprepared for counter-insurgency, with both its army (above) and police (below) small forces that had never been tested by combat. Relatively quickly, both forces became much larger and more effective. (Marks photos)

of three in a regiment, with the other two battalions comprised of reservists. In reality, only one regiment had its two "volunteer" battalions. None of the reserve component units was on active duty; all were under-strength and armed with outdated weapons. Single armor, artillery, signal, and combat engineer regiments were also only under-strength battalions. At one time, approximately a third of the "volunteer" personnel themselves, as opposed to their units, were on active duty to make up manpower shortages in regular units. Communal disturbances had already stretched available units so tightly that air force and navy men regularly performed as foot soldiers. Air support was minimal,[48] the navy a small coastal flotilla.[49]

These, then, were the forces called on to grapple with the complexities of irregular warfare. Initially, in the months after July 1983, there was the expected chaos of gearing up for internal conflict. In March 1984, however, it appeared a new approach was at hand. Oxford-educated Lalith Athulathmudalai, a possible successor to President Jayewardene, was named head of a newly created Ministry

Unity of Command: In 1984, Oxford-educated Lalith Athulathmudalai (left; shown with army head, Hamilton Wanasinghe) was appointed to head a newly created Ministry of National Security, thus bringing the counter-insurgency under one leader. A second position as deputy Defense Minister effectively gave him authority to command all security force assets, as well. (Marks photo)

of National Security as well as Deputy Defense Minister. (Jayewardene himself was Defense Minister.) This effectively placed control of the armed services and counter-insurgency operations under one man. Intra-service coordination improved under a Joint Operations Center (JOC), as did military discipline and force disposition. Still, it was not long before it became evident that the government effort would continue to be plagued by inefficient planning, unimaginative leadership, and continuing indiscipline.

As the military and insurgents blooded each other, delegates from various sectors of Sri Lankan society continued talks with the relative moderates of TULF at an All-Party Congress (APC) designed to seek solutions to the ethnic impasse. There were times when the protagonists appeared near agreement on some form of local autonomy that would satisfy moderate Tamil demands for "independence" yet retain the essential national unity demanded by the Sinhalese. None of these schemes proved successful, falling victim to the increasingly narrow room for maneuver that hemmed in moderates on both sides. As a unitary state, with provinces and districts run by centrally appointed officials, Sri Lanka was unable to view even limited scenarios for the devolution of power as anything other than steps toward separatism. And any partition of "Lanka" was out of the question.

In its particulars, there was much in the mindset of the majority Sinhalese community that was akin to Zionism, with its characteristic pugnacity and rigidity. The Buddha himself, it was taught in Sri Lanka, had chosen the island as his bastion for the faith's survival. His religion had vanished from India, the land of its birth, but in Lanka it was to remain protected and nurtured. Sinhalese legendary heroes aplenty held Tamil invaders at bay that it might remain so. Thus the Sinhalese came to see themselves as a chosen people, living in a chosen land, and following the chosen and one true faith. Their missionaries revitalized decaying Buddhism near and far. By historical circumstances, the Sinhalese view went, other races and religions, notably the Hindu Tamils, had come to be incorporated into the independent state of Sri Lanka, but there was no question in the majority mind as to whose land the island truly was. Those who were not Sinhalese and Buddhist were welcome as guests privileged to have come to the island, but any assault on the system's essential parameters meant an end to the welcome. The resulting misbehavior of the armed forces, comprised of young, ill-educated, rural, Sinhalese-speaking males, was predictable.

In the absence of a well-defined socio-political approach to the problem, a strategy that would cut popular support out from under the self-professed Marxist revolutionaries, the government's counter-insurgency program rapidly became little more than an attempted exercise in human and organizational engineering. Lalith stated in August 1984[50] that improvement in the tactical situation was to take place within a strategic framework that had as its objective the isolation of the insurgents in Jaffna through Sinhalese settlements in the non-Jaffna areas of the insurgents' claimed *Eelam*. This would be carried out using existing government resettlement schemes, a part of the massive Mahaweli Development Programme, to create an equal mixture of ethnic groups—Tamil, Muslim, and Sinhalese—in areas such as Trincomalee and Batticaloa Districts, which then had Tamil-Muslim majorities. The rationale was that in areas of mixed population, there would be a minimum of ethnic conflict and radicalization, because people would tend "to get along." The likelihood that such a scheme would almost certainly be the subject of attack necessitated some form of home guard, but that would be left until later.

Completion of such settlement was envisaged for 1986–88, at which time the insurgents would be effectively isolated demographically in Jaffna. They would have no appeal elsewhere. In Jaffna, Lalith noted, a "hearts and minds" approach was futile, as the cancer of radicalism had already taken root. A solution could only come when a new generation of Tamil leaders emerged within an environment where it had been clearly demonstrated that the government could not be beaten. This might, he concluded, necessitate a willingness to accept "a Northern Ireland" for the following fifteen to twenty years. It was the minister's expectation that Tamils of talent and ability who did not sympathize with the insurgents would leave the Jaffna area.

In some respects this approach was sound. It was based on a realization that the problem had two dimensions: popular Tamil demands, actual or latent, for redress of grievances, on the one hand, and use of those grievances as a vehicle for an assault on the state's integrity by insurgents, on the other. Through the events of July 1983 and the abuse of civilians that followed, a large proportion of the Tamil population had become insurgent sympathizers, especially in Jaffna. Unable to make headway in impeding the growth of insurgent influence there, and faced with insurgent attempts to expand into marginally affected, Tamil-populated areas elsewhere, the logical course of action was to isolate the rebels.

This attempt at human engineering was doomed to failure, of course, because it turned reality on its head. It was based on the premise that if only the insurgents could be controlled, isolated, and eliminated, the majority of the Tamil people would be freed from the grip of fear and free to negotiate with the government in good faith. Yet the Tamil people, generally speaking while allowing for individual exceptions, had not become supporters of the insurgents through insurgent terror, ample as it was. Rather, they had been driven to the rebels by the government's failure to reach a political solution and by its failure to protect them from the abuse of both elements of the security forces and unruly Sinhalese mobs.

Within such a mind-frame, the means soon became the end. Increasingly, the Sri Lankan effort focused on the mechanical aspects of small-unit warfare. Even these were carried out badly. Factions within the government, as well as key military officers, were aware of this critical shortfall but seemed unable to influence policy decisions. It was as though paralysis had set in at every level of Sri Lankan decision-making, beginning with President Jayewardene. The most commonly offered explanation for the lack of movement toward a political solution, fear of a Sinhalese backlash, while not a straw man by any means, eventually became a self-fulfilling prophecy and an excuse for inaction.

By late 1984, insurgent activity had grown to the point that it threatened government control of Tamil majority areas in northern Sri Lanka. Security forces had increased in size and quality of weaponry, but a national concept of operations was lacking. There was serious doubt, in fact, whether some elements of the armed forces in the north, if pressed closely by an insurgent onslaught, would be able to make an orderly withdrawal. Reports forwarded to higher authorities were routinely falsified to put the best possible face on the situation.

The extent to which insurgent capabilities had developed was amply demonstrated in a well-coordinated and executed attack on 20 November 1984 in which a Tamil force of company size used overwhelming firepower and explosives to demolish the Chavakachcheri police station on the Jaffna Peninsula and to kill at least 27 policemen defending it. There followed continued ambushes of security forces, as well as several large massacres of Sinhalese civilians living in areas deemed by the insurgents to be "traditional Tamil homelands." Use of automatic weapons, mortars, and RPG-7 rocket launchers was reported.

Even as these developments took place, it became clear to the authorities that a drastic upgrading of security force capabilities was needed, a task accomplished in remarkably short order amidst the turmoil of a worsening situation. Absence of fulsome assistance by outside powers was initially in stark contrast to the rush that had followed the 1971 JVP outbreak. Rather, Sri Lanka managed largely on its own or by contracting for services. Most significantly, a new police field unit, Special Task Force (STF), was raised under the tutelage of ex-SAS (Special Air Services) personnel employed by KMS, Ltd. STF took over primary responsibility for security in the Eastern Province in late 1984, freeing the army to concentrate on areas of the Northern Province (which included Jaffna).

New units: To conduct specialty tasks within the counter-insurgency framework, a police field force, Special Task Force (STF, above) and four regiments (battalions, below) of army special operations forces were stood up. Both performed well tactically. (Marks photos)

In similar fashion, Israel was approached on the basis of its demonstrated expertise in counter-terrorist operations. In the face of much criticism and amidst fears that the lucrative Middle East market for Sri Lankan expatriate labor might be jeopardized, Colombo allowed the establishment of an Israeli Special Interests Section in May 1984, with the US as the protecting power. Small teams (normally two personnel) from Israel's internal security service, *Shin Bet*, shortly thereafter arrived to train Sri Lankan personnel in intelligence gathering and internal security techniques.

STF proved reasonably successful, despite its not being able to replace the army in counter-insurgency operations totally.[51] The relationship with Israel was not nearly as smooth, particularly given the political complications caused, not only in Sri Lanka's foreign affairs but also in its relations with its large Muslim community. Aside from the fact that Israel was essentially looking for a route to renew diplomatic relations suspended during the Bandaranaike administration (1970–77) and had no desire to become entangled in Sri Lanka's internal fighting, the value of counter-terrorism advice was limited when applied to counter-insurgency.

Who said what and to whom may never be known, but there was a basic similarity between the unsuccessful Israeli approach to pacification of the occupied Arab territories and that practiced in the early stage of the fighting in Sri Lanka. The "population-as-enemy" philosophy, harsh reprisals, and emphasis on the military to maintain order rather than to function as a shield behind which a political solution could be put in place were common components of the Israeli and Sri Lankan strategies.

The results were also identical. With their position in Jaffna consolidated, the insurgents moved in force into areas of the east, which they also claimed as part of *Eelam*, despite a majority of the population being non-Tamil. Additionally, they began to operate in Sinhalese-majority areas, attacking the population. With its forces deployed in "hot" areas, and having violated the tenet to secure first its own base areas before moving out to engage the enemy, the government was unprepared to meet this new threat. Efforts to increase force strengths further and to purchase new equipment (e.g., a dozen Bell 212 helicopters) did little to improve the security apparatus' serious shortcomings.

By mid-1985, then, when the Thimpu talks began, the island was in a state of serious disorder, which the security forces proved unable to alleviate. Most fundamentally, the government was crippled by its inability to set forth a viable political solution within which military operations could proceed. Military success, even when gained, was little more than momentary tactical advantage. Regardless of efforts to improve the military posture, there could hence be little impact on the overall poor security climate.

As the insurgent threat spilled out of Jaffna, the government met it with *ad hoc*, haphazard schemes. Both privately and publicly, Colombo's spokespersons talked not of counter-insurgency but of their "fight against terrorism." This shift in perspective was to be of fundamental import. Focused on terrorism rather than insurgency, Sri Lanka ordered its military leaders to go after the guerrillas and to stamp out the rebellion. There was little movement toward political accommodation that would have isolated the insurgent hardcore, especially the leadership. As the insurgents mobilized the target population, the government could not engage in counter-mobilization, because it had no theme or plan about which such action could be based.

Sri Lanka's position was made immeasurably more difficult by the ability of the insurgents to operate from safe base areas in India's southern state of Tamil Nadu. That democratic India should be involved with Marxist insurgents attempting to form a counter-state within a democratic neighbor was on the surface a paradox but not altogether unexpected given the regional imperialism that had been an essential driving force of New Delhi's foreign policy since independence.[52] Even while the country looked to the West for cultural approval, its alliances during the Cold War were with the Soviet Union. It was, then, Sri Lanka's close ties with Western democracies that played a crucial role in the development of India's succor for the insurgents.

Sitting astride key sea routes, Sri Lanka's geo-strategic position had long been recognized. Britain used the island as a locus for dominating the Indian Ocean. The port that was the headquarters of this effort, Trincomalee, on the eastern coast, was one of the world's finest natural harbors and had an oil storage area of nearly a hundred finely preserved tanks left by the British. There was also a functioning airfield.

Of primary attraction to the West, however, had been Sri Lanka's democratic institutions and its eventual commitment to market mechanisms, despite the formal title "Socialist State of Sri Lanka" adopted by an SLFP government. After President Jayewardene's UNP assumed office in 1977, Western aid-donors became actively involved in major infrastructure projects. The country was regarded as something of a showcase for the developing world. Not surprisingly, in its foreign policies, Colombo was supportive of Western interests, and in the Non-Aligned Movement (NAM), it was consistently a voice of moderation.

Such a posture did not sit well with New Delhi, which prided itself on its own "non-aligned" position even while maintaining extensive military, economic, and diplomatic links with Moscow. An inordinate fear among India's top policymakers at "encirclement" by foreign powers was reflected in what can only be termed paranoid strategic thinking by Prime Minister Indira Gandhi. Washington was judged to be engaged in a strategic design to sandwich India between China, on the one hand, and the smaller pro-Western states of Pakistan, Sri Lanka, and Bangladesh, on the other. Most alarming to the Indians was their conviction that Jayewardene planned to grant American military forces base rights to Trincomalee. This, New Delhi stated publicly and privately, would pose an unacceptable threat to Indian national security.

In reality, neither Washington nor Colombo appear ever to have discussed a military base in Trincomalee, although the Sri Lankans were keenly interested in the commercial development of the port's oil tank farm and, in fact, called for joint venture bids to accomplish this. That American firms were favored by Sri Lanka was held up by India as further proof of menacing US intentions. Placed within the context of bitterly resented American ties with Pakistan and Washington's warming relations with Bangladesh, New Delhi was sure it had spied out a looming threat. Sri Lanka was to pay the price.

To gain better intelligence on developments concerning Trincomalee, RAW established links in early 1982 with the then-small Tamil insurgent groups operating in the Sri Lankan north. Members of PLOT and TELO were put through standard commando training, with special emphasis on reporting back on ship movements and port calls at Trincomalee. The Marxist orientation of these groups, we have already noted, was ignored—to the detriment of RAW's original aims. Rather than getting intelligence operatives, it found itself ignored by its trainees, who moved back into their parent groups and became instructors. They were joined by compatriots who had received similar training from international liberation movements such as the PLO.

Not all major Tamil insurgent groups had relations with Indian intelligence at this time, but the situation changed following the communal rioting of July 1983. Guided by a new set of instructions, RAW became involved with the other groups not already under its tutelage. Domestic calculations played a role in Mrs. Gandhi's instructions, but more central were the same geopolitical considerations that had prompted the original involvement with the insurgents. That is, she was piqued at President Jayewardene's abandonment of the non-aligned stance of his predecessor—Mrs Sirimavo Bandaranaike, a close personal friend of the Indian leader—in favor of his more pro-Western posture. Seeing a chance to resolve the problem under the guise of humanitarian concerns, and reap domestic political benefit in the bargain, Mrs Gandhi ordered a separate program, quite apart from the training of the Tamil insurgents being conducted in Tamil Nadu. This was nothing less than the formation of an invasion force for a "Bengali solution," as had been done in the creation of Bangladesh, of Indian-trained indigenous personnel for an invasion that would be accompanied by Indian forces posing as guerrillas.

Diplomatic pressure from the US and Britain combined with what seemed to be a less pressing situation in Sri Lanka during early 1984 to cause a postponement of Indian invasion plans, yet by this stage the Indian training effort had taken on a life of its own and continued to operate based on the domestic reasons cited above. At first limited to instruction, this continuing program in Tamil Nadu eventually included providing weapons and equipment. With such assistance, the insurgents were able to gain the upper hand in some areas of the country.

As the conflict grew in scope and intensity, Colombo turned to foreign sources. Israel and Britain were not the only places Sri Lanka sought assistance. Washington, for instance, provided important foreign aid and increasingly was drawn, with London, into active diplomatic support for Colombo in its often bitter exchanges with New Delhi. Pakistan and Saudi Arabia helped to obtain arms, with Islamabad becoming involved in training Sri Lankan security personnel and home guards at sites in Pakistan itself. China became a prime source of small arms and equipment, as did Singapore and Belgium. South African armored vehicles were obtained. In the end, India's involvement with the insurgents led to precisely the result it so feared—a Sri Lanka linked not only with extra-regional forces but also with New Delhi's chief regional rivals, Pakistan and China. For their part, the other states of South Asia saw India's role in the Sri Lankan affair as but further evidence of New Delhi's hypocritical regional imperialism and so gave what assistance they could.

State Search for a New Approach

Changes in the Indian political landscape provided some alternatives, yet the insurgents were adamant that *Eelam* was their only acceptable goal, and Colombo was just as adamant that the territorial integrity of the island would be preserved. Buttressing its position was the demographic reality that at no time, then or later, did a majority of the Tamil population live in the areas claimed by *Eelam*. Rather, more than half of all Tamils continued to reside in Sinhalese-dominated areas.

Regardless, Rajiv Gandhi, after endeavoring to reverse his mother's position, found himself forced to seek political cover. Though New Delhi had upped its profile and finally become a direct participant in the Thimpu discussions, it was unable to influence the outcome. For its troubles, it paid a high domestic price. An upsurge of Dravidian nationalism led to protests in Tamil Nadu and challenges to "Hindi authority." When President Jayewardene told the influential *India Today* in November 1985 that he saw no option to "decisive military action," Rajiv decided to cut his losses. While continuing to express his desire for a diplomatic solution and to send representatives to Colombo for talks, the Indian leader apparently turned the actual handling of the situation back to the same subordinates whose strategic logic was so flawed.

They proceeded to harangue Colombo at every turn on the need to negotiate with the insurgents. That there realistically could be no middle ground between the positions of Sri Lanka, as a sovereign state, and the insurgents, as a budding counter-state demanding not only independence but delivery from the evils of capitalism and imperialism, was ignored. In actions and words, New Delhi's stance moved back toward the unproductive policy of Indira Gandhi. Policy results were the same: strained relations with Colombo and greater Sri Lankan determination to avail themselves of all possible sources of aid. Israel, for instance, even began to fit Sri Lankan security force amputees with artificial limbs. When New Delhi learned of Colombo's use of foreign pilots for training and administrative flights, it warned against external involvement in the conflict. From Colombo's perspective, a more disingenuous position would have been hard to imagine.

New personalities were brought into play, such as Lieutenant General Cyril Ranatunga, appointed Sri Lankan Joint Forces Commander, but these had little impact on the conduct of the counter-insurgency campaign. Troops were scattered in defensive positions, generally of such limited strength as to make only holding their own fortifications possible. There was little attempt at the conduct of stability operations and no use of the classic "oil spot" technique for the systematic restoration of government writ to alienated areas.[53] In particular, the government effort was hamstrung by the failure of political leaders to set forth clearly a proposed political solution, a goal toward which military operations could be directed. Success in the field, therefore, while not altogether uncommon, was not directed toward the accomplishment of any strategic purpose and was thus largely meaningless.

Despite its overwhelming parliamentary majority, the ruling UNP was keenly aware that its dominant position was largely due to electoral mechanics (i.e., winner-take-all voting districts) rather than actual popular dominance. Faced with a situation where a strong opposition was working actively to tap ubiquitous Sinhalese fears and passions, the UNP opted for a path of short-term political expediency and seeming safety. It sought to wear down the insurgents militarily while placing its faith in the ability of Indian pressure, to be exerted sometime in the future, when, it was assumed, New Delhi would realize the self-destructive folly of backing insurgents based on its own unstable soil.

While possible in the short-term, such a strategy had little likelihood of long-term success, for it guaranteed that the conflict would remain open-ended, a posture Colombo found difficult to sustain, economically or politically. Economically, for instance, the 1986 budget contained an estimated deficit of Rs. 26,986 million (USD 983.1 million) against expenditures of Rs. 67,800 million (USD 2.47 billion). The Ministry of Defence alone was slated to spend 70% over its budgeted amount. These massive outlays, which were beyond the capacity of the economy (built on tea, tourism, and textiles) to endure for long, were heavily dependent on foreign grants and loans.

Ironically, all was not well in insurgent ranks, either. Gains for the combatants came even as divisions within the *Eelam* movement and the Tamil community itself became more apparent. LTTE turned on its ENLF partners in April and May 1986, all but wiping out TELO, but the government was unable to turn such events to its advantage.

Nevertheless, states possess inherent capabilities for human and fiscal mobilization that, if used properly, can provide the wherewithal to wage war. Sri Lanka did just that. Although it did not put together the necessary campaign plan for ending the insurgency, Colombo did come up with an approach for the military domination of insurgent-affected areas. Pacification of the east and near-north left only Jaffna as an insurgent stronghold as 1987 began. The green light for an all-out assault came when a rash of insurgent outrages occurred in April 1987, including bombings in Colombo and the massacre of Buddhist monks in the east. President Jayewardene responded by ordering a "Liberation I" offensive in May.

By this time, murderous fighting within the *Eelam* movement had left LTTE more dominant. This was significant, because, as indicated, LTTE was more militarily oriented than its rivals, increasingly drawing inspiration from terrorism, especially suicide tactics. LTTE combatants wore cyanide capsules around their necks and fought tenaciously in defense of what they called their "sacred soil." As their position in Jaffna Peninsula collapsed, the Tigers became more fanatical,[54] but this could not hold off security force consolidation over all save Jaffna city. On the verge of launching "Liberation II" to seize that final Tamil stronghold, in which the insurgents had concentrated for a last stand, the Sri Lankans found themselves stymied by India.

Miscalculation: The first Indian casualties suffered during the intervention of IPKF. Though initially welcomed, the Indian intervention
quickly succeeded in alienating not only the Tamils but the Sri Lankan
state. LTTE inflicted severe casualties in the three years that followed.
(Marks photo)

New Delhi, responding to domestic pressure and making a geo-strategic virtue out of its internal dilemma in Tamil Nadu, entered the conflict directly as an Indian Peacekeeping Force (IPKF). In reality an invasion, New Delhi gave Colombo no choice but to "invite" intervention.[55] Sri Lankan forces returned to barracks, and India assumed directly responsibility for overseeing implementation of a to-be-agreed-upon cessation of hostilities. The insurgent groups were pressured to cease their armed campaigns, hand over their weapons, and work out a compromise with the state.[56]

Groups other than LTTE proved more prepared to adjust to what one insurgent leader called "the realities of our situation." They structurally reflected the Marxist-Leninist form of political movements that commanded armed forces. Shelving military plans, while surrendering (as demanded by the Indians) their ("less useful") weapons, did not rob their liberation campaigns of vitality. These groups merely prepared to emphasize political organizing. In contrast, LTTE had increasingly moved away from ideology and saw all things as coming from its combatants. Its political movement had become decidedly secondary to armed struggle. This left it to emphasize circumventing the agreements reached.

The result was Indian military assault against LTTE commencing 10 October 1987.[57] Conflict quickly became general, with Indian forces endeavoring, as foreigners, to duplicate, in the north and east, the counter-insurgency campaign previously conducted by the Sri Lankans. The Indian presence, while having some tactical advantages, was strategically disastrous, because it not only reinforced the nationalist aspects of the *Eelam* appeal amongst the Tamil mass base but also provoked a Sinhalese nationalist reaction tapped by the dormant JVP. The causes that threw up the JVP manpower were the same as had produced the 1971 explosion. The new conditions only provided the spark.

Return of the JVP Counter-State

As the Indians attempted to deal with the Tamil insurgents, the Sri Lankans were forced to move troops south to deal again with people's war. The failure of the government to resist Indian intervention prompted widespread rioting in Sinhala-speaking areas and gave the Maoist JVP a second lease on life. Exploding nationalist passions saw an attempted assassination of President Jayewardene on 18 August 1987. A later move was made against Rajiv Gandhi, as well, when he arrived in Colombo for discussions. The assassination attempts were only the tip of what appeared to be a very large iceberg of discontent and anger directed at the ruling UNP for its perceived authoritarian drift and abuse of power. The presence of

Indian troops served as a rallying-point for the otherwise fragmented and lackluster opposition. Even Buddhist monks joined in anti-government rioting; a number of them were arrested with stolen semi-automatic weapons in their possession. Exploding nationalist passions once again exposed the dark side of Sri Lanka. Power grows from the barrel of a gun, opined Mao. And in the absence of functioning politics, he might have added, there is no recourse save the gun. That much should have been clear to Sri Lankan decision-makers in light of the origins of the Tamil insurgency. In the absence of a viable opportunity-structure there is nowhere else for popular discontent to go save the streets or the ranks of the insurgents. Colombo had not understood this with the Tamils and did not understand it with the Sinhalese.

That politics could be assessed as struggling in Sri Lanka seems a contradiction in a nation that since independence in 1948 had maintained a functioning parliamentary democracy. But if politics may be further defined as shaping the human environment, Sri Lanka's system had failed. Behind the facade of democracy, successive governments had taken procedural steps that had diminished the constitutive system. Electoral mechanics saw the nearly 50–50 split in the popular vote in the 1970 and 1977 elections reflected in lopsided parliamentary majorities for either of Sri Lanka's major political parties. The UNP, in power since 1977, ruled with an enormous parliamentary margin, as had the rival SLFP during 1970–77, despite losing the popular vote. Both parties used this statistical gift to centralize decision-making and authority, roundly abuse opposition voices, curb individual freedoms, and censor the media. Rules were even pushed through allowing the replacement by party officials of any MP who had the courage to criticize his own party, this for MPs who, in any case, were not required to reside in the districts they represented.

Some two decades of such actions resulted, predictably, in a political system manned by individuals owing their allegiance not to their constituencies or to higher principles but to their parties. Electoral corruption, intimidation, and manipulation of voting rules prevented popular discontent from fielding alternate representatives. Rather than see its four-fifths majority endangered in 1982, a crucial level because it allowed amending the constitution at will, the UNP held a referendum to extend the life of the parliament another term. Although the UNP won the vote, the narrow margin of victory reflected the true polarization of the electorate.

Fueling popular resentment was the increasing isolation of the government bureaucracy from the population. Without the political system acting as overseer (it was too busy looking after its members' needs), the permanent cadre in official positions turned to their own concerns. Corruption reached considerable proportions even as basic services deteriorated island-wide. The worsening lives of the people escaped notice in many quarters, foreign and domestic. Progress in economic macro-indicators served to conceal serious problems in the micro-world of Sri Lanka's majority, problems of health, nutrition, livelihood, and opportunities for advancement. Large segments of the population had limited access to health care, malnutrition was widespread, unemployment and under-employment were double-digit. Educational attainment frequently proved a dead end due to the unavailability of suitable employment.

The discriminatory legislation and regular episodes of anti-Tamil rioting, which culminated in the nationwide explosion of July 1983, were passed off by the world as communal conflict. Actually, as noted, they reflected attempts by the Sinhalese majority to claim from the successful Tamils their slice of what increasingly was viewed as a zero-sum distribution of rights, resources, and privileges. Faced with a system unwilling to provide for their well-being or even to protect them, the conservative Tamil populace turned to the only available option championing their interests, the Marxist insurgent movements.

The steadily escalating fiscal and manpower demands of the campaign to fight Tamil insurgency, in turn, further curtailed Colombo's human and economic development efforts. Yet in another of Sri Lanka's many ironies, the Tamils earlier had become prominent in business and government service precisely because of their need to escape the structural conditions that were different only in degree from those afflicting the Sinhalese majority. Tamil areas were the poorest of the island, with limited carrying capacity. Hence migration to and employment in the larger Sri Lankan community were imperative. Driven back into itself, Tamil society had little choice but self-defense.

Similarly, the factors discussed above drove the Sinhalese community to self-defense. Contrary to a view fashionable in many circles of the Colombo elite, the JVP had not caused the insurgency, any more than it had caused the 1971 upheaval. Neither—again—could it even be said to be leading it. It was racing to keep up with it. What the JVP had demonstrated was a new tactical sophistication that allowed it to ride each wave of discontent as it swelled.[58] Previously sympathetic to the Tamil cause, it flip-flopped and adopted a hard-line pro-Sinhalese stand when it became clear that such was to its advantage.

This served it in good stead when the Indians entered the picture, because it allowed the party to wrap itself in the mantle of nationalism. Indeed, JVP documents said virtually nothing of party ideological stance, concentrating instead on the "betrayal" of the country by its rulers. It was but a logical next step to advance a simple connection: "the same people who sold you out are responsible for the poor conditions of life in which you find yourselves" (my phraseology). Yet this linkage was normally reserved, in its most explicit forms, for instructions to JVP cadre. It was to be introduced to the masses only when the party felt conditions were safe.

Predictably, a government that had steadily isolated itself from the people was not likely to recognize the root of its problems. As violence escalated, the administration reacted in fumbling fashion. Security forces were deployed, but because their presence did not protect socio-economic-political measures designed to deal with the structural basis for the problem, their activities could only place a temporary damper on the violence. In their rear the insurgency gained strength. Whole areas of the country effectively became "no-go" areas after dark, and urban unrest grew dramatically. Anonymous "struggle committees" functioned in virtually all businesses and closed them down at will simply by posting notices instructing work to cease lest reprisals be taken.

By using terror to murder prominent examples of those who did not comply with their demands, the JVP insurgents gained authority far beyond their numbers. The industrial sector, for instance, thoroughly cowed by a spate of well selected assassinations, was functioning at a mere 20% capacity. Such economic paralysis, in turn, fed the JVP cause. Many businesses reported they were unable to meet their loan and tax obligations. They concentrated only on at least paying their workers. As this, too, became impossible, the ranks of the unemployed provided fertile ground for JVP recruiters. Sri Lanka staggered.[59]

What followed was significant. A change in leadership, with Ranasinghe Premadasa replacing the retiring Junius R. Jayewardene, brought a government approach that again turned the tide. Crucial to this was the employment of the *techniques* that had gradually come to be standard in dealing with the Tamil insurgency, such as a coordinated command and control structure. The military, unlike in 1983 (or even 1971), had gained an understanding of what it should have been doing in counter-insurgency. Having become a more effective, powerful organization, it now deployed to areas where, among other things, it spoke the language of the inhabitants and had an excellent intelligence apparatus.[60]

Superimposed on the tactical organization of the army was the counter-insurgency structure itself. Administratively, Sri Lanka's nine provinces were already divided into districts, twenty-two in all, each headed by a Government Agent (GA) who saw to it that services and programs were carried out. To deal with the

246

Experienced force: Sri Lankan brigade commander Janaka Perera talks with villagers in Eastern Province during 1987 operations. As special operations commander, he was to lead the unit that captured the JVP leadership. (Marks photo)

insurgency, these GAs were paired with Coordinating Officers (COs), whose responsibility it became to handle the security effort in the district. Often, to simplify the chain of command, the CO would be the commander of the battalion in the district. The brigade commanders, in turn, acted as Chief Coordinating Officers (CCO) for their provinces[61] and reported to Area Commanders. Areas 1 and 2 divided the Sinhalese heartland into southern and northern sectors, respectively. Area 3 was the Tamil-populated zone under IPKF control.

Used historically with considerably effect by any number of security forces, particularly the British (or the Thai and Filipinos), this system had the advantage of setting in place security personnel whose mission was to win back their areas. They could be assigned assets, military and civil, as circumstances dictated. COs controlled all security forces deployed in their districts; they were to work closely with the GAs to develop plans for the protection of normal civilian administrative and area development functions. For this work, they were aided by a permanent staff whose job it was to know intimately the area. In particular, intelligence assets remained assigned to the "Coord" headquarters and guided the employment of operational personnel. They did not constantly rotate as combat units came and went.

The framework culminated in the Joint Operations Center (JOC). This, though, never really hit its stride as a coordinating body. Instead, manned by senior serving officers, it usurped actual command functions to such an extent that it *became* the military. The service headquarters, in particular the army, were reduced to little more than administrative centers. Attempts to rectify the shortcomings resulted only in a JOC that functioned as a weak supreme command, with the service chiefs rotating as head at 3-month intervals. This clumsy arrangement eventually fell by the wayside, too, as operational requirements became more pressing. But the essential confusion of roles remained.

Although often lacking precise guidance from above, local military authorities nonetheless fashioned increasingly effective responses to JVP insurgency. In contrast to continued unrest in Colombo, the rural areas, although unsettled, were gradually brought under control. This was possible, because the Coordinating Officers and operational commanders, older and wiser after their tours in the Tamil areas, proved more than capable of planning their own local campaigns. Tactically, then, the Sri Lankan security forces demonstrated a knowledge of counter-insurgency techniques and theory surprisingly advanced for so young a force. Strategically, however, they felt that the national leadership had failed them.

So intense was the animosity amongst the security forces toward the political leadership that it was at times surprising there were no moves "out of the barracks," as happened in other cases we have considered in this work. This was a credit to the professional ethos. For there was no shortage of individuals, both civil and military, who recognized that there had to be a political strategy for dealing with the issues that were allowing the insurgents to gain strength. "These politicians are always making things a shambles," a second lieutenant observed from the base where he commanded a two-platoon force. "They go for short term popularity. In a few years, they can leave office. But the army and the police don't get to leave. We have to deal with the problems they have left behind. What we need is honesty and a plan."[62] Indeed, these two issues, corruption and the lack of a plan, cropped up over and over again.

"It is the children of our battered peasantry who are joining the JVP," analyzed a GA as his Coordinating Officer partner nodded in agreement. "The root cause of these troubles is landlessness." "We are in a race for the minds of our children," added the CO. "I don't believe in body count, but the politicians do. How are we going to resolve this problem? We have been at this for 18–19 years [he was a veteran of the 1971 insurrection]. These people aren't thinking. We need a solution!"

Opined a brigade commander in another area, "The army can only do so much. It can restore the situation to a point. But if there is no effort to address the socio-economic causes, all this will come back. We have to have some sort of plan to guide us. But I doubt if we'll get it. The politicians have made a real mess of things. We can't expect people who are a part of the problem to recognize it." One of his battalion commanders noted, "Our corrupt power-holders are the major reason we have this situation. If you take the sympathizers, they're not really JVP. They're just anti-government." A company commander of the battalion observed, "The mechanisms for hearing people are not very effective. There are real reasons why people are on the road. But there are no real solutions being offered."

As on a ship at sea without a compass, each "captain" made do as best he could. The Achilles heel of their efforts, of course, was that in the absence of strategic coordination and operational guidance, each commander constantly had to reinvent the wheel and to deal with tactical problems the ultimate cause of which was beyond his control. He could only ameliorate their local impact. "Look at this map," said a Coordinating Officer, pointing to the wall:

The green areas are small river valleys where the people are clustered. They were driven from their land when the British took it over for the estates [tea and rubber in this particular area]. Now, with population growth, there are too many people for the land. And where can the people go? See these villages here? They can't even be reached by road. It takes five hours to get to the nearest school. So the children grow up without an education and no hope for meaningful employment. So they're stuck in their poverty. But all around they see what was once their land, and they see the people living on it getting rich. And those people are Indians [i.e., Indian Tamil estate workers]. Now the Indian laborers are followed by Indian troops. Then along comes someone who tells them he'll set all this right, that he'll get rid of the government that sold out the country and made everyone poor. Is it any wonder people join the JVP? I do what I can but. . .

Thus the commanders sent their troops out on daily operations, primarily cordon and searches, as well as night ambushes, generated by intelligence leads. Units appeared to have little trouble getting information once they established their presence in an area. One commander visited in 1989 was deluged by a hundred letters a day, 80–90% of which he estimated contained accurate information.

Why was there such a response? Paradoxically, army presence eliminated the worst abuses of the system. It did this by enforcing a standard of conduct the system itself was unable to provide. Most people, to be clear, did not want to become insurgents. Rather, when the immediate abuses of the system were halted, they were only too willing to go back to figuring out how they were going to put rice on the table. And, because most retained faith that ultimately the democratic system would respond to them, they were only too willing to inform on the JVP once they saw that there was a viable hope for functioning democracy. The JVP added to this trend by its widespread and increasing resort to terror.

The danger inherent to such a posture, however, was that it could not go on forever. "The situation requires a political solution," observed a CO. "The security forces are only suppressing what the problems throw up. My troops are tired. We have been at this for six straight years, first in the north, now here. The boys cannot go home on leave [due to the JVP terror campaign]; their families are not safe. We are still holding up, but everyone has his breaking point."

Ultimately, intense pressure for local solutions combined with the strains engendered by limited resources and an intense operations tempo to bring about a terrible end to the JVP problem. Put simply, though such was not systemic, some individuals and units dispensed with the tedious business of addressing grievances, of targeted response, and of legal process. Those suspected of subversion were simply eliminated. In the process, old and new scores on both sides were settled, although alleged JVP sympathizers certainly comprised the bulk of the victims. The dead apparently figured at the level of the previous JVP upheaval, and included the key members of the JVP leadership.[63] In ending the second JVP insurgency, however, the security forces were able to turn their attention again to the Tamil insurgency.

Return to the Tamil Counter-State

For all had not gone well for IPKF. Grown to 80,000 men (more than 40 infantry battalions), it had proved incapable of dealing with the LTTE challenge. Further, Indian use of the non-LTTE *Eelam* groups as a "Tamil National Army" (TNA) compromised them as quislings, thereby contributing still further to LTTE dominance. Tactical errors of force employment ensured that the IPKF would be ineffective in combating LTTE guerrilla and terror tactics.[64]

Consequently, by the time of IPKF withdrawal, in January–March 1990, almost three years and several thousand IPKF casualties later,[65] LTTE was more firmly established than on Indian arrival. This was compounded by further LTTE entrenchment during a subsequent Colombo-LTTE negotiation period, which the Tigers used to decimate TNA forces. When LTTE abrogated the talks, renewed hostilities left the security forces facing mobile warfare (or main force warfare), LTTE units attacking in massed units, often of multiple battalion strength, supported by a variety of heavy weapons.

Deaths numbered in the thousands, reaching a peak in July–August 1991 in a series of set-piece battles around Jaffna. The 25 days of fighting at Elephant Pass, the land bridge that connected the Jaffna Peninsula with the rest of Sri Lanka, saw the first insurgent use of armor. Elsewhere, terror bombings and assassinations became routine. Even national leaders such as Rajiv Gandhi[66] and President Ranasinghe Premadasa, fell to LTTE bomb attacks (on 21 May 1991 and 1 May 1993, respectively), as did numerous other important figures, such as Lalith Athulathmudalai and members of the JOC upper echelons. Heavy fighting in Jaffna in early 1994, as the security forces attempted to tighten their grip around Jaffna city, resulted in

Mobile warfare: Tamil home-made tank in the front lines of Elephant Pass camp, mid-1991. Built on a powerful bulldozer chassis, the vehicle, one of a number of such behemoths, had frontal armor so thick that 106mm recoilless rifle fire failed to penetrate. LTTE powerfully demonstrated that its three-year battle against the Indians had left it capable of main force warfare. (Marks photo)

government casualties approaching those suffered by LTTE in the Elephant Pass action. The conflict had been reduced to a tropical replay of the First World War trenches.

Only with the election of a coalition headed by the SLFP in August 1994, followed by the November presidential victory of SLFP leader Chandrika Bandaranaike Kumaratunga, were politics again introduced into the debate on state response to insurgent challenge. The SLFP sweep ended 17 years of UNP power and led to a 3-month ceasefire, during which Colombo sought to frame a solution acceptable to both sides. The effort came to an abrupt halt when LTTE again, as it had in every previous instance, unilaterally ended the talks by a surprise attack on government forces.

Significantly, the wave of assaults thrust to the fore the military side of what at its core remained a political conflict. LTTE techniques included using underwater assets to destroy navy ships, as well as the introduction of SA-7 surface-to-surface missiles into the conflict. The former involved divers planting underwater demolitions; the latter use of the SAMs to down air force transports, later at least one helicopter gunship. Armor and artillery were already in use by both sides. What had begun as a campaign of terror had grown to main force warfare augmented by terror and guerrilla action.

Much more had changed, as well. With the end of the Cold War, LTTE quietly dropped all talk of Marxism, though it continued to portray itself as socialist. New Delhi, although still closely linked to Moscow, had seen its patron collapse and cautiously reached out to establish more normal relations with the US and other supporters of Colombo. There was no objection raised when in mid-1994 the US agreed to begin a series of direct training missions conducted by special forces elements.[67]

New circumstances, in particular a new administration, dictated a review of approach. In mid-1995, therefore, the government held a series of meetings designed to settle on a revised national strategy for ending the conflict.[68] The meetings, of which there were at least three primary sessions, did not go well. A plan was articulated for devolution that came close, in all but name, to abandoning the unitary state in favor of a federal system. Still, while all official bodies basically agreed that LTTE would have to be defeated militarily in order for the political solution to be implemented, there was considerable disagreement on the plan of operations.

On the one side were those who saw no option but to end the LTTE hold on Jaffna, the Tigers main base area, by direct, conventional assault. Principal advocate of this approach was Anuraddha Ratwatte, a presidential relative and, effectively,

Minister of Defence.[69] He was joined by a body of military officers who felt the effort had to be made.

Opposed was an equally distinguished and senior body of officers, both active and retired, who demurred. They cited the considerable success that had been achieved by the systematic domination of areas using force as the shield behind which restoration of government writ. This approach, they argued, while much slower, would be considerably less costly in lives and financial resources and would play to Sri Lanka's strengths, especially the by then well developed framework for counter-insurgency outlined above.

Financial aspects were especially important, because by 1995 interest payments to service government debt were of themselves 29.9% of current expenditures, with a figure of close to 48% reached if amortization and interest payments were considered as a combined figure of true debt cost. High intensity operations, regardless of purely military considerations, were bound to worsen this financial situation.

So intense became the debate that some critics were sidelined. Army commander, LTG Gerry de Silva, a Sandhurst graduate, found himself very much in the middle. His important contribution after assuming command on 1 January 1994 had been to rationalize the command and control structure of a force grown to 76 infantry battalions alone (drawn from three sources: active, reserve, and national guard).[70] With even his own staff divided on the merits of a Jaffna assault, he was torn between demands from above that he lead the charge and from below that he back another course of action.

The arguments of those sidelined were important, given later developments. They advocated continuing systematic domination of human terrain while taking the battle directly to the insurgents using raids, especially by special operations forces. These were the tactics that had been used successfully in JVP II. Principal weapon for raids was to be a Reserve Strike Force that had been formed in July 1994 as an integral part of refining the command structure. Under it fell the four battalions of what had been the Special Forces Brigade,[71] as well as six infantry battalions, mechanized and airmobile, and three armor battalions. As such, it was a potent, mobile force that could respond in virtually any fashion to a threat anywhere in the country.

Rather than being used in the manner intended, however, these forces became the spearhead for the approach that came out of the strategy meetings: a conventional response to an unconventional problem. As a first step, a multi-divisional assault on the heavily fortified Jaffna area was ordered. This was carried out successfully, but with no overland link to government positions thus established, the forces in

Jaffna became a bridge too far, a classic case of strategic overreach with LTTE enjoying interior lines.

Fiscal overreach was also an issue, as the Jaffna offensive alone was estimated to have cost USD 500–750 million in new arms and equipment, as well as operational funding. Intense fighting developed as the Sri Lankan military endeavored to secure its lines of supply and communication from south to north. LTTE adroitly used a combination of main force and guerrilla units, together with special operations, to isolate exposed government units and then overrun them. These included headquarters elements, with even brigade and division headquarters being battered. In the rear area, LTTE used a suicide truck bomb to decimate the financial heart of Colombo in February 1996, killing at least 75 and wounding more than 1,500.

Much worse was to come, though, as over-extension of forces and an inability to handle the complexities of main force, conventional operations left the Sri Lankan military badly deployed. Debacle was not long in coming, and on 17 July 1996, an

Debate on strategy: Sri Lankan commandos depart on operation in 1995. Under the new SFLP government, a military-driven response was initially successful but ultimately failed badly, setting the stage for stalemate. (Marks photo)

estimated 3,000–4,000 LTTE combatants, using the techniques earlier worked out in the 1991 Elephant Pass attack, isolated and then overwhelmed an under-strength brigade camp at Mullaitivu in the northeast, inflicting at least 1,520 dead total on the security forces. This exceeded the total death toll for 1994, which had been 1,454,[72] and shattered army morale. Desertion, already a problem, rapidly escalated. There followed stalemate.

LTTE, having only to exist as a rump counter-state that mobilized its young for combat, had demonstrated the ability to construct mechanisms for human and fiscal resource generation that defied the coercive capacity of the state. Linkages extended abroad, from whence virtually all funding came (as already discussed), and diaspora commercial linkages allowed obtaining necessary weapons, ammunition, and supplies.[73] Although the security forces could hold key positions and even dominate much of the east, they simply could not advance on the well-prepared and fortified LTTE positions in the north and northeast, which, in any case, were guarded by a veritable carpet of mines.

Political disillusionment again followed, increasing as LTTE continued to pull off spectacular actions that sapped morale: the most sacred Buddhist shrine in the country, the Temple of the Tooth in Kandy, was attacked by suicide bomb in 1998. President Kumaratunga herself narrowly missed following Premadasa as a presidential victim, surviving a 1999 LTTE bomb attack but losing an eye. The Elephant Pass camp that had previously held out against such odds fell in 2000, and in July 2001, a sapper attack on the international airport in Colombo left eleven aircraft destroyed. It was not altogether surprising that in the December 2001 parliamentary elections, the UNP, led by Ranil Wickremasinghe, returned to power.

This left the political landscape badly fractured between the majority UNP and its leader, the prime minister, and the SLFP's Kumaratunga, still the powerful president in Sri Lanka's hybrid system similar to that of France. That the two figures were longtime rivals, with considerable personal animosity, did not ease the situation. Again, it was changes in the international arena that dealt a wild-card. The "9-11" terrorist attacks in the US and the resulting "Global War on Terrorism" caused Western countries finally to move to cut off LTTE fundraising activities on their soil. For reasons that remain unclear, LTTE suddenly offered negotiations to the new UNP government, in February 2002. The government accepted the offer, and an uneasy truce commenced.

Talks to arrive at a political settlement were brokered by Norway, but the cessation of hostilities was a very mixed bag. LTTE used the restrictions on Sri Lankan security forces to move aggressively into Tamil areas from which it had previously been denied, and rival Tamil politicians, most survivors from the decimation of the TNA after India's withdrawal, were ruthlessly intimidated and assassinated. Throughout Tamil-populated areas, Tamil-language psychological operations continued to denounce the government and the Sri Lankan state, particularly its forces.

LTTE intransigence led the UNP government to flirt with ideas that came close to dismembering the island, even if only *de facto* rather than *de jure*. Its major concern was to resurrect the economy, for which a peaceful resolution of the conflict was essential, and even the decades-old emergency provisions had been allowed to lapse. Mrs Kumaratunga watched uneasily and then moved, in early November 2003, while Wickremasinghe was in Washington meeting with US President George W. Bush. Claiming that the UNP approach was threatening the "the sovereignty of the state of Sri Lanka, its territorial integrity, and the security of the nation," she fired the three UNP cabinet ministers most closely associated with the talks, dismissed Parliament, and ordered the army into Colombo's streets.

LTTE watched, but in the April 2004 parliamentary elections that were held as a consequence of talks between the dueling Sinhalese parties, SLFP unexpect-edly swept back into power at the head of a United People's Freedom Alliance that included the JVP, still clinging to life and earlier allowed back into the legal mainstream in return for giving up its calls for revolution. Hence the Tigers withdrew from negotiations. By mid-1996 conflict had again returned to the island.[74]

Conclusions

What is noteworthy in the Sri Lanka case is its sheer complexity and the high level of violence. The lowest figure now used for lives lost during the Tamil insurgency is some 65,000, which is likely a serious undercount (and to which must be added as many as 40,000 lost in the two JVP Maoist insurgencies). Nevertheless, these losses and the complexity discussed throughout this chapter serve to highlight Colombo's *relative* success in meeting the challenge and continuing as a viable political and economic entity. Perhaps more than that, whatever the harsh edges of the counter-insurgent campaign, the state did not find it necessary to suspend or destroy its democratic system. The rule of law continued, in all its imperfect particulars, and fierce debate raged throughout the contest as to both means and ends that ought to be used and pursued. Changes in the forms used (e.g., from a pure parliamentary system to a mixed parliamentary-presidential system) derived largely from the inter-party competitive dynamic as opposed to the exigencies of internal war.

Though the system remained intact, certainly mistakes of strategic approach and operational implementation were made, beginning with the persistent failure to assess the insurgency in realistic terms appropriate to framing a correct response. In this, Colombo's experience foreshadows what we see happening in the global war on terrorism; that is, the focus on the symptoms rather than the causes of the violence and the misinterpretation of that violence once it has appeared.

To be sure, Sri Lanka had its analytical work cut out for it in assessing the nature of the threat. All insurgencies, JVP and Tamil (within which, to reiterate, there were at one point in time more than 40 groups, each pursuing its own approach), used terror as a central element, thus making it comprehensible that "terrorism" absorbed the attention of the state. Insurgency, though, was the goal of the militants all along, with revolutionary war the precise aim. Terror, although used extensively, was never intended as an end unto itself. It was to be method rather than logic. From its use as one weapon among many in the effort to form a counter-state, it became a strategy for insurgency: to inflict so much pain on the "occupying force" that it would have to quit the field. This did not mean abandoning the people's war approach.

Use of the term "people's war" here is important, because it highlights the point made in the introductory remarks of this work: The template arrived at by Mao, perfected by the Vietnamese, is not dependent on communist ideology. That was a mistake made by the French in Algeria, where officers often claimed FLN nationalism was a part of the same communist thrust they had earlier faced in Indochina. JVP insurgency, of course, explicitly claimed to be Maoist, so it was logical that it used the people's war approach. Yet being merely "Marxist" did not prevent the Tamil insurgent groups from examining and utilizing the same approach. That they eventually emphasized the terror weapon, to the point that it became insurgent strategy, should not serve to obscure the methodology being used and end sought. It was the adroit use of "war of interlocking" techniques (though not called such) that baffled the Sri Lankan military response.

What could have arrested the process was addressing the grievances of the mass base early on. Although leaders and followers were thrown up by the same injustice, they responded in dissimilar fashion. Leaders sought structural change, revolution, as the route to liberation; followers looked to redress of immediate issues. Had the state driven a wedge between the two, what became a profound threat to the security of the state would likely have remained a law and order problem.

Indeed, it was the very scale of state abuses (claimed and real) against Tamil civilians that galvanized both the Indian and the Sri Lankan diaspora Tamil communities to open their hearts and their wallets to the insurgent groups (even as the same issues involving Sinhalese did not provoke such a response). As these latter transformed, becoming ever more violent and divorced from any sense of compromise, their identity as avenging angels was maintained as a powerful motivating force by alienated Tamils abroad. These could thus lash out vicariously in redress of their own grievances and frustrations.

To focus on the tactical acts of terror, whether carried out by the JVP or *Eelam* groups, was precisely the wrong approach by the state. Certainly repression was a necessary element of response, but the security forces should only have been the instrument for the accomplishment of the political solution. This was realized by any number of actors within the conflict, but they were rarely in the right spot at the right time, hence unable to alter the course once set. Still, it is noteworthy that a developing world state, with very limited capacity and resources, was able to put together a response that came within a whisker of delivering a knockout punch. Learning and adaptation were a constant feature of an approach that, even if imbalanced, tilted toward repression as opposed to accommodation, nevertheless proved capable of dealing with not only the complex Tamil insurgent threat but also two rounds of Sinhalese Maoist upheaval.

Although any number of criticisms may be leveled at Sri Lanka's imperfect command and control arrangements, together with flawed coordination and force deployment, these should not blind us to the reality that Colombo had sought out models, chosen correctly if not wisely, and endeavored to implement its selections. The counter-insurgency structure and procedures used, which emphasized unity of command and long-term presence in affected areas, did prove capable of dealing with the situation, but the test was not completed.

It is impossible to say definitively what would have happened in July 1987 had Colombo been allowed to land its hammer blow. One school of thought would hold that, in the absence of systemic reform, another round of Tamil insurgency would have arisen, even had the current crop of radical leadership been eliminated. Another school, however, would point to the evidence that populations savaged in the course of a struggle tend to be inoculated against repeat infections. The two rounds of JVP insurgency would seem to support the former, but other cases, from abroad, the latter, such as the aversion to renewed action that the resurrected Communist Party of the Philippines found in the former centers of Huk Rebellion recruitment.[75]

In any case, international forces made moot the issue. World-historical timing obviously matters a great deal in any such situation. The role of India was driven

Test not completed: Sri Lankan forces (above with author) performed well but were unable to overcome the geostrategic handicap of being neighbor to democratic but hegemonic India. Strong counter-insurgency performance against avowedly Maoist insurgencies could not be duplicated against Marxist Tamil groups in the face of Indian intervention.

not only by its geo-strategic prerogatives but by its position within the Cold War equation. Though Indian sources tend to emphasize New Delhi's need to respond to the domestic forces unleashed by Tamil suppression, evidence supports the conclusion that equal weight was given to perceptions of alleged foreign threat facilitated by Sri Lankan fecklessness.

That New Delhi had based its actions on a flawed analysis of the situation was cold comfort for Colombo, because it was the three-year IPKF interlude that allowed LTTE to not only recover from its desperate situation in July 1987 but to move to the mobile warfare stage of insurgency. Fielding main force units in conjunction with guerrilla and terror actions, the insurgents emerged in 1990 as a truly formidable force.

As such, the experience, driven as it was by resistance against foreign occupation, had taken on the characteristics associated with all manner of "wars of national liberation." In these, the goal was invariably to inflict so much death and destruction on the enemy that he would decide the campaign was not worth the price being paid. It was entirely logical, then, that no actions were off-limits to LTTE in its quest to inflict pain. It engaged in everything from massacres of Sinhalese communities to bombing cities and temples to executions of prisoners to attempts to use poison gas.

Faced with such a foe, the state often responded in kind. It is significant, however, that instances of indiscipline declined dramatically among the security forces as the struggle wore on. From an initial position of feeling terrorized by the security forces, and especially there inability to protect innocent civilians from communal reprisals, the Tamils settled back into Sri Lankan society. Nothing illustrated this more than the continued presence of a majority of the Tamil population within "Sinhalese-controlled territory."

A different dynamic played itself out in each of the JVP uprisings, but even there the instances of virtual death squad activity were not policy and often resulted in action being taken against perpetrators. The upshot was that, considered as a whole, it was the stark realities of an extraordinarily brutal conflict that increasingly were at issue as opposed to disproportionate or inappropriate response.

Most state actors, whether leadership figures or members of the security forces, had a reasonable understanding of the issues at stake and the means necessary to accomplish them. Whether endeavoring to maneuver battalions or carrying out special operations, individuals, many of whom had risen rapidly due to force expansion and been thrust into senor leadership positions, performed extraordinarily well given the circumstances. How else to explain the ability of units to carry out area domination missions in, say, the Sinhalese south even as riots rocked Colombo and families were at risk from terror action?

Little appreciated in any such struggle is an elemental fact: If the security forces will not crack, challengers for state power, whatever damage they may inflict, can not succeed. Sri Lanka had its fill of problems with desertions and indiscipline, but it also had signal success in using the British regimental model to build and field new units of relative cohesion and effectiveness. Particular efforts were made to maintain morale through a variety of rewards and incentives.

On the other side, the insurgents did the same. Most frightening about LTTE success should be what it tells us about the ability of a radical, institutionally totalitarian movement to recruit, socialize, and deploy manpower so rigidly indoctrinated that combatants prefer death by cyanide or self-destruction to capture. Having gained control of certain areas early on, LTTE was able to recruit manpower at extraordinarily young ages and then guide them in ways such that entire units were comprised of young boys and girls who had never known alternative modes of existence.

In the world created by LTTE leadership, Sinhalese were demons, and a world beyond the insurgent camps did not exist. Even sex lives, especially sex lives, were rigidly controlled by draconian penalties. Combatants knew only their world and each other and behaved accordingly when unleashed on targets.

As relative moderates passed from the leadership scene, those who knew other worlds vanished, their places taken by a hard core who had risen in the movement. They generally spoke no language save Tamil and had limited life-experiences. Brutality was simply a weapons system. The ability of the insurgents to keep their manpower isolated was thus an important factor in maintaining control and movement cohesion. The simple lack of alternatives, real or imagined, kept LTTE combatants from defecting.

What was extraordinary was that young people did flee such an environment, balking when faced with instructions to end their own lives. This did not occur in numbers sufficient enough to make a difference. Though a pronounced decline in the average age of LTTE combatants was noticed as the conflict wore on, at no time were manpower shortages a factor as to influence insurgent strategy or operations. To the contrary, human wave assaults continued throughout to be the essential tactic of engagements. Still, in the very existence of defectors was evidence that a repentance campaign pushed forward by information warfare is a necessary element in any counter-insurgency.

To what, then, was owed LTTE participation in the recent ceasefire? It may have been a simple matter of tactics. Prabhakaran has demonstrated a shrewd capacity for combining violent and non-violent action, armed strikes with information warfare, local with international action. He may well have simply decided to open up space for a repair of his fund-raising apparatus damaged by the post "9-11" moves against it, or he may have sensed that a Sri Lanka in some disarray as to its own course was ripe for an appeal to a "political solution."

The two are not mutually exclusive, and the ceasefire certainly gave LTTE all that it had been unable to acquire through its campaign of political violence: well-nigh complete control over the Tamil population in the area delimited as *Eelam*. In this sense, it played its cards shrewdly. It used the hunger for normalcy to make the state complicit in meeting LTTE's own ends, formation of a counter-state.

Notes

[1] For a dated but still fairly comprehensive treatment of various aspects of Sri Lanka, see K. M. de Silva, ed., *Sri Lanka: A Survey* (Honolulu: University Press of Hawaii, 1977).

[2] Information on the subject of Sinhalese-Tamil relations has been gathered generally from several sources and augmented by fieldwork conducted over several decades. Excellent discussions are contained in A. Jeyaratnam Wilson and Dennis Dalton, eds., *The States of South Asia: Problems of National Integration* (Honolulu: University Press of Hawaii, 1982); see especially C. R. de Silva, "The Sinhalese-Tamil Rift in Sri Lanka," 155–74, and A. Jeyaratnam Wilson, "Sri Lanka and Its Future: Sinhalese Versus Tamils," 295–312.

[3] See Jane Russell, *Communal Politics Under the Donoughmore Constitution, 1931–1947* (Dehiwala, Sri Lanka: Tisara Prakasakayo, 1982).

[4] An excellent source is K. M. de Silva, A *History of Sri Lanka* (London: C. Hurst, 1981); also valuable for its discussion of Sri Lanka's cultural influence on the region is Jean Bois-selier, "South-East Asia: Sri Lanka," in Jeannine Auboyet et al., *Oriental Art: A Handbook of Styles and Forms*, trans. Elizabeth and Richard Bartlett (New York: International Publications, 1980), 97–130. For details on a majority of the British period see Lennox A. Mills, *Ceylon Under British Rule, 1795–1932* (New York: Barnes & Noble, 1965).

[5] Detailed discussions are contained in S. Arasaratnam, "Nationalism, Communalism, and National Security in Ceylon," Chapter 12 in Philip Mason, ed., *India and Ceylon: Unity and Diversity* (London: Oxford University Press, 1967); B. H. Farmer, "The Social Basis of Nationalism in Ceylon," *Journal of Asian Studies*, 24.3 (May 1965), 441–89; and Robert N. Kearney, "Sinhalese Nationalism and Social Conflict in Ceylon," *Pacific Affairs*, 37.2 (Summer 1964), 125–36 . See also Michael Roberts, ed., *Collective Identities, National-isms, and Protest in Modern Sri Lanka* (Colombo: Marga Institute, 1979); Social Scientists Association, *Ethnicity and Change in Sri Lanka* (Colombo: Karunaratne, 1984).

Notes

⁶ Robert N. Kearney and Janice Jiggins, "The Ceylon Insurrection of 1971," *Journal of Commonwealth and Comparative Politics*, 13.1 (March 1975), 49.

⁷ See Janice Jiggins, Caste *and Family in the Politics of the Sinhalese, 1974–1976* (Colombo: K. V. G. de Silva, 1979); Tissa Fernando, "Elite Politics in the New States: The Case of Post-Independence Sri Lanka," *Pacific Affairs*, 46.3 (Fall 1973), 361–83; and Robert Oberst, "Democracy and the Persistence of Westernized Elite Dominance in Sri Lanka," *Asian Survey*, 25.7 (July 1985), 760–72.

⁸ See Robert N. Kearney, "The Marxist Parties of Ceylon," Chapter 7 in Paul R. Bass and Marcus F. Franda, eds., *Radical Politics in South Asia* (Cambridge, Massachusetts: MIT Press, 1973), 400–39, and George J. Lerski, "The Twilight of Ceylonese Trotskyism," *Pacific Affairs*, 43.3 (Fall 1970), 384–93.

⁹ The name JVP was adopted shortly before the 1970 elections in May.

¹⁰ The precise structure of the JVP during this period remains to be worked out. See Kearney and Jiggins, 52.

¹¹ A useful summary is found in Kearney and Jiggins, 54–55; see A.C. Alles, *Insurgency: 1971*, 3rd edn. (Colombia: Mervyn Mendis, 1976), 42–46; and Fred Halliday, "The Ceylonese Insurrection," *New Left Review*, 69 (September–October 1971), 75–78.

¹² Principal sources on the 1971 insurrection are: Paul Alexander, "Shared Fantasies and Elite Politics: The Sri Lankan 'Insurrection' of 1971," *Mankind*, 13.2 (December 1981), 113–32; Alles; S. Arasaratnam, "The Ceylonese Insurrection of April 1971: Some Causes and Consequences," *Pacific Affairs*, 45.3 (Fall 1972), 356–71; Blackton; Halliday; Janice Jiggins, "Caste and Insurgency of 1971," in Jiggins.; Robert N. Kearney, "A Note on the Fate of the 1971 Insurgents in Sri Lanka," *Journal of Asian Studies*, 36.3 (May 1977), 515–19; Kerney, "Educational Expansion and Political Volatility in Sri Lanka: The 1971 Insurrection," *Asian Survey*, 15.9 (September 1975), 727–44; Kearney and Jiggins; Gananath Obeyesekere, "Some Comments on the Social Backgrounds of the April 1971 Insurgency in Sri Lanka (Ceylon)," *Journal of Asian Studies*, 33.3 (May 1974), 376–84; W. A. Siswa Warnapala (pseudonum, "Politicus"), "The April Revolt in Ceylon," *Asian Survey*, 12.3 (March 1972), 259–74; Warnapala, "The Marxist Parties of Sri Lanka and the 1971 Insurrection," *Asian Survey*, 15.9 (September 1975), 745–57; and A. Jeyaratnam Wilson, "Ceylon: A Time of Troubles," *Asian Survey*, 12.2 (February 1972), 109–15.

¹³ Halliday, 80, claims that the JVP was not involved in this attack. Other sources disagree.

¹⁴ *Ibid.*

¹⁵ Alexander, 124.

¹⁶ Alles, 137.

¹⁷ See Obeyesekere, as well as Kearney and Jiggins, especially p. 44; and Alles, Chapter

22 (256–67) and 23 (268–81).

[18] Alles, 280–81.

[19] The term *pelantiya* is not the precise equivalent of "landed aristocracy" or local gentry, but the structural position appears to justify equating the two. Alexander (120) has defined *pelantiya* as "a putatively endogamous group of landlords, living a common lifestyle modeled on a vision of the feudal past, and controlling all local government offices." It is important to bear in mind that in the argument being advanced here, the "national *pelantiya*" had ceased altogether functioning as an actual landed aristocracy.

[20] See Gananath Obeyesekere, *Land Tenure in Village Ceylon* (London: Cambridge University Press, 1974).

[21] Historically, regardless of identity of ownership, the dominant form of land organization in the tea sector has been the "estate," where 80% of the labor force was comprised of Indian Tamils.

[22] Alexander, 121: "The economic activities of the *mudalali* were concentrated in four areas: transport (trucks, buses and hire cars); rice milling and rice purchasing; fish and vegetable wholesaling; and retailing through village shops and market stalls."

[23] This latter development is detailed for Anuradhapura District in James Brow, "Class Formation and Ideological Practice: A Case from Sri Lanka," *Journal of Asian Studies*, 40.4 (August 1981), 703–18. The author, however, is principally concerned with aspects of the process itself as sharecroppers are replaced by wage labor and does not consider causes for the transition. See also Barrie M. Morrison, M. P. Moore, and M. U. Ishak, eds., *The Disintegrating Village: Social Change in Rural Sri Lanka* (Colombo: Lake House, 1979). For historical background, see Tilak Hettiarachchy, *The Sinhala Peasant in a Changing Society* (Colombo: Lake House, 1982).

[24] Wilson, 111.

[25] See Alexander, 122: "The colonial policy of financing food imports (distributed as free or subsidized rations) with the earnings from plantation agriculture, provided no incentives for the development of peasant agriculture. By 1970, irrigation systems had broken down, crop increasing techniques such as transplanting and careful weeding were not widely used, and the condition of the fields seemed pitiful in comparison with Java or South India. Although the increasing cost of food imports and the technical developments of the Green Revolution, [*sic*] led to changes in government policies in the late sixties, for the most part the policies were mere paper plans."

[26] Jiggins, 125.

[27] As measured in the October 1971 census, the population was 12,747,755.

[28] Kearney and Jiggins, 41.

[29] Alexander.

264

[30] This state of affairs has come to pass, he notes, because all accounts draw on the same sources: government press releases or news reports, especially those of the Western media, all frequently inaccurate and misleading.

[31] *Ibid.*, 127.

[32] Premier reference for the formative years of the Tamil insurgency remains M.R. Narayan Swamy, *Tigers of Lanka: From Boys to Guerrillas*, 3rd edn. (Delhi: Konark, 2002).

[33] By 11 July 1979, the government claimed 14 policemen had been killed by LTTE and other groups.

[34] As related by Swamy, 69: "Prabhakaran was furious when the academic [Anton Stanislaus Balasingham, a Marxist academician who eventually became LTTE's second ranking figure] argued that it was important to politicize people before taking to the gun. 'What people, people, you talk about?' he burst out. 'We have to do some actions first. People will follow us.' When the academic persisted, Prabhakaran commented with undisguised contempt, 'You (arm chair) intellectuals are afraid of blood. No struggle will take place without killings. What do you want me to do? You people live in comfort and try to prove me wrong. So what should I do? Take cyanide and die?"

[35] In this attack, a busload of LTTE guerrillas, disguised as soldiers, penetrated Anuradhapura, the site of Sri Lanka's capital from the Fourth Century BC to the Tenth Century AD, and opened fire indiscriminately on Buddhist pilgrims paying homage to one of the country's most sacred shrines, the *Sri Maha Bodhi*, a *bo* tree revered for having been grown from a sapling of the tree under which Buddha attained enlightenment. After first attacking the bus station, the insurgents assaulted worshippers at the shrine itself. All too predictably, in a consequence apparently anticipated by the assailants, attacks on Tamil civilians followed at the hands of enraged Sinhalese mobs.

[36] Useful, although not always reliable on military particulars, is Mark Tully and Satish Jacob, *Amritsar: Mrs Gandhi's Last Battle* (New Delhi: Rupa, 1985). For the military view, see Kuldip Singh Brar, *Operation Bluestar: The True Story* (Delhi: UBS, 1993). A more recent interview with then-MG Brar is contained in "Operation Bluestar, 20 Years On," <www.rediff.com/news/2004/jun/03spec.htm>.

[37] Field work, southern India, summer 1984. I discuss this point in greater detail in "Marxist Tamils Won't Stop at Separatism," *AWSJ*, 8 May 1986, 6 (rpt. as "Tamil Rebels Aim Beyond Autonomy," *AWSJW*, 26 May 1986, 12); "The Ethnic Roots of Sri Lanka's Ideological Struggle," *AWSJ*, 12 August 1987, 8 (abridged under the same title: *AWSJW*, 31 August 1987, 12); and "Book Review—Stanley Tambiah, *Sri Lanka: Ethnic Fratricide and the Dismantling of Democracy,*" *Issues & Studies*, 23.9 (September 1987), 135–40.

[38] Anton S. Balasingham, *Liberation Tigers and Tamil Eelam Freedom Struggle* (Madras: Political Committee, LTTE, nd), 42. Put in plain English: we'll only be free when we get

rid of both the Sinhalese and capitalism.

[39] The two had been arrested in May 1982, together with several followers, after trading shots on a crowded Madras street.

[40] Dixit's last assessment of the Tamil case (before passing away of natural causes) is contained in J.N. Dixit, ed., *External Affairs: Cross-Border Relations* (New Delhi: Roli Books, 2003), "Sri Lanka," 47–96. It is necessary reading, both for its astute analysis as to many matters, as well as its fundamental inaccuracies concerning alleged foreign plots (especially US) to use Sri Lanka as a base from which to threaten India. Revealing is his claim to "definite information" (i.e., intelligence) concerning US motives and actions even as he outlines in detail the shortcomings of the source of those assessments, Indian intelligence agencies, in their efforts concerning Sri Lanka.

[41] A 19-year old LTTE guerrilla, following his captured in August 1986, offered the following brief description of such sessions, "The leaders always spoke about Marxism. They wanted a Marxist *Eelam*. That was their main idea." An older, higher ranking captive, in another discussion, observed, "We were hoping to establish a Tamil socialist state in the north and east." As put by Anton S. Balasingham, number two in the LTTE hierarchy and leading theoretician for the movement, "The political objective of our movement is to advance the national struggle along with the class struggle, or rather, our fundamental objective is national emancipation and socialist transformation of our social formation." Balasingham, 42. Consideration of Tamil insurgent ideology has been neglected. Even as fine a work as A. Jeyaratnam Wilson, *Sri Lankan Tamil Nationalism: Its Origin and Development in the 19th and 20th Centuries* (Vancouver: University of British Columbia Press, 2000), has precisely one entry in the index under "Marxist ideology" (pg. 128; it deals in passing with the Marxism of the EPRLF). Yet in my own field work, when I talked with Tamil insurgent leadership figures, Marxism was the analytical framework within which all analysis took place.

[42] Balasingham, 42.

[43] EPRLF leader K. Padmanabha was uncharacteristically open when he told a Sri Lankan journalist in 1985, "When Eelam is set up there will be no democracy there. The choice is between fascism and communism. I think the people will opt for the latter."

[44] Field work, Tamil Nadu, India, August 1984.

[45] The precise position of Marxism within LTTE has in many respects been driven by the personal relationship between undisputed LTTE leader Prabhakaran and the decade-older (now deceased) penultimate figure, Balasingham, a relationship sources have variously characterized as son/father or pupil/teacher. That Balasingham was a committed Marxist is beyond dispute; that Prabhakaran found ideology useful up to a point but secondary to combat is equally true. The instruction in Marxism that was a part of the daily training

schedule in the early years of the movement was allowed to lapse as the military elements of the struggle became more salient.

[46] In this episode, members of the 1st Battalion, Rajarata Rifles Regiment, were disciplined after taking retaliatory actions against civilians. In protest against the measures, nearly a hundred other soldiers went on strike and deserted. The entire battalion was consequently disbanded; the deserters, once rounded up, were cashiered, as were key members of the chain-of-command. The remaining unit members were combined with another under-strength regular battalion to form the first unit of an entirely new regiment.

[47] Weaponry was likewise woefully inadequate. There was no single infantry rifle. Even the venerable 1941 Lee Enfield was in use in some units. Heavier backup was a mix of British, Chinese, Soviet, and Yugoslav arms.

[48] Fourteen aircraft—five HC-1 "Chipmunks," six Cessna-150 Skymasters, and three Devon Doves—were based in a flying wing that spent most of its time training new pilots. A transport squadron had eleven heavier aircraft ranging from the DH-114 ("Heron" and "Riley" versions) to the Dakota DC-3 to the Cessna 337 (utility version).

[49] Ten fast attack craft (PCF) with guns were the heart of the Sri Lankan Navy, though at any one time several were laid up for repairs. The two newest vessels were indigenously produced 40-meter craft built at Colombo Dockyards and launched in mid-1983. The remaining eight craft consisted of seven *Sooraya*-class (ex-Chinese *Shanghai* II) and one ex-Soviet *Mol*-class gunboats. Aside from a single lighthouse support vessel, the remaining members of the naval inventory, some 21 vessels, were little more than patrol craft of diminutive size and capability.

[50] Interview with author, Colombo, August 1984.

[51] See Marks, "Sri Lanka's Special Force: Professionalism in a Dirty War," *Soldier of Fortune*, 13.7 (July 1988), 32–39.

[52] Portions of this section have appeared in Marks, "India is the Key to Peace in Sri Lanka," *AWSJ*, 19–20 September 1986, 8 (reproduced under the same title in *The Island* [Colombo], 5 October 1986, 8; abridged under the same title in *AWSJW*, 22 September 1986, 25) and "Peace in Sri Lanka," *Daily News* (Colombo), 3 parts, 6–8 July 1987: "I. India Acts in its Own Interests," 6 July, 6; "II. Bengali Solution: India Trained Personnel for Invasion of Sri Lanka," 7 July, 8; "III. India's Political Solution Narrow and Impossible," 8 July, 6. Published under the same titles in *Sri Lanka News*, 15 July 1987 (cont), 6–7; in *The Island* as "India's Covert Involvements," 28 June 1987, 8, 10.

[53] Details in Marks, "Counter-Insurgency in Sri Lanka," *Soldier of Fortune*, 12.2 (February 1987), 38–47.

[54] In the months that immediately preceded the 19 July 1987 accord that gave the Indians the legal cover necessary to enter Sri Lanka, ominous events demonstrated that LTTE was about

to move wholesale into imitation of the suicide tactics favored by radical Islamic movements. A "land torpedo," for instance, a truck packed with explosives, had been used to demolish the main Jaffna telecommunications center. Its atomized driver, "Commander Miller," had joined the growing pantheon of LTTE "martyrs," who were celebrated in regular ceremonies and services. A "Black Tigers" suicide commando had likewise been formed to carry out one-way attacks. There remains considerable debate as to precise inspiration for this shift.

[55] Refer to sources in note 52.

[56] Details in Marks, "Sri Lankan Minefield: Gandhi's Troops Fail To Keep the Peace," *Soldier of Fortune*, 13.3 (March 1988), 36–45.

[57] Certainly the most poignant aspect of these events was the final LTTE delegation that visited the Indian battalion commander with whom the Tigers had maintained daily contact, LTC T. P. S. ("Tipi") Brar, headquartered in the Jaffna Fort. They came to tell him that they understood he was only doing his duty in carrying out orders to attack them. Brar, in another of the many ironies evident throughout this chapter, was the younger brother of the LTG Kulip Singh Brar, who had commanded Operation *Bluestar* against the Sikh militants in Punjab. "Tipi" was to become a LTG himself and command XVI Corps in counter-insurgency operations in Jammu and Kashmir.

[58] Good overviews are C.A. Chandraprema, *Sri Lanka: The Years of Terror–The JVP Insurrection 1987–1989* (Colombo: Lake House Bookshop,1991), and Rohan Gunaratna, *Sri Lanka: A Lost Revolution? The Inside Story of the JVP* (Colombo: Institute of Fundamental Studies, 1990).

[59] Details in Marks, "In Sri Lanka, Despair Explodes into Violence," *AWSJ*, 16 August 1989, 6 (abridged as "Sri Lanka's Despair Breeds Violence," *AWSJW*, 21 August 1989, 15).

[60] Details in Marks, "Professionals in Paradise: Sri Lanka's Army Gears Up for "Tiger" Hunt," *Soldier of Fortune*, 15.1 (January 1990), 48–55, and "Chaos in Colombo: Sri Lanka's Army Awaits its Marching Orders while Politicians Dither," *Soldier of Fortune*, 15.2 (February 1990). 48–55.

[61] Only as the conflict progressed did the army place its battalions under permanent, numbered brigades—though these remained continually changing in composition—and its brigades under divisions. In theory, there was a brigade for each of Sri Lanka's nine provinces. These were grouped under three division headquarters, only two of which were operational at this point in time, because the third was designated for the area under Indian occupation.

[62] For this and quotations that follow, see sources in note 60. Therein, particulars and circumstances of citation are related.

[63] A Sri Lankan general's analysis of the campaign seems fitting: "We have done terrible things, terrible things."

[64] For details, see Shankar Bhaduri and Afsir Karim, *The Sri Lankan Crisis* (New Delhi: Lancer International, 1990).

[65] Official figures are 1,155 dead, 2,984 wounded for the 32-month deployment. Rohan Gunaratna, *Indian Intervention in Sri Lanka: The Role of India's Intelligence Agencies*, 2nd edn. (Colombo: South Asian Network on Conflict Research, 1994), 315.

[66] Details in Marks, "Toying with Terrorists: India's Sri Lankan Creation Runs Amok," *Low Intensity Conflict (LIC) International* (Washington, DC), 1.1 (December 1992), 6–8.

[67] These were initially scheduled in advance, two per year, as a part of the normal training cycle of the US special operations units concerned. As Sri Lankan needs were further clarified, both individuals and teams returned as dictated by circumstances. Interestingly, these trainers were never threatened by LTTE, much less attacked. Evidence indicates that a decision was made by the insurgents not to risk an aggressive US response to an overreaction by LTTE. When all was said and done, went the insurgent logic, US aid would have, at most, minor tactical impact; while a lashing out by Washington, even if only in the form of increased aid, could have operational or even strategic impact.

[68] For background and context of this effort, to include discussion of personalities, see Marks, "Sri Lanka: The Dynamics of Terror," *Counterterrorism and Security*, New Series 1.1 (1994), 19–23; "Sri Lanka: Terrorism in Perspective," *Counterterrorism and Security*, New Series 2.3 (Fall–Winter 1995), 16–19 (rpt. as "Dynamics of Terror in Sri Lanka," *Sunday Times* [Colombo], 31 December 1996, 7; concluded, 7 January 1996, 7); and "Sri Lanka: Reform, Revolution or Ruin?", *Soldier of Fortune*, 21.6 (June 96), 35–39.

[69] He was actually Deputy Minister, but the President herself was the minister, so Ratwatte ran the security forces. A reserve lieutenant colonel, he had himself recalled to active duty and eventually promoted to four-star rank. This chain of events occasioned considerable controversy.

[70] Growing from its mere four infantry battalions (recall that a fifth battalion was disbanded for indiscipline), the army went to 24 battalions that were nearly twice their predecessors' size. They had grown not only numerically but also in effectiveness and equipment. Essential to this expansion process was the use of the regimental system. Each of the country's five regiments—Gajaba, Gemunu Watch, Vijayabahu Infantry (all of these first three named after great kings), Sri Lanka Light Infantry (which traced its ancestry to the colonial Ceylon Light Infantry), and Singha ("Lion")—had five component battalions, numbered one through five (with one regiment having not yet produced its fifth battalion). Each infantry battalion, in turn, was given seven companies: five line, a headquarters, and a support weapons. This 1,200-man body allowed the most experienced officers to maneuver their fledgling charges, a necessary adaptation to rapid expansion and its consequent influx of green recruits, both officers and men. It was a difficult unit to control, though, given the dispersed deployment

requirements of irregular war. As soon as adequate numbers of junior officers became available to allow for promotions throughout the system, the size of a battalion was cut back by one line company, bringing strength down to about 900. Further pruning of the structure progressed as officer resources allowed, resulting in the final 76 figure with 600–850 men per battalion.

[71] When the early insurgent threat in Sri Lanka was one of terror actions, with attacks including strikes by Tamil groups against Colombo's commercial air links, a small army commando force had been formed. It had only two squadrons, one devoted to rapid response missions, principally anti-hijacking, the other to VIP security. As actual hostilities progressed, the commandos found themselves in counter-guerrilla operations, as well. The shortage of such personnel led to the formation of a separate Special Forces Regiment, primarily for jungle operations. Leaving permutations aside, the end result was that both the commandos and the special forces eventually evolved into forces of two battalions each (of 450 men rather than the standard infantry 600–750 strength), task organized in a Special Forces Brigade.

[72] LTTE filmed the entire operation, which featured suicide personnel clearing defensive minefields by blowing themselves up and the defenders overwhelmed by repeated "human wave" assaults. Indeed, the LTTE name for the assault was Operation Oyada Alaikhal, or "Endless Waves." Details in Paul Harris, "Bitter Lessons for the SLA," *Jane's Intelligence Review* (October 1996), 466–68.

[73] Details in Anthony Davis, "Tamil Tiger International," *Ibid.*, 469–73. Davis puts LTTE funding at this point at an estimated USD 2 million *monthly*, 60% from abroad, principally from Western locales. He further notes (p. 473): "Perhaps predictably, alleged involvement in the narcotics trade has been a contentious piece of the LTTE financial jigsaw."

[74] Useful for tracking events is *South Asia Intelligence Review* (*SAIR*), a New Delhi internet weekly published by the Institute for Conflict Management available at <www.satp.org>.

[75] Refer to Ben Kerkvliet's fieldwork in central Luzon discussed in Chapter 4. He found that former Huk areas, having been through an intense round of insurgency in the earlier struggle, had no desire to relive the experience.

Chapter 6

Terror as Insurgent "Driver": The Communist Party of Peru in the Shining Path of Mariategui

Obviously, Peru does not lie in Asia (see Figure 6.1). Developments there neverthe-less had a serious impact on what is to be discussed in the next chapter, on events in Nepal, and hence it is necessary to discuss the Peruvian case briefly.

Certainly, its dénouement is known to most, more so now that it has featured in a superb film, *The Dancer Upstairs*. On 12 September 1992, even as it prepared for what many observers, both foreign and domestic, saw as a possible "Red October" final offensive against the tottering Peruvian state, the people's war of the Maoist group Shining Path, or *Sendero Luminoso*, lost its top leadership to a government raid in Lima. Included in the haul by DINCOTE, a special police intelligence unit, were *Sendero* supremo, Abimael Guzman Reynoso, the self-proclaimed "fourth sword of Marxism" (the other three being Marx himself, Lenin, and Mao) and several members of the inner circle. Just as important a prize, however, taken in other raids, were the movement's master computer files. In the days that followed, the government raced to detain insurgent personalities before they could vanish. Hundreds were detained. As though taking in a collective gulp of air, the country then waited for the *Sendero* response. The sigh that followed was all but audible as it became clear, the government's miscues in handling its good fortune notwithstand-ing, the insurgents were truly staggered.

Not soon enough, however, to prevent Peruvian Maoists from becoming the darlings of the international Maoist movement, such as it was by the 1980s and early 1990s, when even China had renounced Maoism. Associated with the chaos and death toll of the Great Proletarian Cultural Revolution, the "internalization of the dialectic" continued, following Mao's death, to be championed by his widow,

271

Figure 6.1

Chi Peng and her intimates, the so-called "Gang of Four," the term thereafter associated with "radical Maoism" and the extreme forces such an effort unleashed as man turned against man.

This was Maoism as adopted by insurgents of the post-Mao era. Its essence was to push forward terror as insurgent driver (within the "violence" line of operation) at the expense of mobilization achieved by the mass line and the united front mechanisms. It could not even be called "militaristic," simply violent, which meant political warfare and international action were relegated even further into the background. The approach convulsed Peru to the extent that the death toll is still being tallied and the sums regularly increased.

Growth of Insurgent Challenge to the Old-Regime

Ayacucho, the highland department of Peru where *Sendero* was born, was an impoverished area twice the size of El Salvador. Forty-eight hours by single, one-lane road from the center of power, Lima, its 566,000 people (one-tenth the population of El Salvador), 90% of whom were Quechua Indians, lived in isolated poverty. Small wonder, therefore, went the early belief, that in 1980 they responded to the clarion call for revolution sounded by the "Communist Party of Peru in the Shining Path of Mariategui" (Mariategui is the father of Peruvian Marxism) when the first incidents occurred. Small wonder, too, that their pent up anger took on, at times, horrific forms, to include torture and mutilation of terror victims. *Sendero*, it was argued, could be judged a logical outgrowth of its environment, in the same vein with fundamentalist explosions worldwide. This was true as far as it went, but the explanation foundered on larger realities. "The 'Inca's Last Rebellion' explanation is bullshit," stated a Peruvian analyst pithily in 1989.[1] Added a well-versed foreign observer, flatly: "There is no peasant revolt in this country in the traditional agrarian revolt pattern. . . The societal problems here are necessary but not sufficient to explain *Sendero*."[2]

Peruvian national conditions, they were saying, were not those that should have led to insurgency. First, whatever the 1980 poor state of life in Ayacucho itself, the economy as a whole was expanding. Secondly, there was the fact that Peru in 1980 was a democracy. Its democratic institutions were only just emerging from twelve years of military rule (1968–80), but these had been reformist in nature as opposed to oppressive. To the contrary, major foreign investments had been nationalized, relations established with the socialist world (especially the Soviet Union, which became Peru's chief source of military aid and advice), and extensive agrarian reform carried out.

When the complexities of running the country proved unduly vexing, the men on horseback decided a return to the barracks was in order. This was a much welcomed move, and while it did not occur without assurances that past abuses of power would not be made into an issue by democratic process, the point was that options for legal democratic activity were expanding at the very time *Sendero* was revolting against the system. "The Marxist left had even garnered 36% of the vote for representation at the constitutional convention that accompanied the end of military rule," observes David Scott Palmer, dean of American *Senderologists*.[3] There seemed plenty of "democratic space" within the system for resolution of grievances, no matter how profound. Local conditions in Ayacucho might be awful, but there were other regions—the neighboring department of Huancavelica, to cite an illustration—where objective circumstances were considerably worse. What needed factored in was the subjective element.

This had appeared in Ayacucho in 1962 in the presence of Guzman. Taking up his first job as a university instructor, he served initially as a professor of philosophy in the Education Department of the re-opened (1959) National University of San Cristobal de Huamanga (founded 1677). Already a member of a Maoist splinter from the mainstream, Soviet-oriented Communist Party, his quarrels with the Maoist party leadership, as well, eventually led to *Sendero*'s formation. To those on the scene at the time, it seemed little more than another "coffee-house discussion" group of radicals. Further, the commitment of its members to action amongst the populace dovetailed neatly with the university's own orientation toward service. The school's various departments and majors were tailored to meet the specific needs of the highlands and its Indian population. Nearly three-quarters of the student body were Quechua-speaking, native to the region.

Yet as they were trained to return in service roles to their communities, especially as teachers—Education was the largest department—the Indian youth, the flower of a regional generation, were indoctrinated by Guzman and other *Sendero* members. This effort became more comprehensive as Guzman moved up the university hierarchy. Ultimately, as the university, which had been a small establishment of some 550 students and 40 faculty, grew to approximately 4,500 students and 200 teachers, Guzman emerged as the director of the teacher training school; later, as Personnel Director for the university (1971–74). As such, he was able to stack the deck with fellow true believers and maintain absolute control over the school from 1968 to 1972 (and substantial influence until 1975). He used the time to develop the cadre for *Sendero*'s insurgency.

Ironically, all of *Sendero*'s top leadership, to include Guzman himself, were outsiders to Ayacucho. In the laboratory that was the University of Huamanga, however, they became completely committed to the struggle. Faced with the suffering of the downtrodden, they threw themselves into the effort to make a Maoist revolution. The entire *Sendero* Central Committee, drawn from fewer than half a dozen families, was comprised of former faculty and students. In May 1980, they declared people's war. At the time, *Sendero* numbered 150–200 militants at most.

Their first act was symbolic, the burning of a ballot box in a small town. It was seemingly an inauspicious beginning for the revolution. Only a decade later, the movement had grown powerful and widespread enough to have been directly responsible for more than 69,000 deaths and property damage equivalent to one-third to one-half of the GNP! What allowed for this stunning development was, on the one hand, *Sendero*'s strategic finesse, and, on the other hand, the weakness of the system and the government's inability to respond appropriately.[4]

Ample fuel for a fire: Ayacucho highland town. Characterized by economic neglect, social marginalization, and political impotency, the Quechua-speaking Indians and their plight were targeted by Shining Path as its initial mass base. (Marks photos)

Constructing the Counter-State

The movement's strategic acumen came directly from China. Between 1965 and 1974, it is now known, almost every Central Committee member made at least one extended trip to the PRC. Guzman made three. There, amidst the chaos of the Great Proletarian Cultural Revolution, the *Sendero* elite was trained, ideologically, in "Gang of Four Maoism," politically and militarily, in the mechanics of people's war. When the Maoists were ultimately vanquished in China, Guzman, under the *nom de guerre* President Gonzalo, became the self-appointed heir to the "true" Marxist legacy, his template for Peru's future, "Gonzalo Path."

Although his heavy reliance on terror might seem out of step with Mao's emphasis on united fronts and the mass line, it is now better understood how important violence actually was to people's war in China. As such, it was little different from the methodology adopted by the Maoist "southern branch," the Vietnamese communists, whether in their Viet Minh or Viet Cong incarnations.

Sendero initially focused more on organizational work and bringing politics to those who lived on society's margins. Violence, of course, was always present, because there were those who objected to the connection of local grievances redress with ideological membership. But it was not random violence, no matter how brutal. It was calculated terror.

From neutralizing individuals who would oppose it, *Sendero* sought to neutralize the state in all its functions. By 1989, 25% of all local justices-of-the-peace and 35% of all mayorships were vacant, citizens being too frightened to fill them. In a typical Maoist campaign, in the run-up to the November 1989 municipal elections, 120 mayoral candidates were struck down. Consequently, more than 400 others resigned in fear. In Ayacucho, 85% of the populace did not vote.

What made terror so effective was the absence of anywhere to turn for help. "There has traditionally been no government presence in many areas," observed the editor of a leading Peruvian news magazine at the height of the conflict. "There are no liberated areas, only abandoned areas."[5] In such a vacuum, it took only a few armed men to establish *Sendero*'s writ.

Once the "revolutionary struggle" was inaugurated, however, after the 17-year gestation period, the death rate rapidly soared to 500 per year, with 2,000-plus dead in 1983 alone. This translated to about 100 deaths per 100,000 population per annum, far surpassing the murder rates of such US crime centers as Detroit or Washington, DC. Further, it was not just the numbers but the *way* those 500 were usually killed—butchered would have been a more appropriate term.

276

Integral to every insurgent murder was a message, often associated with Indian myths since the target population was Indian. Thus feet would be cut off and sewed on backwards to prevent the walk to heaven, or an entire community would be forced to inflict a knife wound on a writhing victim so that all would be implicated, and hence involved.

An American Embassy official observed:

It [*Sendero*] is not committing genocide. We are not witnessing pent-up rage exploding. Rather, we are seeing carefully designed and calculated terror. They target individuals in advance, then execute them in ways that have symbolic meaning. *Sendero's* most recent tactic is the "armed strike." Cadre pass out leaflets that in 72 hours there will be a strike. Subsequently, *Sendero* will kill several who violate the strike, bomb several businesses. and burn some transport. Horrible methods of execution will be used, ways that are symbolic in a mythological sense. For example, one of the most common is to slice the throat of the victim, because then the soul cannot escape from the mouth.[6]

Such a level of killing had an increased impact because of the very lay of the land. Although almost the whole department was mountains, with peaks rising as high as 5,453 m (17,890 ft), the jumble of crags was cut by innumerable river valleys.

Ayacucho in 1989: A journey that might have taken less than half an hour by helicopter would require days on foot. (Marks photo)

277

A patrol might require equipment suitable to a Himalayan climbing expedition one moment, a group of Arizona rattlesnake hunters the next. Snow-capped peaks torn by fierce winds overlooked cactus-filled desert. A journey that might have taken less than half an hour by helicopter would require days on foot. To make the Alice-in-Wonderland geographical transition complete, in the northeastern reaches, high jungle brought to mind stretches of Southeast Asia. Lush vegetation embraced strategic hamlets guarded by militias and marines. Society, in other words, was atomized, so a brutal action in a small community had a disproportionate impact.

The point of such brutality was to carve out a counter-state, to eliminate all who opposed *Sendero* and both to remove state presence and to sever linkages between the state and the population. The new Maoist order was to be all for the people in the target zone.

In organizational terms, there was little to distinguish *Sendero*'s approach from that considered throughout this work.[7] The key individuals in the villages were the cadre. Contacts were first made with a community through acquaintances or relatives.[8] This gave *Sendero* sufficient local presence to make some converts, who then formed the "Nucleus" of a "Popular Committee."

The Committee's leadership normally consisted of five individuals. At the head was a political commissar (*Comisario Secretario*). He was assisted by individuals charged with: (1) security—organized mechanisms of control and defense (all travel, in particular, was controlled); (2) production—determined matters of provision and logistics (in particular, which crops would be grown); (3) communal matters—administered normal societal functions such as justice, marriage, and burials; and (4) organization—classified the population by sectoral group: children, juveniles, women, peasants, or intellectuals. These divisions were then used for study sessions and other activities.

This political organization existed in the open and maintained influence in part through its ability to call on a *Sendero* armed column for support. The columns normally carried out violent action. Such actions were particularly intimidating, because the local communist party organization of *Sendero* remained underground in clandestine three-man cells, each with a secretary, sub-secretary, and an information specialist. The result is that no one knew for sure who was informing on them. This paralyzed attempts to fight back. Given the virtual absence or intermittent nature of the government's presence, there simply was no one to whom villagers could have recourse.

Throughout its preparatory years, the movement expanded its political sway largely through persuasion. In the process, it benefited from the political space provided by the military government's (1968–80) efforts to mobilize the peasantry behind its reform measures, efforts taken without the concomitant capacity to implement them effectively in a region Lima did not consider important. *Sendero* hence garnered considerable sympathy and support among the Ayacucho population by addressing grievances initially raised by the military itself.

Nevertheless, popular sympathy could carry the movement only so far. Eventually, the moment came—precisely at what point is being explored in on-going research—when *Sendero*'s leadership felt that it had to resort to force to consolidate the gains made and to expand further. The counter-state already in place was the vehicle for expansion. Terror and guerrilla action served to protect it and give it power.

At this point the crossover occurs in an insurgency: the impetus behind the movement is no longer grievances as such but the mechanisms of organization. These manifest themselves, in particular, in recruiting. Because an alternative political body has come into existence, with all the coercive mechanisms that adhere to such status, it need no longer rely only on those with grievances derived from structural injustice to fill its ranks. Instead, it can appeal to a more complex mixture of motives. "Human factors considerations," in other words, come to the fore.[9] At one extreme, potential recruits see the movement as a viable alternative for social participation; at the other, they simply recognize that it, effectively, has become the state and must thus be obeyed. It recruits, socializes, deploys, and controls. In between will be an array of motives.

The advance and consolidation of *Sendero* in this respect was highly methodical. When a region targeted was deemed to have sufficient popular committees, a Support Base could be declared. According to several sources in Peruvian intelligence, the annual production in such areas was divided in half, with 50% going to the people, the other 50% going to the *Sendero* apparatus for stockpiling and use during operations.[10] In Ayacucho, there were twenty such bases known to be in existence in 1989, with an additional eighty Popular Committees. Such were healthy figures even if not particularly large.

There thus existed an extensive dual web enmeshing the people: the overt system of sectoral organizations, coordinated by the Revolutionary Front for the Defense of the Village (*Frente Revolucionario de Defensa del Pueblo*), and the covert system of the party, with its cells. These party cells, in turn, were coordinated by Local Committees (*Comites Locales* or CL), which themselves fell under Sub-Zones (*Sub Zonales* or SZ). The Sub-Zones belonged to Zones (normally referred to as CZ after the Spanish *Comite Zonal*), the Zones to Regional Commands.[11]

Nothing in this infrastructure would have surprised a member of the CPT or CPP or JVP.

Apparently, boundary changes were the responsibility of the regional commands, each headed by a secretary and sub-secretary, working with five other staff members responsible for military operations, logistics, security, agitation and propaganda, and administrative organization. Peru's size made these Regional Commands quite independent. Yet they did not appear to have the degree of autonomy enjoyed by, say, a CPP regional body.

At the apex of this pyramidal scheme were the central organs, of standard Leninist form. A Politburo and Central Committee, together with a Permanent Committee, or Secretariat, existed to direct party operations. These party operations were conducted in six regions nationwide, each headed by a party Regional Committee: south, central, north, northeast, the metropolitan area (Lima), and "the principal area" (Ayacucho). That Ayacucho rated its own regional committee stemmed from its being the birthplace of *Sendero*.

Although the Maoists formed a number of front organizations, these were never particularly strong. Political warfare was virtually non-existent. At no time, for instance, did *Sendero* offer to negotiate with the government. International action, carried out through the Revolutionary Internationalist Movement (RIM) was minimal, despite the central role in RIM mytho-history carved out for this new, latest hope for international revolution.

To illustrate how this system worked in practice, we need only consider Ayacucho. As just noted, it was one of six regional commands. Actually, as the Maoists expanded, the Ayacucho Regional Committee came to embrace more territory than the department of Ayacucho alone. Ayacucho Department thus comprised four of the Regional Committee's five Zones. The other Zone, however, was to the west in the neighboring department of Huancavelica. Regardless, all five Zones were further divided into a varying number of Sub-Zones, normally three or four.[12]

Given the increasing salience of violent action in the movement, it should not surprise that the lines of command became increasingly vague between the political counter-state just outlined and *Sendero*'s military component. In an orthodox people's war framework, the primacy of politics dictates a chain of command that is quite standard—all military formations are controlled by party organizations. A district guerrilla unit, to cite a hypothetical illustration, would report to and take orders from the district party apparatus.

Not so, it would seem, for *Sendero*, where Guerrilla Zones (ZG is the Spanish acronym) were defined by operational necessity and might straddle any number of

SZs. Principal authority was supposed to lie with the Political Commissar of the ZG, but there were growing reports, as time passed, of military commanders taking charge. Since the latter, like the commissar and the three other ZG staff members (logistics, information, and organization), was a party member, the division was possibly not serious. Nonetheless, it was unorthodox and serves to highlight the obvious but often underestimated fact that must be decided in all insurgencies: Who wields power? Those who "talk" or those who "fight"? Invariably, combatant ascendance results in a bloodier conflict, because decisions begin to be driven by considerations of force.

Leaving aside questions concerning precise command and control arrangements, within each ZG was to be found the classic insurgent tripartition of forces into main, regional, and local, called in the *Sendero* setup, respectively, the Principal Force, the Local Force, and the Base Force. Together, these comprised the Popular Guerrilla Army (*Ejercito Guerrilla Popular* or EGP).

Numbers were never *Sendero*'s strength. In its Ayacucho heartland, for instance, in mid-1989, the Principal and Local forces fielded just in the neighborhood of 250 personnel each, the Base Force, 750. Only the Principal Force was armed with modern firearms, normally AK-47s captured from the police, mixed with some RPG-7s. The counter-state this armed force was intended to protect, of course, was much larger, but was never estimated at more than 20–30% of the population in even the worst-hit areas of *Sendero* operations, such as Ayacucho.

Recruitment was standard, with local forces gaining manpower from the most promising base force personnel, the principal force drawing from the best local force men. "Men," it may be added, was certainly a misnomer, since as much as half of any *Sendero* unit might be comprised of women. This high percentage of female combatants prompted any number of explanations, none wholly convincing.[13]

"Manpower," of whatever gender, required support. Initially, *Sendero* relied on forms of revolutionary taxation. When these failed to generate the income necessary to support movement expansion, a battle was waged with the "other" insurgent movement within Peru, the Tupac Amaru Revolutionary Movement (MRTA, *Movimiento Revolucionario Tupac Amaru*), for control of the Upper Huallaga Valley and its coca crop. At the time, Peru was the source of perhaps 65% of the world's raw coca, from which cocaine was produced, and the 3,000 square-mile Upper Huallaga Valley was the major production area.

In an economy that increasingly became effectively bankrupt, coca planting remained virtually the only growth industry, and, certainly, the only livelihood for tens of thousands of peasants. Capitalizing on the ill-will aroused by government eradication efforts, *Sendero* was able to establish a mass base in coca-producing areas. Unlike the 10–15-man columns of Ayacucho, actual companies (60–120 men) were formed in the Upper Huallaga, and deals with drug lords reportedly provided M-60 medium machine-guns, 81mm mortars, and grenade launchers, a considerable upgrading of armament.

The complete preoccupation of the United States with the drug war did not make the situation easier for the Peruvians. Wedded to a strategy of crop eradication, Washington financed a counter-narcotics base at Santa Lucia, north of Tingo Maria in Huanuco Department (population: 609,200), from which Drug Enforcement Agency personnel operated with Peruvian forces. Lima was constantly pressed to go after growers and refineries more aggressively. Yet, pointed out a high-ranking military officer:

> The US has its own priorities and strategy. We fit in only because of the drugs. Our attitude is simple. Coca is just raw material. It is the refining that gives it astronomical value. It is the people on the distribution end who have the power and influence. The growers are small fish. Still, in the States there is no serious campaign to fight drugs. Down here, we have 150,000 *campesinos* who earn their living off the stuff. To go after them is a mistake. It is the drug lords who are the real threat. We help the US right now, because as far as our security is concerned, there is no distinction between the drug lords and *Sendero*. [But] our policy is to solve the security problems first, to get rid of *Sendero* and then the drugs. Our first priority must be attacks on the system.[14]

It was a dilemma. Buoyed by its successes in the Upper Huallaga, *Sendero* pressed its organizational efforts in other parts of Peru, especially in the critical breadbasket of the Mantaro Valley, located to the east of Lima in Junin Department (population: 542,900). Additionally, it tried hard to work in Lima's teeming slums. There, paradoxically, where conditions seemed most ripe for revolt, *Sendero* had uneven success. Still, it was ultimately, as indicated earlier, in a position to launch a climactic offensive. This skipped the mobile warfare phase entirely and would seem to smack of *focismo*. The reason such was possible lay in the more prominent role given terror rather than political mobilization.

State Response to Insurgent Challenge

What allowed the Maoists, then, to operate with virtual impunity was Peru's sheer size (an area equal to Texas, New Mexico, and Arizona, with the same population, then 20 million) combined with the incapacity of the government. Militarily, initial ignorance of *Sendero* led Lima simply to ignore it. When authorities did respond, they did so brutally, with repression producing insurgent recruits.

Lima had early been slow to react to the communist challenge at all. The newly installed civilian government of President Fernando Balaunde Terry was sure that military demands for committing forces, made as early as 1980, were but a screen for their renewed involvement in politics. So it sent instead the Civil Guard, which, through its brutality, promptly created *Senderistas* out of previously uncommitted peasants, *campesinos*. Finally, as 1982 ended, Lima relented and deployed army units. An Emergency Zone was declared in Ayacucho and neighboring areas. Battle was joined. By this time, of course, *Sendero* was deeply entrenched. Those who did not go along willingly were forced by terror to toe the line. Army atrocities made the situation worse.

There matters remained, as under Balaunde's uninspired administration, the country drifted. In particular, the economy, for all practical purposes, collapsed. Great hopes were raised when April 1985 brought to office Alan Garcia Perez, a 35-year old social democrat, who represented the centrist-leftist *Alianza Popular Revolucionaria Americana* (the American Popular Revolutionary Alliance or ARPA). He seemed a breath of fresh air. He proved, instead, something of a cyclone run amok.

Unilateral decisions, such as declaring that Peru would no longer fully service its substantial foreign debt, led to a cutoff in much foreign aid and to the flight of capital. Having charted a path to financial ruin, Garcia reaped the whirlwind. Hyperinflation, matching that of post-Second World War China, had by 1990, when he left office, reached the staggering rate of 7,600% per year. The economy was contracting rapidly. Corruption and mismanagement were rife, and the armed forces completely demoralized.

At that point *Sendero* had become a nationwide force, seemingly financially secure, because of an influx of protection money from the drug trade, and in the driver's seat strategically. Its clandestine infrastructure was growing in the capital itself. Still, it should not have been surprising that there were individuals who could see their way clear to solutions. Although a deeply flawed state, Peru was nevertheless a democratic system, even if a struggling one. Remarkably astute, for instance, was the analysis of a government advisor connected with a leading official think-tank, himself a former high-ranking general officer and government official:

> An oligarchy rules this country. The military knew this when it took power in 1968. Then, we had a social pyramid where one percent had everything. The military

283

Military committed late: Peruvian soldiers (above), their youth and lowland origins apparent, in Ayacucho. Fear of the military caused Peru's democracy to move cautiously in the years following its 1980 restoration. This gave Shining Path ample opportunity to utilize terror effectively. When security forces were committed, they were brutal, as still remembered (below) in the folk art of the region. (Marks photos)

[1968–1980] set out to change this. It was very difficult, but it was necessary. Our problem was strategic—how to do that? Various ways with which you're familiar were tried, including widespread land reform. The purpose of the military was right, but it is possible that in the execution we were in error. We have a version of the same problem now. It's logical that the oligarchy doesn't want to lose its privileges. That is the principal conflict [in Peru]. They don't put their profits back into development of the infrastructure and [thereby] increase employment. Velasco[15] tried to impose his will on these people. We should have avoided confrontation by relying more on persuasion. You can't turn the country against foreign investment, as we inadvertently succeeded in doing. We also forgot the attitude of the revolutionary populace. We thought because we were a popular government, there would be no space for a subversive recruitment. In this we were incorrect. *Sendero* ideology is very complicated, a hybrid of all manner of doctrines. But they found the proper space for development of their forces. We weren't taking decisive action to develop areas such as Ayacucho, and they sought out those areas. The problem was compounded after the military left power. The Balaunde government failed to move vigorously against the guerrillas, because he was too afraid the military would use its strength to get back into power. . . Now we are caught in our current dilemma. When Garcia got into power, he was very popular. Yet he has exacerbated the very conditions that created the opening for the subversives. Mass communications has made the situation even more unsettled, because publicity strengthens the terrorist image. . . . . We need to revive our earlier plans and be very self-critical. We must look for the enemy within, not as a manifestation of outside forces. Special operations must be used against revolutionary operations. You have to look at the problem with a strategic vision. You must support economic and social actions of the government, because it is these contradictions that produce the conflict. In the mountains the government must take actions to lift the level of life. Further, we have not yet integrated the regions of insurgency—as well as many others—into the national life. Our country is so large and so diverse. It is not integrated. We don't have a nation-state. We have a meeting of regions. The real problem of Peru is integration.[16]

Such analysis was not an exception. Obviously, the crucial question was whether these sentiments, expressed in Lima, could be translated into action on the ground in places such as Ayacucho. Increasingly, even while Garcia remained president (he was to be replaced in 1990), they were. As in the other cases we have examined, military officers, rather than their civilian superiors, took the lead in this effort. In the forefront was the army.

Peru's army just prior to the 1990 presidential election was fairly large, with some fifty infantry battalions. It was organized in a fairly standard format: divisions, which were in reality brigade-size, headed by brigadier-generals; battalions—the term really meant nothing in a formal organizational sense, since *ad hoc* arrangements predominated—were three per division; three to four companies per battalion; three platoons per company; three 10-man squads per platoon.

Personnel arrangements were weak. Too many officers were kept occupied with "other duties." The non-commissioned officer corps was not a viable entity. Military occupational specialty training existed only for the officers, leaving troops to learn what they could on-the-job. Further, units were not deployed as such. Groups of individuals were simply put together. Most tellingly, for what it said about the lack of priority the insurgency held in the upper echelons, the heaviest concentrations of forces, complete with armor, mechanized artillery, and air support, were along the borders with Ecuador and Chile, with which Peru had fought wars in the past.[17]

In such a framework, the character of individual commanders assumed salience. It was indicative of just how weak the *Sendero* position was that whenever a competent commander was present in an area, the Maoists experienced extreme difficulties. An illustration was provided in 1989 when Brigadier-General Howard Rodriguez was given command of the 2nd Division in Ayacucho.[18] He sought to use his four battalions in the most efficient manner. The area of operations was divided into nine zones, each with a variable number of BCGs (*Base Contra Guerrilla*), sited in key locations where they could protect population concentrations and civic action projects.

Altogether, the BCGs numbered around fifty. Each, in turn, was manned by fifty men broken down into three officer-led patrols of fifteen each. The extra men comprised the headquarters element. (It may be noted that the 50 BCG x 50 men comes to 2,500, which would appear a near-total deployment of four battalions.) There was no long logistical tail. Two helicopters serviced the entire enormous area that was Ayacucho. At any one time, one of the 15-man patrols was out on long range operations (defined as 3–5 km of straight-line distance, which would normally be much more when terrain was considered). The second was closer in, on local operations, and the third was present in the BCG for security and training.[19]

Although the top priority for patrols was to seek out the enemy, civic action was also a normal part of the routine. That the troops were at times faced by profound decisions caused by the nature of the war was obvious from the number of orphans who had been "adopted" by the division and who lived at the headquarters. Naturally, there were other, more ambitious projects at hand. One major effort was to punch

286

Reform from within: Howard Rodriguez, 2d Division commander in Ayacucho in 1989. He typified the reform leadership which, in a series of introspective sessions, reoriented Peruvian security force strategy. The results were startling. (Marks photo)

Domination of human terrain: Peruvian army patrol in Ayacucho in 1989. Deploying numerous BCGs (*Base Contra Guerrilla*), the 2d Division used small unit tactics to clear areas of insurgents so that democracy could again function. (Marks photo)

through the eight kilometers of road from Huancayo to Ayacucho. The intent was to cut substantially the days required to make that tortuous journey. It was a trek regularly undertaken by the populace because of traditional linkages between the towns. A regular road would immeasurably lighten the burden. Other projects that were being undertaken by the two engineer battalions at hand had similar goals: to improve the quality of life.

That the "hearts and minds" approach was making headway was obvious from the numbers enlisting in the *rondas campesinos*, or local defense forces. Though the *rondas* term enjoyed virtually universal use, especially among the people, the government itself differentiated between self-generated self-defense (the *rondas*) and government-generated self-defense, which took the designation *Comités de Autodefensa*. The two forms had different legal bases but eventually were merged into the latter.

Frequently maligned by the Peruvian left, the militia (as was the case, for example, in Thailand, the Philippines, and Sri Lanka's south) were seen as the lynchpin of the counter-insurgency effort. In the late 1980s, they were still spread unevenly and in various states of organization.

In Ayacucho, they frightened many urban bureaucrats, because they had sprung up spontaneously in widespread areas of indigenous communities. Frequently they were armed only with sharpened stakes and knives, yet they had attacked *Sendero* cadre, even units, and begged the authorities for arms. They were at times given old shotguns, but in Lima, at the time, a fierce debate raged concerning the wisdom of passing out weapons on a more widespread basis.

In time, this was done nationwide. Pending the formal decision to arm the militia, however, which would follow the 1990 election, the main military aim was to link them, whatever their weapons, to the BCGs with effective communications. Troops could thus respond to calls for assistance. Backing up both the troops and the militia were reaction forces. The BCGs and militias secured their area by establishing a government presence and by taking the countryside away from the insurgents. They were, in effect, an anvil. The hammer was provided by the reaction forces.[20]

Even before the change in governments, this combination—regular patrolling by the BCG units, militia static defense, and strike force reaction by the special companies—appeared to be having an effect on *Sendero* operations. In Ayacucho itself, the situation had stabilized, yet the focus of insurgent action simply shifted elsewhere, in particular to a renewed effort to isolate Lima.[21] Such activity was important, not only in its tangible form but also for the damage it did to Peruvian

The people numerous and armed: Armed peasants (above) listen to a self-defense leader, while (below) army control officer engages in discussion with a regional self-defense official. Ultimately, the numbers of mobilized peasants in Ayacucho were astonishing and swamped Shining Path. (Marks photos)

Special companies: "Lynx" reaction unit trains in Ayacucho in 1989. While regular units and local forces dominated populated areas, elite reaction forces were kept on standby to pile on once a Shining Path column was located. The creation of such a "grid" made it increasingly difficult for *Sendero* to muster the power needed to intimidate villagers. (Marks photo)

morale. Whatever progress was being made in areas such as Ayacucho was not reflected in the streets of Lima. There as elsewhere, violence and the desolate economic scene dominated concerns.

State Search for a New Approach

Desperate, in 1990 Peru elected to the presidency a virtual unknown, Alberto Fujimori, Rector of the Agrarian University of Peru and lacking prior political experience. He won by a margin of 57 to 34%. "El Chinito," as Fujimori was nicknamed during the campaign, promptly instituted a draconian economic solution and various reforms, especially numerous micro-development programs aimed at uplifting the poorest members of rural society (the Indians). Resistance to his approach, though, culminated in his *autogolpe* of 5 April 1992, a self-coup against his own government. Congress was disbanded, although, subsequently, elections for a new body were held under a new constitution, approved narrowly by plebiscite. These actions cost Peru dearly in international alienation and cutoffs of foreign aid, particularly from the US, yet such factors did not prove crucial, because in September 1992 Guzman was captured.

Found in Lima through old-fashioned detective work, Guzman was detained together with, ultimately, much of his Politburo, as well as members of the Central Committee and hundreds of other cadre of various degrees of importance.[22] So centralized had *Sendero* become that cutting off the head dealt the movement a body blow. Hundreds of guerrillas surrendered, and insurgent incidents nationwide dropped markedly, even as Fujimori's economic reforms, notably his privatization efforts, caused the economy to grow at roughly 7% per annum.

Most crucially, the specter of demoralization that had set in was lifted. The populace abandoned its defeatist mind-set. Simultaneously, Fujimori considerably expanded arming militia formations nationwide and the tempo of counter-insurgency operations by regular forces.[23] Until his administration, authorities had refused systematically to arm the people at the receiving end of *Sendero*'s depredations. The new president, recognizing the power in the popular groundswell, ordered them to be given shotguns, training, and radios for communication. Officials conducted ceremonies where priests blessed the arms.[24] A change in law in 1992 recognized the people's right to self-defense.

In summer 1993, a massive parade of local defense forces was held in Lima. Units came from throughout the country. Critics charged that it was all a massive publicity stunt. *Sendero* knew better. *Rondas campensinas* became the government's most potent weapon. Working in shifts, they dramatically multiplied the government's available manpower and made it impossible for *Sendero* to continue to operate in the local defense areas. By mid-1993, there were 4,205 authorized Committees of Self-Defense (*Comites de Autodefensa*), or *rondas*, spread throughout the country. They totaled 235,465 individuals and had 16,196 weapons.[25] *Sendero* was squeezed out of local space.

Conclusions

What had transpired? Paradoxically, Fujimori's "anti-democratic" moves, in fact, had been grounded in popular desires to a greater extent than was the case with the actions of the corrupt system he displaced. Thus *Sendero* found itself out-mobilized. That the people turned from it stemmed from its violations of the covenant that had linked an isolated, impoverished Indian world to the ideological solutions of urban leadership. In desperation, the people turned to a government that, even if imperfect, was an improvement, not only on that which it replaced, but on any conceivable alternative *Sendero* could offer.

Providing security: Members of a patrol base (with author) during security operations. Faces are concealed to prevent identification by insurgents, who utilized terror as their weapon of choice.

Particularly startling is the entire time span covered in the events above: some 17 years spent by *Sendero* in patient preparation of its counter-state, followed by a dozen years until the capture of Guzman, with another several years after that devoted to definitively breaking the back of the movement. How could a group that in 1980 numbered about 180 people have brought a system the size of Peru to its knees, whatever its shortcomings? It was the sheer magnitude of the violence that the insurgents inflicted. Terror as insurgent strategy incapacitated a system already profoundly lacking in capacity.

This is a salient point we shall encounter in the next chapter as we examine Nepal. *Sendero* was able to grow because the system was so incredibly weak, systemic response so inappropriate. When the momentum of its original appeal to grievances had run its course, *terror became the weapon of choice as opposed to one tool among many.* Terrorism as a method of action began to approach terrorism as a logic of action. Consequently, the mass base, which had never shared *Sendero*'s ideological goals, turned on it and was the key to its destruction.

Notes

1 Interview with author in Lima, 18 August 1989.
2 Interview with author in Lima, 15 August 1989.
3 Personal communication, 30 November 1993. Essential for an initial understanding of *Sendero* is David Scott Palmer, ed., *The Shining Path of Peru,* 2nd edn. (New York: St. Martin's Press, 1994). Palmer, who at one time shared an office with Guzman, has produced a number of other works that have been important to understanding the Peruvian Maoists. These include "Expulsion From a Peruvian University," Chapter 14 in Robert Textor, ed., *Cultural Frontiers of the Peace Corps* (Cambridge, Massachusetts: Harvard University Press, 1966), 243–70; "The *Sendero Luminoso* Rebellion in Rural Peru" in Georges Fauriol, *Latin American Insurgencies* (Washington, DC: Georgetown University Center for Strategic and International Studies/National Defense University, 1985), 67–96; "Rebellion in Rural Peru: The Origins and Evolution of *Sendero Luminoso*," *Comparative Politics,* 18.2 (January 1986), 127–46; "Terrorism as a Revolutionary Strategy: Peru's *Sendero Luminoso*," Chapter 5 in Barry Rubin, ed., *The Politics of Terrorism: Terror as a State and Revolutionary Strategy* (Baltimore: Johns Hopkins University Press, 1989), 129–52; and (certainly his most comprehensive work) "The Revolutionary Terrorism of Peru's Shining Path," Chapter 12 in Martha Crenshaw, ed., *Terrorism in Context* (University Park: Pennsylvania State University Press, 1995). Exception to his work, as well as that of Cynthia McClintock, was taken by Deborah Poole and Gerardo Renique in their hortatory piece, "The New

Chroniclers of Peru: US Scholars and Their 'Shining Path' of Peasant Rebellion," *Bulletin of Latin American Research*, 10.2 (1991), 133–91. More balanced and useful is their *Peru: Time of Fear* (London: Latin America Bureau [Research and Action], 1992). Illustrative works by McClintock are: "Why Peasants Rebel: The Case of *Sendero Luminoso*," *World Politics*, 37.1 (October 1984), 48–84; and "Peru's *Sendero Luminoso* Rebellion: Origins and Trajectory," Chapter 2 in Susan Eckstein, ed., *Power and Popular Protest: Latin American Social Movements* (Berkeley: University of California Press, 1989), 61–101.

⁴ Indispensable are Gustavo Gorriti, *The Shining Path: A History of the Millenarian War in Peru* (Chapel Hill: University of North Carolina Press, 1999), and Steve J. Stern, ed., *Shining and Other Paths: War and Society in Peru, 1980–1995* (Durham, North Carolina: Duke University Press, 1998).

⁵ Interview with author in Lima, 17 August 1989.

⁶ Interview with author in Lima, 15 August 1989.

⁷ Details, to include maps, may be found in a number of my earlier works: "Making Revolution With Shining Path," Ch. 10 in Palmer, ed., *The Shining Path of Peru*; "Making Revolution: *Sendero Luminoso* in Peru," *Small Wars and Insurgencies* (London), 3.1 (Spring 1992), 22–46; and *Maoist Insurgency since Vietnam*, Chapter 5, "Making Revolution: *Sendero Luminoso* in Peru as Maoist Conclusion, 1980–[?], 253–84." Given that Poole and Renique specifically took McClintock to task for using estimates of *Sendero*'s strength and organizational structure drawn from "the right-wing mercenary magazine *Soldier of Fortune*," a measure of academic gallows humor is in order. My original data on which I built the works just named is (I assume) the offending material and was published in a three-part series in *Soldier of Fortune*: "Corner of the Dead,"15.3 (March 1990), 44–51; "The Guerrilla Myth," 15.5 (May 1990), 56–59, 65–68; and "Peru's Fatal Distraction," 15.7 (July 1990), 30–33. Much the same data appeared nearly simultaneously in my "Terrorism vs. Terror: The Case of Peru," *Counterterrorism and Security* (Arlington), 2.2 (May–June 1990), 26–33.

⁸ For details, see James Anderson, *Sendero Luminoso: A New Revolutionary Model?* (London: Institute for the Study of Terrorism, 1987). Although accurate in particulars, some caution is necessary when considering the monograph's analytical thrust. The title is suggestive of the problem: "A New Revolutionary Model." In the first two pages of the introduction (11–12), he thrice calls attention to *Sendero* as "a unique variety of guerrilla movement" expanding in unique fashion with hitherto unseen speed. This confusion seems to stem from unfamiliarity with "people's war" as opposed to the Guevarist *foco* approach that had dominated Latin American revolutionary impulse prior to *Sendero*'s appearance.

⁹ See Andrew R. Molnar et al., *Human Factors Considerations of Undergrounds in Insurgencies* (Washington, DC: American University, 1965).

¹⁰ Field work, Ayacucho, August 1989

[11] It should be borne in mind that in each case what is being described is a level of organization working in an area of operation. What is being rendered as "Zone," for example, was actually a "Zone Committee," in Spanish, exercising a span of influence and control over a physical area and human population. There was no rigid system for the assignment of territory. Sub-zones generally corresponded to government provinces, the components of the larger departments, but this was not always the case and could be modified at will.

[12] One anomaly I was never able to work out to my satisfaction was that each of the Ayacucho zones appeared to have, on an equal status, not only the sub-zones but also a certain number of local committees. The operational reason for this was unclear, though it might have been as simple an explanation as the few local committees in question having progressed to the point that they might eventually be given sub-zone status.

[13] Some noted that women joined as a route to freedom from the horrible conditions of marriage most endured in the highlands (Interview by the author in Lima, 17 August 1989). An alternative possibility was offered by a longtime aid worker: "Women are not mistreated *per se* in the *sierra* [mountains]. There is a great deal of beating both ways. In truth, it is women in the *sierra* who control the purse-strings. They function as equals, so it's perfectly logical that they should simply join *Sendero* like anyone else, not because they're particularly downtrodden" (Interview with author in Lima, 20 August 1989).

[14] Interview with author in Lima, 26 August 1989.

[15] General Juan Velasco Alvarado led the 3 October 1968 coup and what came to be called "the Peruvian experiment."

[16] Interview with author in Lima, 19 August 1989.

[17] As one wag pointed out to me in 1989, in explaining this seeming anomaly of military deployment, "All Peruvian heroes are men who died fighting Chile in hopeless situations. They haven't gotten over that." Chile, for that matter, won the war in question, 1879–83, and captured Lima, an episode that apparently remains a searing memory for many military Peruvians, together with the subsequent seizure by the Chileans of a portion of Peru. A border war with Ecuador in 1941 sputtered to life in 1995 with disastrous results for Peru.

[18] For a view of *Sendero Luminoso* threat at this time in the division area of responsibility, see *Folleto de Inteligencia Para la "OEB"* [*Intelligence Handbook for the Order of Battle*] (Ayacucho: G2 [Intelligence], 2d Division, undated).

[19] In addition to the officer commanding the patrol, each included an NCO, an RTO (i.e., the radio operator), and a "sanitation man." Normal patrols lasted anywhere from 15–20 days. Rations of corn, rice, and sugar were carried in field packs. The universal garb was a black pullover sweater with fatigue trousers and a black ski cap (most equipped with pull-down masks to conceal the face during operations in areas where anonymity was important). Standard battle rifle was the Belgian-made 7.62x51mm FN FAL, though in every patrol at

least one soldier carried a shotgun. Belgian 7.62mmx51mm FN MAG 58 machine guns were in the inventory but were in my experience not often taken on patrols. A wide variety of other weapons were present. Patrol leaders often favored the H&K 9mm MP5 submachine gun. For communication the US-made A/N-PRC-77 and the French TRC 372 were used, though the rugged terrain played havoc with radio effectiveness.

[20] In Ayacucho in 1989, the strike force was comprised of *Compania Lince*, or "Company Lynx." Although it had some special equipment, its strength principally came from its rigorous training in the ranger/commando tradition.

[21] An excellent overview of this campaign can be found in Gordon H. McCormick, *From the Sierra to the Cities: The Urban Campaign of the Shining Path*, RAND Paper R-4150-USDP (Santa Monica: RAND, 1992). McCormick had earlier authored a number of works on Shining Path, to include another RAND study, *The Shining Path and the Future of Peru* (1990), as well as his earlier "The Shining Path and Peruvian Terrorism," in David C. Rappoport, *Inside Terrorist Organizations* (New York: Columbia University Press, 1988).

[22] These arrests stemmed from the lesser known operation, mentioned earlier, the capture of the master records of the movement. As concerns the capture of Guzman himself, though the credit naturally redounded to Fujimori's credit, DINCOTE was a creation of his (rightly maligned) predecessor. Nevertheless, to the victor belong the spoils. When the snatch was made, Fujimori-led Peru was in a position to take advantage of it. Among the many consequences of the *autogulpe* housecleaning was a revamping of a compliant judiciary that had regularly turned loose *most* insurgents detained. This was ended, and a system of "faceless judges" instituted to ensure both their honesty and survival.

[23] Details in Marks, "End of the Nightmare? Peru's Fight against Terrorism," *Counterterrorism and Security*, N.S. 1.3 (Spring 1975), 26–30, and "'Shining Path' to Oblivion? Fate Breaks Peru's 'Fourth Sword of Marxism'," *Soldier of Fortune*, 21.7 (July 1996), 54–57.

[24] In 1991, 10,000 Winchester Model 1300 shotguns were distributed, along with a variety of surplus pistols.

[25] Details can be found in Marks, "Peru: Securing the Peace," *Soldier of Fortune*, 24.3 (March 1999), 48–51. Imbalance between manpower and weapons is handled by patrolling in shifts. Sarhua, for instance, a 1,000-person town in a 3,113 person district of the same name, fielded in the late 1980s a *ronda* of sixteen groups of ten to twenty men each. Fifteen of the groups were comprised of Catholics, the remaining group of evangelical Protestants. They had fifteen shotguns between them, the heaviest the ever-present Winchester, and passed the weapons between groups.

Chapter 7

Back to the Future:
The Insurgency of the
Communist Party of Nepal (Maoist)

Important as the case of *Sendero Luminoso* was on its merits, it was more so because, in a post-Cold War world that often saw strategic victory over communism confused with operational realities, die-hard elements of discredited Marxist-Leninism looked to the Peruvian Maoists as their standard-bearers. This was as true in Nepal as elsewhere.[1]

What makes the Nepali case all the more compelling is that it has played itself out in the manner intended by the Maoists in the cases considered in previous chapters of this work. Indeed, in many ways all the elements are present, especially when compared to the Thai case, but they have unfolded in dissimilar fashion and thrust the Nepali Maoists to the threshold of victory—what no other Maoist group in Asia has been able to accomplish since the end of the Vietnam War.

Insurgency in Nepal has existed for perhaps five decades but burst into the open as a serious force only with the declaration of people's war on 13 February 1996 by the Communist Party of Nepal (Maoist) or CPN(M), the most radical offshoot of the leftwing spectrum in Nepali politics.[2] Desultory action ended when the "Maoists," as they are universally known, unilaterally abrogated on-going talks with the government and launched a nationwide general offensive in November 2001. There followed a steadily increasing level of violence that by April 2006 had left some 13,000 Nepalis dead, a majority of them in not quite four years.[3] In that month, the old-order was toppled, much as had happened in Thailand in October 1973, and a similar drama began to play itself out as occurred 1973–76—with important distinctions.

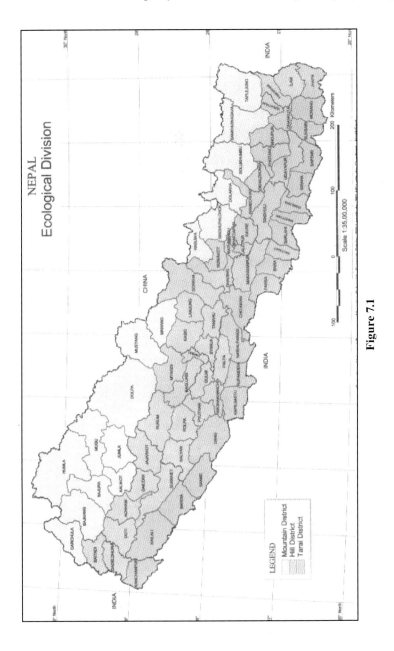

Figure 7.1

Growth of Insurgent Challenge to the Old-Regime

Known as a premier tourist destination, the site of the mighty Himalayan Mountains, the tallest the majestic Mount Everest, Nepal would hardly seem a candidate for a raging communist insurgency. Indeed, if anything, its population was recognized not as rebels but for its loyal service as Gurkhas, perhaps the single most legendary infantry in the world.

The combination, however—dominant peaks and service as infantry in foreign armies—actually goes to the heart of the matter. It is not accidental that over the past nearly two centuries, a small, land-locked mountain kingdom has sent hundreds of thousands of its young men into combat for others. To the contrary, Nepalis have flocked abroad not because of martial bent or any other characteristic, rather for the oldest reason known to recruiters: need.

Far from being Shangri-la, Nepal (see Fig. 7.1) is 24 million people competing for their livelihoods in a country but the size of Florida (139,670 sq. km land area for the former *versus* 139,671 sq. km for the latter), which has a population of 16,713,000.[4] Roughly a fifth of the national territory is the Himalayas, with, consequently, a mere fraction of the population. The lower approximately one-third of the country, the *tarai*, scrub jungle now largely cleared, until recently hold 32.1% of the populace. It could not even be settled until the 1970s when several virulent strains of malaria were conquered. This resulted in a popular concentration, 67.2%, in the central one-third, or the hill country. Lest the point be lost, some 16 million people were sandwiched into "one-third of Florida."[5]

The result, according to a World Bank study done in 1973, was "population density per square kilometer of arable land is probably as high as 1,000, a concentration similar to that found in certain Asiatic deltas, but where, in contrast, the soil is more fertile and the climate allows two to three crops a year." Conditions of livelihood, among the worst in the developing world,[6] were exacerbated, because an effective lack of any industrial base meant 90% of the population was rural, 80% of the total population working directly on the land. Although 90% of farmers were classified as owner-operators, this impressive figure was achieved only by severe division: 50% of all households endeavored to engage in agriculture on plots of less than half a hectare; 7.8% were completely landless.[7]

The economy thus has a current Gross Domestic Product (GDP) of only USD 5.5 billion, an annual budget of just USD 1.1 billion. In contrast, numerous US public school districts have greater budgets.[8] The official leading source of foreign exchange, tourism, was supplemented by foreign aid put at anywhere from

40–60% of the total budget figure. Foreign remittances consequently have become increasingly important.[9] It should come as no surprise that the United Nations lists Nepal as among the poorest countries in the world: 80% of the populace, surveys consistently find, must do outside work to survive. Limited development, however, ensures that such work is scarce. The result is a skewed distribution of resources, in which some have and many do not. The only solution readily available has been out-migration and participation in the global economy.

Historically, for certain hill tribal groups, this has meant enlistment as soldiers in the British Indian Army. Such opportunities, although they declined substantially in British service after Indian independence in 1948, have continued in the forces of India, but still have no possibility of absorbing even a sizable fraction of hill tribe job-seekers much less others.[10] Indeed, Nepalis of all communities seeking relatively well-paid expatriate work have largely opted for service work abroad, with the largest single employer apparently being Japan, if India, which has an open border with Nepal, is not considered.[11] Regardless, most job-seekers are unable to obtain external employment, regardless of destination, and so find themselves mired in poverty. Statistics show that at least 20% of the population lives in extreme, abject circumstances.

Considering only economic matters, Nepal would have been a candidate for serious dislocation. Exacerbating the situation further, however, were social parameters: issues of caste, ethnicity, and language. On the surface, Nepal was a picture of unity, the world's only official Hindu kingdom. The constitutional monarch, a living god to much of the population even in the 21st century, sat atop a society 86.5% Hindu and 9% Buddhist, a society in which every aspect is dominated by caste.

In reality, beneath this picture of unity, is fragmentation. There are sixty recognized caste and ethnic groups. Only slightly more than half the population, 56.4%, is actually embraced by the caste system. More than a third, 35.5%, are classified as ethnics, tribal groups outside the caste system. The four largest of these have just over a million members each: Magar, Tharu, Newar, and Tamang. (Magars apparently have supplied a plurality of Gurkha manpower in the British system.[12]) A further 3.6% of the people are classified as belonging to religious communities (e.g., Sikhs, Muslims), and 4.5% are simply "others."

Significantly, half of the caste figure is comprised of the top two castes, Brahmins and Chhetris, the historic priestly and warrior castes at, respectively, 16.1% and 12.9% of the total population. Therefore, 29% of the population is structurally positioned, by religious mandate, to dominate. This they have done, effectively controlling all positions of power and influence.[13] Not surprisingly, this leads to charges of unfair advantage, where disproportionate influence and possession are replicated by religious sanction.

Linguistically, there is also severe division. According to the 1991 Census, Nepal's people speak thirty-two languages, with only 50.3% claiming Nepali, the national language, as their mother tongue. Although the second language, Maithili, 11.9%, is a distant second, the Census notes that some ethnic and caste groups, which have their own tongues, are not even reflected in the total figure of languages spoken. Needless to say, the top castes are brought up in and are totally at ease with Nepali, while other groups often struggle, even as linguistic competence is a key factor in access to coveted bureaucratic employment, whether in the government or private sector.

Given such socio-economic divisions, it would have been expected that politics play a significant role in mediating contending demands. For the country was, constitutionally, a parliamentary democracy. Here again, there was more than met the eye. A democracy since only 1990, Nepal suffered from all-too-familiar problems of the genre "emerging democracy": corruption, inefficiency, and lack of focus.[14] Compounded by a lack of state integration, the political system was able to foster little save a lack of legitimacy.

Nepal emerged as a country in 1774–75.[15] As it reached its present boundaries, then sought to expand into territory claimed by British India, it found itself bested in an 1815 war with the East India Company. As a consequence, most of the *tarai* was lost, and Nepal was forced to agree to what effectively was British suzerainty.[16] A prime ministerial coup of sorts led to more than a hundred years of hereditary Rana rule, 1846–1951, during which Nepal was closed to the outside world, save limited British representation. This ended in November 1950 when India, which desired a greater role in Nepal's affairs for defense reasons, supported a royal restoration.[17] The king assumed direct control in December 1960, and only in 1990–91 did democratic forces emerge triumphant.

This proved a mixed blessing. The era of Rana rule was not improved on by the subsequent ten years of chaotic transition and the thirty years of monarch-guided democracy, the so-called *panchayat* system. Thus, even as Nepal had all the organizational and bureaucratic trappings of a modern nation-state, in reality it remained a backwater. The writ of its administrative apparatus barely extended beyond district capitals, and most areas could be reached only on foot. There were five regions (plus a capital region which is essentially the Kathmandu Valley[18]), 75 districts, and 3,913 Village Development Committees (VDC), the legal manifestation of what other Asian countries would refer to simply as "villages" with their constituent hamlets.[19] Development was at a primitive level. Little changed.

Into this dynamic: Maoist political demonstration during a ceasefire the first half of 2003. Left wing political thought has had a strong following in Nepal, as might be expected in a country with severe socio-economic challenges. The legal left controlled a majority of local government leadership positions at the time the Maoists declared people's war in February 1996. (Marks photos)

Heightened expectations that democracy would make a difference in the lives of the populace were dashed.[20] Although there were improvements, particularly in health and education, these were minor bright spots in an overall dark picture of self-absorption by the major political parties. The Nepali Congress ruled for all but roughly a single year of the democratic era (prior to the October 2002 crisis; see below), with the legal leftist coalition, the United Marxist-Leninists, the major opposition. The monarch, who might have been expected to serve a mediating and leadership role similar to that played effectively by King Bhumipol of Thailand, was killed in June 2001 in the so-called "Royal Massacre" and replaced by his brother, who to many lacked legitimacy.[21]

Into this dynamic, the left had early interjected itself as an active player, even heading the government for slightly less than a year. Yet, as happened in Peru with the restoration of democracy in 1980, the expectations and passions unleashed, which surfaced particularly vigorously within the left, saw the proliferation of ever more radical options. The result, in the early 1990s, was the CPN(M),[22] a body that in its formative stages consciously modeled itself on *Sendero Luminoso*.

Committed, then, to "Gang of Four" Maoism, CPN(M) members had been linked to RIM and other international Maoist movements from their earliest days as radical activists. Not surprisingly, they demanded a solution to Nepal's problems by the establishment of a Maoist people's republic.[23] Politically, this necessarily meant an end to the monarchy, to be achieved through a constituent assembly that would rewrite the constitution. The party also demanded an end to "Indian imperialism." Economically, there was to be an end to capitalist exploitation; socially, an end to caste, ethnic, religious, and linguistic exploitation. Since the system would not simply accept these demands, people's war was to be used to force the issue.

People's war, though formally declared in 1996, had been discussed and planned in the early 1990s, if not before, and was by that time a well tested and efficient mechanism for seizing state power. If we apply the framework advanced in the chapters of our discussion, we find:

(1) *Mass line*: As its principal targets, the party worked in hill tribe areas, especially in the Midwestern Region, and among *dalits* or untouchables (the lowest caste in the Hindu system). There was no shortage of grievances (as well as hopes and aspirations). Prior to being banned, cadre of the CPN(M) functioned as did the representatives of any other party, but they endeavored to use their solutions to local dilemmas to form an embryonic counter-state. In this respect, they functioned very much as did the other Maoist groups we

have studied, especially *Sendero Luminoso* prior to its own 1980 declaration of people's war. What was different from the Peruvian case was the extent to which, during the pre-1996 period, it was the cadre of rival political parties who found themselves engaged in violent confrontations with Maoist cadre.

(2) *United front*: Just as there was no shortage of issues for the mass line, so were there innumerable causes about which could be mobilized those who sought activism of a non-Maoist stripe. Issues of education, for instance, allowed mobilization of students who, although apparently not formally CPN(M) members, nevertheless acted as virtual wings of the party. Similarly, tribal fronts, ostensibly seeking more equitable treatment, were also very active. Most prominent was the *Akhil Nepal Rashtriya Swatantra Vidyarthi Union (Krantikari)*, the All Nepal National Independent Students' Union (Revolutionary), or ANNISU(R).

(3) *Violence*: As will be seen below, the CPN(M) used violence in a manner which would have been familiar to our book's earlier insurgents. Indeed, studying those cases, particularly that of Peru, the Maoists judged that a mistake had been to accept the protracted war as a given rather than exploiting success as it developed. If, in other words, events unfolded in such manner as to present opportunities for shortening the insurgency, then openings should be exploited. Thus the CPN(M) aggressively sought to reinforce success, to enhance the momentum of its campaign. It felt it was entering Phase 2 with its general offensive (November 2001). This was then solidified through the actions that led to government reverses,[24] which resulted in the present Phase 3, driven by united front action.

(4) *Political warfare*: To undermine the will of government units, the CPN(M) emphasized its ostensible desire for a "political solution" to the issues in dispute. The words are deceptive, because what the Maoists mean is that they would prefer not to fight and are quite willing to negotiate the terms whereby the old order will disassemble itself. CPN(M) used its participation in "peace talks" as a cover for military preparations prior to launching its November 2001 general offensive. It did the same with the seven months of talks that ended with unilateral Maoist attacks in August 2003.[25] The present period (see below) has seen the demand for "peace" serve as a cover for coercion that has progressively neutralized all remaining centers of resistance.

(5) *International action*: Although not a prominent element during the Chinese civil war itself, this had become more important as people's war had devel-

oped. In conflicts such as the war of liberation in Algeria by the FLN and the insurgency of the Viet Cong in the Vietnam War, international pressure on the counter-insurgents played a decisive role. The CPN(M) recognized early that in South Asia and within Western society it had allies, Maoist bodies yet committed, whatever the outcome of the Cold War, to radical restructuring along lines advocated by the so-called "Gang of Four," the key adherents to radical Maoism. To that end, regular coordination was effected in the West with the constituent members of the Maoist umbrella group, RIM. RIM in turn provided a variety of services, such as seeking to block assistance to the Nepalese government. Closer to home, a Coordination Committee of Maoist Parties and Organizations of South Asia (CCOMPOSA) was created in July 2001 after a meeting of nine South Asian Maoist parties in West Bengal.[26] Eventually, however, it was clandestine arrangements reached with India that sealed the fate of the old-order. What India was incapable of seeing to fruition in Sri Lanka with its support of Tamil insurgents, it has sought in Nepal.

In implementing its approach, the CPN(M) examined the numerous people's war struggles that had been carried out in the post-Second World War era. The two insurgencies that exercised the most influence early on were Peru's *Sendero Luminoso*,[27] as already mentioned, and the so-called "Naxalites," or Indian Maoists.[28] The former is fairly well known in the West, the latter less so, though a virtual icon amongst international leftists. It began as a minor Maoist-inspired upheaval in 1967 in the small Indian district of Naxalburi, which sits up against Nepal's southeastern border. It was snuffed out but then revived in "copycat" left-wing upheavals throughout India, some of which eventually required deployment of the military. Remnants remain active in perhaps a dozen Indian states.[29] Links were established with them.

The practical result was that the CPN(M) initially looked for inspiration to two of the more radical insurgent movements to have appeared in recent years. There is some irony in this, since the CPN(M)'s leadership, like that of both *Sendero* and the Naxalites (not to mention the Maoist movements examined in this volume), is overwhelmingly drawn from the very "class enemies" attacked by the party's doctrine. For instance, the two key figures in the 9-man Politburo for most of the period under discussion, Pushpa Kamal Dahal, "Prachanda," and Baburam Bhattarai, are both Brahmins with educational backgrounds.[30] (At one point, Ram Bahadur Thapa, "Badal," an ethnic Magar, was the party's military wing commander and hence an exception.) The similarities in their trajectories to those of the Khmer Rouge (Cambodia) upper leadership are startling.[31]

Mass line: Maoist performers at a Dang District political rally during the 2003 ceasefire (above, Marks photo). As with any political party, the Maoists sought to win allegiance by advancing the CPN(M) as the only force capable of addressing popular grievances. After early emphasis upon Maoist forms copied from Chinese agitprop (below, Salyan District), the Maoists switched to propaganda built upon modified but traditional Nepali cultural forms. (Photo: Rajaram Gautam in Author Collection)

Leadership from the exploiters: Dr. Baburam Bhattarai, number two in the Maoist hierarchy and the intellectual source of Maoist plans for socio-economic-political transformation. His Ph.D. dissertation (see bibliography) echoes the unsuccessful visions of societal transformation favored historically by Marxist-Leninist groups, most tragically by the Khmer Rouge. As invariably the case in insurgencies, leadership figures of the Maoists are overwhelmingly drawn from the "exploiting classes." (Marks photo)

That leaders of a revolutionary movement should come from the elite is consistent with patterns discussed throughout this study. So, too, as in Peru, is the prominence of leadership figures with an educational background.[32] Followers, as might be expected, are drawn from altogether different strata, the marginalized of society, those who become the so-called "grievance guerrillas." That the CPN(M) has had little difficulty tapping such individuals stems from the abundance of socio-economic-political contradictions discussed earlier compounded by gender issues. Women have been prominent in the recruiting profile.[33]

Prior to going underground and becoming illegal, central members of what is now the CPN(M), guided by their "progressive" ideology, focused their political efforts on just such strata, even sending representatives to Parliament in the early period of transition to democracy.[34] The areas of this electoral strength, the same Midwestern Regional hill districts that form the subject of so much development literature, remained the Maoist heartland.

Organizationally, there was nothing unexpected in the CPN(M)'s approach in those areas. Using the mass line in areas where they were present in strength, the united front in areas of government presence (especially urban centers), cadre emphasized winning the allegiance of the people by tapping local grievances and then connecting solutions with membership in the CPN(M). Logically, this meant there were oftentimes contradictions between the subjective pronouncements of Maoist publications and objective realities on the ground.[35]

Where the population hesitated, terror ensured compliance. This increasingly was the case as the party moved out of the areas where it previously had an electoral base. Statistical analysis of casualties showed a near majority to be upper caste victims, an expected result in a society where those castes were dominant.[36] As a mass base was mobilized, it was incorporated into the counter-state, the alternative society of the CPN(M). This structure at first essentially replicated that of the government, merely standing up a radical alternative. The Politburo issued directives with the assistance of a Central Committee of approximately twenty-five members. As time progressed, however, radical programs were implemented, particularly seizure of land and property from the rural gentry.

The precise relationship between the emerging political infrastructure and the so-called "Military Wing" was a matter of some conjecture, but the degree of independence ostensibly enjoyed by the latter from the party was undoubtedly overemphasized.[37] The main armed component early on, for instance, six guerrilla main force units ("battalions"), could only launch a military action in response to instructions relayed through the chief commissar, who was a Central Committee member.[38] Similarly, the united front apparatus, while also existing as a separate entity, appeared to be under firm party control.[39]

Leaders and followers, then, as we would expect from Scott's framework, were mobilized, in the final analysis, by the same "causes," but approached the issues quite differently. Leaders, drawn overwhelmingly, even at this point in time, from elite strata, sought structural change to deal with issues. Followers, also seeking solutions, wanted direct, local redress.[40] Preliminary systemic response involved sending ill-prepared police, both from local stations and regional response units, into affected areas, where their behavior, actual and perceived,[41] thrust self-defense into the equation as a major theme for Maoist recruitment.[42]

Armed political movement: Maoist milita in Rukkum. Weapons are .303 Lee Enfield rifles captured from police. (Photo: Mukunda Bogati in Author Collection)

Heartland of the early Maoist position: Insurgents in Rukkum. Mobilized initially by self-defense, tribal manpower in the Midwestern Region provided the Maoists with a viable base from which to expand to other areas of the country. (Photo: Rajaram Gautam in Author Collection)

The heartland of the early Maoist position was the area straddling either side of the border between the districts of Rolpa and Rukkum in the Midwestern Region. There, Kham Magars responded to CPN(M) guidance and became guerrillas generally supported by the population.[43] Further expansion proved more difficult, and the level of popular involvement was commensurately lower. Indeed, even as the Maoists were able to dominate the six districts of the so-called "Red Zone"—Pyuthan, Rolpa, Rukkum, Salyan, Jajarkot, and Kalikot (see Figure 7.1)—an area as near to the epicenter of the uprising as western Rolpa, Gharti Magar territory, witnessed a counter-state structure so thin that mere handfuls of cadre sufficed to maintain control through their ability to call on guerrilla manpower for enforcement of their writ.[44]

Consequently, the human terrain the Maoists were able to dominate, the districts in the Mid-Western Region, served as base areas in the manner of the Jiangxi Soviet. It is useful to emphasize further that these were among the very poorest regions in the country—not because of the issues of exploitation posited in party literature but for more mundane reasons of overpopulation, poor techniques of agriculture and animal husbandry, and limited soil and water regimes. The result was the virtual absence of the sort of social engineering one would expect to find in a "liberated area," apart from taking from those who "had" to give to those who "had not." Very limited enhanced resources became available to the liberation movement.[45]

In the absence of external input, as provided, for instance, by drugs in the case of *Sendero Luminoso*, the CPN(M) was forced to rely on the more traditional but limited insurgent methodology of criminal activity, especially bank-robbing, smuggling (e.g., rare animal hides and certain aphrodisiac roots), kidnapping for ransom, and extortion[46] to generate funds. Such activity could at times produce windfalls but was unable to meet the demands of rapid expansion.[47] Neither could external links make up shortfalls, since the allied movements of CCOMPOSA were actually in an inferior position logistically to their Nepali compatriots. These stark realities left the movement with a character, in many areas, as much *jacquerie* as disciplined insurgency.

Constructing the Counter-State

Progress thus was steady but more a product of government lack of capacity than insurgent power.[48] Methodology was predictable and mirrored that of other insurgent movements following the people's war approach. While "winning hearts and minds" was important in the base areas, terror was indispensable for expanding into contested populations. This was supplemented by guerrilla action and ultimately, with the launching of the November 2001 general offensive, the mobile warfare phase.[49]

Regardless of what occurs at the main force level of people's war, the key is the cadre. Doctrinally, armed political cadre should enter an area and gradually mobilize the counter-state that challenges the state. Movements in all of our previous cases, to include *Sendero Luminoso* prior to its 1980 declaration of people's war, have essentially followed this approach. More common in recent insurgencies in general, however, as illustrated by the Naxalites in India and Colombia's FARC (which uses people's war doctrine, though it is not Maoist[50]), is to lead with violent action, "capturing" a target population and then reorganizing it according to ideological dictates. This was the approach CPN(M) relied on after 1996.

In a typical action, in Muchook, a small village a half-day's walk from the district capital of Gorkha (the capital is also Gorkha), a Congress Party representative and Maoist opponent, a "big landlord" (two hectares), was awakened at 10:30 PM by a knock on his door. Confronted by seven Maoists, armed mainly with agricultural implements, he was dragged from his home and told he was to be made "to suffer the way you made the people suffer." His legs and feet were then systematically broken with hammers. Carried to a hospital in Kathmandu, he survived, but his absence deprived the village of a natural rallying-point. For there existed no government presence in Muchook, no police station, for example. Police who did venture to the area found nothing, but they could not stay, and so the Maoists effectively took control of the village and its surrounding area, one of Nepal's 3,913 basic building blocks, or VDC. This process was repeated time and again. Complementary moves were carried out to neutralize the state completely. District and VDC offices, for example, were systematically razed, their records and equipment destroyed. In Gorkha, the single month-and-a-half period prior to May 2002 saw 34 of the district's 66 VDC offices completely eliminated. The 60-odd police stations were helpless: they had fewer than 500 men spread out over the size of a US county (3,610 sq. km), with more than a quarter of a million people to cover and no real means to do so save on foot. (The only paved road in the district connected Gorkha town to Kathmandu.)[51] Nationwide, then, by the beginning of 2003, more than 1,400 VDCs no longer existed, and virtually all no longer functioned, their personnel, elected locally, having almost universally fled.[52] The influence of terror was illustrated by the reality that fewer than thirty VDC chairmen had actually been assassinated (again, of a theoretical total of 3,913).[53]

All other elements of the state likewise found themselves attacked. Roads were cut; bridges, dams and hydropower facilities, aqueducts, telephone towers and electric lines, airport control towers were systematically destroyed.[54] By the same early-2003 date noted above, more than 440 post offices, most but rudimentary facilities, had been gutted.[55]

Such action was the essence of the approach of *Sendero Luminoso* and the Khmer Rouge.[56] To all appearances, the goal was to sever links with the existing system, isolate the population into a self-contained entity, and return society to the proverbial revolutionary "Year One," when remaking the new world would begin. The guide for this transformation was to be the thoughts and dicta of the leader, "Prachanda Path," a deliberate echoing of *Sendero Luminoso*'s "Gonzalo Path." (Recall that "President Gonzalo" was party leader Abimael Guzman Reynoso).

Although the essence of the campaign was rural-based, as would be expected from the people's war approach (as it had evolved, particularly through the Vietnam War experience[57]), urban action was not eschewed. Just as *Sendero* eventually extended its campaign into urban spaces, so did the CPN(M). These, in any case, were limited in Nepal, so the main targets were the three most important cities and their surrounding productive lands: Kathmandu, the capital; Pokhara, to the west, on the doorstep of the Midwestern Region; and Nepalgunj in the *tarai*. United front activity of the CPN(M)'s United Revolutionary People's Council was most important, supplemented by a terror campaign of bombings and assassinations initiated in August 2002.[58] The most prominent victim was Inspector General of

Police bear the brunt: Police perform morning calesthentics in Labang, Rolpa District, in early 2003. A largely "watcher" force, the undermanned and under-armed police suffered terribly in the insurgency and took serious casualties. (Marks photo)

Armed police as link: Armed Police Force (APF) recruits go through basic training in 2003. Modeled after the Indian approach, APF was stood up as a police field force, thus giving the police themselves a response capability beyond their slender local resources. (Marks photo)

313

Police Mohan Shrestha, commanding officer of the police field force (Armed Police Force or APF), killed in January 2003. Even as terror forced society in on itself, the main target of guerrilla action was the 46,500-man police force, the first line of armed defense—for Nepal possessed no local forces of any kind.[59] An essentially unarmed "watcher" force, two-thirds of whom carried nothing heavier than a patrol stick, the police were unprepared for the demands of counter-insurgency. Emergency response units, which in any case were armed with the 1941 version of the .303 Lee Enfield (a bolt action rifle), were likewise found lacking. Patrols sent to the scenes of incidents were ambushed; numerous small police stations were overrun, attacked in the dead of night in assaults initiated with homemade explosives, then overwhelmed by human assault waves. Efforts to stand up a more properly armed and equipped police field force, Armed Police Force (15,000 men[60]) made slow progress under the pressure of operational demands. By January 2003, the Civil Police had suffered 985 dead, the APF, 108 dead.[61]

Predictably, the only possible police response was to abandon outlying stations and consolidate in a defensible mass. In the hills, where terrain, lack of communication, and difficulty of movement favored the guerrillas, this process was inexorable across the entire breadth of the country. Rolpa, in the insurgent heartland, was typical (see Fig. 7.2).[62] In 1996, there were 33 stations in the district, with the largest but 75 men, most less than 20.[63] When the post at Ghartigaun, in western Rolpa, was attacked in 1999, for example, it had a complement of 19. Fifteen were killed, the others wounded. The station was totally destroyed and not re-garrisoned. In 1998, two such stations were abandoned; in 1999, a further 16; in 2000, six more; in 2001, another four; and in 2002, three—leaving a total of just two for the entire population of nearly 211,00.

Such was the lack of national integration that, once the police presence was eliminated, the insurgents became the state. All that remained to serve as a reminder of far-off Kathmandu were the minor functionaries, who could not flee lest they lose their meager salaries: the likes of teachers, postmen, and VDC personnel. Heads of VDCs, as mentioned previously, almost universally fled,[64] but school staff and postmen generally stayed. In most areas, once the initial spasm of destruction had been completed, it ended—with comparatively lower levels of destruction in those areas where the Maoists held sway and made use of facilities, such as VDC offices. Land was gradually seized or redistributed, and schools were progressively forced to change the normal, centrally determined curriculum in favor of a more "progressive" version. Private schools were generally closed. Maoist combatants carried out civic action projects of sorts, such as improving trails and constructing bridges, even as

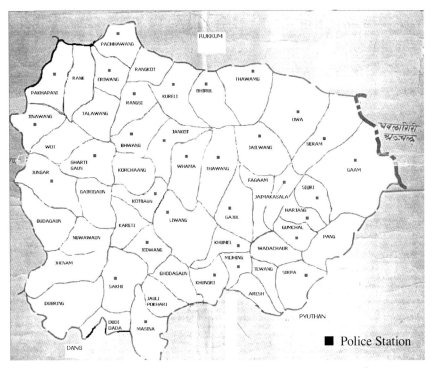

Figure 7.2

government development personnel charged with doing the same tasks were refused entry. Only in those core areas of longstanding insurgent presence did anything "new" surface, although various people's governments and projects, in reality, were but efforts to make earlier forms more equitable and responsive.

Cadre were of remarkably uneven quality and presence. It would be expected that the level of ideological knowledge would be low among movement "followers," but this generally was the case for the cadre, as well. Participation in the movement resulted from a variety of local and personal factors,[65] and cadre generally did their best to reproduce the procedures and symbology of the movement, but outside the core areas, they held sway through terror, through their ability to call on guerrilla formations to act as enforcers.[66]

This reality revealed a peculiarity observed by virtually all observers: the dependence of the Maoist campaign in its crucial formative years on tribal manpower,

315

A staple of Maoist agitprop: Maoist political theater dramatizes the attacks by "police" on villages in Rukkum. Tapping the desire for self-defense allowed the Maoists to build a base area in the Midwestern hills, which was used to push out into the remainder of the country. (Photo: Rajaram Gautam in Author Collection)

especially Magars. That guerrilla formations early on were dominated numerically by Magars stemmed from the ethnic composition of the core areas in which the Maoists had long worked, such as the Rukkum-Rolpa border corridor. That entire tribal communities would become involved in the insurgency was predictable once government miscues allowed the CPN(M) to tap the self-defense dynamic. A staple of Maoist agitprop in such areas remained skits featuring blue-clad "policemen" burning villages and brutalizing the villagers, only to be routed by combatants under the party's leadership. The similarity with the Hmong case in Northern Thailand is striking. That tribal links were being exploited was further illustrated by Magar dominance of guerrilla formations as far away from the core Midwestern areas as Dolakha District, where Magars were less than 2% of the population (as per census).[67]

If this dynamic fingered the early CPN(M), in a sense, as a tribal revolt, a different process was at work in more mixed areas. In those, cadre were the movement, and they, as indicated, were a product of local realities and thus of mixed ethnic and class composition. Although they did participate directly in terror actions, especially in villages targeted for movement expansion, within their own areas of responsibility, they were more likely to call on outsiders, the local guerrillas of the militia.[68]

These guerrillas, initially in small units, were eventually linked (certainly by early 2003) to main force units, battalion facsimiles of 400–600 men each. Through 2003, single battalions were found in the Eastern and Central Zones (as per the Maoist framework), four battalions in the Western Zone.[69] By the end of 2004, there were perhaps three times as many battalions. Their weaponry was similar to that possessed by the government, a mix of old and new. The latter were primarily captured pieces and those bought on the black market using looted funds.[70] For early training, ex-servicemen were both coerced and hired, with ex-Indian Gurkhas more prominent than any other single ex-servicemen's group.

As the structure of military response became more complex, so, too, did the Maoist combatant organization. When the Royal Nepalese Army deployed brigades under divisions, the CPN(M) adopted the same organization and terminology, although it could not match the unit particulars.[71]

Even were terror not the most salient issue in the minds of villagers, contact between them and the guerrillas would be a recurring fact of life, since the combatants were dependent on villagers for daily necessities. All movement, for instance, involved the preparation of caches of necessities, ranging from food and water to firewood, and such activity occurred by orders issued to villagers by the cadre at the behest of the guerrilla chain of command. Similarly, mandatory attendance by villagers at political rallies was enforced by the combatants, with the cadres issuing the orders and fingering those who resisted or malingered. The end-product was a high level of fear but an inability to do anything save reach accommodation, unless flight was adopted as a course of action. At the time of the 2003 ceasefire, a growing number of villagers appeared already to have opted for this.[72]

State Response to Insurgent Challenge

Only with the November 2001 general offensive by the Maoists did Nepal take the necessary step of reinforcing the overwhelmed police force by invoking martial law legislation and committing the 54,000 troops of the RNA.[73] Spread throughout areas of the country that could be reached by road, quartered in battalion but more often company cantonments, the RNA had been a largely ceremonial force better known for its contribution to UN peacekeeping missions than for its martial prowess. Indeed, even companies did not often deploy as such. The result was a number of serious reverses as the RNA went through the painful transformation required for dealing with irregular warfare. In several instances, company equivalents were overrun. By January 2003, it had suffered 244 dead and 345 wounded.[74]

Faced with the Maoist campaign, the state reeled.[75] Response was hampered by the political shortcomings already detailed. Not only did governments change with startling rapidity, on average one per year, but governance was only possible due to the formation of various intra- and even inter-party coalitions. Self-interest was the order of the day, illustrated by rampant corruption, and administrative drift meant than even substantial foreign development assistance was not incorporated systematically. The appearance of an insurgency, therefore, was seen as but another minor factor among many and parceled out to the security forces for action, which prior to November 2001 meant the police.

Under some enlightened commanders, local police operations could have passed for those who had proved successful for our case studies discussed herein. Others, however, were more repression than development in thrust. One advantage for the state was that numerous individuals, both civilians and security force, had served abroad with the UN in peacekeeping.[76] They were thus well versed in the "hearts and minds" approach to internal pacification as opposed to pure repression. It was in a sense predictable, then, that approximately a year before the Maoist general offensive, the RNA, although still in its barracks as concerned stability operations, was nevertheless deployed in limited fashion in support of a government Integrated Security and Development Programme (ISDP).

The RNA, it was intended, would serve as the security shield for bringing government presence to underdeveloped areas, which would then see an interjection of activity designed to improve conditions and promote livelihood. As things worked out, the RNA was the only element of the government that actually fulfilled its role. Although a half dozen districts were designated, with Gorkha as the pilot project, and RNA battalions deployed in area domination patrols, the civilian input was limited to selecting projects by local government bodies. The result was that the RNA used its limited assets to build roads, dig wells, and provide rudimentary medical attention to villagers, yet none of this was done on a scale that made the slightest difference to the actual situation on the ground.[77]

With the November 2001 offensive, the ISDP was suspended, and the RNA deployed to engage in area domination. The highest formation for command and control was the brigade, but this gradually gave way to divisions and a planned corps, both of these more area commands than deployable military entities. Solid individual training could not be channeled into results-oriented operations because of shortfalls of arms and equipment, as well as severe shortcomings in leadership and technical skills.

A critical weakness was intelligence, central to any counter-insurgency effort. Nepal's various sources for information gathering and processing—the police, Armed Police Force, RNA, and National Investigation Department—were quite unprepared for the demands of internal war and generally deficient in information gathering and intelligence production/dissemination.[78] Exacerbating the situation, these bodies functioned as separate entities with little coordination or data-sharing. Only at the very highest levels of the bureaucracy was raw input brought together for analysis, but this, too, was provided for in an *ad hoc* and undermanned fashion.[79]

Still, strides were made in standing up the command and control architecture necessary for counter-insurgency. With the prime minister as commander-in-chief, the National Security Council was charged with prosecuting the campaign. Because the council itself consisted of top government leaders, in actual terms it was the council's Executive Secretariat that undertook planning and coordination. At various levels, but especially in the districts, coordinating committees—comprised of the local police, RNA, civil, and intelligence representatives—met to determine policy and implementation. A unified command, with the RNA having actual authority over all elements of the armed response, eventually came into existence, giving fiber to the *ad hoc* but functioning coordination cells that had been formed at RNA headquarters. APF platoons were deployed as if they were "light" RNA units, and the police were given primacy in the defense of most urban areas.[80]

Difficulties occurred in overcoming the substantial baggage of past political inadequacies. The police, for instance, were not trusted by the RNA, being seen as corrupt, inefficient bullyboys for the ruling party, which normally had been the Nepali Congress. The new APF, in turn, had received a good portion of its initial manpower draft from various Nepali Congress youth groups and so was likewise not trusted by either the Civil Police, who did have a good many within the officer corps who were well trained and had substantial experience, or the RNA. For its part, the RNA was viewed as loyal first and foremost to the Palace and as a possible threat to fledgling democracy. A highly centralized decision-making machinery meant that even the best of motives could often not overcome bureaucratic inertia or implement decisions when they were forthcoming.

Foreign support hence became crucial in overcoming these flaws. Britain, as might be expected from its long and deep involvement in Nepal, played an important role in training of all kinds. India, concerned lest it see another security headache develop on a crucial border—Nepal was a buffer between New Delhi and Beijing—initially responded with training and material support, eventually moving to suppress substantial Maoist activity within its own borders. Finally, the United States, long a major development actor through USAID, moved promptly in all areas, from supplying arms and equipment to training. An emergency appropriation brought the combined military aid (Foreign Military Financing) for Fiscal Years 2002 and 2003 to USD 17 million. Assessment teams from all three of the countries just named were supplemented by personnel for actual training, to include US Special Forces.

Where no amount of foreign input could compensate, however, was in overcoming the inertia of a traditional system that organizationally manifested itself in extreme deference to authority and a consequent lack of initiative. This, combined with the intelligence shortcomings cited above, resulted in a failure to come to grips with the struggle operationally and tactically even as the general strategic grasp of overall parameters could be judged reasonably accurate. While it was understood with considerable clarity how socio-economic-political shortcomings had produced the insurgency, it was not grasped how to respond.[81] Consequently, a comparatively weak insurgent movement, which drew its combatant strength from minimally armed tribal revolt and could expand beyond core regions only through terror orchestrated by voluntarist action, was allowed to go unchecked for want of applying a systematic counter.

Further, as this uncoordinated, haphazard, armed response moved forward, political realities further hobbled efforts. For virtually the entire post-November 2001 period, the government was in a state of crisis, with the Nepali Congress splitting into two rival factions, and the UML refusing to accept the reigns of government. Finally, in October 2002, the situation became so bad that the King, using extraordinary powers granted to him by the Constitution—but highly controversial nevertheless—disbanded Parliament and appointed a government made up predominantly of members from minority political parties. As the King's own legitimacy was not secure, this made the government's even less so, and the ousted parties, through mass action, wasted no time in attempting to test the new administration's staying power. So tainted were the political parties by their own corruption and ineptness, however, that they were initially unable to rally a viable challenge.

Seeking to exploit the situation, the Maoists in January 2003 offered a ceasefire and renewed negotiations. The reason had already been provided by Bhatarrai in December 2002: "The situation is now peaking toward a climax after the fratricidal and regicidal 'king,' Gyanendra, and his notorious son, Paras, have staged a retrogressive coup d'etat against the supine parliamentary democracy on Oct. 4 and restored autocratic monarchy in the country."[82] Nonetheless, the country eagerly embraced the proffered respite.[83]

Earlier negotiations, detailed above, had been unilaterally terminated by the CPN(M) in November 2001 in order to go over to the offensive, yet links had never been completely severed. The UML, in particular, because its stated ideology continued to incorporate the notion of "revolution," had kept channels of communication open as had any number of other actors. Human rights groups, for instance, tried to act as mediators. Eventually, the Palace and its appointed government used these channels to renew discussions. Just how they would fare remained anyone's guess, because neither side showed any sign of altering its basic positions. These, to be clear, were irreconcilable on such basics as the nature of the state and the position of the monarchy. Both sides continued to train, re-equip, and acquire armaments.

In this situation, it was the Maoist position that was of most moment. From the previous ceasefire, captured documents and pictures, to include video footage, together with interrogations of prisoners, showed cadre telling the mass base that negotiations were a tactical gambit, that the cause of the revolution would never be betrayed or given up until a "people's republic" was established. That such remained the CPN(M)'s position had been stated directly. The real question was whether the party saw the new talks as but a tactical pause for regrouping or a more strategic effort to gain by non-violent means that which until then it had been unable to gain through violence, the standard political warfare approach. The latter course seemed likely, with the CPN(M), in its own calculations, moving from a position of strength into fractured Nepali politics.

The CPN(M), in the circumstances of the moment, felt it could not lose and would be able to defeat the enemy in detail, much as Lenin had in the chaos between the ouster of the czar and the final Bolshevik coup.[84] Directly and through its front organizations, as in 2001, it aggressively used political space, in which it could operate freely, to divide its foes further. In closed-door meetings, it made common cause with both the political parties and the monarchy (through its appointed government), the end-game to use one against the other, then to out-maneuver the survivor in the organizational contest to follow.

Crucial in this strategy was the "constituent assembly," through which the monarchy was to be neutralized, in particular separated from its armed base, the RNA, in the name of establishing a "republic." Integration of the CPN(M) combatants, as was being demanded, would further ensure the RNA's inability to respond to provocation. In such an environment, co-optation would serve in place of armed confrontation. Indeed, the CNP(M)'s "75 Points"[85] were structured as such a multitude precisely so that no one or minor grouping was objectionable. It was the platform's totality, to be achieved by persistently emphasizing that the smaller, "moderate"[86] compromises provided the only route to a "lasting peace," that was intended to produce a totally transformed whole.

The CPN(M) had not changed its basic positions but, like the Provisional Irish Republican Army (PIRA) in Northern Ireland, saw the moment as ripe for pushing ahead with non-violent means even as violence was held in reserve.[87] This formulation was theoretically of particular interest, because it advanced that a sub-state actor held the same rights as the state. In particular, the state was no longer granted a monopoly of legitimate force. To the contrary, having lost this status by illegitimate action, the state, it was claimed, had to negotiate with the sub-state actor, which had access to its own purportedly legitimate force.[88]

The Maoists hence claimed to have emerged, through the use of violence, as an equal to the state. The state controlled the urban areas, argued the CPN(M), the sub-state actor controlled the rural ones. The clash between the thesis and antithesis, hitherto a violent affair, had given rise to the demand for the realization of a new synthesis through non-violent negotiation. Violence had been necessary to arrive at the point of "political solution," but it could now be superseded by political warfare. The destruction wreaked principally in the hinterland, therefore, although having various tactical and operational goals, such as area domination, strategically was intended as political communication, irrefutable evidence for the old order that the CPN(M) was a force that could not be ignored.[89]

None of this precluded the Maoists' inclusion of more immediate concerns, although Bhattarai, as the head of the Maoist negotiations team, had begun to emphasize that the CPN(M)'s "75 Points" was a document of strategic goals rather than tactical demands. He claimed for the party a willingness of the movement to accept intermediate steps (e.g., a "bourgeois republic" with a constitutional monarchy), a determination to move beyond an early attraction for the approach of *Sendero Luminoso* or the Naxalites in order to arrive at a unique, situationally appropriate "Nepalese Maoism."[90] Specifics of application, for the building of a new Nepal, were to be found in an expansion of Bhattarai's PhD dissertation released in May 2003.[91]

Even if this formulation had been accepted at face value, there would have been grounds for pessimism. Maoist excessive rhetoric, especially attacks on the RNA, and a bargaining emphasis on broad, often utopian, declarations at the expense of specifics, led to a situation where the two sides were talking past each other. Undoubtedly, the RNA saw little but a cynical effort to weaken it. In the field,

Maoist cadre and combatants had been briefed that the major goal of the round of talks was the "national army."[92] Simultaneously, the Maoist representatives in Kathmandu focused on ending international assistance to the government (which, as indicated above, was crucial to enhancing the capabilities of the security forces), all the while demanding that the RNA "return to the barracks." Under no such restrictions themselves, Maoist forces continued to move and train, funded by undiminished criminal activity.

Further, unsure of their position *vis-à-vis* Nepal's international supporters in the era of the global war on terrorism, the Maoists stridently attacked them, in particular the US. This furthered the impression of Machiavellian maneuvering, although it would seem more correct to find the inspiration for such CPN(M) verbiage in the party's parochial origins and operational environment. Put simply, the Maoists had a painfully limited understanding of the global forces and processes in play.[93] This lead to a degree of paranoia and mistaken bargaining positions.[94] The entirely predictable result was an increasing alienation of key elements of society even as the Maoists saw themselves as courting those elements. The situation's difficulty was compounded by the movement, in May 2003, of the estranged political parties into a phase of active resistance against the state. Although they continued to voice support for a favorable outcome in the government/CPN(M) negotiations, they committed their own efforts completely to confronting the palace and its appointed government.

In such an environment, the only real surprise came when the Maoists on 27 August 2003 abruptly terminated the ceasefire and again resorted to a variety of armed actions, including targeted assassinations of important government personnel in Kathmandu. The surprise came from the obvious quarter: Government disorientation and lack of focus seemed to be providing the CPN(M) with ample leeway to make progress, through "political" means, progress that would surely be more difficult in a state of armed conflict. Indeed, faced with renewed assassination efforts, the government promptly restored legal prohibitions and asked international organizations to assist in apprehending leadership figures. Thus people's war was again in full swing.[95]

As the "stir against regression" likewise intensified, the absorption of attention and resources created the space for dramatic Maoist gains in the first half of 2004. Murder, robbery, and kidnapping grew dramatically, particularly the latter, with its forced drafts of young people into Maoist ranks. Plans to stand up a local security capacity were stillborn, however, when "EU objections" claimed that such would contribute to the deteriorating human rights environment.[96]

Lack of leadership seriously affected security force response, yet an element of personal animosity toward the king seemed as much at issue with the leaders of the "five parties" as an actual desire for a solution. Koirala, for instance, relishing his role as the grand old man of Nepali democracy, its living link with the past struggles to institute parliamentary rule, seemed to have few plans for a solution beyond name-calling and stirring rancor. Most controversial to the general public was the involvement, through party mechanisms, of young people in street demonstrations marshaled by "professional students."

When a compromise of sorts was put together in early June, with Deuba being returned as prime minister, there was a collective sigh of relief, but the reactions of the "stir" movement was guarded. Although the UML cautiously embraced the step as one in the right direction, Koirala dismissed it and pronounced the struggle would continue. Another lackluster performance by Deuba led to a final dismissal in 1 February 2005 and assumption of direct rule by the king. This polarized the political situation still further. Foreign reaction was negative, as was that of the Nepali expatriate community.

United Front as Decisive Weapon

It was this polarization that led to a situation in April 2006 not unlike that in Thailand post-1973 or certainly post-October 1976—with the monarchy in a role quite the opposite. Mass action led to the collapse of the royal "martial law" regime and a restoration of parliamentary rule. If in Thailand Bhumipol had proved a rallying point for reform, in Nepal, Gyanendra was to prove a Marcos-like figure around which all opposition could rally. This provided the Maoists with the basis for a viable united front, precisely what had alluded them in all of the post-Vietnam cases we have examined thus far. A boycott of a government effort to restore local VDC politics, aided by the actions of international actors present in Nepal, notably European-based NGOs, provided the immediate context that brought the main opposition legal parties—the Seven Party Alliance (or SPA)—into alliance with the CPN(M). Behind the scenes, democratic India, again pursuing geopolitical ends not unlike those seen in the Sri Lanka chapter, hosted the meetings that produced the alliance and then ensured its power in the streets by cutting off ammunition and other supplies to the Nepali security forces. The result was a united front upheaval in April 2006 that echoed People's Power in February 1986 Manila.

The collapse of the old-order began with the late 2005 issuing of a 12-point letter of understanding between SPA and the Maoists (SPAM, as wags had it). Therein, it was claimed, as advanced by the leader of the legal (Parliamentarian) Marxists, UML General Secretary, Madhab Kumar Nepal, the public face of the agreement, that the Maoists had "developed a new maturity," had reached a conclusion that they were unable to complete their "capture of state power through the barrel of the gun." Consequently, they were willing to proceed peacefully, which meant "if the Maoists resort to arms again, those in power will have to take the blame." For good measure, he threw in, "If the well-equipped Shah of Iran was uprooted by unarmed people, there is no reason why it can't happen in Nepal."

Waving this flag, the political parties temporarily stormed back onto center stage in Nepali politics, making a bargain which was altruistic, Machiavellian, or simply suicidal, depending upon how the cards fall after publication of this volume. However this may be, their long-running battle with the palace had caused them to play "peace" as the hand that would gain them both power and breathing room from their mortal foes, the Maoists. There was no "peace," went the stated logic, because there was no "democracy"; and there was no "democracy" because "the Palace" insisted upon violence. That this was historical falsification of the first order was apparent to anyone who had even notional familiarity with the political history of Nepal, but it was also irrelevant.

There was insurgency in Nepal, of course, due to shortcomings of the system that evolved during the democratic era. Those most responsible were the same individuals who had reached the deal with the Maoists—not just the same parties but the same individuals. That this well-documented reality could somehow be blamed upon the Palace was a position that emerged in vibrant form only with the "Royal Massacre" that replaced the previous monarch, Birendra, with his less-popular brother, Gyanendra. The latter's missteps served to elevate the parties to the position as advocates of a "democracy" they had never practiced, either in power or within their own ranks.

In reality, it was the nature of "democracy" that had been the issue all along in the Nepali struggle, as it had been in our other case studies. For the Maoists, the choice had never been between "absolute democracy" and "autocratic monarchy," the terms used in the 12-point agreement. It had been between parliamentary democracy and "people's democracy," a clash seen perhaps most vividly in the Philippine illustration. In Nepal, parliamentary democracy was portrayed as a Western concept. People's democracy was certainly also a Western concept but was portrayed as "Maoist." The very Western origin of Maoist ideological beliefs was regularly on display at the CPN-M's public gatherings, where place of honor was occupied by the pantheon of "white gods plus one"—Marx, Engels, Lenin, Stalin, and Mao—but this contradiction too was irrelevant.

What "absolute democracy" (*loktantra*) meant for the Maoists, operationally, was the ability to knock from the battlefield their only tangible obstacle, the monarchy. What it meant strategically was the ability to move beyond the gun to the ballot at the early 2006 juncture in the struggle. It was what the Sandinistas had done so adroitly in Nicaragua, moving rapidly within "democracy" to solidify what they had been after all along—a Marxist-Leninist version of democracy, in our terms here, "people's democracy." Apologists went to some lengths to avoid discussing this aim, but it was the concrete manifestation of the "dictatorship of the proletariat."

That the Maoists had no intention of abandoning their strategic goal was made clear to cadre in a series of meetings in Rolpa. Whether they tactically would go the route of the Provisional Irish Republican Army (PIRA) in Ulster, actually decommissioning their arms, was subsequently agreed to but remained to be seen as this book went to press. There were too many unknowns, not least the nature of the Maoists' links with the newly formed Communist Party of India-Maoist, CPI-Maoist, created through a merging of the two principal Maoist insurgencies in India, and aggressively committed to violence as the only route to political power and social justice. In their statements, the two Maoisms have stated clearly that peaceful means are useful only so long as they facilitate the violent end.

A central role in the emerging situation, as noted above, was played by members of the Indian "legal Left," a catch-all term for those Marxists who participate in parliamentary democracy while disclaiming its ultimate legitimacy—the same position taken by the UML in Nepal. On the one hand, Indian Left participation offered some grounds for optimism, since the legal Left there did not engage in insurgency (which was not the same thing as eschewing violence, something PIRA demonstrated well in the Catholic ghettos of Ulster in the late 1990s). On the other hand, it was also grounds for profound disquiet, since the "terms of reference," as reflected in the 12-point agreement, were vague and contingent upon the effective surrender of the Nepali Royal Government. This only heightened Nepali nationalist suspicions that what was being set in motion was a "Sikkim solution," though Bhutan might have been the more apt comparison, a nominally independent nation-state, strategically located, compliant with New Delhi's strategic wishes.

The turning point came with the government's early 2006 effort to hold local elections. SPAM cooperation consequently reached a new level, and the mass demonstrations of April resulted. That the government decision to hold local elections was considered controversial demonstrated the degree to which polarization and mistrust had poisoned the Nepali polity. Exploiting the estrangement between the

Palace and the parliamentary parties, the Maoists emerged as advocates of "peace," declaring a ceasefire and using military pressure outside Kathmandu Valley even as SPA demonstrations proceeded in the Valley and other major population centers. "Negotiations" were held up, went the Party propaganda line, because of government intransigence and insistence upon pursuing counter-insurgency. In reality, as stated directly in the RNA's campaign plan, the goal was that counter-insurgency would restore legitimate government writ in such fashion and to such extent that the Maoists ultimately would agree to re-incorporation within the political system.

The rub was that the Maoists were not interested in re-incorporation. They did not even accept the common understanding of "negotiations." To the contrary, evidence supported a conclusion that the point of their ceasefire was to further the armed struggle. Maoist exhortations to combatants continued to state that the old-order could only be addressed with violence. Fellow-travelers, continued the Party line, would be accepted as long as they were useful, but they would not have a meaningful role in the shaping and execution of "New Democracy." Nevertheless, it was felt by the Party that the political parties could play an important role, "with all forces against the autocratic monarchy centralizing [focusing] their assault against the autocratic monarchy from their respective positions, thereby creating a nationwide storm of democratic protest."

Absent the "nonviolent" delivery of operational victory, however, plans were laid for the resumption of the Maoist military assault within the overall strategy for the seizure of power. The "nationwide storm"—April 2006—only had worth so long as it delivered by "political means" that which could only be gained at greater cost through violent means. If this was the strategy, operational intent was to include demonstrations in urban areas and attacks in rural areas to force the government to fight on two fronts. The RNA was aware of this to some extent, but it was unable to do much about it due to two pressing failures: inability to engage in the nonmilitary aspects of counter-insurgency, and an inability to provide local security.

The failure to address the information warfare side of the equation caused especially serious problems with respect to India. A key aspect of an information warfare campaign should have been to bring the Indian government back into the game in a positive manner. Instead, the impression of "failure" and of "democracy destroyed" that allowed the Indian legal Marxists to support the elements of the ruling coalition at Delhi that sought to meddle in Nepal's affairs. The issue was rarely stated as such, but there were left wing elements (within India) who viewed India's own democracy as problematic, so they sought to "act out" against whatever force in Nepal could serve as a surrogate target. To that end, bringing the monarchy to its knees served their immediate purposes. This was not in India's best interests, keenly aware as it was that it had a growing Maoist problem on its hands within its own borders. The joint statements and activities of the Nepalese and Indian Maoists, together with an upsurge of activities on the ground in India, had led to the Center's becoming much more energized in its approach to the lackluster State anti-militant campaigns. Still, the particulars of India's own domestic politics resulted in a virtual legal Marxist foreign policy in much the manner Tamil Nadu had for years conducted its own Sri Lanka policy (which also included backing insurgents whose primary tactic was use of terror).

The failure to implement a solution to the local security dilemma was the second major issue and placed the security forces in an impossible situation. The invariable reason given in Kathmandu for having no local security in place was "the EU." Foreign donor objections to local security mechanisms were real (with most NGOs quietly honoring Maoist extortion demands and more than a few actively siding with them against the government), but local security was indispensable. There was no way to proceed in its absence. As has been discussed time and again in preceding chapters , the precise form of local security must be determined—it need not even be armed capacity. But it must be the capacity to inform and/or resist, pending reinforcement by the security forces.

The security forces, it bears observation, had improved, led by advances in the quality of RNA junior and middle grade officers. In many ways, in fact, the senior service, the RNA, was not the same force it had been several years before. Tactical and operational improvement, however, could make no headway in the absence of a strategy for victory. This highlighted the heart of the matter: Even as events of the first half of 2006 developed, there was still no articulation of "why we fight," much less a comprehensive state (national) plan for counter-insurgency. There was an RNA plan, and this did bring along elements of the state at times, but there was no designated command authority that could bring together all facets of state power—much less the actual application of those assets. This remained centralized in the Palace, where there was an inability to respond in timely manner to emerging issues.

Instead, it was the Maoists who demonstrated an ability to move rapidly and with strategic precision. The changing correlation of forces demanded a recognition that the violent line of operation had reached its culmination point. An earlier Prachanda-Bhattarai debate had been over just this issue: whether military action (violence) should still lead, or if the path could be forged by any of the other (four) lines of operation. If we return to these four, as discussed early in the chapter, we find:

(1) *Mass line*—The Maoists had consolidated a political base in the west. It had been achieved by armed political action. Terror, always important, could by 2006 give way to menace. The base areas had been consolidated relatively quickly and at acceptable human cost. Though the numbers were awful enough, what had been lost in the entire conflict in Nepal was probably shy of what Sri Lanka lost in either of the two efforts against the Maoist JVP. Yet the Nepali Maoists had found it increasingly tough going to do anything decisive strategically from those base areas.

(2) *United front*—February 2005 provided the chance for a strategically decisive shift by delivering the political parties into the Maoist hands. That the political parties made a "mistake" was quite irrelevant to the fact that the mistake was made. A combination of "ceaseless waves" protest inside with armed action outside, all held together by dramatically enhanced use of terror against the state and security forces (especially through Improvised Explosive Devices, or IEDs, and unconventional actions) was seen as an unbeatable combination. The most significant element in Prachanda's various statements was his advancing the next step in the united front process: he proposed that the political parties jointly form an army with the Maoists, sharing all positions and authority. He further proposed that democratic elements within the RNA join with the Maoists and the parties. He raised the question as to who controlled whom, monarch or RNA. The bottom line was the same: The Maoists recognized that the military, as in every case in this book, was the tactical and operational lynchpin. If it could be neutralized, the game was over.

(3) *Political warfare*—Here again, developing circumstances delivered up to the Maoists a "blue chip" item, "peace." The longing for peace was so great that the Maoists could use it as a term over and over to undermine the will of all concerned to continue the struggle. It mattered not one whit that "peace" meant nothing tangible. It mattered not that the Maoists had created the situation, or that the political parties were the very ones who enabled their progress. The longing for "peace" could be used at all levels of war (strategic, operational, and tactical) to neutralize the ability of the government to continue.

(4) *International*—What the Maoists saw was a global situation where the trends were in their favor. Even those international elements opposed to the Maoists' dated, Cold War views were unwilling to grapple with the situation due to their preoccupation with violent radical Islam (which the Nepalese Maoists claimed to support). As the CPN(M) saw it, everything was flowing its way. At least

in part, the Party declared its ceasefire as a tactical gambit to see if it could neutralize government armed action. This did not happen, but strategically the government took a black eye as the entity that refused to "give peace a chance." That the Maoists used the interim to prepare for operations was winked at by many who saw the existing system as irredeemably flawed. India, as the prime offender in this regard, decided that playing its usual version of "the Great Game" was preferable to supporting the Kathmandu government. New Delhi was not totally committed negatively, but, in logic virtually identical to that which had prevailed in its Sri Lanka adventure, seemed to think it could contain the Nepali situation by fostering a "West Bengal solution" (i.e., legal Maoists participating in democratic governance).

This left "the government" in a tight spot. The April 2006 restoration of parliamentary supremacy was followed by a series of agreements that revolved around Maoist disarmament and participation in an interim government pending

Terror as driver: Most common Maoist IEDs converted common containers, such as rice cookers, into lethal weapons. Mines and booby traps were ubiquitous, as was the use of home-made explosive charges during assaults. (Photo: Rajaram Gautam in Author Collection)

a constitutional convention and transfer of sovereignty to a new regime, the form to be determined by the convention. Though technically ruling, the parliamentary government had surrendered its future and power to a process not unlike Thailand 1973–76, with the tremendous difference that the security forces were prevented from maintaining even public order out of concern that their actions might jeopardize the ongoing "ceasefire." In such a situation, the Maoists thrived, with menace driving their organization, fundraising, and subversion efforts to new peaks. As always, the task at hand was to discern insurgent intentions.

The Maoists are portraying themselves as having had a change of heart. That is not true at all: they have simply chosen to lead with a different combination, to fall back upon a boxing metaphor. They see violence and nonviolence as complementary, just as did the Provisional Irish Republican Army (PIRA) in its famous maxim that it would fight with a ballot in one hand, an *Armalite* in the other. It may be recalled that when the PIRA moved to emphasize the ballot, the question was whether the shift was "real." The intelligence was very mixed. On the one hand, significant steps were taken that indicated a PIRA willingness to participate peacefully in politics. On the other hand, there were serious actions that demonstrated the armed option was not being foreclosed (such as working with FARC in Colombia). In the event, in Ulster, the strength of the state and the willingness of the insurgents to reintegrate produced a tenuous peace. Neither of those factors is present in the Nepali case. To the contrary, in the Irish case, "reintegration" was the end-state.

In Nepal, the Maoists are offering the terms of surrender. Though they claim they are willing to accept the outcome of a vote on the future shape of the system, they refuse to allow political action that would create a level playing field. SPA cadre are effectively blocked from any action outside major urban centers or district capitals. Rather, as the Sandinistas did in Nicaragua, the Maoists, having altered the playing field and gained armed control of the areas which will produce an anticipated "democratic" vote in their favor, have made a strategic decision to allow "peaceful measures" to hold sway. The movement, in other words, is on Maoist auto-pilot: its strategy has not changed, only emphasized a different campaign element (or "weapons system," if you like). Violence and nonviolence are still but two sides of the same coin.

Conclusions

By this point, much should be obvious. In particular, the success of any insurgency using the people's war approach is as much dependent on state incapacity as on its own capacity. The two go hand-in-hand. What has changed since the end of the Cold War, particularly as terrorism itself has become an overarching factor, is the incorporation of terror as insurgent weapon of choice into the Maoist approach. Mao would not have approved, but it is noteworthy that the final two cases discussed, where such approach was used—Peru and Nepal—displayed a lack of state capacity perhaps beyond anything Mao could have imagined. Strategic contempt for one's enemy was one matter, he cautioned. Taking him lightly operationally was another altogether. Yet we now see states so lacking in institutional glue as to be of minimal competence across the spectrum, in strategy, operational art, and tactics.

Those being recruited mirror this reality. Nepali youth have flowed into the CPN(M) counter-state not because of a sea-change in life-circumstances objectively but subjectively. This process has been seen globally. New awareness of options in a world of globalism has produced upheaval in a wide variety of states. Radical political actors, whether Islamists in Pakistan, Afghanistan, and Saudi Arabia, or Maoists in Nepal, have brought incorporation to the margins, or, more correctly, the "margins of the margins." The incorporation, however, is into the counter-state.

Any insurgency seeks such an end. It, of course, is a practitioner of political violence. Mao, although setting forth some astonishingly violent rhetoric, constantly sought to keep winning allegiance and "struggle" balanced, because he recognized the disruptive effect imbalance could have on a liberation movement. It can surely be argued from the foregoing pages that only the CPT, for all its other mistakes, at least had this balance correct. Just as surely, it can be argued that the Maoists have got the balance wrong and have paved the way for their own demise.

The outcome will depend on the temporal element. Any military conflict has a way of even small mistakes turning into larger disasters because of the friction of war. It always was unlikely that the CPN(M) could defeat the state outright, or even nibble it to death; international actors were willing to invest enough aid to see to that, and the Nepali insurgents had no prospect of resource enhancement from the likes of drugs or seriously lucrative smuggling. What was possible within such parameters was depressing: a bloody stalemate. It was to this reality that drove the Maoist shift in emphasis between its lines of operation.

Such shift by leadership highlights a fundamental point: Changes in personalities do make a significant difference. In all of the previous cases, dramatic changes of leadership put in place correct counter-insurgency approaches that produced victory for the state over the counter-state. Sri Lanka, of course, can be used to support either side of the point, though it still supports the general thrust, as changes in leadership were associated with each of the major positive shifts in the conflict. It should not be forgotten that the Maoists were twice vanquished and that the *Eelam* movement was on the verge of liquidation when India intervened. In Nepal, we see the consequences of inadequate leadership when outmatched in a fashion simply not seen in the other cases. That such occurred in a struggling democracy should prove sober cause for reflection.

Crisis in democratic states can produce various solutions. In our cases, the changes at the helm were especially salient in those conflicts that most resemble Nepal in their people's war parameters: Thailand (to Prem), the Philippines (to Aquino), and Peru (to Fujimori). In political parameters, Sri Lanka might be the more apt comparison—democracy mired in corruption and inefficiency—but only if one forgets the pronounced drift that had taken hold in Thailand under Thanom/Praphas, the Philippines under Marcos, and Peru under Garcia. In short, all four of our Asian cases (and Peru) were struggling with major challenges posed by the very factors that had facilitated insurgent mobilization. That the public was more willing to support reform as opposed to revolutionary action allowed the old-regimes to prevail.

The Nepali public is likewise inclined. There is little revolutionary impulse visible—as opposed to mobilization of a youth population for which, to quote the famous explanation for an explosion of rioting in Los Angeles, "There is no Little League in Watts." That is, where there are no alternatives, becoming part of something, whether a gang or a riot, is a potent tool for mobilizing, especially by a counter-state that seeks to do just that. Inevitably, as state response gathers momentum, a rethinking of choices and hence of options will occur.

This should not be interpreted as a mere "The good guys are gonna win." At the end of the day, in our "most like Nepal" cases, the old-order was finished. States that emerge victorious from insurgent challenges rarely if ever come out looking as they went in. Thailand began as a military-dominated oligarchy and ended as a parliamentary democracy. The Philippines saw democracy restored after more than a decade and a half of martial law. Peru swept away the old political elite, went through a period of authoritarianism, and ultimately emerged a more democratic state, especially in the areas where *rondas campesinas* dominated—self-defense, as the Greeks and the Roman Republic understood, the most potent mobilizing element for transformation of subjects to citizens. The same could well happen in Nepal.

Most sources claim such was already happening even as the insurgency germinated. An entire stratum of talent had already demonstrated itself fully capable of existing in the "multi-tasking environment" of the global environment. That such individuals do not presently run Nepal may require little explanation beyond the obvious: to earn "real money," Nepalis may attend to various careers, but politics is certainly not one of them, unless one has found a way to divert public income to private gain. But our cases have demonstrated that the mobilization of new talent that is an inevitable part of a war effort produces demands for new approaches and procedures. This can be seen especially within the security forces but is not limited to them. The inevitable counter-argument is that cultural factors will prevent such from ever moving beyond the theoretical, that the hierarchical structure of Nepal, with its deference to authority and aversion to risk of any sort (most of all, seemingly, decision-making), will prevent change sufficient to "save the system." There is more than a little tautology in these arguments, set forth most prominently in claims that the Nepali monarchy—unlike all others throughout history and around the globe, most particularly the Thai—is incapable of reform and adaptation.

What needs to be advanced first and foremost is that Nepali culture has not prevented certain forms of action that lead to ends selected by the participants. Micro-development projects, for instance, a fundamental component of the Peruvian counter-insurgency, are standard fare in Nepal, as is local government. That the local gentry frequently end up playing an important role in both of these only highlights the obvious fact that all societies turn to local power for local solutions. The CPN(M) claims to be mobilizing new local powers but shows little sign of doing so. Its leaders remain overwhelmingly estranged members of the old-order elite, especially teachers and politicians.

Neither has their culture prevented Nepalis from assuming leadership positions and roles, both at home and abroad. This is not to attempt to deny the very real drag hierarchy appears to play on decision-making in the Nepali context, rather to point out that the same arguments have been used in all of the cases above to explain inaction, most saliently for Thailand. A more convincing case, then, will have to be made to support a notion that Nepali culture and its structure negate human agency.

There is a delicate matter that surfaces at this point: the role of the donor community. Their central position makes it inevitable that just as they are part of the solution, so they are part of the problem. Nepal, although never legally a colony, is as thoroughly colonized as any aid-dependent state can be in the new age of donor imperialism. Donor priorities, uncoordinated and at best theoretically linked to a national plan, take precedence, in a view widely held, over state concerns, even its own survival. This plays itself out in a weak state such as Nepal in a particularly pernicious way, by introducing confusion as to the proper course of action, lack of unity in approach and planning, and dispirited implementation of plans once conceived.

War is always controversial, both in its essence and parameters. In the US, the North could not even agree among itself whether it really wanted to fight to preserve the Union when the South seceded to initiate the American Civil War in 1861. War in Nepal was no different. The natural lack of unity concerning a proper course of action, to be expected in a democratic state, even one facing a ruthless foe, was exacerbated by the welter of contradictory foreign advice heaped on Kathmandu, much of it designed to serve donor not Nepali interests and often based on little save ideological inclination that saw counter-insurgency or even counter-terrorism as illegitimate or certainly beyond the world of donor concern.[97]

What a Saiyud Kerdphol (Thailand), or a Victor Corpuz (the Philippines), or a Lalith Athulathmudalai (Sri Lanka), or an Alberto Fujimori (Peru), therefore, would have recommended be done seems rather straightforward, when considered against the backdrop of people's war history in Asia (and elsewhere):

(1) *A coordinated national effort was necessary*, as appropriate for grappling with the most serious crisis to confront Nepal since its transition to democracy in 1990–91. No matter how challenging that earlier upheaval, it paled in scope and casualties to what occurred post-13 February 1996. Yet the counter-insurgency remained essentially a matter delegated to the security forces. There were, for instance, no local forces of any sort. Neither, at the other end of the spectrum, was there a clear articulation of "why we fight." The security forces were not given the minimum adequate resources necessary to proceed.

(2) *A key component in a national response should have been a strategic plan*, with operational components delimited and responsibilities assigned. This would necessarily have involved all elements of national power and driven a multi-faceted, coordinated response to the insurgency. Jointness should have been central, but even the police were marginalized. Civilian components of the state, which should have taken the lead, were conspicuous only by their absence. The heart of the plan should have been domination of human terrain rather than focus on insurgent combatants. Local security remains the key to restoration of normalcy. This can take a variety of forms but above all must give to the people an organizational capacity to secure lives and property.

(3) *Socio-economic-political reform should have assumed pride of place in any such plan*. Although the operational driving force behind insurgent expansion was provided by terror, the strategic environment of the failed state that is Nepal was thrown up the historic moment the Maoists sought

to exploit. Democracy has been corrupt and ineffective, the political class distracted and self-absorbed. Consequences in the economic and social spheres have consequently been exacerbated. Leadership should have set in place solutions that could have provided inspiration for mobilization. The role of the security forces was to provide the shield behind which restoration of government writ and reform could have occurred. Nepal even had a legal basis for such a campaign in its 1999 act implementing the VDC structure. Local political control, with access to resources (through micro-development), always is what inspires a willingness to engage in local security, with the result a growth of democratic capacity.

If we seek to examine the future, one is left to emphasize a central logic: "Hope is not a method." One can not look at the present situation and be sanguine as to where "peace" will lead Nepal. It is often forgotten that negotiated political solutions to recent insurgencies have involved one of two options: either one side has dominated the other, so that the loser was willing to talk; or both sides have beaten each other senseless, so that both were willing to talk. The case of Thailand illustrates the former, El Salvador (not discussed here), the latter. Nicaragua and Northern Ireland (also not among our case studies) perhaps fall somewhere in between. In the former, the role of the *contras* in bringing the communist government in Managua to its knees is often conveniently forgotten.[98] The Sandinistas did not simply decide to hold an election. The same may be said for the PIRA, which had been placed in something of a strait-jacket by the British security apparatus to the extent that non-violent means appeared a more reasonable alternative to continued armed struggle. Thus did it decide to opt for the ballot box, even while reserving for itself the right to resort to armed action.[99]

As concerns people's war groups specifically, there has not been a case of genuine negotiations being engaged in during hostilities. All internal documents point to the contrary, to the use of non-violent means to achieve violent ends. What they are willing to do, historically speaking, is to negotiate the terms on which their demands will be accepted. This is not the same as normally meant by "negotiations," and no "confidence building steps" can overcome the sort of duplicity that historically has been at the heart of all such Maoist efforts to date, to include that of the Nepali Maoists. Advocating "talks" as a solution sidesteps the crucial issue of insincerity.

Counter-insurgency, in contrast, seeks to change the temperature of the water, to engender democratic capacity to the citizenry such that governance can take place. It is not a menu of violent techniques for human engineering but rather an approach that uses necessary violence to secure a campaign that empowers citizens at the local level

Unresolved conflict: Author in Rolpa. Insurgency in Nepal has switched emphasis from its violent line of operation to its four "other" lines. Though allegedly "peaceful," the Maoist campaign functions as would any gang in a Western urban setting, relying upon menace and criminal activity, overt violence as necessary, to maintain control.

so that they are both more capable of controlling their own destinies and securing them. Counter-insurgency is subversive of existing order if that old-regime is not based on democratic access. Democracy, then, is both end and means. All violent action must serve as a shield for restoration of the government writ and fostering local democratic capacity. Micro-development is a key component for economic development, while the social consequences of generating a local security capacity are increased democratic capacity and greater sense of citizenship. Such action takes place in both rural and urban spaces and is tied together in a systematic reclaiming of those areas lost to insurgents. For Nepal, what might have been has given way to contingency, a roll of the dice in a game played with those whose terror has forced their inclusion at the table.

Notes

[1] An early version of this chapter appeared as Marks, *Insurgency in Nepal* (Carlisle: Army War College, 2003). See also Marks, "At the Frontlines of the GWOT: Insurgency in

Nepal," *The Journal of Counterterrorism and Homeland Security International*, 9.4 (Fall 2003), 28–34.

[2] For a sympathetic treatment of historical context, see Arjun Karki and David Seddon, "The People's War in Historical Context," in Karki and Seddon, eds., *The People's War in Nepal: Left Perspectives* (Delhi: Adroit Publishers, 2003), 3–48.

[3] The closest thing to "official" figures for the conflict are those compiled by the Informal Sector Research & Study Centre (INSEC) and published both periodically and in an annual. They were undoubtedly compiled in good faith and widely accepted, but it is difficult to take at face value a compilation that, for key years, listed Maoists killed while engaged in insurgency as those "victimized by the state," or as "political workers" who were "victims killed by state." The National Human Rights Commission also publishes periodic and annual reports. These are more carefully worded, though not in the detail of the INSEC papers. See, for example, *Human Rights in Nepal: A Status Report 2003* (Kathmandu: National Human Rights Commission, 2004).

[4] Lest confusion set in, in my earlier work, I compared Nepal to North Carolina because of the similarity of shape and size (126,161 sq. km). The population of the latter I listed as 6.5 million using an earlier census; this has now reached some 8.2 million. Florida is a more perfect fit, although the terrain of North Carolina continues to make the comparison useful. Maps of Nepal, displaying a wide variety of data, are readily available. See, for example, Prem Sagar Chapagain, Pawan Kumar Ghimire, and Rajesh Thapa, eds., *New EKTA School Atlas*, 2nd edn. (Kathmandu: EKTA Books, 2002); and S. H. Shrestha, *Nepal in Maps*, 5th edn. (Kathmandu: Educational Enterprise, January 2002). The single best source for detailed sheets is Maps of Nepal, S. M. Trading Centre (New Baneswor, Kathmandu), <aditi@ccsi. com.np>.

[5] All statistics are drawn from government documents but seem to occasion no end of controversy. Some recent sources, for example, have nearly half the population now in the *tarai*. Others have some 7% in the Himalayas, which would seem to depend largely upon where draws the line of settlement. The critical points that should not be lost amidst the debate: first, no one seems quite clear who is in Nepal and where they are, but, second, all agree they have exceeded the carrying capacity of the land and are driving a growing search for livelihood.

[6] In 1971, when Nepal's population was but 12 million, average life expectancy was 37 years, and the infant mortality rate (per 100,000 births) was a staggering 172. Adult literacy was put at 13%. By 1998, despite substantial improvement, a Nepali could still expect to live but 58 years; the infant mortality rate was 72; and adult literacy was 38%. *Civics in Nepal*, Grade 12 textbook, Contemporary Society Course (Kathmandu: Creative Press, 2001). Such trends became still more pressing as a rapidly growing population produced an age

distribution whereby, as per 2001 census estimates, 50% of the population was 19 years old or younger.

[7] For discussion of structural issues engendered by traditional patterns of landholding, see Mahesh C. Regmi, *Landownership in Nepal* (Delhi: Adroit Publishers, 1999 [1st Indian edn.]), and Shanker Thapa, *Historical Study of Agrarian Relations in Nepal (1846–1951)* (Delhi: Adroit Publishers, 2000).

[8] Fairfax Country, for instance, to the west of Washington, DC, was reported to have budgets between USD 1.3 billion and USD 1.6 billion during the period of research.

[9] This phenomenon is examined in David Seddon, Jagannath Adhikari, and Ganesh Gurung, *The New Lahures: Foreign Employment and Remittance Economy of Nepal* (Kathmandu: Nepal Institute of Development Studies, 2001).

[10] The United Kingdom establishment has been run down to just two infantry battalions and limited support units, with another battalion-equivalent (three rifle companies) assigned to round-out under-strength British infantry battalions. Brunei, where one of the two battalions is based on a rotational basis, has two Gurkha battalions of its own, though they apparently have declined in strength after agitation concerning pay and allowances. Manpower for these two battalions comes from prior-service British Gurkhas who are recruited on separation from UK service. Singapore Police has a Gurkha battalion which is recruited as part of the normal British scheme. India apparently has at least 42 battalions of Gurkha infantry and some 10–12 battalions of other formations, such as Assam Rifles, which, though not nominally "Gurkha," are in fact manned by them. At an 11 May 2003 presentation in Kathmandu, Major (Ret.) Deepak Gurung presented figures that placed 35,000 Nepalese in the Indian Army, with over 115,000 receiving pensions, and 3,500 men in the British establishment, with 26,000 receiving pensions. If the number of "other formations" is included, it would appear that the number of Nepali citizens serving in the Indian armed and paramilitary forces is possibly as high as 50,000. Field notes, April–May 2003.

[11] As of the end of 2001, there were officially 1,870,000 Nepalis working abroad, although the numbers can not be considered accurate, as there is no way to measure returnees. Large numbers were thought to be in Japan. More purportedly precise figures stated that Saudi Arabia had 71,895 working there, with another 44,226 in Qatar. More than 53,000 Nepalis apparently sought employment in Malaysia the same year. Statistics for Nepalis working in India are unreliable, but one data set put the figure at 587,243 in 1991, with a further 418,982 Nepalese born in India. See Harka Gurung, *Nepal: Social Demography and Expressions* (Kathmandu: New Era, 2001), 16–18. For a comprehensive look at a particular community, see A. C. Sinha and T. B. Subba, *The Nepalis in Northeast India* (New Delhi: Indus Publishing, 2003). Independent estimates figure at least USD 1 billion is remitted to Nepal from overseas annually. Field notes, November 2002.

[12] Useful is Gary Shepherd, *Life Among the Magars* (Kathmandu: Sahayogi Press, 1982). Particularly good for the situation in the Nepali hills generally is J.P. Cross, *The Call of Nepal*, Series II: Vol. 17 of *Biblioteca Himalayica* (Kathmandu: Mandala Book Point, 1998; 1996 original); on the Gurkhas themselves see Cross, *In Gurkha Company* (London: Arms and Armour, 1986). For details of recruiting, a variety of sources are useful; see particularly two works by Lionel Caplan, *Warrior Gentlemen: "Gurkhas" in the Western Imagination* (Oxford: Berghahn Books, 1995), and *Land and Social Change in East Nepal*, 2d edn. (Kathmandu: Himal Books, 2000); as well as Tony Gould, *Imperial Warriors: Britain and The Gurkhas* (London: Granta Books, 1999). For insight into the "Victorian Mentality" see a reprint of a 19th-century work, Ministry of Defence, *Nepal and The Gurkhas* (London: Her Majesty's Stationary Office, 1965). For the present Indian forces, the best readily available work is Rajesh Kadian, *India and its Army* (New Delhi: Vision Books, 1990). For historical recruiting patterns of Nepalese, see Purushottam Banskota, *The Gurkha Connection: A History of the Gurkha Recruitment in the British Army* (New Delhi: Nirala, 1994), and Kamal Raj Singh Rathaur, *The Gurkhas: A History of the Recruitment in the British Indian Army* (New Delhi: Nirala, 1987).

[13] British presentation to June 2002 Donors Meeting in United Kingdom: "In 2000 upper castes accounted for 35% of the population, but 95% of the civil service, 98% of army officers, 78% of political leaders, including—ironically—the Maoists." Less dominant figures may be found in the literature, but even the most favorable see the two upper castes represented in all major areas in proportion at least double to their societal fraction. See the extensive data presented in Harka Gurung, especially the tables in the appendices.

[14] See, for example, Martin Hoftun, William Raeper, and John Whelpton, *People, Politics, and Ideology: Democracy and Social Change in Nepal* (Kathmandu: Mandala Book Point, 1999), and Dhruba Kumar, ed., *Domestic Conflict and Crisis of Governability in Nepal* (Kathmandu: Centre for Nepal and Asian Studies, Tribhuvan University, 2000). In the latter, Chapter 6 (163–96), Pancha N. Maharjan, deals specifically with the Maoist challenge and offers a wealth of data.

[15] Excellent recent overview, which includes discussion of present events, is John Whelpton, *A History of Nepal* (New York: Cambridge University Press, 2005).

[16] A lasting result was the treaty that allowed Britain to recruit Nepali hill people, Gurkhas, for armed service.

[17] The Indian political left played an important role in this process. Useful for what it has to offer concerning later trends discussed in this paper is Santwana Tewari Chaube, *Democratic Movement in Nepal and the Indian Left* (Delhi: Kalinga Publications, 2001). For a more general discussion of the crucial role India played ideologically, see D. P. Adhikari, *The History of Nepalese Nationalism* (Kathmandu: Jeewan Printing Support Press [Personal imprint], 1988).

¹⁸ Various renderings of Kathmandu are possible, with use of the "h" being most common (e.g., *Kathmandu Post*). American media have recently begun to use "Katmandu." Nepali youth-television commentator Sumina Karki has noted that use of the "t only" spelling changes the actual meaning: "Kathmandu is derived from *Kasthmandap* or a temple made up of a single tree. And the temple is still in *Kathmandu*. *Kath* means wood. So using *Katmandu* instead destroys the meaning of the name." Personal communication, 18 May 2005.

¹⁹ For population figures and maps of VDCs within their districts, see Central Bureau of Statistics (Nepal), *Population of Nepal: Village Development Committees/Municipalities (Population Census 2001)* (Kathmandu: w/UNFPA, June 2002).

²⁰ Useful for a discussion of this issue at the local level is Ganga Bahadur, ed., *Promoting Participatory Democracy in Nepal: An Assessment of Local Self-Governance* (Kathmandu: Political Science Association of Nepal, 1998).

²¹ The entire royal family was shot and killed by the elder son, angered at his inability to secure parental consent to marry the woman of his choice. He subsequently turned his weapon on himself but did not die immediately, presenting the country with the bizarre situation where a murderer was, prior to his death, the crowned king (which occurred even as he was in the intensive care unit). For further details, see, for example, Jonathan Gregson, *Massacre at the Palace: The Doomed Royal Dynasty of Nepal* (New York: Hyperion, 2002).

²² All researchers dealing with this early period are indebted to the Deepak Thapa, "Day of the Maoist," *Himal*, 14.5 (May 2001), internet attachment received, n.p. Also noteworthy is Mukunda Raj Kattel, *Sociology of the "People's War" in Nepal: The Genesis, Development and Aftermath*, MA thesis (Sociology), submitted to Central Department of Sociology and Anthropology, Tribhuvan University (Kathmandu), 15 December 2000.

²³ CPN(M) claims that this is not the "immediate" but the "long term" goal are not altogether convincing given the considerable freight that accompanies all Marxist-Leninist protestations of support for intermediate objectives compatible with democratic impulse.

²⁴ As stated by Baburam Bhattarai, the CPN(M)'s chief ideologue at the time and then head of the International Department of the party: "The revolutionary people's movement (which is popularly known as People's War) undergoing for the past seven years has now created a parallel people's power, army, economy and culture in large parts of the country, except the cities, and a situation of strategic stalemate has developed in the overall sense." See interview conducted via the internet by Chitra Tiwari with Bhattarai, "Maoists Seek a Democratic Nepal," *Washington Times*, 14 December 2002.

²⁵ Bhattarai: "We have always remained amenable to a negotiated settlement of the problem, but it is the feudal autocratic monarchy that has sabotaged all our earlier attempts. The 'ice' will be hard to break unless the monarchy is made to realize that its days are now numbered and it has to make a graceful exit from the stage of history."

[26] From India: Communist Party of India/Marxist-Leninist (People's War), or CPI/M-L (PW), based in Andhra Pradesh and known generally as "People's War Group" or PWG; Maoist Communist Centre, or MCC, based in Bihar, the large Indian state on Nepal's southern border; the Revolutionary Communist Centre of India (Maoist); and the Revolutionary Communist Centre of India (Marxist-Leninist). From Bangladesh: Bangladesher Samyabadi Dal (M-L); Purbo Bangla Sarbahara Party (CC); and Purbo Bangla Sarbahara Party (MPK). From Sri Lanka: the Ceylon Communist Party (Maoist). The ninth attendee, of course, was the CPN(M) itself. More recently, a Bhutanese Communist Party (Marxist-Leninist-Maoist) has emerged and called for "people's war" to overthrow the reigning monarchy. This organization is not yet a CCOMPOSA member but can be expected to seek such status. Field notes, May 2003. It remains unclear whether this hitherto unknown party is an ethnic Bhutanese phenomenon or an outgrow of CPN(M) efforts to penetrate the country's ethnic Nepali community. The latter has been in a state of turmoil since the late 1980s as a result of official Bhutanese efforts to promote nationalism through a variety of socio-economic-political measures. See Michael Hutt, *Unbecoming Citizens: Culture, Nationhood, and the Flights of Refugees from Bhutan* (New Delhi: Oxford University Press, 2003).

[27] Possibly the single most cited essay comparing the cases of Peru and Nepal is R. Andrew Nickson, "Democratisation and the Growth of Communism in Nepal: A Peruvian Scenario in the Making?" *Journal of Commonwealth and Comparative Politics*, 30.3 (November 1992), 358–86. I am indebted to Nickson for elaborating on the article's contents during a discussion in Asuncion, Paraguay, 15 August 1993. Building upon this work, see Marks and Scott Palmer, "Radical Maoist Insurgents and Terrorist Tactics: Comparing Nepal and Peru," *Low Intensity Conflict and Law Enforcement*, 13.2 (Autumn 2005), 91–116.

[28] Key works include: S. Banerjee, *India's Simmering Revolution: The Naxalite Uprising* (London: Zed Press, 1984); E. Duyker, *Tribal Guerrillas: The Santals of West Bengal and the Naxalite Movement* (Delhi: Oxford University Press, 1987); and A. K. Samana, *Left Extremist Movement in West Bengal: An Experiment in Armed Agrarian Struggle* (Calcutta: Firma KLM), 1984. Particularly good at placing the Naxalites within regional development context is Partha Chatterjee, *The Present History of West Bengal: Essays in Political Criticism* (Delhi: Oxford University Press, 1997).

[29] To include West Bengal, Bihar, Jharkhand, Orissa, Andhra Pradesh, and Maharashta. The most vibrant of these were People's War Group (PWG) of Andhra Pradesh and the Maoist Communist Centre (MCC) of Bihar, both CCOMPOSA members, but now united as the Communist Party of India (Maoist), formed in 2005.

[30] Both were born in 1954 and entered politics in their university years. Prachanda earned a graduate degree (MA) in agriculture, Bhattarai in (PhD) urban planning (his wife, Hishila Yemi, is an architect/engineer and also a member of the Maoists). Both have been widely

quoted as advocating social transformation through violence—Bhattarai is credited with the intellectual authorship of the "Class Enemy Elimination Campaign" launched in 1996. Asked for personal details by Tiwari, he replied, "As per your query about my individual background, you can take me as a typical representative of a Third World educated youth of peasant background, who finds the gross inequality, oppression, poverty, underdevelopment and exploitation of the overwhelming majority of the population in a class-divided and imperialism-dominated world just intolerable, and grasps Marxism-Leninism-Maoism as the best scientific tool to change it positively."

[31] For a recent discussion of the Khmer Rouge leadership, see Philip Short, *Pol Pot: Anatomy of a Nightmare* (New York: Henry Holt, 2004), together with the excellent review of the same, James Fenton, "The Cruel Carpenter," *The New York Review of Books*," LII.10 (9 June 2005), 28–311. Essential reading on the Khmer Rouge would include: Ben Kiernan, *The Pol Pot Regime: Race, Power, and Genocide in Cambodia Under the Khmer Rouge, 1975–79* (New Haven: Yale University Press, 1996) and *How Pol Pot Came to Power: A History of Communism in Kampuchea, 1930–1975* (London: Verso, 1985); David P. Chandler, *Brother Number One: A Political Biography of Pol Pot* (Boulder, Colorado: Westview Press, 1992) and *Voices From S-21: Terror and History in Pol Pot's Secret Prison* (Berkeley: University of California Press, 1999); Kenneth Quinn, "Political Change in Wartime: The Khmer Krahom Revolution Southern Cambodia, 1970–1974," *Naval War College Review*, 28 (Spring), 3-31, and *The Origins and Development of Radical Cambodian Communism*, PhD dissertation, University of Maryland, 1982; Karl D. Jackson, ed., *Cambodia, 1975–1978: Rendezvous with Death* (Princeton, New Jersey: Princeton University Press, 1989); Michael Vickery, *Cambodia, 1975–1982* (Chiang Mai: Silkworm Books, 1999); Elizabeth Becker, *When the War Was Over: Cambodia and the Khmer Rouge Revolution* (New York: Public Affairs, 1986); and Chandler, Kiernan, and Chanthou Boua, *Pol Pot Plans the Future: Confidential Leadership Documents From Democratic Kampuchea, 1976–1977*, Monograph Series 33/Yale Southeast Asia Studies (New Haven: Yale Center for International and Area Studies, 1988).

[32] Fieldwork in the important district of Gorkha (from which the term "Gurkha" is derived) revealed, as per police statistics for the period November 2001–March 2002, that fully 40% of those arrested were teachers (79 of 196). Field notes, March 2002.

[33] Impressionistic analysis of admittedly incomplete data indicates that one-tenth to one-fifth of the cadre and combatants may be women. (This is a revision of earlier work, wherein I placed the proportion somewhat higher.)

[34] Contesting the 12 May 1991 Parliamentary elections as the United Peoples' Front of Nepal, or UPFN, the Maoists won nine seats of the 205: one from the Eastern Region (Siriha); four from the Central Region (Ramechhap, Kavrepalanchok, Lalitpur, Chitwan); and four from the Mid-Western Region (Rukkum, Rolpa x 2, Humla). This is a fascinating

mix of some of the most and least educated areas of the country. By comparison, the Nepali Congress captured 110 seats, the Nepal Communist Party (United Marxist-Leninist), the "legal left," 69 seats. Figures supplied by journalist Rajaram Gautam of Kantipur Publications.

[35] A "big landlord" in the hills, for instance, might be a man with two hectares of land; but objectively this does not fit the definition of such. The point is fundamental, for if the essence of Nepal's problems lies, as it does, in the population exceeding the carrying capacity of the land, no ideological restructuring can adequately address issues of livelihood. The result is bound to be, as it was in Cambodia, tragedy.

[36] A preliminary analysis of all Maoist civilian victims of terror actions in 2002 produced 323 names, 145 of which could be identified as Brahmin, Chhetri, or 44.9%. Of the remaining 178 names, 52 were tribals (16.1%; called "ethnic community members"); 82 could not be identified (25.4%). These four categories amounted to 86.4%. Victims were virtually all male. Their numbers were exceeded by the number of security force dead, especially the police.

[37] The tension that did exist appeared to stem from a logical source: the high proportion of hill tribe manpower in combat formations. Many of these foot-soldiers saw themselves as involved in a self-defense dynamic as opposed to an ideological crusade. Thus they were dealt with carefully by the leadership as it engaged in the tactical maneuvering so typical of a Leninist organization.

[38] Field notes, April–May 2003. This conclusion is based on interviews with Maoist combatants in Rolpa. It may be further noted that each battalion also has a vice commissar with equivalent powers to the chief commissar.

[39] Most active in the united front campaign are student and ethnic liberation groups. The latter have not proved particularly vibrant, but the former function openly and appear to execute instructions issued by the CPN(M) leadership.

[40] For a discussion of motives, see Li Onesto, *Dispatches From the People's War in Nepal* (Chicago: Insight Press, 2005).

[41] This is an important issue, because the limited scholarly work produced to date has relied principally on "circular" journalistic accounts of actual events, the result being that hearsay has taken on a life of its own. One police operation, in particular, *Kilo Sierra II* (June 1998), is now consistently cited as mobilizing hill people in self-defense; but its particulars are normally conflated with other operations, such as the earlier *Romeo* (November 1995), which are then arrayed as if a consistent pattern of systemic repression. Examination of contemporaneous data, though, such as the field reports for *Romeo* (Field Notes, November 2001), raises questions as to what occurred objectively—quite a different issue from what occurred subjectively. Subjective issues can not be ignored and may be crucial in any insur-

gency; for instance, what could seem to be limited repression objectively might nevertheless culturally be perceived as substantial. Yet consideration, when dealing with a voluntarist movement, must be given to the possibility that limited, even unexceptional, actions can be exploited through shrewd ideological campaign by insurgents.

[42] Figures on CPN(M) strength did not inspire confidence, but government estimates provided in early 2003 would seem reasonable: 5,500 combatants; 8,000 militia; 4,500 cadre (referred to in Nepalese English as "cah-dres"); 33,000 hard core followers; and 200,000 sympathizers.

[43] See especially Anne de Sales, "The Kham Magar Country: Between Ethnic Claims and Maoism" in David N. Gellner, *Resistance and the State: Nepalese Experiences* (New Delhi: Social Science Press, 2003), 326–57. There are five separate groupings within the general Magar category.

[44] Field notes, Rolpa, April–May 2003. Discussions with donor representatives in February 2004 served to challenge this point, but I found their contention that limited numbers of cadre were incapable of cowing populations to be a fundamental misreading of the terror dynamic.

[45] This statement must be used with some care. Though it holds as a general proposition, areas differ. Further, as the Maoists have consolidated their hold, they have sought to implement priorities and programs that hitherto have been lacking. See e.g. Kishore Nepal, *The Maoist Service Provision in Parts of Mid and Far West Nepal* (Kathmandu: Center for Professional Journalism Studies, March 2005), as well as the individual selections in Michael Hutt, ed., *Himalayan People's War: Nepal's Maoist Rebellion* (Bloomington: Indiana University Press, 2004). These may be profitably compared to a selection of the best examinations of similar activity by the Vietnamese insurgents. See Eric M. Bergerud, *The Dynamics of Defeat: The Vietnam War in Hau Nghia Province* (Boulder, Colorado: Westview Press, 1991); Stuart A. Herrington, *Silence Was a Weapon: The Vietnam War in the Villages* (Novata, California: Presidio, 1982); Jeffrey Race, *War Comes to Long An: Revolutionary Conflict in a Vietnamese Province* (Berkeley: University of California Press, 1972); William R. Andrews, *The Village War: Vietnamese Communist Activities in Dinh Tuong Province, 1960–1964* (Columbia: University of Missouri Press, 1973); and James W. Trullinger, *Village at War: An Account of Conflict* (Stanford: Stanford University Press, 1994).

[46] Local variations make generalization risky, but extortion, classified by the Maoists as "revolutionary taxation," was until 2004 apparently "reasonable" in an objective sense. Small shopkeepers in Rolpa in April 2003, for instance, cited payments of NPR 50 per month (about USD 0.66); government personnel remaining in "liberated" areas (e.g., teachers, postmen) paid amounts equal to one day's wages per month. NPR 100–200 (USD 1.32–2.64) was often cited by teachers who were making approximately NPR 7,500 per month (roughly

USD 98). Reports of excess from collecting cadres were comparatively rare. In contrast, kidnapping-for-ransom was common, despite efforts by the Maoist hierarchy to deny such activity, and far more arbitrary. The amounts frequently were steep by the standards of rural Nepal. A case, not atypical, in Rolpa involved a small innkeeper held until ransomed by his family for NPR 30,000, or nearly USD 400. He subsequently fled to India, leaving his family adrift. Field notes, April–May 2003. Equally lucrative for the movement, of course, is extortion from businesses associated with the commercial economy. A typical trekking group of foreigners, for instance, stopped in October 2001, was allowed to proceed once the guide had paid NPR 2,000 (about USD 26), a normal amount and an order of magnitude greater than what can be gained in taxing the impoverished population. In the case just cited, a receipt was issued, and the trek reported no further demands. Field notes, December 2001. It is this activity, extortion, that grew completely out of control by 2004, to the extent that it was forcing the shutdown of even donor-funded projects. Demands as high as 10 percent of contract value were reported. Field notes, June 2004.

[47] For example, government statistics for the first several days of the November 2001 offensive put losses to CPN(M) bank-robberies at some USD 2 million. Field notes, November 2001. No reliable data exists on total CPN(M) funding, but it would seem logical to suggest a high figure of some millions of US dollars. Most local collections are likely not to find their way to higher organs.

[48] For discussion of this point in general, see Paul B. Rich and Richard Stubbs, eds., *The Counter-Insurgent State: Guerrilla Warfare and State Building in the Twentieth Century* (New York: St. Martin's Press, 1997).

[49] The basic pattern of mobile warfare, as discussed at length previously in this work, may again be conceptualized as follows. Terror facilitates or establishes the "space" necessary for the insurgent political campaign. It eliminates societal rallying-points, the synapses such as local gentry and minor government officials. Terror further generates demands for protection. Answering this demand, police forces respond. Once they predictably spread out, they are attacked in guerrilla actions, with small patrols and stations overwhelmed. Unable to defend themselves, the police invariably consolidate forces, thus exposing still larger swaths of the population to insurgent domination. Behind the scenes, certain guerrilla units (i.e., a proportion of guerrilla combatant strength) are "regularized," to use Mao's term, turned into mobile warfare units (main force units). When the government inevitably deploys its military to reclaim "lost" areas, these units (normally the army) find themselves, first, harassed by guerrilla action, which demands small unit saturation patrolling, then, defeated in detail by the mobile warfare units (which fight using "guerrilla tactics"). Only in Phase 3, when mobile warfare gives way to the so-called "war of position," do insurgents endeavor to hold ground.

⁵⁰ See Tom Marks, "Colombian Army Counter-insurgency," *Crime, Law and Social Change*, 40 (2003), 77–105. For state response, see Marks, *Sustainability of Colombian Military/Strategic Support for "Democratic Security"* (Carlisle: Army War College, 2005).

⁵¹ Field notes, May 2002.

⁵² This was not only an administrative blow but a key step in establishing Maoist political dominance. For VDC candidates were affiliated with the major political parties. The result was that the legal left bore the brunt of the Maoist assault, since some 2,600 VDC Chairmen of the 3,913 possible were UML members. *Ibid.*

⁵³ Field notes, November 2002. The first year of the Maoist offensive (November 2001–November 2002) saw 1,321 VDC buildings completely destroyed, according to government figures, as per the following breakdown by regions: Far West, 316 of 383 (82.5%); Mid-Western, 165 of 575 (28.7%); Western, 221 of 865 (25.5%); Central, 334 of 1,199 (27.8%); and Eastern, 285 of 893 (31.9%). VDCs continued to be destroyed at such a clip, though, that the statistics were already surpassed at time of release.

⁵⁴ For an effort to study the targeting dynamic, see Shyam K. Upadhyaya, *Maoists' Strikes on Hydropower Plants: Any Policy Lessons?* Equitable Hydro Working Paper 3 (Kathmandu: Winrock, November 2003).

⁵⁵ Field notes, November 2002.

⁵⁶ It is significant that Maoist leaders steadfastly maintain no inspiration from (or knowledge of) the Khmer Rouge case. It is ironic, then, as per Bhattarai to Tiwari, to read a claim such as: "There is no independent and authentic account of events in Cambodia under the Khmer Rouge available so far. Whatever is emanating from the Western media appears to be highly exaggerated to us." Such, of course, is an untenable position that ranks with "Holocaust Denial" but is representative of many *ad hoc* CPN(M) pronouncements.

⁵⁷ See Marks, "Urban Insurgency," *Small Wars and Insurgencies* (London), 14.3 (Autumn 2003), 100–61.

⁵⁸ By the declaration of the ceasefire in late January 2003, an apparent twenty-one assassinations had been carried out in the Kathmandu Valley, to include two Nepalese security personnel employed by the US Embassy. The goal of united front activity, as per Bhatarrai to Tiwari, is transparent: "In the current triangular balance of forces –namely [between] the monarchists, parliamentary democrats and revolutionary democrats—if the latter two democratic forces are able to mount a joint struggle against the feudal aristocratic forces, there are strong chances that democracy will be consummated in the country in the near future."

⁵⁹ In a move that increased the vacuum of authority in rural areas, the authorities systematically confiscated weapons, most for hunting, from the populace. Examination of security force statistics citing "weapons captured" reveals a predominance of "musket guns." Best

evidence indicates these are weapons confiscated from civilians and not pieces actually captured from guerrillas. For a discussion of local forces, see Marks, "At the Frontlines of the GWOT: Colombia Success Builds Upon Local Foundation," *The Journal of Counterterrorism and Homeland Security International*, 10.2 (Summer 2004), 42–50.

[60] Field notes, November 2002. The force was rapidly expanding and slated for an ultimate strength of 25,000.

[61] In contrast, a total of 850 civilians were listed as having been killed since the declaration of people's war on 13 February 1996. Nearly 5,000 more had been mutilated.

[62] Data that follow as well as map from field notes, April–May 2003.

[63] Field notes, April–May 2003: Local records could not provide total police strength in the years under discussion, but it clearly was but in the hundreds. Even today, there are but 300 police personnel assigned to the district.

[64] In Rolpa, the VDC heads numbered 51, affiliated with the major parties as follows: UML, 23; NC, 18; RPP [the successors to the conservative backers of the old *panchayet* regime), 8; and Independent, 2. Field notes, April–May 2003.

[65] In one village studied, there were but three cadre, well known to villagers. They were normally referred to as the Opportunist, the Criminal, and the Young Lenin. The first was a former Nepali Congress (NC) member who, following his own kidnap and ransom, had become a Maoist, apparently to safeguard the family property. Other members of his family, having moved to the *tarai*, remained prominent NC politicians. The second had spent ten months in jail for his previous Maoist activities and had been released under the terms of the ceasefire. He was the most dangerous of the lot and was eager for "payback." The third was a high school student who had effected Leninist dress and seemed a true believer. Yet he attended classes faithfully and, according to his instructors, caused no difficulties. Field notes, April–May 2003.

[66] The Opportunist discussed above, for instance, had seven months prior to my arrival accused the village postman of being a spy and had summoned a section (i.e., squad) of guerrillas who had taken the man away, bound. He has disappeared, despite the efforts of his family (a wife and four children) to locate him. Likewise, the Criminal worked closely with guerrillas in the area and regularly threatened villagers, at one point telling a teacher that but for the ceasefire, he was dead. Finally, the Young Lenin, despite all his admirable characteristics, and probably precisely because of his clean-cut, wholesome appearance, had apparently been tapped to make regular trips to Kathmandu to work with surveillance teams preparing targets for the urban terror campaign. *Ibid.*

[67] Census figures (projections) put the 2001 population of Dolakha at 204,229, of whom a plurality were Chhetri, 58,183, or 28.5%. Another 18,791 (9.2%) were Hill Brahmins; 27,619 (13.5%) were Tamang; and just 3,392 (1.7%) were Magars. Yet guerrilla units in the area

were visibly dominated by the latter and drew support from Magar communities.

[68] All communications observed, whether between cadre and guerrillas, or within and between guerrilla units, were by hard copy message although later reports have indicated this changed as technological fixes began to enter the hills due to greater resources available to the movement. Field notes, April–May 2003.

[69] Field notes, April–May 2003. It is noteworthy that efforts to draw guerrillas into discussions concerning their relationship to terror actions invariably led to responses such as: "Lower level party cadres are involved in such actions, not the battalions. We just fight." This could well have been true, since it was neither possible to establish affiliation of guerrillas observed engaging in enforcement activities during field work in Rolpa, nor to determine the extent of independent guerrilla formations outside the battalion structure. It was noted that half-sections and sections from battalions were constantly moving through the hills, and this accords with villager descriptions of such-sized units carrying out terror actions. After my field work, the number of battalions increased dramatically, though strength figures varied.

[70] Captured weapons predominated, with the most common high-powered firearm being the .303 Lee Enfield taken from the police. SLR's taken from the RNA were uncommon enough to be relegated to leadership figures, such as Section Leaders. Efforts to tap the extensive arms black market in South Asia met with some success. There was evidence of attempts to look further afield, though. One intercepted shipment of high-powered firearms was coming from Burma. There have been reports of corrupt Chinese officials also providing surplus weapons for a price. *Ibid.*

[71] Field notes, June 2004.

[72] The dimensions of this phenomenon are difficult to assess. INSEC's *Human Rights Yearbook 2003* (pg. vii) listed 17,564 displaced persons for 2002, a modest figure that would seem too low. As CDO [Chief District Officer] Rolpa, Tejprasad Paudel, noted, when commenting on the high number of passports his office had been issuing daily: "And you do not even need a passport to go to India. Lots of people have been leaving." My own observation in western Rolpa counted roughly 20% of the houses abandoned in village centers. These appeared to be the residences of local gentry. Field notes, April–May 2003.

[73] Field notes, November 2002. Precise figure at the time was given as 54,245. This later increased substantially.

[74] Taking the figures detailed so far, the Maoists had at this point killed at least 2,187 individuals; 50% (1,093) were police, another 11.1% (244) RNA, and the remaining 38.9% (850) civilians.

[75] British figures for only the period 23 November 2001 to 23 October 2002 cite the following losses: police, 456 dead, 358 wounded; RNA, 208 dead, 189 wounded; civilians

Back to the Future: The Insurgency of the Communist Party of Nepal (Maoist)

attacked by Maoists, 304 dead, 191 wounded; and presumed subversives, 4,434 dead, "heavy" wounded. This total of 5,402, if compared to an 8,000 total (an estimate, to be sure), yields 67.5%. Field notes, November 2002.

[76] Now dated but still useful is Bishwa Keshar Maskay and Dev Raj Dahal, eds., *Nepal's Participation in the United Nations Peace Keeping Operations* (Kathmandu: United Nations Association of Nepal, 1995).

[77] Field notes, November 2001.

[78] See especially Sukumar Basu, "The Role of Intelligence in Conducting a Counter-insurgency Campaign Against the Maoist Rebels in Nepal," unpublished paper. My own research found the police consistently to be best informed as to local realities. Indeed, the intelligence center set up in 2002 as a section of operations in police headquarters, Kathmandu, was as close to that required in counter-insurgency as existed in Nepal. Field notes, November 2002.

[79] The concept of an All Source Intelligence Center (ASIC) at the lowest possible tactical levels, a staple of Western (especially US and British) security force procedures, did not enter the Nepalese organizational architecture, this despite extensive efforts by, in particular, the British. Field notes, April–May 2003.

[80] Until early 2003, the Civil Police had primacy in the defense of the Kathmandu Valley. This then passed to the RNA Valley Division command. Other urban areas, though, remained principally a police responsibility, at least at the cutting edge.

[81] This was in contrast to Nepalese performance, both of individuals and units, in Gurkha and United Nations service (though some, in private correspondence, have disputed this characterization, claiming Nepalese martial conduct to be invariably lackluster). What is crucial, of course, is that these experiences occur outside the Nepali cultural matrix as given tangible form in societal structure.

[82] Tiwari.

[83] Background and discussion in SAP-Nepal [South Asia Partnership], *Quest for Peace*, 2nd edn. (Kathmandu, 2003).

[84] The CPN(M) draws heavily on Lenin's work in its calculations, an orientation reflected at this time in what appeared to be a conscious effort by senior party members to imitate Lenin's mode of dress (in contrast to earlier efforts to imitate Chinese or Khmer Rouge models). This mode stood in sharp contrast to more traditional Nepalese forms, especially the Maoist use of the worker's cap instead of the ubiquitous *topi*.

[85] Readily available. See, for example, "75 Points of the Maoists," *New Business Age* (Kathmandu), May 2003, 28–33.

[86] Bhattarai to Tiwari is instructive in this regard: "Our party, our party Chairman Prachanda and our various publications have time and again stressed that our immediate political

350

agenda is to consummate a democratic republic in the country. Please note that we are not pressing for a 'communist republic' but a bourgeois democratic republic. For what we have advanced the immediate slogans of a round-table conference of all the political forces, an interim government and elections to a constituent assembly, which have been increasingly endorsed by an overwhelming majority of the population. As the constituent assembly is the highest manifestation of bourgeois democracy in history, we fail to understand why anybody claiming to be a democrat would shy away from this."

[87] Particularly useful, amidst the myriad works devoted to the Ulster conflict and the IRA/PIRA, is Richard English, *Armed Struggle: A History of the IRA* (London: Macmillan, 2003). His discussion focuses on insurgent intentions and calculations in the struggle.

[88] For a fascinating work dealing with CPN(M) efforts to expropriate cultural idioms to validate its own legitimacy, see Maric Lecomte-Tilouine, "Regicide and Maoist Revolutionary Warfare in Nepal: Modern Incarnations of a Warrior Kingdom," *Anthropology Today*, 20.1 (February 2004), 13–19.

[89] I base this formulation on discussions with Maoist leadership figures during field work, April–May 2003, especially an interview with the second figure in the hierarchy, Baburam Bhattarai, 13 May 2003.

[90] Interview with Baburam Bhattarai.

[91] Baburam Bhattarai, *The Nature of Underdevelopment and Regional Structure of Nepal: A Marxist Analysis* (Delhi: Adroit Publishers, 2003).

[92] Field notes, April–May 2003.

[93] A telling illustration is provided by the pantheon given pride of place at Maoist functions: Marx, Engels, Lenin, Stalin, Mao, and Prachanda. That the public veneration of (at least) several mass murderers might be taken as chilling testimony of a new "Kampuchea" in the making is simply not understood by the Maoist hierarchy. The legal Nepali left, it may be noted, suffers from the same myopia.

[94] It should be further noted here that the representatives of the CPN(M) who were present in Kathmandu for negotiations were among the most worldly and well-educated in the Party. This lead to questions as to both the scope of their authority and the degree to which their positions accurately reflected those of the entire leadership. Though CPN(M) decision making is apparently a collective enterprise, Prachanda dominates through majority support in the Politburo. His views especially concerning the extent to which compromise may be exercised in the present negotiations are unknown despite the claim by Bhattarai that he and his peers are but a reflection of the party will.

[95] Just how intense the struggle had become was indicated in the rapidly escalating casualty figures amongst the security forces. From 27 August to 17 December 2002, the army (RNA) suffered 82 more dead and 127 wounded; the police (CP), 105 dead and 157 wounded; and

the armed police (APF), 171 dead and 205 wounded. Field notes, January 2004.

[96] Field notes, January–February 2004. The term "the foreigners who would be gods" was freely used in RNA circles to describe those who advanced critique but no solutions to issues of local security beyond vague conceptions of "confidence building steps" within a strategic approach of "conflict resolution." The ideological basis for such position was of little use to Nepali villagers, but some within the donor groups concerned claimed that the RNA was the greatest foe and that "their Nepalis" (i.e., those connected relevant donor-funded aid projects) were able to cut deals with the Maoists that safeguarded their lives and property.

[97] The role of donor security officers unintentionally contributed to the Maoist campaign of terror by validating Nepali fears. Concerned to stay one step ahead of threats, they disseminated (prior to 1 February 2005) schedules of CPN(M) armed strikes (*bandhas*) and issued warnings to their people. These, in turn, were picked up by Nepalis, especially the press, who used them as proof that such strikes indeed had been declared or that threats were real. In fact, declared or not, the Maoist armed strikes were invariably so weak in an objective sense that they could have been easily brushed aside had it not been for the pervasive atmosphere of fear created with foreign assistance.

[98] For details, see Timothy C. Brown, *The Real Contra War: Highlander Peasant Resistance in Nicaragua* (Norman: University of Oklahoma, 2001).

[99] Refer again to English, *Armed Struggle: A History of the IRA*.

Chapter 8

Conclusions:
Insurgency in a Time of Terrorism

And so we return to the query posed several hundred pages earlier: Of what relevance is the study of the people's war approach today, in the post-Cold War world beyond Nepal, particularly one dominated by violent Islamist upheaval? Of central importance. For Mao's methodology has continued to be used throughout the globe, both operationally and as analytical tool, whatever the ideological particulars at issue.

It is the latter that is perhaps of most interest. People's war components—mass line, united front, violent action, nonviolent action (political warfare), and international action—are the essential elements of any insurgency. Particular circumstances will call forth differing combinations, appropriate to the battle at hand, but none of the elements can be ignored. This is true even if a movement does not consciously follow the template or ignores it altogether.

Insurgencies are, after all, of a piece. They are armed political movements that seek ends by the employment of ways and means. To focus solely upon their stated ideologies is to miss the forest for the trees. Even those not explicitly political (e.g., those that claim to be religious) must in the end aim for the seizure of political power, in some shape or form, in order to implement whatever social or economic changes are demanded. Seizure of power requires an approach.

People's war, as a form that has migrated through insurgent Promised Land, therefore, is not dependent upon Marxist-Leninism. Cold War insurgencies, in any case, never were strictly ideological. Even the *most* ideological of them, such as that of *Sendero Luminoso* in Peru, with an elite leadership for which Maoism offered a blueprint for a new, more just world, still had to recruit followers by mobilizing those alienated from the system, followers for whom ideology meant little or nothing but for whom grievances were central. This meant working among the marginalized Indian populations for nearly two decades.

Likewise, even the apparently *least* ideological of insurgencies, such as that of the Tamils in Sri Lanka, had to have an explanation for the cause of alienation. This explanation was provided by Marxist-Leninism, an ideology openly espoused at one point by all major Tamil insurgent groups. Operational particulars were derived from careful study of people's war and other methodologies of insurgencies worldwide. Obviously driven at the grievance level by concerns for ethnic justice, these *Eelam* groups, at the conceptual level, required explanations for both situation and solution. In the end, their strategy was, in all its particulars, perhaps more faithful to people's war than that of the overtly Maoist JVP.

Are we to argue, then, as I stated initially would not be done, that all successful movements are actually people's war? Not at all; rather we must recognize that any insurgency must perform certain functions, but the manner in which they actually do these functions will be particular to time and place. Use of violence as a tool for mobilization, for instance, has always gone on. Excessive use of terror is a mistake often made by insurgents. Yet mistake or conscious design, such use does not mean something "new" has appeared. Too much emphasis has been placed on what remains an insurgent tactic that has incorrectly—or correctly, if it succeeds!—been elevated to strategy. It certainly does not mean insurgency itself has been transformed[1] or that warfare has entered a new generation.[2]

How to conceptualize these groups that appear consciously to reject any element of the people's war approach save violence? A word of caution. What a group appears to be in its formative stages, when its numbers are few, its weapons few, is not necessarily indicative of its nature or its plans. LTTE certainly appeared to be "just a band of terrorists" early on but had plans for a counter-state. Likewise, the fire can be missed when concentrating on the smoke. To think that suicide bombers (or violence in general) is all there is to Hamas and Hizbu'llah is to miss the essence of those insurgencies.[3]

Let us conclude, then, with an exercise of sorts. Let us concede that the world has changed a great deal, to the extent we have: "pure people's war" being waged in the likes of Nepal and India; a perverted form of people's war being waged in, for instance, Colombia; and "something else" being waged in other areas such as Iraq, Afghanistan, and Jammu & Kashmir (India). How can we tie these together in such manner as to highlight the continued relevance of people's war, as well as its position within a larger matrix of what we shall call "insurgency in a time of terrorism"?

Insurgency is Armed Politics

An insurgency, Mao would argue, is an armed political movement aimed at the overthrow of a constituted government, or separation from it, through use of subversion and armed conflict. It is a protracted politico-military struggle designed to weaken government control and legitimacy while increasing insurgent control. Political power is the central issue in an insurgency.[4]

To overthrow the existing social order and reallocate power within China required that the CCP mobilize human and materiel resources in order to form its alternative to the state. This alternative was the communist counter-state. Mao's desire to form a counter-state grew from the same causes that galvanize any political campaign. These causes ranged from the desire for greater equity in the distribution of resources to a demand that foreign domination end. China had them all.

Naturally enough, a counter-state was useless without a population. A fundamental people's war goal, therefore, was to capture the support of the populace, to mobilize rather than compel them to side with the new order. Violence was always a central element in the insurgency, but successful mobilization provided active and passive support for the insurgency's programs, operations, and goals. This played itself out thus:

- At the strategic level of war, mobilization grew out of dissatisfaction by some elite members (e.g., "Mao the school teacher") with existing economic, social, or political conditions.
- At the operational level of war, these marginalized elite members built links with followers by bringing them into the counter-state.
- At the tactical level of war, the recruitment was done by local movement representatives, the cadre, who addressed local grievances.

Signally, the local solutions were credited by the cadre to the insurgent movement. Loyalty was normally won through deeds rather than appeal to abstract principles, though the accomplishment of deeds was explained through slogans (e.g., end hunger, eliminate poverty). The support of the people—*legitimacy*—was for Mao the center of gravity.[5] Support had to be gained in whatever proportion was necessary to sustain the insurgent movement.

As in any political campaign, all levels of support were relative. The goal was mobilization such that the enemy could be defeated. This necessarily depended as much upon the campaign approach (i.e. operational art) and tactics adopted as upon more strategic concerns of "support."

Insurgent Doctrine

Insurgent doctrine is critical in determining how the insurgents will actually implement their effort.[6] Mao could have chosen an alternative approach, for there are actually two basic options:

- A first approach, which we see Mao choose, is to emphasize mobilization of the masses. This course places a premium upon political action by the cadre in local areas, with strategic and operational directives coming from above. Cadre will be the central component of the movement.
- A second approach emphasizes armed action. This course favors violence rather than mass mobilization, with the combatants themselves the bulk of the movement. Cadre play a much more limited role than in the mass mobilization approach (and may be completely absent, especially in the early stages of movement action).

The first approach will be sustained by a mass base. The second approach will have only a much smaller support base. The support base will not have the numbers of the mass base generated by the mobilization approach.

Mass Mobilization Approach

A mature insurgent organization of the first approach, built upon mass mobilization such as found in the people's war model of the Chinese and Vietnamese, normally consists of four elements: the leadership; the combatants (often deployed, whatever the terminology, as main forces, regional forces, local forces); the cadre (often called, "the militants"); and the mass base (the bulk of the membership). The proportions relative to the larger movement depend upon the strategic approach adopted by the insurgency.

To the extent state presence has been eliminated in particular areas, the four elements can exist openly. To the extent the state remains a continuous or occasional presence, the elements must maintain a clandestine existence.

If we examine each of the elements, we find:

- Leadership figures engage in command and control of the insurgent movement. They are the idea men and the planners. They see solution to the grievances of society in structural terms. Only altering the way the institutions and practices of society fit together will result in real change. Reforms and changes in personalities are deemed insufficient to "liberate" or "redeem" society.

- The combatants do the actual fighting and are often mistaken for the movement itself. This they are not. They exist only to carry out the same functions as the police and armed forces of the state. The combatants maintain local control, as well as protect and expand the counter-state. Combatants who secure local areas are the local forces. Combatants who link local areas and provide regional security are the regional forces. Both of these elements normally are tied to specific areas. Main forces, in contrast, are the "heavy" units of the insurgent movement and may be deployed in any area. Rather than engaging in terror and guerrilla warfare (as are the main activities of local and regional forces), they engage in mobile warfare and war of position, both subsumed under the "conventional warfare" rubric but different in emphasis when used by insurgents.

- The cadre are the political activists of the insurgency. This does not mean they are unarmed but that they are concerned first and foremost with mass mobilization activities. They are called militants since they are actively engaged in struggling to accomplish insurgent goals. Following guidance and procedures provided by the insurgent movement, the cadre assess the grievances in local areas and carry out activities that satisfy those grievances. They then attribute the solutions they have provided to the insurgent movement itself. Deeds are the key to making insurgent slogans meaningful to the population. Larger societal issues, such as foreign presence, facilitate such action, because these larger issues may be blamed for life's smaller problems.

- The mass base consists of the followers of the insurgent movement, the population of the counter-state. Mass base members are recruited and indoctrinated by the cadre. Mass base members may continue in their normal positions in society, but many will lead either second, clandestine lives for the insurgent movement, or even pursue new, fulltime positions within the insurgency (e.g. combatants normally begin as members of the mass base before becoming armed manpower).

What results, as in any armed conflict, is a contest of resource mobilization and force deployment. In the mass mobilization approach, the combatants exist to facilitate the accomplishment of the political goals of the insurgent movement as defined by the leadership.

In local areas, terror (i.e., terrorism as a *method of action*) and guerrilla warfare are used to eliminate resistance, either from individuals who are opposed to the movement or from the local armed representatives of the state, normally the police. Main force units, which are guerrilla units that have been "regularized," turned into rough copies of government units, are used to deal with the inevitable deployment of the military by the state.

The purpose of main forces is to engage in mobile (or maneuver) warfare. The intent is force-on-force action, to destroy government main force units. This allows the insurgents to secure and expand their counter-state (which may be clandestine in all or parts). The intent of mobile warfare, however, is not to seize and hold position as in conventional warfare. This occurs only in "war of position."

- Classic mobile warfare was that fought by the North Vietnamese Army (NVA) and Viet Cong (VC) against the United States in the 1965–73 period. US forces frequently faced battalions and regiments (i.e. brigades), even as terror and guerrilla action continued.
- Classic war of position was seen in the Vietnam War three times: the Tet Offensive that occurred in January–February 1968; the Spring 1972 "Easter Offensive," which resulted in the permanent alienation of portions of South Vietnamese territory; and the Spring 1975 offensive, which saw the fall of South Vietnam and its absorption into the larger unified Vietnam. In all of these battles, enemy divisions and even corps were utilized, with terror and guerrilla action assuming the role of special operations in support of operations.
- More recently, in El Salvador, where the US successfully supported the counter-insurgency, government forces twice, 1981 and 1989, had to beat back "war of position" offensives designed to seize widespread areas, including portions of the nation's capital. In Nepal, as discussed in Chapter 7, widespread use of terror and guerrilla action has been complemented by mobile warfare to overrun government positions up to company strength. Mobile warfare targets were chosen operationally (i.e., as part of campaign planning) to position the CPN(M) for anticipated "war of position" offensives, notably against major population centers.

Armed Action Approach

Significantly, if emphasis is upon the second approach, armed action, the political goal is to be accomplished primarily by violence rather than mass mobilization. This Mao claims emphatically is a mistake, by which he means (without using the terms) that it is all too easy for unbridled terror to degenerate from method to *logic of action*. The insurgent loses sight of his real target, the support of the population. Instead, he attempts to inflict such a level of casualties and destruction that the counter-insurgent is incapable or unwilling to continue (and his foreign supporters unwilling to stay the course).

In this approach, the combatant force rarely moves beyond terror and guerrilla warfare, with units small and more specialized, frequently no more than squad or platoon strength. Sympathizers provide recruits for the support base but are generally involved actively only occasionally, though they are often central to the information warfare component of the insurgent campaign.

- Illustration of this approach was "The Troubles," 1968–98, in Northern Ireland (Ulster), only mentioned in the text. An initial mass mobilization approach followed by the Provisional Irish Republican Army (PIRA) allowed state penetration and hence was abandoned in favor of a cellular "Active Service Unit" (ASU) methodology. At normally no more than 300-man strength, the ASU network engaged almost exclusively in terroristic actions and was sustained by a support base that numbered but in the thousands, of a total 1.5 million population in an area the size of Connecticut. Sympathizers came overwhelmingly from a minority within the Catholic community, thus from a minority within a minority. At its peak, however, this sympathetic base proved capable of mustering 17% of the votes in democratic elections and served to keep open to question the legitimacy of British rule, which was actually favored by a substantial majority. That terrorism remained throughout a *method of action* as opposed to a *logic of action* is precisely the reason why most sources, whatever popular and official "terrorists" terminology, maintained that PIRA was analytically best assessed as an insurgency. Certainly it was counter-insurgency that was the British response, with counter-terrorism as a significant sub-campaign.[7]
- More recently, this approach has been used by the insurgents in Iraq and Afghanistan.[8] Terrorism (as a *method of action*) and low-level guerrilla warfare have been focused upon indigenous supporters and infrastructure

of the new regimes in Baghdad and Kabul. Simultaneously, attacks upon US forces have sought to inflict casualties to break the will of the US public to continue. It is recognized by the insurgents that the indigenous regimes can not continue in the short-term without US backing and assistance. Neither, as the US begins to withdraw, will the new regimes be able to continue if their populations can be suitably terrorized into sullen neutrality.[9]

Mao did not consider this approach to be viable. Communist insurgents doctrinally rejected terror as anything save an adjunct to the more fundamental organizational effort. This was their basic disagreement with the anarchists in the earlier age of terrorism that swept Europe and especially Russia during the late 19th and early 20th Centuries.[10] Later, there were significant exceptions, and, with the benefit of hindsight, a clear line is visible from the atrocities of the Khmer Rouge to those of *Sendero Luminoso* to those of the Nepalese Maoists. They were made increasingly possible by consigning the opposition to the category of "other," hence expendable. This shift, now commonplace enough, especially when we examine the various campaigns of the Islamist extremists (and perhaps others), was one the Maoists accomplished rhetorically (e.g., a category, the *bourgeoisie*, labeled *enemy*) and in their mechanisms of state terror but did not incorporate into people's war as tactic, operational art, or strategy. In contrast, many movements of our *Armed Action Approach* did this.

Protracted War

The two approaches are different in another way, their manner of unfolding. Insurgencies following the mass mobilization approach will pass through common phases of development. Not all insurgencies experience every phase, and progression through all phases is not a requirement for success. The same insurgent movement may be in another phase in other regions of a country. Successful insurgencies can also revert to an earlier phase when under pressure, resuming development when favorable conditions return.

Be all this as it may, the normal progression will be that envisaged by Mao. It states that insurgents are first strategically on the defensive (Phase I), move to stalemate (Phase II), and finally go over to the offensive (Phase III). Strategic movement from one phase to another incorporates the operational and tactical activity typical of earlier phases. It does not end them. The Vietnamese explicitly recognize this reality in their "war of interlocking" doctrine, which holds that "all forms of warfare" occur simultaneously, even as a particular form is paramount ("is the driver" might be the current terminology).

Political organization occurs throughout. While on the defensive, however, in Phase I, a movement will necessarily fight the "war of the weak," emphasizing terrorism (as a *method of action*) and guerrilla warfare. It is through main force action that stalemate, Phase II, is achieved. This allows Phase III, "war of position," to unfold.

The terminology is drawn from Western, especially Soviet, usage. Nevertheless, US sources in particular insist upon conceptualizing the process as "organization, guerrilla, conventional warfare," which misrepresents what occurs. Except as illustrated by tactical exceptions, insurgent organization does not occur without violence, certainly not at the operational or strategic levels. Insurgency is by definition an armed political movement.

This is all the more visible if the insurgents adopt the second approach, a strategy of armed action. In this case, the phases just discussed do not necessarily apply. Emphasizing the combatants envisages "level of pain" as the "driver" throughout the insurgency. There will be no need to form main force units. In this approach, campaigns (operational art) dictate tactical action, with an active support base used to make armed action possible.

It could be argued that there is a third approach, what has been called "economic insurgency." Therein, the insurgents neither mobilize nor terrorize so much as they plunder. Calling such individuals "insurgents" is an unfortunate misuse of the term. In fact, there has been a decided tendency since "9-11" to lump all internal war phenomena into the category "insurgency." This should not be.

Certainly, throughout history, there has been no shortage of insurgencies that have degenerated to criminality, particularly as the "movements proper" have disintegrated, and elements have been cast adrift. From the state's perspective, this has normally been held that such disintegration is desirable, because it takes what is truly dangerous, an ideologically inspired body of disaffiliated individuals motivated by ideology, and replaces it with what is less dangerous, a more diverse body normally of very uneven character. The former is a security threat; the latter a law-and-order concern. Still, this should not be interpreted as denigrating armed capacity of a law-and-order threat, as the various movements in the Gold Coast area of Africa would appear to illustrate.[11]

The African groups appear to raise another issue: Criminal "warlordism," while it may exist in a strategic posture of estrangement from the state—which some have labeled "insurgent"—should not be confused with actual insurgency. Were we to make such an analytical leap, we would be conducting "insurgent studies" on alienated, disaffiliated impoverished areas the likes of East Los Angeles or Rio de Janero. What has long been discussed is the capacity of such areas for mobilization by insurgent actors, much as Afghanistan was appropriated by Taliban and then used as a platform of operations by Al Qaeda. In the event, it has proved exceptionally difficult for insurgents to establish presence in such areas worldwide where they remain integrated into the larger state, precisely because of the barriers stand-alone criminal activity throws up to ideological mobilization.

Most insurgent movements have at one time or another, particularly in their early phases, established relationships with criminal elements (e.g., Mao in the 1920s). Ideologically sound movements regularly move against elements that seek to exploit criminal activity for personal as opposed to movement gain. Ascendance of criminality creates an altogether different level of concern and would seem to dictate stability operations (as presently conceptualized) rather than counter-insurgency. Reduced to bare bones, stability operations and counter-insurgency have much in common, but the latter certainly must place greater effort upon the classic "hearts and minds" activity that serves to divide insurgent leadership from manpower. It is precisely the ideological inspiration of insurgent leadership that separates insurgency from traditional rebellion and resistance.

Counter-insurgency Approach

Does the fact that so many insurgencies are at this moment using the armed action approach influence response? Yes, certainly, for the simplest of reasons. Intelligence being the imperfect art and science that it is, there is no way around the need, beyond all else, for eyes and ears on the ground. If the insurgents are truly prepared to die to the last man (and woman), the counter-insurgent is looking at extraordinary commitments of manpower needed to dominate the ground. No objective force level guarantees victory for either side. It is frequently stated that a 10:1 or 20:1 ratio of counter-insurgents to insurgents is necessary for counter-insurgency victory. In reality, no firm ratios exist. As in conventional war, in insurgency all correlations of forces depend upon the situation. Of necessity, however, commitment by the state is bound to be manpower intensive.

This commitment of manpower in a strategic campaign of counter-insurgency should not be confused with *counter-terrorism*, whatever present security realities. *Counter-insurgency* is the neutralization by the state of the insurgency (with one component terrorism as a *method of action*) and its effort to form a counter-state. As the most potent insurgent doctrine yet, people's war has been the opponent against which counter-insurgent doctrine has been put to the ultimate test. It has succeeded as often as it has failed.

Counter-insurgency is so difficult, however, because it contains an inherent contradiction. It is imperfections of the existing system that feed the insurgency. Simply returning to the status quo is not an option. Reform is necessary, but reform is a matter for the state, utilizing all of its human and material resources. Security forces are only one such resource. The response must be multifaceted and coordinated, yet states typically charge their security forces with "waging counter-insurgency." This, they can not do alone.

To the contrary, *the state* first decides upon its goal (restoration of legitimate government writ), then produces *a plan* to accomplish that end. *All elements of national power* are assigned their roles in carrying out the plan. The *legal framework* is put in place to enable plan implementation, and *command and control (C2) arrangements* are established.

- The legal framework normally includes a series of extraordinary measures as are associated with emergency situations or even martial law. It frequently will expand military powers into areas delegated solely to the police in "normal times."
- Historically, effective C2 architecture has involved setting up local coordinating bodies with representation from all key parties. These run the counter-insurgency campaign in the area concerned, though one individual will have the lead. Minimally, such a coordinating body includes appropriate representatives from civil authority, the military, the police, the intelligence services, and (though not always) the civil population. The most effective use of coordinating bodies has given permanent-party individuals (e.g. a district officer) responsibility for counter-insurgency C2 in their areas and given them control over any assets, whether civil or military, sent into their areas. Reinforcing intelligence bodies, in particular, have been assigned as permanent party.

All operational and tactical elements of the multifaceted approach support the accomplishment of the strategic goal. Individual campaigns, such as attacking insurgent financing, must be coordinated and weighted as appropriate to the circumstances. There is inherent danger in mistaking an operational center of gravity (e.g., insurgent generation of funding) for the strategic center of gravity (i.e., legitimacy).

Security forces, sent into an area to engage in counter-insurgency, perform as follows:

- Strategically, they serve as the shield for carrying out reform.
- Operationally, they systematically restore government control.
- Tactically, they eliminate (through either death or capture) insurgent leadership, combatants, and cadre so that that local populations (who also provide the insurgent mass base) are secure and able to engage in normal activities.

The counter-insurgency plan will secure the critical infrastructure of the state and the government's centers of power. It will detail the scheme to reclaim what has been lost. Priority of effort and time-line are established. A key part of the scheme will be a sub-campaign against terrorism (as a *method of action*).

As a general principle, the government moves from strength to weakness, "holding" in areas of lesser priority while successively concentrating assets in priority areas.

For the security forces, the strategic counter to insurgent organization and operational patterns is to address the insurgent approach in a correct and sustainable fashion.

- A correct approach will balance elimination of grievances (i.e., reform) and security force action that eliminates the insurgents. The security forces provide the protection necessary for the restoration of government presence and control.
- A sustainable approach is defined by the state itself. It must be willing to bear the human and fiscal cost of the approach it seeks to implement.

With a correct and sustainable approach in place, the counter-insurgent "plays for the breaks," those shifts in the internal or external situation that work against the insurgent and favor the state. This normally involves an extended period of time, a "protracted war." This makes it difficult for democracies to sustain counter-insurgent campaigns, particularly in the present world-environment where there is little agreement upon strategic ends and means, much less operational and tactical concerns.[12]

What is fundamental, beyond all else, is to have a plan for approaching the threat. This naturally presupposes that both state and foreign benefactors will have carried out what Clausewitz called "the first of all strategic questions and the most comprehensive": "to establish . . . the kind of war on which they are embarking; neither mistaking it for, nor trying to turn it into, something that is alien to its nature."[13]

People's war, therefore, is here to stay. Though Asia has remained its heartland, we may expect yet another volume to be necessary. It will be more international in scope, with a mix of "the good, the bad, and the ugly" as concerns fealty to the approach. Its cases will seem hauntingly familiar.

Notes

[1] See Metz and Millen.

[2] This is the unfortunate position of a term such as "Fourth Generation Warfare" or "4GW," which has gained popularity since declaration of the "War on Terrorism." 4GW adherents claim there has been a fundamental shift in warfare, because its methods now target enemy will. See Thomas X. Hammes, *The Sling and the Stone: On War in the 21st Century* (St. Paul, Minnesota: Zenith Press, 2004), as well as the much shorter but informative Hammes, "Insurgency: Modern Warfare Evolves Into a Fourth Generation," *Strategic Forum*, 214 (January 2005), 1–8. To his credit, Hammes advances a more informed, nuanced argument than some proponents of 4GW, but in the end the miscue remains the same. For cogent critique, see Antulio J. Echevarria II, "The Problem With Fourth-Generation War," undated paper distributed by internet.

[3] See Shaul Mishal and Avraham Sela, *The Palestinian Hamas: Vision, Violence, and Coexistence* (New York: Columbia University Press, 2000), and Amal Saad-Ghorayeb, *Hizbu'llah: Politics and Religion* (Sterling, Virginia: Pluto Press, 2002).

[4] Definitions such as those discussed here are well within the mainstream of revolutionary studies, though they do not always mesh completely with official US government definitions. The essence of what is provided in this and following paragraphs, ironically, was included in my submission for Chapter 1, "Overview," in the U.S. Army's Interim Field Manual, FMI 3-07.22 *Counterinsurgency Operations* (October 2004). Necessarily, what was issued differed in many particulars from the draft. As per US military "rules of the game," the doctrine of subordinate organizations cannot contradict the published doctrine of superior organizations. This led to even the definition of insurgency being incomplete compared to that stated here. That such "rules" make reform or even accuracy not always possible hardly needs emphasis. Best single look at the doctrinal process with respect to insurgency is Wray

Conclusions: Insurgency in a Time of Terrorism

R. Johnson, *Vietnam and American Doctrine for Small Wars* (Bangkok: White Lotus, 2001). Equally well done, for the U.S. Marines, is Keith B. Bickel, *Mars Learning: The Marine Corps' Development of Small Wars Doctrine, 1915–1940* (Boulder, CO: Westview Press, 2001). Useful background to the material in both of these books is Andrew J. Birtle, *U.S. Army Counterinsurgency and Contingency Operations Doctrine 1860–1941* (Washington, DC: Center of Military History, U.S. Army, 1998).

   [5] American military sources, relying upon their own misinterpretation of Clausewitz, often assert that there can be but one center of gravity. This is not correct. Best discussion on the controversy (in general) is "Clauswitz and War: Two Perspectives on Center of Gravity," *Joint Force Quarterly*, No. 35 (undated); therein, Antulio J. Echevarria II, "Center of Gravity: Recommendations for Joint Doctrine," 10–17; Christopher Bassford, "Interpreting the Legacy of Clausewitz," 18–19; and Joseph L. Strange and Richard Iron, "Center of Gravity: What Clauswitz Really Meant," 20–27. Echevarria has dealt with the issue at length in his *Clausewitz's Center of Gravity: Changing Our Warfighting Doctrine—Again!* (Carlisle: Army War College, 2002).

   [6] Bard E. O'Neill, *Insurgency and Terrorism: Inside Modern Revolutionary Warfare* (Herndon, VA: Brassey's 1990), divides insurgency into seven "types"—anarchist, egalitarian, traditionalist, pluralist, secessionist, reformist, and preservationist—a division Cable, *op.cit.* (p. 229) usefully simplifies in observing: "While insurgency exists in two forms, offensive and defensive, with the distinction being drawn upon the basis of the overarching political goal, a radical restructuring of the social-political matrix in the case of the former or the assertion of autonomy by a distinct social, cultural linguistic group with respect to the latter, the process which produces the end result of armed conflict is the same."

   [7] See English, as well as J. Bowyer Bell, *The Secret Army: The IRA*, 3rd ed. (New Brunswick, NJ: Transaction, 1997).

   [8] No sources have emerged yet that can be cited as benchmark works for discussing these two counterinsurgencies. Useful for the Iraq case, in all save its opening remarks, is Richard Lowry, "We're Winning: How the U.S. Learned the Art of Counterinsurgency in Iraq," *National Review*, 9 May 2005, 29–37; for the Afghanistan case, Vance Serchuk and Tom Donnelly, "Nation Building, After All," *The Weekly Standard*, 11 April 2005, 20–29.

   [9] At first blush, this seems the approach of Che Guevara and his *foco* theory, but it is not. *Focismo*, while purporting to engage in mass mobilization through the example and reality of guerrilla action conducted by the revolutionary organization, indeed was a variant of the armed action approach. Without even an adequate support base (much less a mass base), the *foco* was inevitably decimated and Che executed in the 1967 Bolivia fiasco. That *focismo* was not "terrorism" stemmed from the conscious effort to avoid terror as a *logic of action*. In fact, unlike the insurgents in Iraq and Afghanistan, who have been quite indiscriminate

366

in their targeting, Che endeavored to avoid attacking civilians altogether. Such parsing of motive was lost on Che's victims, and so he was labeled a "terrorist."

[10] Three works in *Terrorism and Political Violence*, 16.1 (Spring 2004) are useful for establishing particulars of this era and for illuminating the philosophical differences that emerged between rival radical revolutionary approaches: Benjamin Grob-Fitzgibbon, "From Dagger to the Bomb: Karl Heinzen and the Evolution of Political Terror," 97–115; Richard Bach Jensen, "Daggers, Rifles and Dynamite: Anarchist Terrorism in Nineteenth Century Europe," 116–53; and Lindsay Clutterback, "The Progenitors of Terrorism: Russian Revolutionaries or Extreme Irish Republicans?", 154–81.

[11] See e.g. William Reno, "The Failure of Peacekeeping in Sierra Leone," *Current History* (May 2001), 219–25. Therein, Reno makes the challenging assertion, "Conflict in collapsed states is fundamentally different from wars between ideological rivals who mobilize mass followings and build 'liberated zones' to practice their ideas of governance." Useful as well is Stephen Ellis, *The Mask of Anarchy: The Destruction of Liberia and the Religious Dimension of an African Civil War* (New York: New York University Press, 1999).

[12] This formulation was outlined for me by the legendary Sir Robert Thompson shortly before his death. For transcript of interview, see Tom Marks, "The Counter-Revolutionary: Sir Robert Thompson—Grand Master of Unconventional Warfare," *Soldier of Fortune*, 14/10 (October 1989), 58-65/77-80. Thompson's seminal text remains as useful today as when it was written, regardless of the precise ideology adopted by the insurgents: *Defeating Communist Insurgency* (NY: Praeger, 1966).

[13] Carl von Clausewitz, *On War*, trans. Peter Paret (Princeton, NJ: Princeton University Press, 1976), 88–89.

Bibliography

Books

Adhikari, D. P. *The History of Nepalese Nationalism*. Kathmandu: Jeewan Printing Support Press, 1988.

Adloff, Richard. *The Left Wing in Southeast Asia*. New York: William Sloane Associates, 1950.

Alexander, Don W. *Rod of Iron: French Counterinsurgency Policy in Aragon During the Peninsular War*. Wilmington, Delaware: Scholarly Resources, 1985.

Alles, A. C. *Insurgency: 1971*. 3rd edn. Colombia: Mervyn Mendis, 1976.

Anderson, James. *Sendero Luminoso: A New Revolutionary Model?* London: Institute for the Study of Terrorism, 1987.

Andrews, William R. *The Village War: Vietnamese Communist Activities in Dinh Tuong Province, 1960–1964*. Columbia: University of Missouri Press, 1973.

Arquilla, John and David Ronfeldt, eds. *Networks and Netwards: The Future of Terror, Crime, and Militancy*. Santa Monica: RAND, 2001.

Auboyet, Jeannine et al. *Oriental Art: A Handbook of Styles and Forms*. Trans Elizabeth and Richard Bartlett. New York: International Publications, 1980.

Bahadur, Ganga, ed. *Promoting Participatory Democracy in Nepal: An Assessment of Local Self-Governance*. Kathmandu: Political Science Association of Nepal, 1998.

Balasingham, A. S. *Liberation Tigers and Tamil Eelam Freedom Struggle*. Madras: Political Committee (LTTE), 1983.

Banerjee, S. *India's Simmering Revolution: The Naxalite Uprising*. London: Zed Press, 1984.

Bibliography

Banskota, Purushottam. *The Gurkha Connection: A History of the Gurkha Recruitment in the British Army.* New Delhi: Nirala, 1994.

Barnett, A. Doak, ed. *Chinese Communist Politics in Action.* Seattle: University of Washington Press, 1969.

Bass, Paul R. and Marcus F. Franda, eds. *Radical Politics in South Asia.* Cambridge, Massachusetts: MIT Press, 1973.

Becker, Elizabeth. *When the War Was Over: Cambodia and the Khmer Rouge Revolution.* New York: Public Affairs, 1986.

Beer, Patrice de. *The Road to Victory: Documents from the Communist Party of Thailand.* Chicago: Liberator Press, 1978.

Bell, J. Bowyer. *The Secret Army: The IRA.* 3rd edn. New Brunswick, NJ: Transaction, 1997.

Bergerud, Eric M. *The Dynamics of Defeat: The Vietnam War in Hau Nghia Province.* Boulder, Colorado: Westview Press, 1991.

Bernier, Olivier. *Words of Fire, Deeds of Blood: The Mob, the Monarch, and the French Revolution.* New York: Anchor Books-Doubleday, 1989.

Bhaduri, Shankar and Afsir Karim. *The Sri Lankan Crisis.* New Delhi: Lancer International, 1990.

Bhattarai, Baburam. *The Nature of Underdevelopment and Regional Structure of Nepal: A Marxist Analysis.* Delhi: Adroit Publishers, 2003.

Bickel, Keith B. *Mars Learning: The Marine Corps' Development of Small Wars Doctrine, 1915–1940.* Boulder, CO: Westview Press, 2001.

Billington, James H. *Fire in the Minds of Men: Origins of the Revolutionary Faith.* New Brunswick, NJ: Transaction, 2004.

Birtle, Andrew J. *U.S. Army Counterinsurgency and Contingency Operations Doctrine 1860–1941.* Washington, DC: Center of Military History, U.S. Army, 1998.

Blanning, T. C. W., ed. *The Rise and Fall of the French Revolution.* Chicago: University of Chicago Press, 1996.

Bonachea, Roman L. and Marta San Martin. *The Cuban Insurrection, 1952–1959.* New Brunswick, New Jersey: Transaction, 1974.

Braun, Otto. *A Comintern Agent in China, 1932–1939.* St Lucia, Australia: Queensland University Press, 1982.

Brown, Timothy C. *The Real Contra War: Highlander Peasant Resistance in Nicaragua.* Norman: University of Oklahoma, 2001.

Butterfield, Henry. *The Fall of Che Guevara: A Story of Soldiers, Spies, and Diplomats.* New York: Oxford University Press, 1998.

Caplan, Lionel. *Land and Social Change in East Nepal.* 2d edn. Kathmandu: Himal Books, 2000.

Caplan, Lionel. *Warrior Gentlemen: "Gurkhas" in the Western Imagination*. Oxford: Berghahn Books, 1995.

Chandler, David P. *Brother Number One: A Political Biography of Pol Pot*. Boulder, Colorado: Westview Press, 1992.

Chandler, David D. *The Campaigns of Napoleon: The Mind and Method of History's Greatest Soldier*. New York: Scribner, 1966.

Chandler, David G. *On the Napoleonic Wars: Collected Essays*. London: Greenhill Books, 1994.

Chandler, David P. *Voices from S-21: Terror and History in Pol Pot's Secret Prison*. Berkeley: University of California Press, 1999.

Chandler, David P. Ben Kiernan, and Chanthou Boua. *Pol Pot Plans the Future: Confidential Leadership Documents From Democratic Kampuchea, 1976–1977*. Monograph Series 33/Yale Southeast Asia Studies. New Haven: Yale Center for International and Area Studies, 1988.

Chandraprema, C.A. *Sri Lanka: The Years of Terror—The JVP Insurrection 1987–1989*. Colombo: Lake House Bookshop, 1991.

Chapagain, Prem, et al. *New EKTA School Atlas*. 2nd edn. Kathmandu: EKTA Books, 2002.

Chapman, William. *Inside the Philippine Revolution: The New People's Army and its Struggle for Power*. New York: W.W. Norton, 1987.

Chatterjee, Partha. *The Present History of West Bengal: Essays in Political Criticism*. Delhi: Oxford University Press, 1997.

Chaube, Santwana Tewari. *Democratic Movement in Nepal and the Indian Left*. Delhi: Kalinga Publications, 2001.

Zhang Chengjun and Che Man, W. K. *Muslim Separatism: The Moros of Southern Philippines and the Malays of Southern Thailand*. Manila: Ateneo de Manila University Press, 1990.

Ch'i Hsi-sheng. *Nationalist China at War*. Ann Arbor: University of Michigan Press, 1982.

Chiang Siang-tseh. *The Nien Rebellion*. Seattle: University of Washington Press, 1954.

Crenshaw, Martha, ed. *Terrorism in Context*. University Park: Pennsylvania State University Press, 1995.

Creveld, Martin Van. *The Art of War: War and Military Thought*. London: Cassell, 2000.

Cross, J. P. *In Gurkha Company*. London: Arms and Armour, 1986.

Cross, J. P. *The Call of Nepal*. Series 2:Vol. 17. Kathmandu: Mandala Book Point, 1996, 1998.

Dallin, Alexander and George W. Breslauer. *Political Terror in Communist Systems*. Stanford, California: Stanford University Press, 1970.

De Silva, K. M. *A History of Sri Lanka*. London: C. Hurst, 1981

De Silva, K. M. ed. *Sri Lanka: A Survey*. Honolulu: University Press of Hawaii, 1977.

De Young, John. *Village Life in Modern Thailand*. Berkeley: University of California Press, 1955.

Della Porta, Donatella. *Social Movements, Political Violence, and the State*. Cambridge: Cambridge University Press, 1995.

Della Porta, Donatella and Herbert Reiter, eds. *Policing Protest: The Control of Mass Demonstrations in Western Democracies*. Minneapolis: University of Minnesota Press, 1998.

Dixit, J.N. ed. *External Affairs: Cross-Border Relations*. New Delhi: Roli Books, 2003.

Dosal, Paul J. *Commandante Che: Guerila Soildier, Commander, and Strategist, 1956–1967*. University Park: Pennsylvania State University Press, 2003.

Doughty, Robert A. et al. *American Military History and the Evolution of Warfare in the Western World*. Lexington, Massachusetts: D.C. Heath, 1996.

Doughty, Robert A. *The Evolution of US Army Tactical Doctrine, 1946–76*. Washington, DC: Center for Military History, 2001.

Duiker, William J. *Sacred War: Nationalism and Revolution in a Divided Vietnam*. Boston: McGraw-Hill, 1995.

Duyker, E. *Tribal Guerrillas: The Santals of West Bengal and the Naxalite Movement*. Delhi: Oxford University Press, 1987.

Eastman, Lloyd E. *Seeds of Destruction: Nationalist China in War and Revolution, 1937–1949*. Stanford, California: Stanford University Press, 1984.

Eastman, Lloyd E. *The Abortive Revolution: China under Nationalist Rule, 1927–1937*. Cambridge, Massachusetts: Harvard University Press, 1974.

Ebon, Martin. *Lin Piao: The Life and Writings of China's New Ruler*. New York: Stein and Day, 1970.

Eckstein, Susan, ed. *Power and Popular Protest: Latin American Social Movements*. Berkeley: University of California Press, 1989.

Ellis, Stephen. *The Mask of Anarchy: The Destruction of Liberia and the Religious Dimension of an African Civil War*. New York: New York University Press, 1999.

English, Richard. *Armed Struggle: A History of the IRA*. London: Macmillan, 2003.

Esherick, Joseph W. and Mary Backus Rankin, eds. *Chinese Local Elites and Patterns of Dominance*. Berkeley: University of California Press, 1990.

Fall, Bernard B. *Viet-Nam Witness, 1953–66*. New York: Praeger, 1966.

Fauriol, Georges. *Latin American Insurgencies*. Washington, DC: Georgetown University Center for Strategic and International Studies / National Defense University, 1985.

Finley, Milton. *The Most Monstrous of Wars: The Napoleonic Guerrilla War in Southern Italy, 1806–1811*. Columbia: University of South Carolina Press, 1994.

Fitzgerald, Frances. *Fire in the Lake*. Boston: Little, Brown, 1972.

Fitzpatrick, Sheila. *The Russian Revolution*. Revised edn. New York: Oxford University Press, 1994.

Johnson, Chalmers. *Peasant Nationalism and Communist Power in China*. Berkeley: University of California Press, 1962.

Fung, Edmund S. K. *The Military Dimension of the Chinese Revolution*. Vancouver: University of British Columbia Press, 1980.

Gat, Azar. *A History of Military Thought*. New York: Oxford University Press, 2001.

Gellner, David N. *Resistance and the State: Nepalese Experiences*. New Delhi: Social Science Press, 2003.

George, T. J. S. *Revolt in Mindanao: The Rise of Islam in Philippine Politics*. Kuala Lumpur: Oxford University Press, 1980.

Gilbert, Marc Jason, ed. *Why the North Won the Vietnam War*. New York: Palgrave, 2002.

Gorriti, Gustavo. *The Shining Path: A History of the Millenarian War in Peru*. Chapel Hill: University of North Carolina Press, 1999.

Gould, Tony. *Imperial Warriors: Britain and the Gurkhas*. London: Granta Books, 1999.

Gregson, Jonathan. *Massacre at the Palace: The Doomed Royal Dynasty of Nepal*. New York: Hyperion, 2002.

Grenier, Yvon. *The Emergence of Insurgency in El Salvador: Ideology and Political Will*. Pittsburgh: University of Pittsburgh Press, 1999.

Guevara, Che. *Guerrilla Warfare*. Lincoln: University of Nebraska Press, 1998.

Guevara, Che, Brian Loveman, and Thomas M. Davies. *Guerrilla Warfare*. 3rd edn. Wilmington, Delaware: Scholarly Resources, 1997.

Gunaratna, Rohan. *Indian Intervention in Sri Lanka: The Role of India's Intelligence Agencies*, 2nd edn. Colombo: South Asian Network on Conflict Research, 1994.

Gunaratna, Rohan. *Sri Lanka: A Lost Revolution? The Inside Story of the JVP*. Colombo: Institute of Fundamental Studies, 1990.

Gurung, Harka. *Nepal: Social Demography and Expressions*. Kathmandu: New Era, 2001.

Hagopian, Mark N. *Regimes, Movements, and Ideologies—A Comparative Introduction to Political Science*. New York: Longman, 1984.

Hagopian, Mark N. *The Phenomenon of Revolution*. New York: Dodd, Mead, 1974.

Halberstam, David. *The Best and the Brightest*. Greenwich, Connecticut: Fawcett Publications, 1972.

Harrison, James Pinkney. *The Long March to Power: A History of the Chinese Communist Party, 1921–72*. New York: Praeger, 1972.

Harrison, Richard W. *The Russian Way of War: Operational Art, 1904–1940.* Lawrence: University Press of Kansas, 2001.

Hart, B. H. Liddell. *Strategy: The Indirect Approach.* New York: Meridian Books, 1991.

Harvey, Neil. *The Chiapas Rebellion: The Struggle for Land and Democracy.* Durham, North Carolina: Duke University Press, 1998.

Headquarters. Department of the Army, *FMI 3-07.22 Counterinsurgency Operations* (Ft. Leavenworth, Kansas: US Army Combined Arms Center, October 2004).

Herrington, Stuart A. *Silence Was a Weapon: The Vietnam War in the Villages.* Novata, California: Presidio, 1982.

Hettiarachchy, Tilak. *The Sinhala Peasant in a Changing Society.* Colombo: Lake House, 1982.

Hoffman, Bruce. *Inside Terrorism.* New York: Columbia University Press, 1998.

Hoftun, Martin, William Raeper, and John Whelpton. *People, Politics, and Ideology: Democracy and Social Change in Nepal.* Kathamndu: Mandala Book Point, 1999.

Horton, Lynn. *Peasants in Arms: War and Peace in the Mountains of Nicaragua, 1979–1994.* Athens: Ohio University Center for International Studies, 1998.

Humble, Richard. *Napoleon's Peninsular Marshals.* New York: Taplinger, 1973.

Hutchcroft, Paul D. *The Philippines at the Crossroads: Sustaining Economic and Political Reform.* New York: Asia Society, 1996.

Hutt, Michael, ed. *Himalayan People's War: Nepal's Maoist Rebellion.* Bloomington: Indiana University Press, 2004.

Hutt, Michael. *Unbecoming Citizens: Culture, Nationhood, and the Flights of Refugees from Bhutan.* New Delhi: Oxford University Press, 2003.

Ingram, James C. *Economic Change in Thailand 1850–1970.* Revised edn. Stanford, California: Stanford University Press, 1971.

Jackson, Karl D., ed. *Cambodia 1975–1978: Rendezvous with Death.* Princeton, New Jersey: Princeton University Press, 1989.

Jacobs, Norman. *Modernization Without Development: Thailand as an Asian Case Study.* New York: Praeger Publishers, 1971.

Jiggins, Janice. *Caste and Family in the Politics of the Sinhalese, 1974–1976.* Colombo: K.V.G. de Silva, 1979.

Johnson, Chalmers. *Autopsy on People's War.* Berkeley: University of California Press, 1973.

Johnson, Wray R. *Vietnam and American Doctrine for Small Wars.* Bangkok: White Lotus, 2001.

Jones, Gregg R. *Red Revolution: Inside the Philippine Guerrilla Movement.* Boulder, Colorado: Westview Press, 1989.

Kadian, Rajesh. *India and its Army*. New Delhi: Vision Books, 1990.

Karki, Arjun and David Seddon, eds. *The People's War in Nepal: Left Perspectives*. Delhi: Adroit Publishers, 2003.

Kaufman, Howard K. *Bangkhuad*. Locust Valley, New York: J. J. Agustin, 1960.

Kerkvliet, Benedict J. and Resil Mojares, eds. *From Marcos to Aquino: Local Perspectives on Political Transition in the Philippines*. Quezon City: Ateneo de Manila University Press, 1991.

Kessler, Richard J. *Rebellion and Repression in the Philippines*. New Haven: Yale University Press, 1989.

Keyes, Charles F. *Isaan: Regionalism in Northeast Thailand*. Ithaca, New York: Cornell University Press, 1967.

Kiernan, Ben. *How Pol Pot Came to Power: A History of Communism in Kampuchea, 1930–1975*. London: Verso, 1985.

Kiernan, Ben. *The Pol Pot Regime: Race, Power, and Genocide in Cambodia under the Khmer Rouge, 1975–79*. New Haven: Yale University Press, 1996.

Klare, Michael T. *War without End*. New York: Vintage Books, 1972.

Knox, MacGregor and Williamson Murray, eds. *The Dynamics of Military Revolution 1300–2050*. New York: Cambridge University Press, 2001.

Kumar, Dhruba, ed. *Domestic Conflict and Crisis of Governability in Nepal*. Kathmandu: Centre for Nepal and Asian Studies (CNAS), Tribhuvan University, 2000.

Laqueur, Walter. *Guerrilla Warfare: A Historical and Critical Study*. 3rd printing. New Brunswick, New Jersey: Transaction, 2002.

Larteguy, Jean. *The Centurions*. New York: Avon Book Division, 1961.

Levine, Steven. *Anvil of Victory: The Communist Revolution in Manchuria, 1945–1948*. New York: Columbia University Press, 1987.

Liu Xiaoyuan. *Frontier Passages: Ethnopolitics and the Rise of Chinese Communism, 1921–1945*. Stanford, California: Stanford University Press, 2004.

Lockhart, Greg. *Nation in Arms: The Origins of the People's Army of Vietnam*. Boston: Allen and Unwin, 1989.

Loh, Pinchon P.Y., ed. *The Kuomintang Debacle of 1949: Conquest or Collapse*. Boston: D. C. Heath, 1965.

McCoy, Alfred W. *Closer than Brothers: Manhood at the Philippine Military Academy*. Manila: Anvil Publishing, 1999.

McGehee, Ralph W. *Deadly Deceits: My 25 Years in the CIA*. New York: Sheridan Square, 1983.

McCormick, Gordon H. *From the Sierra to the Cities: The Urban Campaign of the Shining Path*. Santa Monica, California: RAND, 1992.

Maier, Pauline. *From Resistance to Revolution: Colonial Radicals and the Development of American Opposition to Britain, 1765–1776*. New York: Norton, 1991.

Maloba, Wunyabari O. *Mau Mau and Kenya: An Analysis of a Peasant Revolt*. Bloomington: Indiana University Press, 1993.

Marks, Thomas A. *Colombian Army (COLAR) Response to FARC Insurgency*. Carlisle, PA: Army War College, 2002.

Marks, Thomas A. *Counterrevolution in China: Wang Sheng and the Kuomingtang*. London: Frank Cass, 1998.

Marks, Thomas A. *Insurgency in Nepal*. Carlisle: Army War College, 2003.

Marks, Thomas A. *Making Revolution: The Insurgency of the Communist Party of Thailand in Structural Perspective*. Bangkok: White Lotus Press, 1994.

Marks, Thomas A. *Maoist Insurgency since Vietnam*. London: Frank Cass, 1996.

Marks, Thomas A. *Sustainability of Colombian Military/Strategic Support for "Democratic Security"*. Carlisle: Army War College, 2005.

Maskay, Bishwa Keshar, and Dev Raj Dahal, eds. *Nepal's Participation in the United Nations Peace Keeping Operations*. Kathmandu: United Nations Association of Nepal, 1995.

Mason, Philip, ed. *India and Ceylon: Unity and Diversity*. London: Oxford University Press, 1967.

Mende, Tibor. *The Chinese Revolution*. Worcester: Thames & Hudson, 1961.

Mills, Lennox A. *Ceylon under British Rule, 1795–1932*. New York: Barnes & Noble, 1965.

Mishal, Shaul and Avraham Sela. *The Palestinian Hamas: Vision, Violence, and Coexistence*. New York: Columbia University Press, 2000.

Mithcel, Arthur. *Revolutionary Government in Ireland: Dail Eireann 1919–22*. Dublin: Gill and Macmillan, 1995.

Moerman, Michael. *Agricultural Change and Peasant Choice in a Thai Village*. Los Angeles: University of California Press, 1968.

Molnar, Andrew R., et al. *Human Factors Considerations of Undergrounds in Insurgencies*. Washington, DC: American University Press, 1965.

Morrison, Barrie M., M. P. Moore, and M.U. Ishak, eds. *The Disintegrating Village: Social Change in Rural Sri Lanka*. Colombo: Lake House, 1979.

Nakahara, Joyce and Ronald A. Witton. *Development and Conflict in Thailand*. Ithaca, New York: Cornell University Press, 1971.

Navarro, Edmundo G. *Bed of Nails*. Manila: Personal imprint, 1988.

Nepal, Kishore. *The Maoist Service Provision in Parts of Mid and Far West Nepal*. Kathmandu: Center for Professional Journalism Studies, March 2005.

Nugent, Daniel, ed. *Rural Revolt in Mexico: US Intervention and the Domain of Subaltern Politics*. Durham, North Carolina: Duke University Press, 1998.

Obeyesekere, Gananath. *Land Tenure in Village Ceylon*. London: Cambridge University Press, 1974.

O'Neill, Bard E. *Insurgency and Terrorism: Inside Modern Revolutionary Warfare*. Herndon, VA: Brassey's 1990.

Onesto, Li. *Dispatches From the People's War in Nepal*. Chicago: Insight Press, 2005.

Padover, Saul K. *Karl Marx: An Intimate Biography*. New York: New American Library, 1978.

Pak-wah Leung, Edwin. *Historical Dictionary of Revolutionary China, 1839–1976*. New York: Greenwood Press, 1992.

Palmer, David Scott, ed. *The Shining Path of Peru*. 2nd edn. New York: St Martin's Press, 1994.

Paret, Peter. *French Revolutionary Warfare from Indochina to Algeria: The Analysis of a Political and Military Doctrine*. New York: Praeger, 1964.

Paret, Peter, ed. *Makers of Modern Strategy—From Machiavelli to the Nuclear Age*. Princeton, New Jersey: Princeton University Press, 1986.

Pelton, Robert Young. *The World's Most Dangerous Places*. 4th edn. New York: Harper-Resource, 2000.

Pepper, Suzanne. *Civil War in China*. Berkeley: University of California Press, 1978.

Perry, Elizabeth J. *Chinese Perspectives on the Nien Rebellion*. Armonk, New York: Sharpe, 1981.

Phillips, Herbert. *Thai Peasant Personality: The Patterning of Interpersonal Behavior in the Village of Bang Chan*. Los Angeles: University of California Press, 1966.

Piker, Steven. *An Examination of Character and Socialization in a Thai Peasant Community*. Ann Arbor, Michigan: University Microfilms, 1964.

Pipes, Richard. *A Concise History of the Russian Revolution*. New York: Vintage Books-Random House, 1995.

Poole, Deborah and Gerardo Renique. *Peru: Time of Fear*. London: Latin America Bureau (Research and Action), 1992.

Pribbenow, Merle L. *Victory in Vietnam: The Official History of the People's Army of Vietnam, 1954–1975*. The Military History Institute of Vietnam. Lawrence: University Press of Kansas, 2002.

Quinn, Kenneth. *The Origins and Development of Radical Cambodian Communism*. PhD dissertation, University of Maryland, 1982.

Rabibhadana, Chandra. *A Proposal for a Five-Year Plan of Social Development in Thailand*. Bangkok: Thai Watana Panich, 1973.

377

Race, Jeffrey. *War Comes to Long An: Revolutionary Conflict in a Vietnamese Province.* Berkeley: University of California Press, 1972.

Rappoport, David C. *Inside Terrorist Organizations.* New York: Columbia University Press, 1988.

Rathaur, Kamal Raj Singh. *The Gurkhas: A History of the Recruitment in the British Indian Army.* New Delhi: Nirala, 1987.

Regmi, Mahesh C. *Landownership in Nepal.* Delhi: Adroit Publishers, 1999.

Reid, Ben. *Philippine Left: Political Crisis and Social Change.* Manila: Journal of Contemporary Asia Publishers, 2000.

Reid, Brian Holden. *Studies in British Military Thought: Debates with Fuller and Lidell Hart.* Lincoln: University of Nebraska Press, 1998.

Reid, Robert H. and Eileen Guerrero. *Corazon Aquino and the Brushfire Revolution.* Baton Rouge: Louisiana State University Press, 1995.

Rich, Paul B. and Richard Stubbs, eds. *The Counter-Insurgent State: Guerrilla Warfare and State Building in the Twentieth Century.* New York: St. Martin's Press, 1997.

Roberts, Michael, ed. *Collective Identities, Nationalisms, and Protest in Modern Sri Lanka.* Colombo: Marga Institute, 1979.

Rocamora, Joel. *Breaking Through: The Struggle Within the Communist Party of the Philippines.* Pasig City (Manila): Anvil Publishing, 1994.

Rooney, David. *Guerilla: Insurgents, Patriots and Terrorists from Sun Tzu to Bin Laden.* London: Brassey's, 2004.

Rothenberg, Gunther. *The Napoleonic Wars.* London: Cassell, 1999.

Rubin, Barry, ed. *The Politics of Terrorism: Terror as a State and Revolutionary Strategy.* Baltimore: Johns Hopkins University Press, 1989.

Russell, Jane. *Communal Politics Under the Donoughmore Constitution, 1931–1947.* Dehiwala, Sri Lanka: Tisara Prakasakayo, 1982.

Saad-Ghorayeb, Amal. *Hizbu'llah: Politics and Religion.* Sterling, Virginia: Pluto Press, 2002.

Samana, A.K. *Left Extremist Movement in West Bengal: An Experiment in Armed Agrarian Struggle.* Calcutta: Firma KLM, 1984.

Samudavanija, Chai-anan, Kusuma Snitwongse, and Suchit Bunbongkarn. *From Armed Suppression to Political Offensive: Attitudinal Transformation of Thai Military Officers since 1976.* Bangkok: Institute of Security and International Studies, Chulalongkorn University, 1990.

Schram, Stuart. *Mao Tse-tung.* Middlesex: Penguin Books, 1966.

Schram, Stuart. *The Political Thought of Mao Tse-tung.* Revised edn. New York: Praeger, 1976.

Scott, James C. *The Moral Economy of the Peasant: Rebellion and Subsistence in Southeast Asia*. New Haven: Yale University Press, 1976.

Seagrave, Sterling. *The Soong Dynasty*. New York: Harper & Row, 1985.

Seddon, David, Jagannath Adhikari, and Ganesh Gurung. *The New Lahures: Foreign Employment and Remittance Economy of Nepal*. Kathmandu: Nepal Institute of Development Studies, 2001.

Selbin, Eric. *Modern Latin American Revolutions*. 2nd edn. Boulder, Colorado: Westview Press, 1999.

Selden, Mark. *The Yenan Way in Revolutionary China*. Cambridge, Massachusetts: Harvard University Press, 1971.

Service, Robert. *Lenin: A Biography*. Cambridge, Massachusetts: Belknap Press of Harvard University Press, 2000.

Shepherd, Gary. *Life among the Magars*. Kathmandu: Sahayogi Press, 1982.

Shrestha, S. H. *Nepal in Maps*. 5th edn. Kathmandu: Educational Enterprise, January 2002.

Short, Philip. *Pol Pot: Anatomy of a Nightmare*. New York: Henry Holt, 2004.

Silcock, T. H. *The Economic Development of Thai Agriculture*. Ithaca, New York: Cornell University Press, 1970.

Sinha, A. C., and T. B. Subba. *The Nepalis in Northeast India*. New Delhi: Indus Publishing, 2003.

Social Scientists' Association. *Ethnicity and Change in Sri Lanka*. Colombo: Karunaratne, 1984.

Solzhenitsyn, Alexander. *Lenin in Zurich*. New York: Farrar, Straus and Giroux, 1975.

Sorley, Lewis. *A Better War: The Unexamined Victories and Final Tragedy of America's Last Years in Vietnam*. New York: Harcourt, 1999.

Spector, Ronald H. *The United States Army in Vietnam—Advice and Support: The Early Years, 1941–1960*. Washington, DC: Center of Military History, US Army, 1985.

Spence, Jonathan D. *The Search for Modern China*. New York: Norton, 1990.

Stern, Steve J., ed. *Shining and Other Paths: War and Society in Peru, 1980–1995*. Durham, North Carolina: Duke University Press, 1998.

Stoll, David. *Between Two Armies in the Ixil Towns of Guatemala*. New York: Columbia University Press, 1993.

Sweig, Julia E. *Inside the Cuban Revolution: Fidel Castro and the Urban Underground*. Cambridge, Massachusetts: Harvard University Press, 2002.

Tanham, George K. *Trial in Thailand*. New York: Crane, Russak, 1974.

Teng Ssu-yu. *The Nien Army and their Guerrilla Warfare, 1851–1868*. The Hague: Mouton, 1961.

Textor, Robert, ed. *Cultural Frontiers of the Peace Corps.* Cambridge, Massachusetts: Harvard University Press, 1966.

Thapa, Shanker. *Historical Study of Agrarian Relations in Nepal (1846–1951).* Delhi: Adroit Publishers, 2000.

Thayer, Carlyle A. *War by Other Means: National Liberation and Revolution in Viet-Nam 1954–60.* Boston: Allen & Unwin, 1989.

Thompson, Sir Robert. *Defeating Communist Insurgency.* New York: Praeger, 1966.

Thomson, James C., Jr. *While China Faced West: American Reformers in Nationalist China, 1928–1937.* Cambridge, Massachusetts: Harvard University Press, 1969.

Tien Hung-mao. *Government and Politics in Kuomintang China 1927–1937.* Stanford, California: Stanford University Press, 1972.

Tong, Hollington K., ed. *China Handbook 1937–1943: A Comprehensive Survey of Major Developments in China in Six Years of War.* New York: Macmillan, 1943.

Trager, Frank N. *Marxism in Southeast Asia.* Stanford, California: Stanford University Press, 1959.

Triandafillov, V. K., *The Nature of the Operations of Modern Armies.* Ed. Jacob W. Kipp. London: Frank Cass, 1994.

Trinquier, Roger. *Modern Warfare: A French View of Counterinsurgency.* New York: Praeger, 1964.

Trullinger, James W. *Village at War: An Account of Conflict.* Stanford: Stanford University Press, 1994.

Tucker, Robert C. *The Marx-Engels Reader.* 2nd edn. New York: Norton, 1978.

Upadhyaya, Shyam K. *Maoists' Strikes on Hydropower Plants: Any Policy Lessons?* Kathmandu: Winrock, November 2003.

Van der Kroef, Justus M. *Communism in South-East Asia.* Los Angeles: University of California Press, 1980.

Van Slyke, Lyman P. *Enemies and Friends—The United Front in Chinese Communist History.* Stanford, California: Stanford University Press, 1967.

Vega, Luis Mercier. *Guerillas in Latin America: The Technique of the Counter-State.* New York: Praeger, 1969.

Vickery, Michael. *Cambodia, 1975–1982.* Chiang Mai: Silkworm Books, 1999.

Clausewitz, Carl von. *On War.* Peter Paret trans. Princeton, NJ: Princeton University Press, 1976.

Weatherbee, Donald E. *The United Front in Thailand.* Columbia: University of South Carolina, 1970.

Wedel, Yuangrat (Pattanapongse). *Radical Thought, Thai Mind: The Development of Revolutionary Ideas in Thailand.* Bangkok: Assumption Business Administration College, 1987.

Weekley, Kathleen. *The Communist Party of the Philippines: A Story of its Theory and Practice.* Quezon City: University of the Philippines Press, 2001.

Whelpton, John. *A History of Nepal.* New York: Cambridge University Press, 2005.

Whitson, William W. and Huang Chen-hsia. *The Chinese High Command: A History of Communist Military Politics, 1927–71.* New York: Praeger Publishers, 1973.

Wickham-Crowley, Timothy P. *Guerrillas and Revolutions in Latin America: A Comparative Study of Insurgents and Regimes since 1956.* Princeton, New Jersey: Princeton University Press, 1993.

Wieviorka, Michael. *The Making of Terrorism.* Chicago: trans. David Gordon White. University of Chicago Press, 1993.

Wilson, A. Jeyaratnam. *Sri Lankan Tamil Nationalism: Its Origin and Development in the 19th and 20th Centuries.* Vancouver: University of British Columbia Press, 2000.

Wilson, A. Jeyaratnam and Dennis Dalton, eds. *The States of South Asia: Problems of National Integration.* Honolulu: University Press of Hawaii, 1982.

Womack, John. *Rebellion in Chiapas: An Historical Reader.* New York: The New Press, 1999.

Wongtrangan, Kanok. *Communist Revolutionary Process: A Study of the Communist Party of Thailand.* Ann Arbor, Michigan: University Microfilms International, 1981.

Wright, Mary C. *The Last Stand of Chinese Conservatism: The T'ung-chih Restoration, 1862–1874.* Stanford, California: Stanford University Press, 1957.

Wurfel, David. *Filipino Politics: Development and Decay.* Ithaca, New York: Cornell University Press, 1988.

Wyatt, David K. *Thailand: A Short History.* New Haven: Yale University Press, 1984.

Yabes, Criselda. *The Boys from the Barracks: The Philippine Military after EDSA.* Manila: Anvil Publishing, 1991.

Young, Arthur N. *China's Wartime Finance and Inflation, 1937–1945.* Cambridge, Massachusetts: Harvard University Press, 1965.

Zartman, I. William Zartman. *Collapsed States: The Disintegration and Restoration of Legitimate Authority.* Boulder, CO: Lynne Rienner, 1995.

Articles

Abbreviations

AWSJ	*The Asian Wall Street Journal*
AWSJW	*The Asian Wall Street Journal Weekly*
NYT	*The New York Times*
FEER	*The Far Eastern Economic Review*

Bibliography

Alexander, Paul. "Shared Fantasies and Elite Politics: The Sri Lankan 'Insurrection' of 1971." *Mankind*, 13.2 (December 1981): 113–32.

Allen, David. "Philippines May Charge SEALs with Homicide." *Pacific Stars and Stripes*, 7 January 2001: 3.

Arasaratnam, S. "The Ceylonese Insurrection of April 1971: Some Causes and Consequences." *Pacific Affairs*, 45.3 (Fall 1972): 356–71.

Averill, Stephen C. "Party, Society, and Local Elite in the Jiangxi Communist Movement." *Journal of Asian Studies*, 46.2 (May 1987): 279–303.

Balana, Cynthia D. "'Frolics of Class '61 Sobers Up." *Philippine Daily Inquirer* (Manila), 11 (October 1995): 1, 7.

Bassford, Christopher. "Interpreting the Legacy of Clausewitz." *Joint Force Quarterly*, 35 (undated): 18–19.

Beckett, Ian. "Forward to the Past: Insurgency in Our Midst." *Harvard International Review*, Summer 2001: 59–63.

Beer, Patrice de. "History and Policy of the Communist Party of Thailand." *Journal of Contemporary Asia*, 8.1 (1978): 143–58.

Behrman, Jere R. "Significance of Intra-country Variations for Asian Agricultural Prospects: Central and Northeastern Thailand." *Asian Survey*, 8.3 (March 1968): 157–73

Bell, Peter F. "Thailand's Northeast: Regional Underdevelopment, 'Insurgency', and Official Response." *Pacific Affairs*, 42.1 (Spring 1969): 47–54.

Billingsley, Phil. "Bandits, Bosses, and Bare Sticks: Beneath the Surface of Local Control in Early Republican China." *Modern China*, 7.3 (July 1981): 235–88.

Bowring, Philip, and Paisal Sricharatchanya. "The Power Wielded by a Constitutional Monarch." *FEER*, 19 June 1981: 53–55.

Bowring, Philip, and Paisal Sricharatchanya. "Shaking the Pillars." *FEER*, 19 June 1981: 38–43.

Brooke, James. "Unease Grows in Philippines on US Forces." *NYT*, 19 January 2002: Internet version.

Brow, James. "Class Formation and Ideological Practice: A Case from Sri Lanka." *Journal of Asian Studies*, 40.4 (August 1981): 703–18.

Brush, Peter. "Reassessing the VC Role after Tet." *Vietnam*, February 2002: 34–43.

Burton, Sandra. "People Power Redux." *Time* (Asian edn.), 29 January 2001: 14–19.

Cable, Larry. "Reinventing the Round Wheel: Insurgency, Counter-Insurgency, and Peacekeeping Post Cold War." *Small Wars and Insurgencies*, 4.2 (1993): 228–62.

Cabrez, Vincent. "Balweg: Beyond the Symbol and Myth." *Philippine Daily Inquirer* (Manila), 3 January 2001, sec. A12.

Carland, John M. "Documents of Note—Winning the Vietnam War: Westmoreland's

Approach in Two Documents." *Journal of Military History*, 68.2 (April 2004): 553–74.

Castro, Renato Cruz de. "Adjusting to the post-US Bases Era: The Ordeal of the Philippine Military's Modernization Program." *Armed Forces & Society*, 26.1 (Fall 1999): 119–38.

Chauncey, Helen R. "The Growth of the United Front." *Southeast Asia Chronicle*, No. 60 (January–February 1978): 2–9.

Childs, Matt D. "An Historical Critique of the Emergence and Evolution of Ernesto Che Guevara's *Foco* Theory." *Journal of Latin American Studies*, 27.Pt. 3 (1995): 593–614.

Corpuz, Victor. "Former Red Cadre Intelligence Chief." *Business World*, 24 January 2001: 12.

Coyne, Jim. "Thailand's Battle Road." *Soldier of Fortune*, 7.2 (February 1982): 37–43.

"Critical Time for Thai Communists." *Bangkok Post*, 22 November 1981: 6.

Dorris, Carl E. "Peasant Mobilization in North China and the Origins of Yenan Communism." *China Quarterly*, 68 (December 1976): 697–719.

Eastman, Lloyd E. "Fascism in Kuomintang China: The Blue Shirts." *China Quarterly*, 49 (January–March 1972): 1–31.

Eastman, Lloyd E. "The Rise and Fall of the 'Blue Shirts': A Review Article." *Republican China*, 13.1 (November 1987): 25–48.

Echevarria II, Antulio J. "Center of Gravity: Recommendations for Joint Doctrine." *Joint Force Quarterly*, 35 (undated): 10–17.

Elkins, W. F. "Fascism in China: The Blue Shirts Society, 1932–1937." *Science and Society*, 33.4 (1969): 426–33.

Eto, Shinkichi. "Hai-lu-feng—The First Chinese Soviet Government." *China Quarterly*, 8 (October–December 1961): 161–83.

Farmer, B. H. "The Social Basis of Nationalism in Ceylon." *Journal of Asian Studies*, 24.3 (May 1965): 441–89.

Fernandez, Connie. "Senator Demands New Probe of War Games Deaths." *Philippine Daily Inquirer* (Manila), 20 February 2001, sec. A12.

Fernando, Tissa. "Elite Politics in the New States: The Case of Post-Independence Sri Lanka." *Pacific Affairs*, 46.3 (Fall 1973): 361–83.

Fenton, James. "The Cruel Carpenter." *The New York Review of Books*," LII.10 (9 June 2005): 28–311.

Flood, Thadeus. "The Thai Left Wing in Historical Context." *Bulletin of Concerned Asian Scholars*, April–June 1975: 55–67.

Franko, Patrice. "Defense Decisionmaking and Accountability Structures in the Philippines." *Low Intensity Conflict & Law Enforcement*, 8.1 (Spring 1999): 57–86.

Bibliography

Gillin, Donald G. "Review Article: 'Peasant Nationalism' in the History of Chinese Communism." *Journal of Asian Studies*, 23.2 (February 1964): 269–87.

Grove, Linda. "Creating a Northern Soviet." *Modern China*, 1.3 (July 1975): 243–70.

Halliday, Fred. "The Ceylonese Insurrection." *New Left Review*, No. 69 (September–October 1971): 75–78.

Harris, Paul. "Bitter Lessons for the SLA." *Jane's Intelligence Review*, October 1996: 466–68.

Hawes, Gary. "Theories of Peasant Revolution: A Critique and Contribution from the Philippines." *World Politics*, 17.2 (January 1990): 261–98.

Herrera, Christine F. "Guerrillas in the Mist: Another Group Breaks Away from the Communist Party of the Philippines, Pushing Unity in the Revolution—and Peace—Further Away." *Philippines Free Press* (Manila), 31 July 1993: 4–5.

Hough, Richard L. "Development and Security in Thailand: Lessons from Other Asian Countries." *Asian Survey*, 9.3 (March 1969): 178–87.

Jenkins, David. "The Hit-Run 'Government'." *FEER*, 23 July 1973: 26–27.

Johnson, Chalmers. "The Guerrilla Movement in Northwest China: The Origins of the Shensi-Kansu-Ninghsia Border Region." *China Quarterly*, 29 (January–March 1967): 61–81.

Johnson, Chalmers. "Peasant Nationalism Revisited: The Biography of a Book." *China Quarterly*, 72 (December 1977): 766–85.

Johnson, Chalmers. "The Guerrilla Movement in Northwest China: The Origins of the Shensi-Kansu-Ninghsia Border Region." *China Quarterly*, 28 (October–December 1966): 63–81

Johnson, Chalmers. "The Third Generation of Guerrilla Warfare." *Asian Survey*, 8.6 (June 1978): 435–47.

Kearney, Robert N. "Educational Expansion and Political Volatility in Sri Lanka: The 1971 Insurrection." *Asian Survey*, 15.9 (September 1975): 727–44.

Kearney, Robert N. "A Note on the Fate of the 1971 Insurgents in Sri Lanka." *Journal of Asian Studies*, 36.3 (May 1977): 515–19.

Kearney, Robert N. "Sinhalese Nationalism and Social Conflict in Ceylon." *Pacific Affairs*, 37.2 (Summer 1964): 125–36.

Kearney, Robert N. and Janice Jiggins. "The Ceylon Insurrection of 1971." *Journal of Commonwealth & Comparative Politics*, 13.1 (March 1975): 49.

Kerkvliet, Benedict J. "Martial Law in a Nueva Ecija Village, the Philippines." *Bulletin of Concerned Asian Scholars*, 14 (October–December 1982): 2–19.

Kham, Chiang. "Mountains of Discontent." *FEER*, 2 July 1970: 20–22.

Landingin, Roel. "Mixed Feelings Over US Troops." *Financial Times*, 18 January 2002: 3.

Landler, Mark. "Global Network: US Advisers May Aid Philippine Anti-terror Effort" *NYT*, 11 October 2001: sec. B4.

Lecomte-Tilouine, Marie. "Regicide and Maoist Revolutionary Warfare in Nepal: Modern Incarnations of a Warrior Kingdom." *Anthropology Today*, 20.1 (February 2004): 13–19.

Leifer, Michael. "More Imelda than Teresa." *Times Literary Supplement*, 18 April 1997: 26.

Lerski, George J. "The Twilight of Ceylonese Trotskyism." *Pacific Affairs*, 43.3 (Fall 1970): 384–93.

Long, Millard F. "Economic Development in Northeast Thailand." *Asian Survey*, 6.7 (July 1966): 355–61.

Lopez, Antonio. "Inside Story: Running a Revolution—The Life and Times of the Philippines' Most Formidable Guerrilla Chief." *Asiaweek*, 9 March 1994: 28–41.

McBeth, John. "A Battle for Loyalty in the Jungles." *FEER*, 8 June 1979: 19–21.

McBeth, John. "Communism: Hazards along the Neutral Path." *FEER*, 19 September 1980: 43–48.

McBeth, John. "The Coup That Never Was." *FEER*, 10 April 1981: 10–15

McBeth, John. "In Search of a New Direction." *FEER*, 10 August 1979: 30–31.

McBeth, John. "Insurgencies: The Ideological Crossroads." *FEER*, 8 February 1980: 32–34.

McBeth, John. "A Profile of the Young Turks' Camp." *FEER*, 19 June 1981: 44–53.

McBeth, John. "Revolution to Evolution." *FEER*, 12 May 1983: 24–25.

McBeth, John. "Thailand: In From the Cold (2)." *FEER*, 17 September 1982: 12–15

McBeth, John. "Thailand: Seeking a Strong Local Accent." *FEER*, 22 August 1980: 30–32.

McClintock, Cynthia. "Why Peasants Rebel: The Case of *Sendero Luminoso*." *World Politics*, 37.1 (October 1984): 48–84.

Mai, Pak. "Northern Separatists." *FEER*, 4 April 1980: 7.

Marks, Thomas A. "An Analysis of the Brunner and Brewer Model of Political Development as Applied to the Philippines." *Philippine Political Science Journal*, Nos. 5 & 6 (June and December 1977): 181–211.

Marks, Thomas A. "An Eclectic Model of Thailand's Participation in the Vietnam War." *Peace Research* (Ontario), 11.2 (1979): 71–76.

Marks, Thomas A. "At the Frontlines of the GWOT: Colombia Success Builds Upon Local Foundation." *The Journal of Counterterrorism and Homeland Security International*, 10.2 (Summer 2004): 42–50.

Marks, Thomas A. "At the Frontlines of the GWOT: Insurgency in Nepal." *The Journal of Counterterrorism and Homeland Security International*, 9.4 (Fall 2003): 28–34.

Bibliography

Marks, Thomas A. "Bengali Solution: India Trained Personnel for Invasion of Sri Lanka." *Daily News* (Colombo), 7 July 1987: 8.

Marks, Thomas A. "Book Review—Stanley Tambiah, Sri Lanka: Ethnic Fratricide and the Dismantling of Democracy." *Issues & Studies*, 23.9 (September 1987): 135–40.

Marks, Thomas A. "Chaos in Colombo: Sri Lanka's Army Awaits its Marching Orders While Politicians Dither." *Soldier of Fortune*, 15.2 (February 1990): 48–55.

Marks, Thomas A. "Colombian Army Counterinsurgency." *Crime, Law and Social Change*, 40 (2003): 77–105.

Marks, Thomas A. "Colombian Army (COLAR) Response to FARC Insurgency." *Soldier of Fortune*, 26.9 (September 2001): 56–61.

Marks, Thomas A. "Colombian Army (COLAR) Response to FARC Insurgency." *Soldier of Fortune*, 26.10 (October 2001): 44–49.

Marks, Thomas A. "Colombian Army (COLAR) Response to FARC Insurgency." *Soldier of Fortune*, 26.12 (December 2001): 48–53.

Marks, Thomas A. "Communist Insurgency in the Philippines: How and Why it Happened." *Gung-Ho*, 7.57 (March 1987): 40–45.

Marks, Thomas A. "The Communist Party and the Strategy of the United Front in Thailand since October 1976." *Asia Quarterly* (Brussels), 1980.1, 3–18.

Marks, Thomas A. "Corner of the Dead." *Soldier of Fortune*, 15.3 (March 1990): 44–51.

Marks, Thomas A. "Counter-Insurgency in Sri Lanka." *Soldier of Fortune*, 12.2 (February 1987): 38–47.

Marks, Thomas A. "Deadlock in the Philippines." *National Review*, 15 October 1990: 30–2

Marks, Thomas A. "Dynamics of Terror in Sri Lanka." *Sunday Times* (Colombo), 31 December 1996:7.

Marks, Thomas A. "The Ethnic Roots of Sri Lanka's Ideological Struggle." *AWSJ*, 12 August 1987: 8.

Marks, Thomas A. "End of the Nightmare? Peru's Fight against Terrorism." *Counterterrorism and Security*, N.S. 1.3 (Spring 1975): 26–30.

Marks, Thomas A. "Government Policy as a Reflection of the Development Model: The Case of Accelerated Rural Development (ARD) in Northeast Thailand." *Journal of East & West Studies* (Seoul), 10.1 (1981): 59–95.

Marks, Thomas A. "The Guerrilla Myth." *Soldier of Fortune*, 15.5 (May 1990): 56–59, 65–68.

Marks, Thomas A. "Guerrillas in the Midst of Defeat." *AWSJ*, 26 July 1990: 6.

Marks, Thomas A. "In Sri Lanka, Despair Explodes into Violence." *AWSJ*, 16 August 1989: 6.

Marks, Thomas A. "India Acts in its Own Interests." *Daily News* (Colombo), 6 July 1987: 6.

Marks, Thomas A. "India is the Key to Peace in Sri Lanka." *AWSJ*, 19–20 September 1986: 8.

Marks, Thomas A. "India's Political Solution Narrow and Impossible." *Daily News* (Colombo), 8 July 1987: 6.

Marks, Thomas A. "Insurgency by the Numbers II: The Search for a Quantitative Relationship between Agrarian Revolution and Land Tenure in South and Southeast Asia" *Small Wars and Insurgencies*, 5.2 (Autumn 1994): 218–91.

Marks, Thomas A. "Making Revolution: *Sendero Luminoso* in Peru." *Small Wars and Insurgencies* (London), 3.1 (Spring 1992): 22–46.

Marks, Thomas A. "Manila Starts to Win Hearts and Minds." *Christian Science Monitor*, 18 April 1989: 19.

Marks, Thomas A. "Marxist Tamils Won't Stop at Separatism." *AWSJ*, 8 May 1986: 6.

Marks, Thomas A. "The Counter-Revolutionary: Sir Robert Thompson—Grand Master of Unconventional Warfare." *Soldier of Fortune*, 14.10 (October 1989): 58–65/77–80.

Marks, Thomas A. "The Military and Politics in Thailand: An Analysis of the Two October Coups (1976–1977)." *Issues & Studies* (Taipei), 13.11 (November 1977): 58–90.

Marks, Thomas A. "The NPA Misfires in the Philippines." *AWSJ*, 31 January 1989: 6.

Marks, Thomas A. "October 1976 and the Role of the Military in Thai Politics." *Modern Asian Studies* (Cambridge), 14.3 (1980): 399–440.

Marks, Thomas A. "Peru's Fatal Distraction." *Soldier of Fortune*, 15.7 (July 1990), 30–33.

Marks, Thomas A. "Peru: Securing the Peace." *Soldier of Fortune*, 24.3 (March 1999): 48–51.

Marks, Thomas A. "Professionals in Paradise: Sri Lanka's Army Gears Up for 'Tiger' Hunt." *Soldier of Fortune*, 15.1 (January 1990): 48–55.

Marks, Thomas A. "Sea Change in Negros." *East West*, 8.3 (Spring 1989): 24–29.

Marks, Thomas A. "'Shining Path' to Oblivion? Fate Breaks Peru's 'Fourth Sword of Marxism.'" *Soldier of Fortune*, 1.7 (July 1996): 54–57.

Marks, Thomas A. "Sino-Thai Relations." *Asian Affairs* (London), 5.3 (October 1974): 296–310.

Marks, Thomas A. "Sri Lanka: The Dynamics of Terror." *Counterterrorism and Security*, N.S. 1.1 (1994): 19–23.

Marks, Thomas A. "Sri Lanka: Reform, Revolution or Ruin?" *Soldier of Fortune*, 21.6 (June 1996): 35–39.

Marks, Thomas A. "Sri Lanka: Terorism in Perspective." *Counterterrorism and Security*, N.S. 2.3 (Fall–Winter 1995): 16–19.

Bibliography

Marks, Thomas A. "Sri Lankan Minefield: Gandhi's Troops Fail to Keep the Peace." *Soldier of Fortune*, 13.3 (March 1988): 36–45.

Marks, Thomas A. "Sri Lanka's Despair Breeds Violence." *AWSJW*, 21 August 1989: 15.

Marks, Thomas A. "Sri Lanka's Special Force: Professionalism in a Dirty War." *Soldier of Fortune*, 13.7 (July 1988): 32–39.

Marks, Thomas A. "The Status of the Monarchy in Thailand." *Issues & Studies* (Taipei), 13.11 (November 1977): 51–70.

Marks, Thomas A. "Terrorism vs. Terror: The Case of Peru." *Counterterrorism and Security* (Arlington), 2.2 (May–June 1990): 26–33.

Marks, Thomas A. "The Thai Approach to Peacemaking since World War II." *Journal of East & West Studies* (Seoul), 7.1 (April 1978): 133–55.

Marks, Thomas A. "The Thai Monarchy under Siege." *Asia Quarterly* (Brussels), 1978.2: 109–41.

Marks, Thomas A. "Thai Security during the 'American Era', 1960–1976." *Issues & Studies* (Taipei), 15.4 (April 1979): 61–88.

Marks, Thomas A. "Thailand's Terror Years." *Soldier of Fortune*, 15.8 (August 1990): 30–37.

Marks, Thomas A. "Toying with Terrorists: India's Sri Lankan Creation Runs Amok." *Low Intensity Conflict (LIC) International* (Washington, DC), 1.1 (Dec. 1992): 6–8.

Marks, Thomas A. "Urban Insurgency." *Small Wars and Insurgencies* (London), 14.3 (Autumn 2003): 100–61.

Marks, Thomas A. "Victory on Panay: Red Tide Recedes From Philippine Communist Stronghold." *Soldier of Fortune*, 14.2 (February 1989): 40–47.

Marks, Thomas A. and Scott Palmer. "Radical Maoist Insurgents and Terrorist Tactics: Comparing Nepal and Peru." *Low Intensity Conflict & Law Enforcement*, forthcoming.

Mariano, Dan. "Opinion Today—Popoy Lagman: A Revolutionary Life." *Today*, 8 February 2001: 9.

Morell, David, and Chai-anan Samudavanija. "Thailand's Revolutionary Insurgency: Changes in Leadership Potential." *Asian Survey*, 19.4 (April 1979): 332.

Munro, Ross H. "The New Khmer Rouge." *Commentary*, 80.6 (December 1985): 19–38.

Napallacan, Jhunnex and Tonton Antogop. "Parents of 2 Boys Killed in Cebu Blast Given P1.5M." *Philippine Daily Inquirer* (Manila), 15 February 2001, sec. A12.

Nickson, R. Andrew. "Democratisation and the Growth of Communism in Nepal: A Peruvian Scenario in the Making?" *Journal of Commonwealth and Comparative Politics*, 30.3 (November 1992): 358–86.

Ng, Ronald C.Y. "Some Land Use Problems of Northeast Thailand." *Modern Asian Studies*, 4.1 (1970): 23–42.

Noland, Marcus. "The Philippines in the Asian Financial Crisis: How the Sick Man Avoided Pneumonia." *Asian Survey*, 40.3 (May–June 2000): 401–12.

Oberst, Robert. "Democracy and the Persistence of Westernized Elite Dominance in Sri Lanka." *Asian Survey*, 25.7 (July 1985): 760–72.

Obeyesekere, Gananath. "Some Comments on the Social Backgrounds of the April 1971 Insurgency in Sri Lanka (Ceylon)." *Journal of Asian Studies*, 33.3 (May 1974): 376–84.

Palmer, David Scott. "Rebellion in Rural Peru: The Origins and Evolution of Sendero Luminoso." *Comparative Politics*, 18.2 (January 1986): 127–46.

Paschall, Rod. "Low-Intensity Doctrine: Who Needs It?" *Parameters*, 15.3 (Autumn 1985): 33–45.

Paul, Anthony. "Insights: Sex and the Single Insurgent." *Asiaweek*, 8 April 1983: 24.

Paul, Anthony. "The Jungle War the Communists Lost." *Reader's Digest* (Asian edn.), (October 1984): 2–6.

Paul, Anthony. "Winding Down a War." *Asiaweek*, 8 April 1983: 16–24.

Paul, Anthony and John McBeth. "Thailand: The Bulldozer Invasion." *FEER*, 8 May 1981: 26–28.

Pepper, Suzanne. "The Political Odyssey of an Intellectual Construct: Peasant Nationalism and the Study of China's Revolutionary History—A Review Essay." *Journal of Asian Studies*, 63.1 (February 2004), 105–25.

"Philippines Finds Mass Graves." *International Herald Tribune*, 9 February 2000: 5.

Piao, Lin. "Long Live the Victory of People's War." *Peking Review*, 4 August 1967: 14–35.

Ping, Ho Kwon. "Thailand, Inc." *FEER*, 23 May 1980: 40–46.

Polachek, James M. "The Moral Economy of the Kiangsi Soviet (1928–1934)." *Journal of Asian Studies*, 42.4 (August 1983): 805–29.

Poole, Deborah and Gerardo Renique. "The New Chroniclers of Peru: US Scholars and Their 'Shining Path' of Peasant Rebellion." *Bulletin of Latin American Research*, 10.2 (1991): 133–91.

Prizzia, Ross. "Thailand: New Social Forces and Re-Emerging Socialist Principles." *Asia Quarterly*, 1975.4: 343–65.

Quinn, Kenneth. "Political Change in Wartime: The Khmer Krahom Revolution Southern Cambodia, 1970–1974." *Naval War College Review*, 28 (Spring 1976): 3–31.

Reno, William. "The Failure of Peacekeeping in Sierra Leone." *Current History*, May 2001: 219–25.

Richardson, Michael. "Military Reform in the Philippines?" *Pacific Defence Reporter*, (Australia) 12.8 (February 1986): 11–12.

Roque, Pat. "Anti-US Feelings in Philippines Rise." *Honolulu Advertiser*, 21 January 2002: sec. A3.

Scott, James C. "Revolution in the Revolution: Peasants and Commissars." *Theory and Society*, 7.1–2 (January–March 1979): 97–134.

Sheehan, Deidre. "Philippines: A Price for Peace—It Will Take More than Brave Talk and Promises for Manila to Win a Lasting End to Revolt on Mindanao." *FEER*, 30 August 2001: 17.

Sheehan, Deidre, and David Plott. "Philippines: A War Grows—A Widening War against Terrorism Brings Together the Military Interests of the US and Philippines." *FEER*, 11 October 2001: 24.

Sison, Jose Maria. "Theoretical and Practical Problems for Contemporary Radicalism." *Progressive Review* (Manila), 1.1 (May–June 1963): 5.

Sricharatchanya, Paisal. "Security: Playing the Same Game." *FEER*, 18 December 1981: 15–16.

Sterba, James P. "Thai Drive Snares Few Red Guerrillas." *NYT*, 26 March 1972: 1.

Sterba, James P. "Thai Insurgents Seen Increasing." *NYT*, 27 March 1972: 18.

Sterba, James P. "Thais Attack a Rebel Stronghold." *NYT*, 18 March 1972: 3.

Strange, Joseph L. and Richard Iron. *Joint Force Quarterly*, 35 (undated): 20–27.

Suwanna, Satha-anand. "Religious Movements in Contemporary Thailand: Buddhist Struggles for Modern Relevance." *Asian Survey*, 30.4 (April 1990): 395–408.

Tanner, Harold M. "Guerrilla, Mobile, and Base Warfare in Communist Military Operations in Manchuria, 1945–1947." *Journal of Military History*, 67.4 (October 2003): 1177–2222.

Tasker, Rodney. "The Hidden Hand: A Military Reform Movement Takes Hold." *FEER*, 1 August 1985: 10–13.

Tasker, Rodney. "Insurgency: A More Peaceful South." *FEER*, 11 October 1984: 28–29.

Tassell, Tony. "Manila Agrees US Defence Deal." *Financial Times*, 28 May 1999: 6.

Teves, Oliver. "Poverty, Not Terror, May be Top Philippine Challenge." *Honolulu Advertiser*, 20 January 2002: sec. A24.

Teves, Oliver. "US Base Camp Set up in Basilan Island Jungle." *Honolulu Advertiser*, 20 January 2002: sec. A24.

Thapa, Deepak. "Day of the Maoist." *Himal* (Katmandu),14.5 (May 2001).

Thomson, John R. "The Burning Mountain." *FEER*, 25 April 1968: 218–20.

Tiwari, Chitra, "Maoists Seek a Democratic Nepal." *Washington Times*, 14 December 2002.

Tome, John Lawrence. "Napoleon's Uncongenial Sea: Guerrilla Warfare in Navarre During the Peninsular War, 1808–14." *European History Quarterly*, 26.3 (1996): 355–82;

Tubeza, Philip C., Andrea Trinidad–Echavez, and Dave Veridiano. "'Ka Popoy' Shot Dead Inside UP." *Philippine Daily Inquirer* (Manila), 7 February 2001, sec. A1.

Turton, Andrew. "The Current Situation in the Thai Countryside." *Journal of Contemporary Asia*, 8.1 (1978): 112.

Van der Kroef, Justus M. "Guerrilla Communism and Counterinsurgency in Thailand." *Orbis*, 18.1 (Spring 1974): 106–39.

Villanueva, Ruffy L., Cheryll D. Fiel, and Michael F. Leonen. "Talks With Reds, MILF Seen Soon." *Business World*, 12 February 2001: 10.

Vogel, Steve. "US Expands War against Terrorism to Philippines." *Honolulu Advertiser*, 16 January 2002: sec. A2.

Warnapala, W. A. Siswa. "The April Revolt in Ceylon." *Asian Survey*, 12.3 (March 1972): 259–74.

Warnapala, W. A. Siswa. "The Marxist Parties of Sri Lanka and the 1971 Insurrection." *Asian Survey*, 15.9 (September 1975): 745–57.

Wei, William. "Insurgency by the Numbers I: A Reconsideration of the Ecology of Communist Success in Jiangxi Province, China." *Small Wars and Insurgencies*, 5.2 (Autumn 1994): 201–17.

Wei, William. "The Guomindang's Three Parts Military and Seven Parts Politics Policy." *Asian Profile* (Hong Kong), 10.2 (April 1982): 111–27.

Williamson, Hugh. "Manila Struggles to Regain Control—Heady Mix of Guns, Clans, Secession and Religion Poses Problems Afresh in Southern Philippines." *Financial Times*, 29–30 April 2000: 4.

Wilson, A. Jeyaratnam. "Ceylon: A Time of Troubles." *Asian Survey*, 12.2 (February 1972): 109–15.

Wright, Mary C. "From Revolution to Restoration: The Transformation of Kuomintang Ideology." *Far Eastern Quarterly*, 14.4 (August 1955): 515–32.

Yoong, Sean. "Philippines, Rebels Agree to Cease-Fire." *Honolulu Star-Bulletin*, 7 August 2001: sec. A11.

Zhang Chengjun and Liu Jianye. *An Illustrated History of China's War of Resistance against Japan*. Peking: Foreign Languages Press, 1995.

Zimmerman, Robert F. "Insurgency in Thailand." *Problems of Communism* 25.3 (May–June 1976): 18–39.

Index

Al-Qaeda: 188

Amarasinghe, Patrick: 205 (photo)

Amendment Six (to Philippine Constitution): 132

America(n): 35, 38–39

    assistance: 79, 156

    civil war: 335

    embassy: 208, 227, 347

    imperialism: 13, 84, 90, 92, 227

    independence: 3

    military: 238

    revolution: 3–4

Amnesty International: 145

Anna DMK (AIADMK): 222

anti-colonialism: 210

anti-communist: 60, 67 *see* communist

anti-guerrilla campaign: 71

anti-Japanese: 64, 88, 94, 134, 135

anti-militant campaigns: 220, 328

anti-Muslim: 186

anti-US: 188

anti-war groups: 44

Antón, Charles: 221

Anuradhapura (Sri Lanka): 222, 223, 286, 265

April Fool's Coup (Thailand): 95

Aquino, Benigno: 159, 177–178

Aquino, Cory (President of the Philippines): 159, 160–163, 167, 178, 182, 186, 333

Arab: 153, 236

Area Commanders (Sri Lanka): 247

Armalite: 331

armed action ("guerrilla action"): 220

Armed Forces: 187, 208, 221

    of the Philippines (AFP; also New AFP): 152, 154, 158, 160, 167, 179, 182, 186, 193

Armed Police Force (APF; Nepal): 313–314, 319

armor: 43, 231, 251, 253, 286

Army of the Republic of Vietnam (ARVN): 43

Arroyo, Gloria Macapagal (GMA; President of the Philippines): 187

Aryans (Sri Lanka): 205

Asia(ns): 13, 85, 115, 119, 127, 271, 297, 301, 333, 335, 365
assassinations: 43, 139, 165, 171–173, 187, 189, 246, 251, 312, 323, 347
Association of Major Religious Superiors in the Philippines (AMRS or AMRSP; Philippines): 145
Asuncion (Paraguay): 342
Athulathmudali, Lalith: 231, 233, 251, 335
authoritarianism: 333
"autocratic monarchy": 325
Ayacucho (Peru): 273–277, 279–288, 290, 301, 311
Ayacucho Regional Committee (Shining Path): 280

Balangiga (Samar): 146
Balasingham, Anton Stanislav: 223, 227–228, 265, 266, 287–288
Balweg, Father Conrado: 151, 186
Ban Nakham (Ubon Ratchathani Province): 68, 69
Bandaranaike, Sirimavo (Prime Minister of Sri Lanka): 236, 260, 252
bandits: 2, 23
Bangkok (Thailand): 57, 59, 62, 64, 65, 67, 70, 78, 79, 81, 83, 85, 93–97
Bangladesh: 238–239, 242
Bangsa Moro Army (BMA): 152
baojia (organizing populace): 29, 31
baolei (blockhouses): 31
baowei tuan (official militia): 29, 51, 53
barangay (*barrio*): 137, 183, 201
base areas: 24, 26–27, 30, 43, 48, 63, 69, 88, 95, 236–237, 310–311, 329
Base Contra Guerrilla (BCG): 286–288
Basilan Island (Philippines): 188
battalions: 14, 42–43
    in China and Vietnam: 42–44
    in Nepal: 308, 317–318
    in Peru: 286, 288, 308, 317, 358
    in Philippines: 147, 150–152, 155, 157–158
    in Sri Lanka: 220, 229, 231, 235, 250, 253, 260
    in Thailand: 100
Batticaloa (Sri Lanka): 233
beans: 25, 139
Beijing: 320

Belgium (-gian): 239, 295,
Bhatarrai, Baburam: 305, 307, 320, 322, 328
Bhumipol (King of Thailand): 303, 324
Bhutan: 222, 326
Bicol (Philippines): 163
"Big Five" (Sri Lanka): 227
"big landlord": 311
Birenda (King of Nepal): 325
Blue Shirts (*Lixingshe*): 33, 50
Bolshevik coup: 321
Bontoc (Philippines): 150,
Borodin, Michael: 36
bourgeois(ie): 10, 12, 35 ,250, 322, 360
Brahmins (Nepal): 300, 305
Braun, Otto: 40
brigade(s): 38, 152, 155, 159–160, 247, 249, 254, 255, 268, 286, 317–318, 358
Britain (-ish): 3, 58–59, 71, 81, 131, 205–206, 210, 228, 237, 239, 247, 249, 267, 283, 300–301,
    319, 336, 339
    Indian Army: 300
    system: 300
Buddhism (ists): 59, 103–104, 112, 206, 211, 232
    "Buddhism, Nation, Monarchy": 103–104
    in SE Asia: 58, 205, 206, 212, 214, 222
    Bulatao, Victor: 145
Bunyen Wothong: 94
bureaucracy(-tic): 301, 319
bureaucratic polity: 59, 60, 81, 84–87, 99, 110, 114–115
business: 32, 34, 61, 69, 98, 112, 153, 163, 174, 182, 245, 250

Cabardo, Jorge: 146
cadre: 7, 14, 35, 41, 43, 60, 64, 67, 75, 89, 100, 158, 161, 176, 244, 246, 274, 278, 288, 291,
    303–304, 308, 310–311, 315–317, 323, 326, 331, 355, 356, 357, 364, 378–379
Cambodia: 43, 52, 92, 93, 94, 110, 304
campesinos: 282–282, 288; *see* peasants (in Peru)
Canton(ese): 21, 22, 30, 37, 39, 53
    Secessionist Movement: 30
capitalist: 9, 12, 84, 95, 129, 131, 149, 211, 216, 226, 228, 303

Cardones, Rene: 167
cash crops: 24
caste (system): 209, 210 212, 215, 300–301, 303, 308
Catarman (Samar, Philippines): 146
Catbalogan (Samar, Philippines): 146
Catholic Bishops' Conference of the Philippines (CBCP): 133
Catholic Church (Philippines): 132–133, 145
Catholic: 326
Catubig Valley (Philippines): 146
Cavalry School (Thai): 97
CBS News: 139
ceasefire: 188, 331
"Ceaseless Waves" (LTTE): 329
Cebu (Philippines): 146, 188 *see* Central Reform Commission
Central Cadre Academy (*aka* Central Government Cadre School; China): 37
Central Committee (KMT): *see* Koumintang
Central Intelligence Agency (CIA): 120, 222
Central Soviet (China): 25
Ceylon: *see* Sri Lanka
Chaovalit Yongchaiyut: 98, 106
Charoen Wanngarm: 64
Chekiang (China): 39
Chhetris (Nepal): 300
Chiang (family): 21, 22, 32, 39,
Chiang Kai-shek (President and Generalissimo): 9, 12, 21–22, 30, 32–40, 94
Chiangmai (Thailand): 85
CHICKS (Negros, Philippines): 174
Chico River (Philippines): 150
Chief of Staff: 100, 154, 160
Chikow (China): 39
Chile (-an): 286, 295
China: 4, 9–10, 12–14, 21–24, 26–28, 30, 34–36, 38–45, 60–61, 70, 84–85, 92–94, 96, 181, 187, 238–239, 271, 276, 283, 355
Chinese:
  Civil War: 304
  communists: 34, 42, 83

Communist Party (CCP): 21–22, 24, 28–41, 93, 355
  Revolution: 21
Chongqing (Chungking; China): 32
Chou En-lai: 36
Christian(-ity): 33, 129, 152, 205
Chulalongkorn (King of Thailand): 65
Chung Li-jieh: 47
cities: 14, 22, 27, 51, 92, 95–96, 144, 179, 180, 260
Citizen Armed Forces Geographical Units (CAFGU; Philippines): 813
civic action: 154, 167–169, 286, 314
Civil Guard (Peru): 283
Civil Police (Nepal): 314, 319
civil rights: 44
civil society: 37
class struggle: 22
class enemies: 305
Clausewitz, Karl von: 365
clergy: 131, 133, 177
coca (cocaine): 282
coconut (crops): 211
Cold War: 6, 125, 237, 252, 260, 297, 305, 329, 332, 353
Colombia: 45, 311, 331
Colombo (Sri Lanka): 205, 220–222, 225, 228, 236–241, 243–245, 248, 251–252, 254–255,
  258, 260–262
colonialism: 127, 206, 211
  domination: 205
  rule, end of: 206
columns (guerrilla): 30, 278, 282
combat forces: 220
Combat Research Division (AFP Operations, J3): 167
Combat: 43
  battalions: 151, 152
  forces: 78, 220
  formations: 155
  power: 11, 12, 41, 42, 229
  units: 248
Comintern: 41, 133

Commandant (FHK): *see* Academy Commandant

Commander-in-chief: 319

Commentary: 172

Commissars: 5, 36

Committee for Coordinating Patriotic and Democratic Forces (CCPDF) (Coordinating Committee for Patriotic and Democracy Loving Forces): 88–90, 94

    Thailand (CPT): 57, 60, 61, 125

    and European Coordinating Committee for Solidarity with the Thai People (ECCSTP): 90

Comite Zonal (Zones, CZ; Shining Path): 95–96, 108, 279–280, 286, 317

communal(-ism): 205, 221, 228, 231, 238, 245, 260, 278

Communism (Marxism): *see* specific entries

communal

    terror: 221

    violence: 205

Communist International (COMINTERN): 40–41

Communist Party (pro-Peking; CP(P); Sri Lanka): 207

Communist Party of India (Maoist) (CPI(M)): 326

Communist Party of Nepal (Maoist, CPN(M)): 297, 303–308, 310–312, 316–317, 321–324, 329, 332, 334, 358

    "75 points": 322

Communist Party of Peru: 273

Communist Party of the Philippines (CPP): 125, 128, 134, 168, 186, 188

    Central Committee: 130, 143

    Politburo: 178

Communist Party of Thailand (CPT): 57–58, 60–65, 67–70, 72–73, 75, 77–79, 82–96, 98–100, 102–108, 110, 113–114

    base areas: 69

    cadre: 93

    counter-state: 77

    forces: 61

    insurgency: 63, 203

    leadership: 92, 103

    Politburo (aka "Executive Committee"): 61, 93, 94

    Fourth Party Congress: 106

    Strategic documents:

        "Mass Organization Plan": 108

coup d'etat: 214, 320
covert: 62, 64, 67, 71, 96, 222, 279
CPM (civil-police-military): 71–72, 97, 99, 101
Criminal Investigation Division (CID; Sri Lanka): 220, 221
Criminal Justice Commission (Sri Lanka): 215
Cuba (as model insurgency): 96
cultural idioms:
    forms: 102
    Thai: 103, 104, 113, 114

Dalits (*also* untouchables; Nepal): 303
Damri Ruangsutham: 94
Davao Oriental Province (Philippines): 187
democracy: 13, 57, 84–86, 88–89, 98–99, 128, 130, 160–161, 164, 168, 176, 179, 274, 250,
    273, 284, 287, 301, 303, 319–320, 324–327, 333, 335–337
    "democracy destroyed": 327
    "emerging democracy": 301
    monarch-guided: 301
    parliamentary: 301, 320, 325, 333
democratic:
    centralism: 4, 38
    empowerment: 24
    governance: 24
demographic(s, ally): 144, 208, 233, 239
demonstrations: 86, 129, 324, 326–327
Despuech, Jacques: 42
Deuba, Sher Bahadur (Prime Minister of Nepal): 324
development: 27, 360
    in China and Vietnam: 46
    in Peru: 275, 285, 291, 300–301, 308, 315
    in Nepal: 318, 320, 334, 336–337
    in Philippines: 145, 149, 151, 156, 165–168, 228, 233, 237–238, 245, 247
    in Sri Lanka: 212–213, 222, 97, 99, 105, 110–111
    in Thailand: 66, 68, 73, 76, 78–81, 83–85,182–183, 185
dictatorship: 99, 132, 147, 161, 188, 189, 348
    of the proletariat: 326
Diem (RVN President): *see* Ngo Dinh-Diem

diplomatic relations: 85, 236
District Guerilla Unit (DGC; CPP): 139, 280
districts: 24, 64, 68, 72, 96, 138, 189, 146, 174, 232–233, 240, 244, 246–247, 299, 301, 308, 310, 318–319
divisions: 29, 30, 36, 42, 92, 94, 143, 155, 241, 278, 286, 301, 317–318, 358
Dixit, J.N.: 225
Dolakha District (Nepal): 316
Dravida Munnetra Kazhagham (DMK): 222
Dravidian: 205
drugs: 282, 311, 332
    Drug Enforcement Agency (DEA): 282
    drug war: 282
Dulo Plan (CPP): 146
Duriappah, Alfred: 219
Dutch (Holland): 205, 206

East and West blocs: 217
East India Company: 301
Eastern Province (Sri Lanka): 221, 234, 247
Eastman, Lloyd: 39
economics(y): 5, 39, 46, 57, 59, 72, 83, 95, 106, 128, 130, 149, 151, 154, 211, 213, 215, 216, 241, 256, 273, 281, 283, 291, 299, 300,
Ecuador : 286
"Edsa Revolution" (Philippines): 163, 187
"Edsa II" (Philippines): 187
education: 32, 303
Eelam: *see Tamil Eelam*
Eelam National Liberation Front (ENLF): 223, 226–228, 241
Eelam People's Revolutionary Liberation Front (EPRLF): 223, 227
Eelam Refugees Organization (EROS): 219, 223, 227
Eelam Revolutionary Organisation of Students (EROS): 219, 223, 227
El Salvador: 273, 336, 358
election(s; electoral process): 64, 129, 131, 132, 159–160, 163, 165, 206–207, 210, 212, 244, 252, 255–256, 276, 271, 286, 288, 326, 336, 359
Elephant Pass (Sri Lanka): 251–252, 255
elite(s): 2, 5, 22, 46, 59, 64, 66, 67, 81, 85, 97, 103, 166, 191, 207–208, 210–214, 217, 245, 276, 290, 307, 308, 333–334, 353–355.

"Five Golden Rays" (CPP): 137
"five parties" (Nepal): 324
Five Province Bandit Suppression Conference (China): 30
Flood, Thadeus: 64, 72
Florida: 299
"flower power": 44
Force:
    action: 358, 361, 364
    battalions: 44
    organizations: 35
    strategy: 287
    units: 7, 44, 101, 260, 308, 317, 346, 358, 361
    war: 43
    warfare: xiv, 28, 42, 251, 252
foreign investment: 128, 130 285
Foreign Military Financing (FMF): 320
France (French): 42, 58, 255
    colonial power: 42
Front Guerilla Unit (FGU; CPP): 139
Fronts (organizations): 36, 84, 96, 108, 133, 138, 139, 143, 144, 161, 164, 166–167, 171, 173,
    179, 181, 183, 185–186, 194, 202, 276, 304, 327
Fujimori, Alberto (President of Peru): 291–292, 333, 335
funding: 142, 145, 178, 185, 189, 254, 255, 364

Gandhi
    Indira (Prime Minister of India): 222, 238–240
    Rajiv (Prime Minister of India): 222, 239, 243
Garcia, Alan (President of Peru): 283, 333
gender: 307
general uprising: 41
genocide: 224
gentry: 22, 28–29, 31, 211–214, 308, 334
German(y): 4
Gharti Magar (Nepal): 310
"GIs Leave China" Movement: 38
globalism: 332
gold: 39, 361

yuan: 39
Golden Temple of Amritsar (India): 222
"Golf Committee" (Thailand): 97
"*Gonzalo* Path" (Shining Path): 312
Gonzalo (Shining Path): 276, 312
Gorkha (Nepal): 311–312, 318
government (-al) (-'s): 26–27, 29–31, 33–36, 38–39, 59–61, 208, 216, 217, 219, 221, 223,
     226, 228, 297, 301, 308, 311, 315, 318, 320, 322, 324, 326–327, 329–330, 305,
     330–331, 336
Government Agent (GA; Sri Lanka): 246
goyiyama (caste; Sri Lanka): 215
Great Proletarian Cultural Revolution (China): 271, 276
Greek Republic: 333
grievances: 5–7, 26, 29, 65, 68, 78–80, 82–83, 86, 100, 134, 136, 142, 145, 149, 152, 169–170,
     172, 177, 179, 188, 210, 215, 217, 219, 233, 250, 257–258, 274, 276, 279, 293, 303, 306,
     308, 354–355, 357, 364
"grievance guerillas": 307
Gross Domestic Product (GDP; Peru): 299
growth of:
     the counter-state: 210
     the market economy: 211
Guerrilla Zones (ZG; Peru): 280–281
guerrilla(s)
     action: 2, 7, 26, 28, 146, 154, 187, 189, 220, 252, 279, 311, 314, 346, 358
     forces: 34, 61, 277
     formations: 147, 315–316
     fronts: 181, 186
     movement: 26, 74
     operations: 27, 63
     tactics: 29–30, 226
     units: 26–27, 44, 138–139, 185, 254, 258
     war (warfare): xiv, 1–2, 4, 9, 14, 24, 26–28, 42–43, 79, 231, 357–359, 361
Guevara, Ernesto "Che": xv, 8
     Guevarist: 220
Gurkhas (Nepal): 299–300, 317
Guzman, Abiamel Reynoso (Shining Path): 271, 274–276, 291, 293, 312
Gyanendra (King of Nepal): 320, 324–325, 327–328

Habash, George: 219
Halliday, Fred: 208
Hannibal: 40
Hanoi: 44
Harbin (Manchuria, China): 24
hardliners: 163–164
Harn Leenanond: 98
Harrison, James: 36, 38
Hart, Liddell: xiv
hearts and minds: 318
heavy division: 42
hierarchy: 31, 61, 103, 139, 162, 208, 274, 307, 334
Himalayan Mountains (Nepal): 299
Hindu: 205, 232, 300, 303
Hmong: 72, 74–75, 78, 100, 113, 316
Ho Chi Minh: 41, 60, 62
Ho Chi Minh Trail: 62
Hobbesian: 22
home guard (Nepal): 233
Hood, Robin: 2, 172
Hsien (county, -ies; China): 24
Hsiung Shih-hui (Xiong Shi-hui): 30
Hsu-chou (battle of; China): 39
Hukbalahap (Huks): 134, 216
    Huk Rebellion (Philippines): 127, 134, 146, 151, 258
human rights: 131, 145, 170, 178, 323
Hundred Regiments Campaign (China): 34

ideology: 6, 61, 89, 104, 207, 216, 220, 225–227, 243, 257, 285, 307, 321, 354, 361
Igorots (Luzon, Philippines): 136
Ileto, Raphael "Rocky": 154, 160
imperial(ism): 10–13, 57, 84, 89–92, 227–228, 237, 239–240, 303, 334, 343
incompetence: 171
indentured labor: 210
independence: 210, 217
India Today: 240

India(n): xiii, xiv, 205, 210–212, 217, 221–222, 224–226, 232, 237–243, 249–250, 257–260, 274, 277, 292, 300–301, 303, 305, 311, 313, 317, 319, 326–328, 330, 333, 354
    High Commission: 225
    Peacekeeping Force (IPKF): 243
    Tamils: 205, 210, 212, 217
Indochina: 41–42, 44, 83, 85, 87, 90, 93, 101, 105, 257
Indo-Tibetan Border Force (ITBF): 225
infantry: 43, 100, 147, 155, 220, 229, 250, 253, 286, 299
inflation: 38, 86
Information Bureau (i.e. Political Department; China): 37
infrastructure(s): 29, 31
    counter-state: 3, 44
    development: 81, 104
injustice: 5, 29, 133, 162, 257, 279
Insurgency (ent, ies): xiii, xv, 26, 28–29, 31, 36, 40–41, 43, 186, 203, 209, 210, 215–216, 222, 223, 225–228, 298, 304–305, 311, 314, 316–317, 320, 325–326, 331–333, 335–337
Integrated Security and Development Programme (ISDP; Nepal): 318
intellectuals: 14, 35, 64, 128, 133, 278
Intelligence Bureau (IB; India): 148
Intelligence: 217, 319, 331
Internal Security Operations Command (ISOC; Thailand): 71, 98, 101, 112
internal security: 236
Ireland (Irish): 212, 322, 331, 336, 359
Irish Republican Army (IRA): *see* Provisional Irish Republican Army
Isan (Isaan, Isarn; Thailand*)*: 62, 65–67
Islam(ic, ist): 152, 185, 186, 239, 329, 332, 353, 360
Islamabad (Pakistan): 239
Islamists: 332
    of ASG: 186
Island Party Committees (IPC; CPP): 138, 146
Israel(is): 236, 239–240

Jacquerie: 311
Jaffna (Sri Lanka)
    Mayor: 205, 219, 220, 221
    Peninsula (Sri Lanka): 234, 241, 251

Jajarkot (Nepal): 310

Janatha Vimukthi Peramuna (JVP or "People's Liberation Front"; Sri Lanka): xiv–xv, 207–211, 213–216, 226, 229, 234, 243, 245–250, 253, 256–258, 280, 329, 354
    leader (s) (-ship): 208, 210, 216
    Maoist orientation: 208

Japan(ese): 9–10, 12–13, 30, 32–34, 40, 42, 61, 64, 90, 127, 133–135, 156, 300

Jayewardene, Junius (President of Sri Lanka): 222, 231–332, 234, 237–338, 240–241, 246

Jiangxi (province): 23–24, 29–31, 37, 40,
    Soviet: 30–31, 37

Johnson, Chalmers: 9

Joint Operations Center (JOC): 232, 248, 251

Kadirgamapillai Nallainathan: 220

Kalikot: 310

Kalinga (Philippines): 150

Kandy (Sri Lanka): 206, 255

Kangleon, Edgar: 145

Kansas: 24

karava (caste; Sri Lanka): 215

Kathmandu Valley (Nepal): 301, 311, 314, 323, 327, 330, 335

Kennedy, John F. (President of the United States): 83

Kham Magars (Nepal): 310

Khao Kaeo Camp (Thailand): 65

Khao Khor Mountain Range (Thailand): 106

Khmer Rouge: 93, 172, 305, 307, 312, 360

Khomeini, Ayatollah: 133

Kiangsi (China): *see* Jiangxi

Kilo 11 Incident (Thailand): 66

king: *see* monarch (king), monarchy

Kinmen (ROC): *see* Quemoy

KMS Ltd.: 234

Koirala, Girija Prasad (Prime Minister of Nepal): 324

Koreans: 35

Krathing Daeng (Red Gaur, Thailand): 103

Krong Chandawong: 67

Kung (family; China): 39

Kuomintang (KMT): 9, 12, 21–22, 24, 29, 31–37, 39, 41–42, 94

Labang (Nepal): 313
labor movement: 187
Labrador, William: 176
Lambat Betag ("Net Trap"; Philippines): 166–168, 186
lamp-post killings or lamp-post victim: 228
Land of Buddha: 206
land army: 209
land redistribution (China): 31
language (Nepal): 300
Lao Peoples Revolutionary Party (LPRP): 94
Laopao Sasong: 77
Laos: 43, 61–63, 71, 74, 92–94, 100–101, 105, 110
Laotian Crisis: 67
Latin America(n): 133
Lavao del Sur (Philippines): 153
Le Traffic des piastres: 42
leader (s)(ship): 215–217, 220, 221, 226, 227, 228
Lee Enfield: 309, 314
left (the): 60, 86, 91, 102–103, 105, 112, 132, 156, 161, 303
legitimacy: 6, 59–60, 158, 166, 185, 301, 303, 320, 326, 355, 359, 364
Lenin(ism,ist): 4, 9–10, 12–13, 22, 33, 36, 38, 68, 136, 166, 207, 216, 227, 243, 271, 280, 321, 325
Lert Kanisthanaka: 100
Leyte (Philippines): 147–148, 172–173
Li Tsung-jen: 39
Liao Chung-k'ai: 36
liberated area(s): 13, 23, 84, 143, 276
liberation
    forces: 61
    movement: 310, 332
Liberation Tigers of Tamil Eelam: 218–221, 223–228, 241–243, 250–252, 254–256, 260–262
liberation: 217, 219, 223, 225, 227
Libya: 152
Lima (Peru): 271, 273, 279–280, 282–283, 285, 288, 291
Lin Piao: 13
Lixingshe (Blue Shirts; China): 33

cadre: 323–325
campaign: 315, 318
framework: 317
Indian: 305, 328
militia: 309
Nepali: 322, 328–329, 336
Peruvian: 297
political demonstration: 302
Maoist Insurgency since Vietnam (1996): xiii
maquis: 229
Marco Polo Bridge Incident (China): 32
Marcos, Ferdinand (President of the Philippines): 125, 127, 129–133, 142–143, 146–147,
    150–155, 158–163, 165–167, 170–171, 173, 176–177, 179, 185, 188–190, 324, 333
    ouster: 190
marginalized groups: 215
"margins of the margins": 332
Mariategui, Jose Carlos: 271, 273
Marines
    Peru: 278
    Philippines: 151
market economy: 215
Marshall, George C.: 38
martial law: 87, 127, 129–132, 143, 145–147, 149, 151–152, 154, 317, 324, 333, 363
Marx(ism,ist,ian): 4, 6, 9–10, 13, 16, 33, 60, 104, 129, 133–134, 180–181, 203, 207–208, 213,
    217, 219, 223–228, 237–238, 245, 252, 257, 259, 271, 273–274, 276, 325–328
Marxist-Leninist(ism): 11–12, 21–22, 41, 134, 221, 223, 226, 243, 297, 303, 307, 326,
    353–354
mass activists (Philippines): 137, 139, 142
mass (the masses): 5, 9–11, 13, 22–23, 33, 104, 136, 159–160, 173, 177, 208, 212, 246, 356
    mass base (Sri Lanka): 216, 221
    mass line: 7, 303–304, 306, 308, 329
    mass organization: 9, 11, 104, 108, 110, 112
McBeth, John: 92–93
McGehee, Ralph W.: 69
Meo (Miao): 75–76 *see also* Hmong
mercenary: 57
merit (Buddhism): 60

Middle East(ern): 153, 219, 224, 236
Midwestern Region (-al; Nepal) : 308, 310, 312, 316
militant(s): 217, 219, 226
Military Committee (China): 36
Military Pacification Regions (China): 31
military:
    action: 12, 28, 78, 240, 308, 328
    apparatus: 12, 68
    commanders: 36, 37, 281
    formations: 181, 280
    governments: 71
    leadership/leader(s): 112, 237
    operations: 83, 99, 156, 186, 188–189, 240, 280
    power: 2, 14, 33, 37 63, 147, 30, 63
    units: 4, 31–32, 185
    wing commander: 221
militia: 29, 31, 69, 77–78, 98, 102, 138–139, 142, 151, 160, 168, 170, 173–174, 176, 183, 278, 288, 291, 317
Mindanao (Philippines): 129, 139, 146, 152–153, 167, 180–181
Minister of Justice: 220
Ministry of Defense (China): 36
Ministry of National Defense (Philippines): 162, 167
Ministry of National Security (Sri Lankan): 231
Mison, Salvador: 147–148, 152, 160
Misuari, Nur: 188
mobile war(fare): xiv, xv, 7, 27–28, 43, 181, 251, 260, 282, 311, 346, 357–358
mobilization: xiii, 1, 4, 6–11, 13, 18, 26, 28–29, 30–31, 33–35, 37, 39–40, 64, 69, 86, 88, 103–104, 112, 114, 189, 220, 241, 273, 282, 304, 333–334, 336, 354–360, 362
modernization: 60
monarch(y): 58–60, 65, 81, 86, 91–92, 95, 103–105, 112–114, 300, 303, 321–322, 324–329, 334
Mongkut (King of Thailand): 81
Mongolia: 24
monoculture: 213
morale: 8, 35, 39, 51, 155, 255, 261, 291
Moriano, Clemente: 167
Moro Islamic Liberation Front (MILF; Philippines): 186, 187, 188

offensive: 26

officer corps

    in the Philippines: 155, 156, 158, 159

oil: 128, 150, 153, 167, 237, 238, 240

old-regime crisis: in Thailand: 99, 102, 110, 203, 213

old-regime: 23, 43, 45, 59, 91, 99

oligarchy: 333

Operation *Phu Kwang* (Thailand): 74

operational (level of war), operations: 27, 28, 30, 42, 48, 62, 63, 68, 71, 82, 83, 94, 97, 98, 99,
    108, 109, 114, 139, 146, 147, 156, 157, 158, 163, 164, 166, 167, 173, 178, 182, 183, 185,
    186, 228, 232, 234, 235, 236, 240, 249, 250, 252, 253, 254, 256, 260, 261, 268, 269,
    270, 279, 280, 281, 285, 286, 291, 292, 295, 318, 319, 330, 344, 350, 355, 358, 362

Organisation of the Islamic Conference (OIC): 152

organization(al): 5, 7, 9, 11, 26, 29, 35, 38, 40, 64, 68, 69, 79, 85, 88, 94, 103, 108, 110, 117,
    121, 142, 143, 146, 151, 152, 158, 162, 172, 205, 215, 216, 219, 226, 246, 264, 278, 279,
    280, 281, 288, 295, 317, 331, 342, 344, 356, 361, 364, 366

organized masses: 44, 139, 142

Organizing Committees (OC; CPP): 137, 138, 142,

Organizing Groups (OG; CPP): 137, 138, 139

Outer Mongolia: 24

Pak Mai (Thailand): 94, 121

Pakistan: 205, 238, 239, 332

Palestine Liberation Organisation (PLO): 219, 223, 238

Palk Strait (Sri Lanka): 222

Pama, Honeylee alias "Ibon": 173

Panay (Philippines): 193, 194

Panay Island Regional Party Committee (PIRPC; CPP): 193

Panchayat (Nepal): 301

Paraguay: 342

paramilitary bodies: 225

parliament: 65, 67, 95, 214, 219, 220, 244, 256, 308, 320

Partido Komunistang Philipinas (PKP): 128, 133, 134, 216, 226 see *also* Communist Party of

partisan war: 62, 189

Party Branch (PB; CPP): 137, 138, 139

Party Member (PM; CPP): 37, 63, 64, 137, 139, 142, 173, 196, 281

Pathom Sermsin: 100

Pike, Douglas: 17, 191
Pokhara (Nepal): 312
Pol Pot: 92
Police: 29, 68, 71, 76, 97, 102, 122, 144, 151, 172, 173, 174, 179, 182, 208, 209, 214, 215, 217,
    219, 220, 221, 229–230, 234, 235, 248, 265, 271, 281, 308, 309, 311–314, 316–319, 335,
    339, 343–344, 346, 348, 349, 350, 351, 352, 357, 358, 363
Politburo: 61, 207, 227, 308
Political Commissar (Comisario Secretario; Shining Path): 278, 281
Political Organizing Team (POT; CPP): 162
Political Program for 1983 (CPP): 144
political
    battle: 29
    end: 24
    movement: 7, 26, 78, 243, 309, 353, 355, 361
    officers: 37
    party: 11, 306
    power: 23, 48, 131, 166, 326, 353, 355
    prisoners: 187
    science: 3, 15
    space: 6, 64, 68, 70, 87, 98, 99, 102, 112, 171, 278, 321
    structure: 22, 24, 84, 129, 142, 166, 180
    system: 59, 81, 83, 127, 128, 131, 151, 176, 178, 244, 301, 327
Political
    Department(s): 36–37
    KMT Military Committee: 36
    Warfare: 8, 11, 12, 28, 41, 182, 216, 273, 280, 304, 321, 322, 329, 353
    Whampoa: 36, 37, 52
    Officer (-s, or system): 36, 37, 174
politics: 2, 3, 4, 24, 30, 37, 59, 87, 95, 99, 102, 106, 135, 151, 165, 171, 172, 187, 194, 212,
    215, 244, 252, 276, 280, 283, 297, 301, 321, 324, 325, 328, 331, 334, 342, 355
Popular Committee (Shining Path): 278, 279
Popular Front for the Liberation of Palestine (PFLP): 219
Popular Guerrilla Army (EGP; Shining Path): 281
popular uprising (in Vietnamese conception): 216
population
    of Sri Lanka: 207, 208, 211, 212, 213, 214, 215, 220, 233, 236, 237, 239, 244, 245, 249,
        258, 260, 262, 264

Portugal (-guese): 205, 206
  colonial government: 206
post-imperial: 22
post-Tet of '68: 44
post-Vietnam: 324
power: 37, 70, 86, 202
  military: 2, 14, 33, 37, 63, 147, 363
  state: 4, 7, 24, 40, 63, 80, 88, 209, 261, 303, 325, 32
Prabhakaran, Velupillai (LTTE leader): 219, 220–221, 223, 224 (picture), 228, 261, 265, 266
Prachanda (Pushpa Kamal Dahal): 305, 328–329; Path 312
Praphas: 71, 85, 333
Prayoot Charumanee: 100
Prem Tinsulanond (RTA Cdr. and Prime Minister of Thailand): 71, 95, 97, 99–101, 104, 106, 114, 122, 333
Premadasa, Ranasinghe (President of Sri Lanka): 246, 251, 255
Preparatory Commission for the National Democratic Front (CPP): 130
president(cy): 39, 83, 127, 131, 132, 133, 135, 150, 154, 182, 183, 185, 187, 255, 285, 291
Presidential Assistant on National Minorities (PANAMIN; Philippines): 150
Presidential Memorandum Order No. 88 (Philipines): 186
Presidential Proclamation 2045 (Philippines): 131
Price, Russell: 57
Pridi Panomyong: 60–61
priesthood: 33
Prime Minister (PM) Orders (Thailand): 122
  No. 66/23 [BE 2523, AD 1980] "Policy for the Fight to Defeat the Communists": 99
  No. 65/25 [BE 2525, AD 1982] "Plan for the Political Offensive": 99
Progressive Review: 129
proletariat: 4, 10, 22 , 212, 213, 215, 326
propaganda
  and Peru: 280
  and the Philippines: 136, 167, 178
protracted war: 12, 46, 48, 304, 360–362, 364
Provinces (of Thailand)
  Chiangrai: 111, 113
  Khon Kaen: 89
  Loei, Nan: 72, 73, 77, 127

418

Rondas campesinas (Peru): 333
Royal Nepal Army (RNA): 317–319, 321–323, 327–329
Ruijin (China): 25
Rukkum (Nepal): 309–310, 316
ruling
        class: 211–212
        elite: 66, 213
Russia(n, s): 12, 36, 60

Saigon: 42, 44, 54, 74
Saiyud Kerdphol: 71, 73, 76, 118, 122, 123, 195, 335
Salyan (Nepal): 310
Samaki Tham (United in Dharma Movement; Thailand): 67–68
Samar (Philippines): 138, 139, 145–148, 162, 172, 182, 186, 187, 189, 192, 193, 194, 195, 196, 200
Samar Province: 187, 189
Samudavanija Chai-anan: 90, 119
San Min Chu-i:
        Youth Corps: 33, 37
        Executive Secretariat: 319
sanbao (strategy; China): 31
Sanbao (strategy; China): 31
Sandhurst: 253
Sandinistas: *see also* Nicaragua 57, 181, 227, 326, 331, 336
Sang Patthanothai: 94
Sangha (Buddhist order of monks): 59, 115
Sanha (Sant) Chitrapatima: 100
Santa Lucia (Peru): 282
Sarit Thanarat (Prime Minister of Thailand): 66–67
Sarochna Robbamrung: 99–100, 122
Saudi Arabia: 239, 332, 339
scale (in insurgency): 6, 171, 173, 257
Scott, James: 5–6, 16, 78, 103, 216, 308
SEAL: 188
Second World War: 23, 41–42, 60, 305
        aftermath in China: 13, 23, 26, 52, 283
Secretariat (Shining Path): 280

Sections (CPP): 138, 139
sectors (CPP): 128, 129, 137, 177, 187
security front (Philippines): 186
Self-Defense Corps (CPP): 138
self-reliance: 11, 13
Senderistas (Shining Path): 283
Sendero Luminoso: *see also* Shining Path 271, 295, 297, 303, 304, 305, 311, 312, 322, 353, 360
Senthil (TELF faction; Sri Lanka): 223
separatism:
    and Sri Lanka: 206, 222, 254
separatist (-movements): 186, 222, 227
serfs: 212
Seven Party Alliance (SPA; Nepal): 324, 331
shadow government: 69, 147
Shah of Iran: 325
Shanghai
    CCP/KMT conflict in: 22, 32, 37, 39
Shangri-la (Nepal): 299
Shin Bet (in Sri Lanka): 236
Shining Path: *see Sendero Luminoso* 271, 273, 275, 284, 289, 290, 296
Shrestha, Mohan: 314
Siam: *see* Thailand
Sicuani Province (Szechwan; China): 47
sierra (Peruvian): 295
Sikhs: 222, 268, 300
Sin, Cardinal Jaime: 133
Singapore: 239, 339
Sinhala: 203, 205–206, 211–216, 219–220, 223, 226, 228, 243
    Buddhist: 207
    chauvinism: 207, 212, 213, 216, 226, 228
    factions: 206
    majority: 206, 212, 222
    nationalism: 206
    Sinhalese rural masses: 207
Sinhalese
    differences with Tamils: 206
    youth: 208, 209

Sirkit (Thai Queen): *see* monarch (king) 97
Sison, Jose Maria "Joma": 129, 179–181, 184, 185, 189–190, 191, 197, 199
Sivakumaran, Ponnudarai: 219
Sixth Strong Youth Training Regiment: 34
social: 60
    action: 9, 144–145, 285
    formation: 223
    revolution: 219, 226
    sciences: 210
socialism (ist): 42, 60, 64, 66, 84, 111, 115, 120, 130–131, 133, 149, 199, 207, 210, 212, 218,
    223, 227, 237, 252, 266, 273
society: 210, 223
socialization: 142
Soong Dynasty (family): 39
South African: 239
South Asia: 239, 305
South China Sea: 187
South Sea islands: 203
South Vietnam (ese): 42–44, 62, 67, 93, 154, 358
Southeast Asia: 44, 62, 67, 85, 90, 94, 150, 206, 278,
Southern Leyte Fighting Front (CPP): 173
Sovereignty (of Nepal): 331
Soviet Union (USSR): 44, 61, 92, 237, 273
soviet(s): 21–22, 34, 37
    Central (China): 25
    doctrine (in China): 42
    Jiangxi (China): 25
SPA and Maoists (SPAM; Nepal): 324, 326
Spain (Spanish): 2, 4, 127, 279–280
Sparrows (CPP): 139, 171, 173, 189
Special Forces
    Philippines: 26, 320, 168
    Sri Lanka: 252–253
Special Mass Course (CPP): 137
special operations: 42, 98, 167, 235, 247, 253–254, 260, 285, 358
Special Task Force (STF; Sri Lanka): 234–235
Spence, Jonathan D.: 32

425

Tigers: *see* Liberation Tigers of *Tamil Eelam*
Time (magazine): 172
tobacco: 25
torture: 228, 273
Trincomalee (Sri Lanka): 233, 237–238
Tri-Province Region (Thailand): 74, 106
Trotsky(ism): 11, 207
TULF: *see* Tamil United Liberation Front

Udom Srisuwan: 64
Ulster: 326, 331
Under Fire (film): 57
United Front Commission (CPP): 143
united front(s): 7–8, 11–13, 19, 32, 34, 41, 61, 63, 68, 84–85, 87–94, 108, 112, 128, 130–131, 143, 144, 145, 187, 189, 216–217, 273, 276, 304, 308 , 312, 324–325, 329, 331, 353
United Marxist-Leninists (UML; Nepal): 303
United National Party (UNP; Sri Lanka): 207, 212–213, 222, 237, 240, 243–244, 252, 255–256
United Nations: 300
        peacekeeping missions (Nepali participation): 317–318
United Revolutionary People's Council (Nepal): 312
United States (US): *see* America(n, ns, or US)
United States (US, America, American)
        and China: 187
        and Nepal: 320
        and Peru: 282
        and the Philippines: 129, 134
        and Thailand (COIN influence): 85
United States: 187, 320, 335
        citizen: 188
        commitment of forces: 188
        Embassy: 208
        forces: 187
        position: 188
        presence: 189
University of Eastern Philippines (UEP): 129, 177
Upper Huallaga Valley (Peru): 281

uprising: 216
urban allies: 216
urban mobilization: 189
urban proletariat: 212
urban: 4, 10, 22, 24, 34–35, 38–39, 41, 43, 76, 85, 92–93, 95, 103, 125, 128, 137, 139,
    143–145, 147, 161, 165, 180–181, 189, 210, 212, 216, 246, 288, 292, 312, 319, 322, 327,
    331, 337
US Agency for the International Development (USAID): 320
US Embassy: *see* American Embassy
US Special Forces: 320
US-Marcos Dictatorship: 147, 161, 188–189
USSR: *see* Soviet Union

Vajiralongkorn (Crown Prince of Thailand): *see* monarch (king)
Vajiravudh (King): *see* monarch (King of Thailand)
Vallejera, George: 163–164, 183
Ver, Fabian: 154–155, 159
veterinary science: 210
Viet Cong: 43, 276, 305, 358
Viet Minh: 42, 276
Vietnam (Viet Nam): xiii, xiv, 5, 21, 41–45, 57, 60–62, 64–65, 67, 74, 83, 85, 89–90, 92–94,
    96, 100–101, 110, 154, 156, 163
Vietnam Communist Party (VCP): 60
Vietnam War: xiv, 57, 83, 89, 297, 305, 312, 358
Village Defence Corps (Thailand): 71
Village Development Communities (Nepal): 301
Village Scouts (Thailand): 103, 104
violence: 3, 4, 7–8, 12 14, 28, 66, 78, 79, 80, 86–87, 91, 104, 112, 127, 129, 132, 134, 150,
    166, 170–172, 186, 203, 205, 208, 219–221, 246, 255–257, 262, 273, 276, 291, 293,
    297, 304, 321–322, 325–328, 331–332, 336–337, 354–356, 359, 361
Visayas (Philippines): 145–146, 180–182
Visayas Church Sector Consultation of the CPP: 145
Visayas Commission (CPP): 145–146, 180–181
Visayas Regional United Front Group (CPP): 145
Visayas Secretariat for Social Action (VISSA): 145
Visiting Forces Agreement (VFA): 187–188
Voice of the People of Thailand (VOPT): 61, 89, 90–91, 94

voluntarism: 214

wage labor(ers): 211, 213
War of Resistance (*aka* War of National Resistance; China): 32–33
war(fare): 304, 318–319, 327, 329, 332, 334–335
warlord(s): 21, 22, 32, 158, 162
Warriors for Peace: (Philippines): 179
Washington (US): 129, 159, 183, 188–189, 238, 239, 256, 276, 282
Wasin Isarangkoon: 100
wat (temple; Thailand): 59
Watts (Los Angeles): 333
Weber, Max: 3
Wei An-jen: 48
Wei, William: 31
welfare: 79, 130, 151
West (the)/Western: xiv, 25, 28–29, 42, 62, 81, 83, 90, 102–103, 112, 127, 147, 156, 168,
    209–213, 217, 222–223, 237–238, 255, 280, 305, 310, 312, 314, 317, 325, 329–330,
    337, 361
West Bengal: 305, 330
West Point (US Military Academy): 156
West Virginia: 211
Westmoreland vs. CBS: 139, 192
Westmoreland, William C.: 43, 192
Wijeweera, Rohana: 207–208, 213, 216
Wirat Angkathavom: 64
women: 307
World Bank: 299
World War I: *see* First World War
World War II: *see* Second World War
Wu Shih: 36
Wyatt, David K.: 85

Yangtze: Development Corporation: 39
Years:
    1517–1638: 205
    1638–1796: 205
    1774: 301

Other Books by White Lotus

Ball, Desmond; **Burma's Military Secrets: Signals Intelligence (SIGINT) from the Second World War to Civil War and Cyber Warfare**
This first book on signals warfare provides a unique view into all of the important military and political developments in Burma over the past half century based on the most secret and authoritative intelligence sources, i.e., signals intelligence (SIGINT) which involves radio interception, telecommunications surveillance, crypt analysis or code-breaking, and analysis of supposedly confidential signals. This book is filled with fascinating and explosive revelations about many important issues, such as:

- the special relationship between Burma and China. Over the past decades, China has become Burma's principal ally, major arms supplier, and only secret intelligence partner.
- the opium and heroin trade. Burma now accounts for two-thirds of the world's total production of heroin and the drug armies maintain sophisticated intelligence collection and communications systems.
- the SIGINT activities of the ethnic insurgent organizations, such as the Karen National Army.
- the battles at Manerplaw and Kawmura in January–February 1995, which involved some 15,000–20,000 troops, and which resulted in the loss of these strongholds to the Burmese Army.
- the use of electronic surveillance by the military junta in Rangoon to control dissent and rebellion.
- the organization of Burma's security and intelligence establishment, including the dreaded Military Intelligence Service (MIS) headed by Khin Nyunt, and the new Cyber Warfare Department.
- the build-up of Burma's conventional arms capabilities, giving it the largest armed forces in Asia by the turn of the century.

Ball, Desmond; **The Boys in Black: The Thahan Phran (Rangers), Thailand's Para-Military Border Guards**
This is a study of the Rangers, a volunteer organization founded by the Royal Thai Army in 1978 to combat communist insurgency. They have since become responsible for tile first-line defense of Thailand's border: fighting intruding armed forces, such as the ethnic insurgent armies and the drug trafficking groups in the Thai-Burma borderlands; guarding refugee camps; maintaining peace and security in troubled areas. They are widely known for their involvement in extraneous politically motivated and violent activities. This book

is about life and security in Thailand's borderlands from a Ranger perspective. It is both a critique of an important element of Thailand's border defense regime and an introduction to the complex political geography and human security issues in the borderlands. General Teerawat Putamanonda (ret.) has provided the foreword.

Ball, Desmond; **Militia Redux: *Or Sor* and The Revival of Paramilitarism in Thailand**

This is a critique of the current resurgence of paramilitarism in Thailand. The central organisation is the Volunteer Defence Corps, or *Or Sor*. An agency of the Ministry of Interior since the 1950s, *Or Sor* has a multiplicity of tasks, including maintaining road checkpoints, guarding provincial and district buildings, supervising refugee camps, development assistance, and involvement in the war on drugs. It has also been instrumental in training and supervising rapidly increasing numbers of Village Self-Defence Volunteers (Chor Ror Bor). Since 2002 their numbers have increased in the Thailand-Burma borderlands and in the South, where *Or Sor* and Chor Ror Bor have become a primary target of the insurgency. Despite a generally improving reputation, many paramilitary personnel are also notorious as thugs for local strongmen, and for corruption and inefficiency. This book is the first in-depth study of this uniquely Thai experience of paramilitarism. Professor Suchit Bunbongkarn has provided a foreword.

Johnson, Wray R.; **Vietnam and American Doctrine for Small Wars**

This tome is the first comprehensive treatment of the evolution of U.S. military doctrine for countering guerillas and other irregular forces in small wars. Since its inception, the United States has been engaged in small wars, or low intensity conflict, and has contested irregular opponents in each. The end of World War II ushered in what has since become known as the "counterinsurgency era," its genesis arguably the containment strategy of the Truman Doctrine of 1947, upon which policy-makers and military planners constructed rudimentary counterinsurgency doctrine for combating communist guerrillas in Greece. Yet Vietnam was the real test for counter-insurgency doctrine, and the war in Vietnam has remained the touchstone for American involvement in small wars ever since. With the end of the Vietnam War, small wars doctrine has risen or fallen according to the perceived threat to the national security interests of the United States, concurrent with the success or failure of scholars and military professionals in persuading the national security bureaucracy to make qualitative changes in doctrine and force structure. In that light, this study examines the roots of American military doctrine for small wars and its subsequent evolution from "counterinsurgency" in the 1960s to "stability and support operations" in the 1990s, and concludes with an analysis of the legacy of Vietnam and the implications for emergent military doctrine in the post-Cold War era.